John Kelly

Sermons

John Kelly

Sermons

ISBN/EAN: 9783741183072

Manufactured in Europe, USA, Canada, Australia, Japa

Cover: Foto ©Andreas Hilbeck / pixelio.de

Manufactured and distributed by brebook publishing software (www.brebook.com)

John Kelly

Sermons

SERMONS

BY

FATHER JOHN KELLY, B.A.

LATE RECTOR OF ST. JOSEPH'S, BIRKDALE.

1897.

Manchester:
P. DESCHAMPS, BLACKFRIARS BRIDGE.

INDEX.

	PAGE.
Preface	7

SERMONS ON THE PASSION:

Fallen but Triumphant	13
"Father, forgive them, for they know not what they do"	20
"This day thou shalt be with Me in Paradise".	24
"I thirst"	33

SERMONS ON OUR BLESSED LADY:

The Maternity of our Blessed Lady	40
The Presentation of our Blessed Lady	47
The Assumption	59
Mary (Month of May)	63
The Influence of Mary on Modern Civilization	68
Help of Christians	72

MISCELLANEOUS SERMONS, DOCTRINAL AND MORAL:

The Predominant Passion	85
Covetousness	89
Anger	95
Gluttony	102
Sloth	108
On Lying	114
On Rash Judgment	120
On Calculating the Chances of Salvation	126
The Particular Judgment	138
Divine Hope	139
The Kingdom of Christ doomed to the hatred of the World	145
Martyrdom a Mark of the Church. Part I.	148
Do. do. Part II.	153
Faith a Dissolving View in non-Catholic England	157
On Mixed Marriages	166
The Leafy Month of June	173
"Coeli Enarrant Gloriam Dei"	179

	PAGE
Care of Orphans	186

SERMONS ON THE SUNDAYS AND FESTIVALS THROUGHOUT THE LITURGICAL YEAR:

	PAGE
The Nativity	192
The Epiphany	198
The Holy Name of Jesus	205
Charity. (Quinquagesima Sunday)	210
Blind Bartimeus. (Quinquagesima Sunday)	215
The Temptation in the Desert	221
Walk in Love. (Third Sunday in Lent)	228
Passion Sunday	234
Palm Sunday	240
Easter Sunday	244
Low Sunday	248
The Good Shepherd. (Second Sunday after Easter)	252
The Ascension	258
The Holy Ghost the Spirit of Peace. Whit Sunday	265
Feast of Pentecost. The Use of the Tongue	273
Trinity Sunday	277
Corpus Christi	284
Jesus in the Blessed Sacrament, our Physician	290
The Sacred Heart of Jesus	297
On the Humility of the Sacred Heart	305
The Love of the Sacred Heart	312
Fourth Sunday after Pentecost. No Salvation outside the Church	318
Eighth Sunday after Pentecost	325
Tenth Sunday after Pentecost. The Pharisee and the Publican	331
Twentieth Sunday after Pentecost. "Redeeming the time because the days are evil."	338
Twenty-fourth Sunday after Pentecost	343
All Saints	349
All Souls	356

LIVES OF SAINTS:

	PAGE
St. Joseph	364
St. John of the Cross	371
St. Margaret of Scotland	377

PREFACE.

THE long delay in the appearance of this selection from the Sermons of the late Father John Kelly, which I undertook to publish at the request of a number of his friends, both lay and clerical, has arisen from various causes. More than half a year elapsed from his decease, before I could get possession of his papers. And when at length they came into my hands, many of the manuscripts were found to be in a dilapidated condition, some of them written in pencil, and in places nearly illegible. So that I was not surprised to hear that it had been proposed to burn them as being valueless.

The absolute need of transcribing and correcting them for the printer would have entailed even a longer delay, but for the help rendered freely and generously by several mutual friends, amongst whom particular acknowledgment is due to the Rev. John Donohoe. He was assistant priest to Father Kelly, at St. Joseph's, Birkdale, at the time of his death, and his collaboration has been especially valuable, as he heard many of the sermons actually delivered. My own occupations, too, more numerous and pressing than usual during the past few months, have interfered with my efforts to get the book through the press as speedily as was wished, and may also, I trust, be pleaded in extenuation of the errors, slight, no doubt, but irritating to the reader, which have escaped me in the revisal of the proof sheets.

In justice to Father Kelly, it must be stated (though this will hardly be necessary for any one who knew him) that the publication of these discourses was the thing furthest from his thoughts. But though they would have received many additions and improvements, and often assumed altogether a different form, had he himself prepared them for the press, they will perhaps be more prized by those who had the privilege to hear him, because they now appear just as they fell from his lips.

They were all preached, as far as can be ascertained, during the last fifteen years of his life, to town and country congregations, and the following dates will give sufficiently, in outline, the changes in his missionary career. Born on the 27th of May, 1843, at Castlereagh, in the County of Roscommon, he received his early education at the Catholic Institute, in Liverpool. He entered Ushaw College, in September, 1857, and after a course of studies, in every way distinguished, he taught with the greatest success for five years, and was finally ordained by Dr. Goss, on the 21st of September, 1872.

From October to the following April, he served the Church of St. Anthony, in Liverpool, but was then transferred to St. Vincent's, and acted as Secretary to Bishop O'Reilly during his residence at that presbytery, and afterwards for several years at the Bishop's House, in Rodney St. Dr. O'Reilly had the highest esteem for the prudence and abilities of his Secretary, in whom he had taken a more than common interest from early boyhood. Hence it was, with extreme reluctance, that he acceded to Father Kelly's request to exchange his trying post for the ordinary missionary life, and nominated him Rector of St. John's, Burscough, in October 1878. Within twelve months the Bishop recalled him to Liverpool, to take charge of St. Michael's, West Derby Road, with its large population consisting, in a great measure, of the working class, and its many Institutions. This charge Father Kelly was obliged to resign, through ill-health, in 1887, and after a voyage to the United States and Canada, he was sent to the quiet country Mission of Gillmoss, where it was hoped his strength would be restored. The heavy work, however, in addition to the usual parochial duties, involved in attending the Public Cemetery, and the Cottage Homes, which were situated two miles from the Presbytery, proved a severer tax than had been anticipated; and on the death of Canon Wallwork he was transferred to St. Joseph's, Birkdale, in October 1891; which mission he held, in spite of almost continuous bad health, till his death, after a short illness, on the 16th of July 1895. These few facts are mentioned chiefly to show the varied character of the congregations to which these discourses were addressed.

As to the selection itself, some of the sermons chosen for

publication may perhaps seem unduly imaginative, and to show too free play of the fancy in presenting the incidents of the life of our Lord and His blessed Mother. This is largely a question of taste and temperament. That to many such a style is attractive, and not only helps them to realize and fix the truths more firmly and vividly in the mind, but awakens strong religious emotion, will scarcely be denied. In the sermon, "Mary's Influence on Modern Civilization," will be found a justification of this method " of logically and securely filling in the scanty outline of Mary's life and character as it is painted in the Holy Scriptures—by a constant tradition coming down from the Apostolic age," and he maintains strongly that whilst "to our enemies this amplification of the Scriptural portrait seems altogether gratuitous, it is far from being so." On the other hand, there are discourses which, though more immediately practical and full of instruction and earnest exhortation, may be thought of rather an ordinary type ; and disappointment will perhaps be felt in some quarters at their inclusion in preference to sermons which are known to have moved his hearers profoundly, and which I have been requested to publish. These, however, in many cases, could not be found, or were in a fragmentary state. The truth is that there has been little room for selection. The choice between two sermons, on the same or different subjects, has often been determined not so much by the importance of the matter, the force of the thoughts, or the felicity of treatment, as by the consideration—which of the manuscripts was more perfect, and had fewer gaps, to be filled in as best might be from conjecture.

In addition to the sermon on St. Joseph, I have found a place for one on St. John of the Cross, and another on St. Margaret of Scotland, as specimens of his treatment of the "The Lives of the Saints," which he often made the subject of his Sunday evenings' instruction. In these, whilst the matter is drawn from common and easily accessible sources (chiefly Butler), there will be found original reflections and practical applications to daily life, which seem to have made them not the least effective part of his preaching.

That Father Kelly always held his audience in rapt attention is of course no guarantee that his sermons will have a permanent value. It is the rule, we may say, that a popular preacher, no less than a distinguished speaker in the political world, with its ever changing and passing interests, suffers in reputation from the publication of his discourses. Much of the effect is gone with the living sympathetic voice, the winsome manner, the evident sincerity, the known life and character of the speaker. But it may be said as truly of Father Kelly as of a celebrated fellow countryman, " Nihil tetigit quod non ornavit." Whatever subject he handled, even in familiar conversation, he set it forth with the utmost clearness, force of argument, and happiness of illustration, and though speaking merely pleasantly and in a lighter strain, he yet surrounded everything with an indescribable charm. And when to a highly poetical nature like his, with the keenest sense and love of the beautiful, whether in nature or art, a brilliant imagination, and an overflowing wealth of language, there was added a faith as simple as it was vivid, an enthusiastic loyalty to the Church, and the deepest reverence for the least point of her practice as well as of her teaching, his published sermons will surely be found to have an inherent worth, and a power still to delight and warm the devotion of his readers, and will add, we may hope, to his own reward for the zeal with which he laboured to discharge this most important duty of the pastoral office.

T. CROSKELL.

St. Edwards, Rusholme.
 1st August, 1897.

IN MEMORY OF THE REV. FATHER JOHN KELLY.

DIED AT ST. JOSEPH'S, BIRKDALE, JULY 16.
INTERRED AT AINSDALE CEMETERY, JULY 19, 1895.

I.

And this his grave is--'neath this lowly mound
  Sleep genius, worth, from earth-forged fetters free ;
  The lark, the leaves that rustle on the tree,
Shall stir him nevermore : nor sight, nor sound
Is e'er again for him. The all-profound,
  Dread silence of the grave is his. Ah me !
  That one so good and gifted here should be,
Whose steps scarce yet had faced life's summer round !
Away, deep down beneath this yet fresh sod,
  The father of his flock finds calm repose,
Whose pure life consecrated was to God ;
  Whose sympathies were all with human woes ;
The soul, like star that shines brief hour abroad,
  Returned has to the heaven from whence it rose.

II.

The brilliant mind, the cultured intellect,
  That shone resplendent as the summer beam,
  And sparkled, rich as sun-bathed mountain stream,
Is now past praise or blame, or cold neglect.
What glorious gifts were his ! rich, ripe, unflecked—
  Wit, fancy—all idealist could dream
  Of fragrance and of force ! Strange doth it seem
That death a fane so noble should have wrecked !
That death should strike one to so many dear ;
  Whose very presence was a fragrance sweet ;
Whose words fell grateful on the listening ear ;
  Whose wisdom erred not, though bright-winged its feet :
But mortal vision is horizoned here,
  And God to take him hence had deemed it meet.*

---

*These lines, by Mr. John Hand, Member of the Liverpool School Board, first appeared in the " Daily Post," and were afterwards reprinted in the " Catholic Times."

FALLEN, BUT TRIUMPHANT.

AMONGST the direst consequences of the Fall, beloved Brethren, we have to reckon not death alone, that bugbear of the human race, but the eternal spirit of strife and discord, which has urged men in each successive generation to inflict death upon one another with every grim circumstance of bloodshed and atrocity. The rebellion against God's ordinance was not simply a proclamation of war against the Almighty, but of the perpetual feud of man against man. In the bosom of Adam's family this warfare began, when Abel's blood, shed by a brother's hand, dyed the surface of the newly-accursed earth. And when that family multiplied, and begot tribes and nations, the warfare thus begun was propagated on a larger and larger scale, until the strength of whole peoples was arrayed in deadly mutual antagonism, till the gore of human hecatombs smoked upon the battle field, and the bones of slaughtered men, struck down in forgotten quarrels, were turned up by the plough in every corner of the inhabited globe. Every century that passed heaped up on the earth its evidences of intermidable hate, the ashes of extinguished fires; and printed upon its bosom, in deeper and deeper characters, the undeniable truth, that with sin are bound up, as by a necessary law, mortal dissensions and sanguinary conflict.

But this hideous bequest of bloodshed, beloved Brethren, was only the visible type of another and a deadlier warfare, unseen by the eye, beginning when man listened to the counsels of the adversary of God, speaking through the serpent in the garden of Paradise, and destined to continue till the breath of the last man has been gasped into the air, on the eve of the great Judgment. It is the struggle between God and the devil, for the possession of the souls of men. By his artifices and wiles, Satan seduced the children of God from their Maker and heavenly Father; and it gave the enemy a fierce satisfaction to see the strife begin under auspices so favourable to the realization of his schemes. Man's nature became tainted and prone to evil. With difficulty he distinguished between true friend and treacherous foe; so that the Father of lies, the Arch-Deceiver, had good reason to hope that he could continue to dupe the degenerate descendants of that noble creature of God, whom he had succeeded in misleading even before human nature had been degraded by sin. But, amid the very thunders of the curse, the Almighty had mingled a whisper of comfort for his fallen children, which made Satan tremble with terror. "The seed of the woman," said He, in His compassion, "shall crush the serpent's head." Still the battle was mainly, through the passing ages, in favour of man's enemy. God seemed driven from the field; and the demon stalked proud and haughty, as a slave-master among his serfs, through the crouching nations of the world. With what malignant joy, did Satan, from his firmly fixed throne here below, see the baffled Creator (for baffled indeed He seemed) hurl down from His citadel in heaven the fiery sheets of brimstone, or the long-lashing torrents of the flood, which consigned the sinners in multitudes, as the thralls of war, to the mercies of the cruel conqueror. With what malignant joy did he see his All-Powerful Adversary, the Master of Heaven, visit great sections of the erring race, ever and anon, as the cup of their iniquities overflowed, with epidemic and plague, that made the earth hideous with their sin-defiled carcases; with earthquakes that swallowed them up alive into hell; with inundations, on whose destroying billows their last breath bubbled, as it were, with sin. All these visitations were incidents in the great battle which favoured the demon, no less than those stupendous visible wars, in which the wicked seed of Adam, with blood-dripping spear or sword in hand, wreaked upon one another, unwittingly, the vengance of God, and mowed down countless victims to grace the triumphal car of Satan in his fiery kingdom.

But the day, long deferred, and threatened by many a prophet in mystic phrases that were treasured up in the quaking heart of the fiend—the day on which the seed of the woman should crush the serpent's head, the day in which the tide of battle should be rolled back, in which God should come down and claim his own world—establish his kingdom—make his enemies his footstool—

rule with a rod of iron from sea to sea, to the ends of the earth—break the captive's bonds, shatter the brazen gates, overthrow the powers of darkness, and inflict death on death—that great and tremendous and long-deferred day came round at last. And yet, since the warfare between the two principles of good and evil began, there never had dawned a day, which opened with the prospect of a greater victory for Satan One after another, the patriarchs and the prophets had gone to the grave foretelling ultimate triumph for God's cause, yet invoking its advent in vain. Terror and hot eagerness, which perhaps seemed to the demon despair, animated their accents, as they cried out again and again, in many forms of phrase, "O that thou wouldst rend the heavens and come down." One after another, they had sunk into the earth from which they had sprung, without seeing the chains of hell snapped, or the reign of sin arrested. "Some were racked, not accepting deliverance, that they might find a better resurrection. Others had trials of mockeries and stripes, moreover also of bands and prisons: they were stoned, they were cut asunder, they were tempted, they were put to death by the sword, they wandered about in sheep-skins, in goat-skins, being in want, distressed, afflicted. Of whom the world was not worthy, wandering in deserts, in mountains, and in dens, and in caves of the earth."—*Heb.* xi. 37. 38. 39. Such has been the fate of those who would fain have routed the forces of evil:—a mean and contemptible life, full of distress and hardships, the death of a malefactor or an outcast, and an unavailing cry to heaven for help, smothered in the utterance, like the shriek of a drowning man.

Another prophet had arisen, and the greatest of all the prophets, whose aspect of meekness and humility, and the majesty and beauty of whose veiled godhead, had often struck the great Adversary with terror and dismal forebodings. He had called Himself the Son of God; but in what sense, the devil was unable to divine; and the overtures of the crafty being in visible form, for the purpose of eliciting the truth, had ended only in his discomfiture and shame. The power of this man had never been matched by any prophet before. Not only did nature obey Him, not only did the slime of the earth become medicinal at His touch, and the winds of heaven and the waves of the sea obey His behest; not only were disease and diabolical influence banished by the sound of His voice; but the human heart itself, though coiled round by all the snakes of hell, was loosed by His presence from their hideous embraces, and drawn irresistibly after the odour of His ointments. But now the day had dawned, when He, like the prophets who preceded Him, is to die a miserable death; a death more miserable, in proportion to the greatness of His prestige, and the marvellous character of His works. The Priests have rejected Him with scorn and contumely. Speaking from the chair of Moses, the High Priest has declared that the man must die, lest all the people perish, The Scribes and the Pharisees have proclaimed Him a traitor to Cæsar, and a blasphemer against God; and the ignorant populace stirred up, like the ocean under angry blasts, has roared and clamoured for His blood. A glorious day indeed for Satan: a day that brings a satisfactory solution to all his doubts as to the personality of this singular man. This latest and greatest of God's champions on earth is to perish from amongst the kinsmen, whom He laboured to save, by the ignominious death of a blasphemer and a traitor. He is to add another name to the long roll of prophets, who have cried to God in vain. He is to ensure to Satan, by His death, a new term of undiminished power, and to rivet afresh the fetters of man's bondage.

"It is your hour," said our Blessed Lord, "and the power of darkness." The terrible day moves on from stage to stage, and from hour to hour; and every second of time inflicts new humiliation or torture upon the Being, who has presumed to raise the standard against the battalions of hell. Never was an ill-starred captain, in all the annals of war, so beaten to the earth, and overwhelmed with disaster. Never was insatiable hate and longing for revenge so fully sated, as the malignant thirst of fiends and synagogue, in this the latest stage of the world's great battle. Yes; glut your eyes upon the spectacle, ye leaders of God's people. There is nothing wanting to the banquet of horrors spread before your gaze. Revel now in the intoxication of your guilty joy; for the cup of vengence is beaded to the brim; and never did the juice of the choicest vintage taste so sweet, nor possess the brain with so maddening an exhilaration. Raise your voices in delirious mirth; lead the jeering cries of the poor deluded multitude; shout and shriek yourselves hoarse, in your glad frenzy. Your arch-enemy is dying by inches; dying the death of a fugitive slave. He denounced you pitilessly in His strength; that tongue, that was so honey-sweet and gentle for all besides, remorselessly tore open your sore wounds, and exposed your shame. Can you not recall even now, as if they were still throbbing on the air, the accents of that awful denunciation; "Woe to you, Scribes and Pharisees, hypocrites! Woe and woe again!" No wonder that the recollection of such words from an upstart, sprung from the dregs of the people, should have stung you to desperate purposes, and given to your revenge of to-day its most acceptable flavour. He lifted the veil of your hypocrisy: behold, He Himself perishes as a hypocrite. The title that stands on His head seems to jibe at His pretensions, and to condemn His ambition—"Jesus of Nazareth, King of the Jews." His friends, whom you feared, have vanished from His side; His disciples have hidden their heads in confusion. He mingles His dying gasps with those of two ruffians, whose lives are a forfeit to the exigencies of law and order; so that "with the wicked indeed is He reputed." Restrain not, then, your feelings of transport :— Wag your heads, and cry: "Vah, thou that destroyest the temple of God, and in three days buildest it up again, save thyself, coming down from the cross, that we may see and believe." Your mockery is echoed, though you hear it not, from the throats of a million demons, who hover in the darkening air around that blood-stained figure, that pants upon the hill of crucifixion.

Pitiable, most pitiable, is the condition of that dying Captain, whom hell and the synagogue have combined to destroy. Unparalleled, since blood began to flow upon the earth, is the gory wreck of that frame, once faultless in its symmetry. A brooding darkness, spreading its mysterious shroud over the world, mercifully obscures the details of the picture; but never did the earth serve as an altar for so ghastly a holocaust. On the rigid beams, prepared for the work of death, He hangs helpless and limp, suspended by great nails, which, with every quiver and spasm of agony, have opened a lengthened gash in hands and feet. From head to foot, there is no spot which has not felt wrench or bruise, or biting stripe; from head to foot, He is one wound; and in His nakedness, the busy heart's blood, welling from many a vein and artery, have woven Him a purple robe, that aids the mocking spirit of the kingly title above His head, and the diadem of piercing thorns upon His brow. Deadly exhaustion adds weight to His nerveless body, and combines with the posture of His sunken head, and the dishevelment of His tattered hair, to make Him appear as the very type of one abandoned by God and man. You would say that despair never found so appropriate an image as that of this dying man; nor a setting so suitable to its ghastliness, as the stormy scene of hostility below, and the unnatural darkness of the sky above. Few are the words that escape from His lips, now baked with feverish thirst, and fringed with the foam of anguish; but these words are gentle and loving, as if from the habit and momentum of a loving and gentle life. Proud Lucifer wonders to hear Him supplicate and plead for those who have hounded Him to such a death; "Father," He says, "forgive them, for they know not what they do." And even in this overthrow and shame, He proves His attraction over the spirits of man, by winning to repentance the thief beside Him; and with a glance of divine compassion, which no suffering could rob of its charm, He promised him a speedy release and happiness:—"This day thou shalt be with me in Paradise." By a new and solemn act too, He locked together the hearts of two beloved beings, who were sharers in His sorrows, in assigning a new mother to His favourite disciple, and a new son to His afflicted mother. Thus life ebbed slowly away with the sands of the ebbing hours; and the demons eagerly looked for the supreme moment, when, the fateful day over, they could claim a signal victory for the gates of hell. It comes at last; and with a thrill of gladness, they hear first that long cry of seeming despair: "My God! my God! why hast thou forsaken me"; and then, bursting from their victim's desolate heart—the acknowledgement of defeat, and the signal for dissolution:—"It is consummated!" His head falls; His soul quits its shattered tenement; the great prophet is dead: the great opponent of hell is overthrown and ruined.

That appalling death-cry, beloved Brethren, which seemed to the demons a confession of defeat, was the proclamation to all the universe, that God had won the greatest victory over the powers of darkness that should ever be recorded. Instantly, heaven and earth bore witness to the godhead of the Crucified. The rocks were rent with earthquake; the graves yawned, and gave up their dead. The twilight of the Jewish dispensation disappeared before a sun-burst, which was to bathe the world henceforward in light; for the veil, that hid the mysteries of the sanctuary, was rent from the top even to the bottom. The Saints were to weep no more, that no man was found worthy to open the book; for "behold the Lion of the tribe of Juda, the root of David has prevailed to open the book and to loose the seven seals thereof." That lion, matchless in strength, was no other than the lamb, matchless in meekness and humility, and long-suffering; whom St. John beheld in his vision "standing as it were slain." "And I saw an angel," says St. John, "coming from heaven, having the key of the bottomless pit; and a great chain in his hand, and he laid hold on the dragon, the old serpent, which is the devil and Satan, and bound him for a thousand years." Bewildered and confounded, the demons, as they plunged into their dungeon of fire, heard afar the echoes of the triumphant pæan, which told of man's liberation from the bondage and tyranny of Satan:—"Thou art worthy, O Lord, to take the book, and to open the seals thereof; because Thou wast slain, and hast redeemed us to God in Thy blood, out of every tribe and tongue and people and nation, and hast made us to God a kingdom, and priests, and we shall reign on the earth." Then thousands and thousands of voices joined the great anthem, crying aloud: "The lamb that was slain is worthy to receive power and divinity, and wisdom and strength, and honour and glory and benediction." And all creation, in its every nook and crevice, seemed to find an answering tongue to this hymn of joy: for "every creature that is in heaven, and on the earth and under the earth, and such as are in the sea, and all that are in them, I heard all saying," continues St. John, "To him that sitteth on the throne, and to the Lamb, benediction, and honour, and glory, and power for ever and ever." And while the demons listened, chafing, to the loud-pealing strains of victory, their hearts told them the same truth, which the awed Centurion, and the guilty crowds that beat their breasts on Calvary, had discovered:—"Truly this was the Son of God."

"FATHER FORGIVE THEM, FOR THEY KNOW NOT WHAT THEY DO."

TO-DAY, beloved Brethren, you are met together to offer your heartfelt sympathy to your suffering Lord, to thank Him for all that He has done and all that he has borne for you; and to bind yourselves more closely and fondly to Him for the time to come. While you will not neglect to dwell to-day upon all the details of His Passion, there is one incident to which I would ask you to give a few moments' consideration.

In the Gospel of St. Luke, we read: "And when they were come to the place which is called Calvary, they crucified Him there; and the robbers, one on the right hand, and the other on the left. And Jesus said: Father, forgive them, for they know not what they do." It is upon this wonderful prayer, breathing the utmost excess of love and kindness, that I would ask you to meditate with me, before you approach to kiss the image of your Crucified Redeemer.

For three long years, from the time of Our Lord's public appearance, the leaders of the synagogue had hated him with a fiendish malice. Their pride was wounded to the quick by the superior wisdom of His words, and the authority with which He spoke: Who was He, that He should put up to teach the people? His origin they thought they knew; is not this the carpenter's son? His hands were hard with manual labour; His life had been passed amongst the poorest of the population; He had never studied under the Masters of the Law; what presumption then to sit in the Chair of the Teacher, and to draw the people after Him as if He were another Moses, or Elias! But that was not all. He was revolutionary in His teaching; a man who would fain supercede the older precepts and maxims, and substitute his own. His cry was; "You have heard it said to them of old:—But *I* say to you." Here indeed was not merely presumption, but most perilous innovation. But to their infinite amaze, chagrin, and perplexity, He confirmed His doctrine by potent signs and miracles: the blind see, the lame walk, the lepers are cleansed. There is no denying that these marvels are wrought by Him. Yet Oh! the blindness of the human heart! They will accept any explanation of His miracles save the obvious one: if He casts out devils, it must be by Beelzebub, the prince of devils. Thus they render their unbelief impregnable; they have entrenched themselves safely against all evidence of His divine mission. Grace cannot come near them. And now their hatred has a free career. The more miracles He works, the more He proves Himself a seducer, and an ambitious man. His very beneficence and goodness in healing upon the Sabbath does but establish beyond doubt that He is a Sabbath-breaker, and one who sets Himself above the law. Let Him do good or evil now—it is all one to these men who have blinded themselves. Thus day by day, their hatred grows, till they openly seek His death. The fearful denunciations which He has hurled at them for their affectation of piety, their alms-deeds down to the sound of the trumpet, their fasts made known to the world by studiously disfigured faces, their respect for outward observances, coupled with an absolute disregard of the inward virtue without which deeds are as worthless rinds and shells without kernel—these fearful denunciations, I say, launched at them in the hearing of the people who once had overrated them as Saints, fill up the vessel of their unappeasable hatred, and ring in their ears wherever they turn. Over and over again, they use all their cunning to entrap Him into speeches upon which they can ground a charge of treason or of blasphemy. They are staggered indeed by the tranquil wisdom which, without any ado, reveals their hidden purpose, and thwarts their carefully-laid schemes. But, like bloodhounds baffled for a moment, they do but take up the chase again with redoubled fury and determination. At last their hour has come, and the power of darkness. The high-priest has said it: "One man must die for the people."

You know, beloved Brethren, the inhuman barbarity with which those Scribes and Pharisees flung themselves, so to speak, upon the long-chased quarry, and tore and mangled His innocent body, till they were drunk with blood. Look at the lamb, as He lies stretched out upon the cross, to which they have hammered Him fast, hands and feet. The story of their cruelty can be read there. Shoulders, back, and sides, one raw sore, from the heavy lashes rained upon Him at the pillar, when they did their utmost to kill Him; one raw sore, exuding great drops and streams of blood; and showing the very ribs beneath, to which the searching scourges have bitten their way. Look at His head: a wreath of great thorns encircles it, piercing into the temples, and shooting agony into the brain. Tangled masses of hair, steeped in blood and sweat, are congealing about the poor shoulders; and the tender hands and feet, pierced through and through, quiver helplessly around the nail-heads. And Oh! the face, that was so sweet, so amiable, how deathlike and ghastly it has grown. There is no light under the heavy drooping eyelid; the features are pinched and the cheeks hollow; and the mouth, covered with foam and blood, is drawn back in gasping pain. There He is, the man that must die for the people;—look at Him ye Scribes and Pharisees, and gloat your eyes with the sight; your work is well done; from the top of His head to the sole of His feet there is no soundness in Him; a worm and no man, the outcast of the people. And what a fire of hellish joy riots and dances in their bosoms. They wag their heads, and mock His torments with taunts and jests. The chief priests with the Scribes and Ancients mocking said: "He saved others, Himself He cannot save. If He be the King of Israel let Him come down now from the cross; and we will believe Him. He trusted in God; let Him now deliver Him if He will have Him: for He said,—I am the Son of God." And what says He, this poor wreck of a human being, what says He to these friends? Has He for these wretches no last word of scorching bale, no everlasting curse, eating to the marrow of their bones, no dying man's malediction, withering their future, and making life and eternity a desert for their feet? No. Stand astounded, ye heavens! His lips move, but not with curses; His eye opens but not to blight. "Father," says He "forgive them, for they know not what they do." Oh! the kindness, the love, the spirit of gentleness and forgiveness, the world of unmeasured compassion, enclosed in this small prayer. It takes you direct to His heart, the inexhausted fountain of meekness and charity.

While its feeble pulse flutters, the life that sustains that heart is, love. He averts His eyes from the sea of mocking faces that surges below; He withdraws His memory from the long roll of injuries and wrongs which He has sustained at the hands of those enemies; He remembers only the blindness and ignorance, self-wrought if you please, which has wrapt them as in a cloud; He bears in mind that seeing they had not seen; His poor enfeebled heart throbs with mercy and yearning for the poor sinners, who are rushing headlong into destruction; and with all the energy of His being, He pleads their cause before His heavenly Father, and shields them, as far as in Him lies, from the consequences of their sin:—"Father, forgive them, for they know not what they do."

Come up then, beloved Brethren, and kiss the feet of your all-merciful Saviour, bleeding for your sins, and praying for your forgiveness. Fear Him not. He is your loving brother. He knows better a thousand times than you do yourselves the darkness of your understanding, the frailty of your will, and the crippling power exercised over you by past habits of sin. He knows how your offences have been often the effect of thoughtlessness rather than malice. There is no excuse you can plead, that He will not plead a thousand times more eloquently. Do but resolve to do better in the future; and though your souls had been red as scarlet with sin, He will make them white as snow. Even though, like the brothers of Joseph, you have sold Him, the favourite of His father, into bondage, be assured when you come to see Him again in the land of His sojourn, with the purple robe of His own blood upon Him, reigning from the cross, His heart will thrill with tumults of joy and gladness to welcome you.

"THIS DAY THOU SHALT BE WITH ME IN PARADISE."

ON this day, eighteen hundred and fifty years ago, it is said that Dionysius the Areopagite and his companion, Apollophanes—both skilled in the science of the heavenly bodies—were standing with their face to Heliopolis, when the full moon was seen, contrary to the laws of nature, to move from the Eastern heavens, and to cover the face of the sun, so as to blacken its entire disc and to plunge the outspread landscape into midnight darkness. For three hours that darkness hung like a pall over the earth; and the preternatural phenomenon so amazed the famous Dionysius that he exclaimed; "Either the God of nature who created the world is in distress, or the world's machinery is falling to pieces."

He spoke the truth. In the capital of Judea, or rather without the sacred precincts of its walls, a tragedy was being enacted through those hours of gloom, which would have appalled the Areopagite, if it had been revealed to his eyes, and the history of which, unfolded to him later by the lips of St Paul, made him not only a Christian, but a saint. The Eternal Word by which all things are made, the King of Kings and the Lord of Lords, was in pain, in excruciating torture, in the throes of a most cruel death, inflicted by the creatures, whom His Almighty hand had shaped from the clay, and animated with the breath of life. And there was a funereal pageantry in the circumstances of His suffering which bore strange witness to the sovereignty of that dying God. He came into the world a King by right of birth, the scion of a royal though discrowned race, the family of the world-renowned David; He came the royal child of prophecy, the Prince of peace, with empire on His shoulder, and on His thigh titles of unmatched grandeur; at His birth, the winged courtiers of heaven sang pæans of gladness and triumph ; and Kings came from the East to adore Him, at the bidding of the long-looked for star, the messenger of light that heralded the advent of the King of glory, and the dawning of the Orient from on high. As a King, I say, He came into the world; and as a King He was leaving it. But strange and weird, and perverse, were the trappings and symbols of sovereignty which surrounded the departing monarch. He was raised high upon a throne, as other monarchs in the pomp of state ; but that throne was the trunk and beam of the dread gibbet, the dais of the cross, whose name was a blight, and whose shadow was a malediction, He wears a crown ; but not such as earthly monarchs wear, beaming with yellow gold, and sparkling with many-coloured jewels. His diadem is wrought for Him by a churlish nature, sin-spoiled and malignant, out of the prickly briars that were sin's creation, and an evidence of the primeval curse. His sceptre He has laid aside, that He may give princely largess out of His bounteous palm, the rubies of His own blood ; the richest gift that monarch ever gave to subject, and the sceptre He bore but now, was a reed or bamboo ; you may find it, wet with blood, in the hall of Pilate. The tattered purple, which a while ago He donned, while knees were bowed in show of homage before Him, has been exchanged for the noblest crimson that ever blushed upon a Kingly form—His heart's blood, spun by miracle into a garment. Over His throne, there is a sky-woven canopy, which Soloman, the wise, could not conjure over his seat of state ; it is the curtain of heaven's thick gloom, which will not be lifted until this death-pageant has traversed its various stages. And lest you should mistake the personality, or the claim of the great King, who is thus lifted above men, you have His title written in three languages above Him :—"Jesus of Nazareth, King of the Jews." The words were written in scorn, but told the truth unconciously, as the High-Priest, in the malice of His heart, was overruled to say : "It is necessary that one man should die for the people."

This King then, this ruler of all the universe, whose realm extended to the furthest star, and whose might was recognised by adoring angels and by shuddering demons alike, was, in a special manner, King of the Jews. He was the expectation of nations, foretold by the patriarch Jacob as to spring from the tribe of

Judah; and the Captain that Micheas had predicted, as owning the same birthplace as David, and destined to rule God's people, Israel. But when He came—this promised Sovereign, ardently desired as He was, and eagerly looked for by the people to whom the promises were made, He came in a manner so inconsistent with their preconceived notions, that, partly from blindness, and partly from an obstinate adherance to their own hopes and baseless visions, they disowned and persecuted Him, ridiculed His claims, and shut their eyes to the miracles, which were His divine credentials to the simple of heart. Left to themselves, the people had acknowledged His princely attributes, and sought to make Him King; but had been thwarted in their purpose by His miraculous disappearance from the midst of the noisy crowd. Later they fell under the influence of their natural guides and rulers; the priests, who offered their daily victims to God, and the Scribes, who were deeply versed in the law, and the Pharisees, who affected to be the law's purest votaries, and most scrupulous adherents. All these, whose vain ambition sought the applause and reverence of men, were amazed, stung, penetrated in every vein and artery with the poison of deadly hatred, when they beheld a common mechanic without respectable connexions, or even ordinary schooling, elevate himself into a professional teacher of religion and morality. The sneer, which His first fame as a preacher won him from their lips, was changed into heartfelt rancour, and the insatiable longing for vengance, when they heard the populace echoing his praises as a man of God. They became aware that the chorus of His ignorant admirers proclaimed Him a wonder-worker; later they heard the scum of their cities (for so they would regard them) hail Him as the Great Sovereign that was promised to deliver them, and talk among themselves of setting Him, the upstart, upon the throne of David, to be the controller of their actions and the arbiter of their lives. But who can conceive the viper-like venom of envy and spite which raged in their vitals, when He, with the reputation of His miracles fresh upon Him, denounced them in the light of heaven, and the hearing of the people, as hypocrites of the darkest dye, and whited sepulchres full of dead men's bones and corruption. That woe, woe! so oft-repeated by lips that spoke so gently to all but them, and had warm eulogies to bestow even upon the converted sinner, rung perpetually in their ears, stirred up their hearts to furious thoughts and mad projects, and left them no remedy for their ravening malice, but to compass His death, and to gloat their unpitying eyes upon the spectacle of His ruin, degradation, public shame and unalloyed anguish. He had unveiled their imposture and pretence before the people; before the people then, who in their simplicity believed Him omnipotent, He should perish as an imposter; as a false prophet, and a sham King; a traitor to Cæsar and to God.

His trial then, was a mere form: His sentence was a foregone conclusion. When in answer to the adjuration of the High Priest, He declared himself to be the Christ, the Son of God, the discordant testimonies of the witnesses were gladly set aside. Flushed with indignation, that claimed to be righteous and holy, the High Priest rent His garments, and cried out: "He hath blasphemed. What further need have we of witnesses? Behold now you have heard the blasphemy, What think you?" But they answering said:— "He is guilty of death." Confronted with Pilate, and asked "Art thou the King of the Jews?" He answered "Thou sayest it." And knowing that He was falsely accused of stirring up the people, knowing that, as the Scripture says, "For envy they had delivered Him," the heathen governor laboured in his own half-hearted way, sickened by the spectacle of their mortal animosity, yet timid of opposing them, to find some plea for rescuing the victim from their toils. He thought to stagger them in their purpose by giving them a choice between releasing Jesus and Barabbas—a robber stained with blood, and notorious for his crimes. All in vain, They will have the murderer released. "What then shall I do with Jesus, that is called Christ? What shall I do with the King of the Jews?":—"Crucify Him," is the savage cry, "we have no King but Cæsar." Appalled at their persistency, and terrified by the responsibility in which he was placed, he strove to silence the voice of conscience, by washing his hands before the wild and excited spectators, saying, "I am innocent of the blood of this just man. Look you to it." And the whole people, possessed by the spirit of Satan, the adversary, shook the very roof of the hall with the awful imprecation: "His blood be upon us, and upon our children."

And so, He who was rejected in favour of an odious brigand and man of blood, must die the death of a defaulting slave, and in company of two other robbers, possibly condemned for their share in the sanguinary scenes, in which Barabbas had been the chief actor. This decision was sweeter to the enemies of Jesus than honey or the honey-comb, or the exhilaration of wine. Unconciously they were filling in the details of the picture which the prophet had painted, when he described the world's Redeemer as "reputed with the wicked." Now would the ignorant mass of the Jews, whose favour this false prophet had courted, see how mean, how vulgar, how degraded, their betters esteem the low-born idol, to whom they have been swearing fealty as Son of God and King of the Jews. Raised up beside Him, therefore, are the two unhappy wretches, their limbs writhing, their faces distorted with agony; and the dim eyes of the dying Saviour, turn they right or turn they left, are scared by these spectres of pain. But above or below or around Him, there is no spot that His eye can rest on without starting fresh fountains of grief and misery within Him. Even His mother's face, so unmoved in its stoney fixedness of grief, is to His sight but an evidence of the ruin that has overtaken all with whom His heart is bound up. But O! the wild saturnalia, more diabolical than the guiltiest rites of pagan worship, more fell and heartless than the dark deeds that Molock's or Bellona's priests perpetrated in their idol's honour, more frantic and unrestrained and inebriate than the orgies of the mad bacchanals, is that which rages amongst the dense multitude at the foot of the Cross. Though unnatural darkness broods over the sinful earth, yet, in the callousness of their fury, the priests and Scribes, and Elders, and Pharisees, moving to and fro in their sweeping robes, wagging their heads and gesticulating like men distraught, urge on with hoarse shouts the passions of the great crowd, and put into their mouths the taunts and cries of derision they are to employ. "Bah, thou that destroyest the temple of God and in three days dost rebuild it; save thine own self; if thou be the Son of God, come down now from the cross, He saved others, Himself He cannot save ; if He be the King of Israel, let Him come down now from the cross, and we will believe Him. He trusted in God; let Him now deliver Him if He will have Him ; for He said, "I am the Son of God." Truly it was their hour, and the power of darkness. It was the very hey-day of Hell's carnival.

But this was not all. Even of the thieves who hung moaning beside Him, one was found to repeat these taunts, and with his dying breath to revile the unknown King. Brutal in thought and feeling, from a life of reckless ferocity, in which animal courage, and a stoicism under torture, were among the qualities most highly esteemed, this man, accustomed to scenes of murder and violence, doubtless felt the deepest contempt for the patient and uncomplaining victim, whose blood-drenched body, scored and opened with a thousand raw gashes, stood out red and ghastly beside him in the twilight. Stimulated doubtless by the wine and myrrh which he had swallowed, and which began to work in his veins, and to tingle in his brain, with a sort of stupor that made light of pain, he was the more ready to scoff at the apparent effeminacy and cowardice of this prophet, transformed among thieves into a criminal, who prayed even for His ruthless murderers, instead of hurling defiance and hatred at them with His dying breath. And so, "he blasphemed Him," says St. Luke, saying, "if thou be Christ, save Thyself and us." Not so, however, with his fellow-culprit. There was still in his heart some remnant of compassion and pity, which he did not seek to repress, and which furnished his dying Saviour with a field for the operation of His mercy and His healing grace. Oh! thrice blessed the impulse of pity, the precious gift of our tender and loving Creator, which opens the door to so many graces, and conducts him, who hearkens to its call, even to the gates of everlasting life. If tradition may be believed, the Incarnate Word already owed a debt of gratitude to the family of that poor robber. For the story is told, that long years before, in that painful pilgrimage to Egypt, when, flying from Herod's myrmidons, he was carried, a tender babe, over the sands of the desert by his youthful mother and foster-father, weary and footsore after a day of laborious travel, the little party looked in vain among the shadows of the barren rocks, and over the far-reaching floor of the wilderness, now darkening under the gathering night, for a place to shelter their heads, and to provide them with some slight repast to keep body and soul together. As it chanced, they stood, without knowing it, in the neighbourhood of a robber's cave; and presently their footsteps brought out the wild denizens of the rocky retreat, who far from ill-treating them, invited them into their abode, and gave them a share of such food and drink as the place afforded. Kindness so unexpected filled the breasts of the travellers with gratitude, which they would fain have testified, but had not the means; when God came to their assistance. Affliction had visited the robber's cave in the form of leprosy, which had fastened upon the latest-born of the family, little Dismas (for such according to tradition was the name); and his mother's heart was rent to see her darling, scaled and discoloured with this loathsome malady. When morning dawned, and the travellers had bidden their rough hosts a grateful adieu, Providence directed the mother to bathe her little leper in the same water, which had been used in washing the divine infant; when lo! to her surprise and unspeakable joy, the leprous scurf disappeared from her boy's limbs, and left them as fresh and fair as they had been before. But her charity (says this beautiful legend) had not its last reward in this miracle: for God's loving eye tracked that child, as it grew through the stages of youth and manhood, and amidst all the deeds of wrong and turbulence, and all the traits of character which he shared with his guilty companions, prepared the greatest grace of his life, by bringing him to a death of torture and ignominy upon this hideous gibbet. As if the mother's humanity still throbbed in that heart, which was so soon to be dust, he felt pierced with compassion for the poor being who, innocent as He was, and overflowing with kindness to all, was suffering the death of the guilty. He could not be restrained, even by the presence of the leaders of the people, who were still crying out their fierce cries, and parading among the crowd, from giving vent to the feelings of indignation which the words of the blaspheming robber had awakened within him. The enemies of this poor stricken man might have it in their power to torture his despised champion and sympathizer; they might wreek their worst vengence upon him; they might rend and tear his flesh, if they would; but he must give utterance to the thoughts that swelled within him, though all the Sanhedrim stood by, and every member of the Council deemed the words a personal affront. Loudly then he answered the other robber, rebuking him in the hearing of the infuriated multitude:—"Neither dost thou fear God (any more than these), seeing thou art under the same condemnation. And we indeed justly, for we receive the due reward of our deeds: but this man hath done no evil."—*Luke* xxiii. 40. When mercy began its work, beloved Brethren, in the robber's heart, we cannot precisely say. But now grace was triumphant. Turning his yearning face to Jesus, he said:— "Lord remember me, when thou shalt come into thy kingdom." Sovereignly gracious, most full of love and tenderness and pity, was the dying King's response. And Jesus said to him: "Amen, I say to thee, this day thou shalt be with me in Paradise!"

Behold! ye wondering angels, who weep over the sufferings of the Son of Man, the first fruits of His bitter passion, and shameful death! The Word that had, at the dawning of creation, said, "Let there be light, and light was," had spoken again in the little world of the sinner's soul; and where the darkness of sin had reigned before, there beamed the sun of Justice, and the sunshine of grace. Chaos had been transformed to order and beauty, not by gradual process of development, but by one syllable from the lips of the Omnipotent King, whom, as the Psalmist says, all things obey. The fire which Jesus came to cast upon the earth, had kindled the heart so long cold, and icy, and benumbed in death; and the crimes of a lifetime, like straw and offal, were instantly consumed in the irresistible flame. Instead of sin, a harvest of virtue. swiftly fostered by the rays of grace, and fed by the fertilizing blood of the Redeemer, sprung up in an instant of time, and made the poor wretch, in the last hour of his extraordinary career, as dear to God, as beloved as he was loving. Ponder upon that sudden growth of supernatural faith, which, through every disguise of humiliation, recognised the great King, that came to save and rule the nations. Ponder upon the penetration of that faith, which understood in an instant what the Apostles were so long in apprehending; that the kingdom of Jesus was not of this world. Ponder upon the fortitude which that faith inspired, and which the Apostles knew not till the descent of the Holy Spirit; a fortitude, which made the poor dying thief brave the utmost resentment of Priest and Scribe and Pharisee, and proclaim to all the frantic multitude that their victim was sinless, and that He, who died as a slave, was the Lord of this world, and the Judge of the world to come. Ponder upon the unhesitating hope and confidence, which the meek companionship of the suffering Lamb of God inspired, when the dying thief, despite his consciousness of a guilty life, begged to be remembered in the realms beyond the grave. Ponder upon the burning flame of charity, which shot up in his soul, when he heard his petition so solemnly received, and knew that he was no longer the outcast of Heaven and earth, but an accepted child and a favoured vassal. Ponder upon the thoroughness of that repentance, which embraced a death so ignominous, and excruciating, as worthy of his deserts, and so publicly proclaimed as his due :—"We indeed suffer justly : we receive the reward of our deeds." Oh! how fervently did poor sorrowing Dismas feel that pining, that passionate regret of the true penitent, which St. Augustine expressed many a generation after in his own eloquent words : "Too late have I known thee, O Ancient Truth, too late have I loved thee, O Ancient Beauty."

Not long, beloved Brethren, yet too long by far, did that awful pageant last. Dismas heard the dying words of his King, his Saviour, and his friend. He heard that plaintive appeal :—"My God, my God, why hast thou forsaken me?" He heard the last word of all—"It is consummated"—and the loud cry, that gave the signal for the heavy head to fall, and the agonizing spirit to depart. He heard the crash of earthquake, and saw the hill of execution burst asunder, and open a chasm between the condemmed robber and his Redeemer. He saw the crowds, subdued and terrified at last, beating their breasts trooping back to the sacred city. He may have seen the dead that rose from their graves, flitting to and fro over the earth. He saw the soldiers come with their crowbars to break his legs, lest his exposed corpse should desecrate the Sabbath. But amidst these terrific sights and sounds, all was joy and jubilee ; gratitude and love cast out fear and overcome pain.

"I THIRST."

THE three dread hours, beloved Brethren, are almost run;—the consummation of protracted suffering and unexampled shame;—and the sacred body of Jesus hangs aloft, limp, heavy and bloodless, save for the gory mantle of clotted blood that wraps it round, in the horror of the unearthly darkness, that veils the day. He has endured a succession of agonies, such as man never endured before, and never will again: and yet no murmur of indignation, no token of impatience has escaped that Lamb of Sacrifice, in fulfilment of the prophet's word: "He shall be led as a sheep to the slaughter, and shall be dumb as a lamb before His shearer, and He shall not open His mouth." The workings of His desolate heart have indeed manifested themselves during that period of the power of darkness; but in immortal words of love and tenderness, compassion and glad self-immolation. He has prayed for His pitiless and bloodstained foes, while their blasphemies have tingled in His ears:—"Father, forgive them, for they know not what they do." He has opened His parched lips to give hope and joy to the robber, who had begun by reviling Him: "This day thou shalt be with Me in Paradise." He has shown how amid all His pains and griefs, His affectionate heart still turns to the mother who gave Him birth, and followed Him from His cradle in the manger, to this rude and knotted couch of wood, that forms His death-bed, with an uninterrupted canticle of sympathy, devotion, and passionate love: "Son," said He to the beloved and virgin Apostle, "behold thy mother." "Mother, behold thy son." He has revealed to us the course of His chief misery, in those words of keenest anguish, which are drawn from

Him by the attitude of His Eternal Father, towards the representative of the guilty race—"My God, my God, why hast thou forsaken me?" "And now, at last, as His hour draws nigh, He would fain make known to us by one short word, that breathes no breath of complaint, one of the greatest of His torments, a torment which through the whole of His passion has been most excruciating, that when He is gone, we might ponder over it, and take to heart the lessons it conveys. "Afterwards," says St. John, "Jesus knowing that all things were now accomplished, that the Scripture might be fulfilled," said :—'I thirst.' "Now there was a vessel set there," he continues, "full of vinegar. And they (the soldiers) putting a sponge full of vinegar about hyssop put it to His mouth. Jesus therefore when He had taken the vinegar, said, 'It is consummated,' and bowing His head He gave up the ghost. The Psalmist foresaw this burning thirst, which the Redeemer of the world was destined to endure, and the draught of vinegar, with which His enemies would mock His agonies; and had cried out with a pitious wail, in the person of the great victim of Salvation: "And they gave Me gall for My food, and in My thirst they gave Me vinegar to drink." Gall and wine they offered Him, when He came to the fatal spot in accordance with the custom observed in carrying out the sentence of crucifixion: for the draught was one calculated to refresh the sufferer after the ordeal of his scourging, and to blunt the sense of pain. But that strengthening potion Jesus would not drink: for as He came to the dregs of the bitter chalice, which His Heavenly Father had commended to His lips, He must needs be fully alive to all their bitterness. "They gave Him wine to drink," says St. Matthew. "mingled with gall, and when He had tasted it He would not drink." But now that every dried cistern of nature gapes with thirst, when the extremity of that torture is come upon Him, having reached its climax of horror; when in response to that heartrending call, "I thirst,"—the soldiers repeated the inhuman jest of offering Him vinegar, a draught which was known to aggravate beyond endurance the pains of the wounded: that nothing might be wanting to the misery of His death, and the fulness of His atonement, Jesus accepted the new agent of pain, and pressed His lips to the moistened sponge. All was over now: the shadowy forms of pain and ignomony and cruel death which had haunted the brains and harrowed up the souls of the prophets, were not so much realized, as outdone, by the innocent victim. "Jesus, therefore, when He had taken the vinegar, said, "It is consummated," and bowing His head He gave up the ghost.

And with good reason, beloved Brethren, did our Blessed Lord proclaim His thirst: for there is no cause which can contribute to such an effect, that is not to be found in the last day of His life. Since He sat in the midst of His Apostles at the last supper, on yesterday evening, far from partaking of any draught that could assuage His thirst, He has undergone every kind of torture, mental and bodily, which could aggravate its agonies. First, in the dew-bedabbled grass of the garden of Gethsemane, beneath those stars which His hand had fixed in the sky, but which looked down as of old, unsympathetic, through all their Maker's sufferings, He had delivered up His soul to the contemplation of the dread prospects awaiting Him: foremost the bitter chalice of suffering, the bitterest ingredients of which would be the ingratitude of friend and foe alike; and in the more distant future, the unchecked outrages of the race for which He gave His life, the ever-renewed crop of sin and ingratitude springing up to the end of the world, and the descent into the pit of myriads, who would fling away the redemption He was about to purchase. Oh! dreadful vision! A terrible outlay of grief and pain for so insignificant a return! The vision grows more vivid! Generations of sinners rise, enact their wicked part, and sink to their doom before His eyes, at sight of which His heart is crushed, and like the red must that comes from the pressed grape, His precious blood is forced out of the very pores of His body by the intensity of His inward agony: and trickling over every limb, more copious than the sweat of the slave who is forced to toil beneath the burning sun, soaks His garments through, and leaves the red print of His knees upon the earth. This loss of blood alone in its physical aspect, would have accounted for a raging thirst in the system so drained; but who shall say how its torture was increased by the feverish excitement produced in Him by such awful visions, and the deadly depression wrought by the approach of the fatal hour. "My soul," said He, "is sorrowful even unto death." Feverish agitation, such as His human nature underwent in the garden, and overwhelming sadness, medical men tell us, are two of the most powerful incentives to thirst: but what medical man will measure that thirst of our Blessed Lord, if it was proportioned to His agitation of mind, His unspeakable sadness, and the physical exhaustion consequent upon His unnatural sweat of blood.

Presently, the voices of His enemies were heard, and the clash of arms; and fitfully flashing lanterns and torches played over the trees and the broken ground of the garden. "Behold," said our Blessed Lord, "the hour is at hand; and the Son of Man shall be betrayed into the hands of sinners." Then came the traitor at the head of the rude throng; and gave them the signal whom to seize with his viper's kiss. How the touch of his perjured lips must have sickened the soul of Jesus, and kindled His pale cheek with the flush of shame, and lacerated His loving heart, at the recollection of all the kindness He had outpoured upon the unfortunate man, all the graces and favours He had lavished upon him in vain. Then began that long and painful series of journeys to and fro through the city of Jerusalem, a few days ago the scene of His homely triumph, now the theatre of His tragic end. First to the High Priest's house; of Annas, father-in-law to the High Priest; thence to the house of Caiaphas, where the chief Priests and the whole Council sought false witness against Him, that they might put Him to death. "He hath blasphemed," cried the High Priest, rending his garments, "what farther need have we of witness?" And they answered in chorus, "He is worthy of death." Then they spit in His face, and buffeted Him: and others struck His face with the palms of their hands, saying, "Prophesy unto us, O Christ, who is he that struck." Oh! beloved Brethren, with a frame already so enfeebled by His sweat of blood, surely amidst all the outrages and all the opprobrium of His persecution, amidst all the mental pangs of unrequited affection from which our Blessed Lord suffered, the cruel fever of thirst, increasing at every new trial, must have been a most distinct and ever present element in His sufferings.

Onwards again moved the soldiers and the rabble, the cortege of the innocent Lamb, covering Him all the way with reproaches, and dealing Him many a blow. He stands before the tribunal of the Roman governor, but He is found to belong, as a Galilean, to the jurisdiction of Herod; and again He is hauled along the streets until he reaches Herod's palace. There failing to satisfy the curiosity of the King, who wished to behold an exhibition of His miraculous power, He was hurried back again, clad in a white garment, as a driveller and a fool, to Pilate's hall. In the midst of the Chief Priests and the Magistrates, He heard the futile and half-hearted pleading of the Roman, who would fain release Him, yet dared not incur the resentment of the multitude; and great must have been the shock, deep the stab in His tender nature, when the chosen people preferred the miscreant Barabbas, to their own King; and when, ringing again and again in His ears, the excited crowds, spurred on by their Priests and leaders, bellowed that cry whose echoes have reverberated wildly in every succeeding age: "Crucify Him! crucify Him! His blood be upon us and upon our children."

But the worst has yet to come. Jesus is bound to the pillar in the governor's hall: and prostrated as He is, scarcely able to stand erect, He is scourged ferociously by men bribed to kill Him under the scourge, and drugged with strong drink to overpower their feelings of humanity. More than forty lashes the Jews are forbidden by law to inflict; but revelations tell us that Jesus received at their instigation five thousand; and this is not incredible, if on the one side we remember that the Jews, fearing he would escape crucifixion through the partiality of Pilate, had set their hearts upon scourging Him to death, and on the other hand that Jesus sustained His weakness by the might of His divine power, under tortures which would, humanly speaking, have occasioned His death many times over. It is simply appalling to the imagination to dwell upon the horrors of that infliction. Thick as the torrents of the winter rain, the blows descend upon His shoulders and sides, and back; dealt with savage purpose, and with the practised skill that knows where to find the most tender parts of the body. Every blow draws blood; the flesh itself is torn off in fragments and strips, and clings to the merciless lash: until the ghastly frame-work of the bones stands revealed to the eye. Truly may He say now, as the Psalmist pictures Him: "They have numbered all My bones." Never did the Wonder-worker, the living Word of God's power, perform a more astonishing miracle than when, under that cruel hailstorm of swift-plied scourges, He maintained Himself in the land of the living, and preserved strength enough to crawl under the weight of His cross to the place appointed for His crucifixion. And what poor mangled wretch upon the field of carnage, when the tide of battle has rolled by, and the moans of the wounded asking piteously for water make the night dismal, ever suffered such pangs of thirst as after so barbarous a scourging did this poor victim, of whom it was truly said—I am as a worm and no man.

But now, beloved Brethren, when I have said so much, I find myself only upon the threshold of my subject: for from the time when His scourging was completed, the thirst of Jesus began to assert itself, as undoubtedly one of the most awful of His many physical pains; and one that must have grown more and more unendurable with every blow He received, every shock, mental or bodily, He underwent, every drop of blood He lost, every breath He drew. From this point I need do no more, nay, I could do no more than indicate the principal phases of His suffering; and leave to your own imaginations to fancy how His thirst must have burnt up His vitals, and preyed upon Him and consumed Him, and worked in His poor brain like a frenzy, at every new development of His passion.

No rest for Him after the diabolical ill-treatment of His scourging; for the soldiers surround Him in the governor's hall; tear from His back His clinging garment; put a scarlet cloak about Him; gird His head round with a thorny diadem; and put a reed into His trembling hand. Then they bowed their knees in mock homage, and cried, "Hail, King of the Jews"; and spat upon Him, and struck His head with the reed, and when they had mocked Him to their heart's content, they tore from His quivering body the garment in which they had clothed Him; and led Him off to crucifixion. O my God! how can we follow Thee through that journey, short indeed in the space traversed, but how vast and endless to Thee in Thy faintness and debility! How can we dwell upon the ruggedness of the way, which so shook Thy enfeebled frame at every step; or upon the ruthless blows from which Thy tottering body shrank, or upon the falls that flung Thee helpless and apparently lifeless under the ponderous cross that bowed Thee down. But imagination must not faint; for, having rejected the draught of wine mingled with gall, Thou art yet to be pierced through the living sinews and nerves of hands and feet, and elevated into the air, amidst howls of cruel triumph and derision, and there, in the ghastliness of the eclipse that covers earth and heaven, with agony upon agony, and gasp upon gasp, for three long hours, into which Thou dost compress the woes of a world's history, Thou dost part with the small remnant of life's current, drop by drop, amidst a thirst that fixes its fangs in Thee like a deadly asp; until, the moment having arrived for Thy release, Thou dost at last declare its pangs in that pregnant and piteous syllable : " I thirst."

But there was another kind of thirst, beloved Brethren, from which Jesus suffered ; a thirst of the soul that knew no bounds, and transcended His physical thirst, as much as the soul's subtlety transcends the coarseness of the body. It was His thirst for your salvation and mine, and the salvation of the whole human race of Adam. As He hung aloft between heaven and earth, He saw the whole world mapped out before Him, with its various forms and fashions of sin, and all the diversities of its abject idolatry. How He longed and panted for the time when His name, and His immolation, would be made known to them all; when His symbol of salvation would be set up among the swarming population of the land of the Nile, and its deserts should be peopled with Anchorites; when many a barbarous tribe of Northmen should bow their stiff necks to His yoke; when Rome should be transformed from the stronghold of pagan superstition into the centre of Christian unity, the beating heart of the great Christian system : when Greece, the mistress of vice as well as refinement, should own the sway of the divine civilizer : when Asia should be traversed by a St. Thomas, a St. Bartholomew, a St. Matthias, a St. Matthew ; and later by His beloved St. Francis Xavier; when those two islands on the confines of the known Western world, should see their Druid groves cut down, and shine as gems on the forehead of Christianity ; when from the hidden seas, more westward still, a mighty world, unknown before, should develop itself to the zeal and charity of its missionaries, and His own bloodless rite, His own clean oblation, well-pleasing and perfect, should take the place of hideous and systematic slaughter, which now labels itself Religion in those far continents. This was the thirst, which more terribly than even its physical counterpart consumed the soul, and wasted the heart of Jesus.

A. M. D. G.

THE MATERNITY OF OUR BLESSED LADY.

THE fact of the Incarnation, beloved Brethren, is a stupendous fact; and the manner in which it was accomplished, is likewise stupendous. That God, the Creator, outraged by His own rebellious creatures, should have decreed to assume their paltry nature, that He might be able to atone in their behalf to His violated justice—an atonement which His creatures of themselves were incapable of offering—this was, indeed, a mystery of mercy, considerateness, and benevolence. But the kindliness of that decree was vastly enhanced by the love and condescension which induced Him to select, as the instrument of His purpose, and the blessed link by which He was to unite Himself to the children of Adam, a poor unpretending girl, rich only in virtue, who was to stand to Him for ever in a relation of the most intimate and tender kind that flesh and blood can beget—the relation of Mother. He, doubtless, in His wisdom and power could have devised some other way, humanly speaking, less humiliating and vulgar, of allying His nature with ours, with a view to the great Expiation, which He contemplated. But no. He chose to have a human mother, though He would have no father according to the flesh; and from her womb He decreed to receive that substance which entitled Him to a place in the category of the fallen family of Adam—through her. He was to be the Son of Man who, as Son of God also, was destined to blot out the handwriting that stood against His fellow-men.

Now, beloved Brethren, let us look this fact in the face, and understand, and humbly and thankfully acknowledge all that it implies. When the Angel Gabriel was sent on that wondrous embassy to the young maiden of Nazareth who, under the shelter of a fond but uncarnal espousal with her kinsman Joseph, was living a life of unsullied continence; when he, that celestial ambassador, dazzled by her spiritual beauty—brilliant though he was himself, as one of heaven's brightest hierarchs, and familiar with the beautiful Spirits that adorned the court of God—in a burst of admiration, inspired by the Holy Ghost—cried out! "Hail to thee, full of grace; the Lord is with thee"; and proceeded to announce to her how God had designed her to be the mother of the promised Emmanuel; the scruples arising from her vowed virginity being removed, Mary bowed her head in submission to the will of her Master, and said: "Behold the handmaid of the Lord; be it done unto me according to Thy word." What happened then? God had waited for her decision; He deigned to let His Incarnation depend upon her consent; He had made her the gate by which He would enter the pale of human nature; and on the signal given, by her gentle whisper of acquiescence, instantly He united Himself to her, and through her to us, becoming in the same moment and the same act her true son, and our true brother. And now henceforth, Mary is bound by the ties, and crowned with the privileges of that unspeakable maternity. He whom she has conceived in her virginal womb can never cease to be her son. She can never cease to be His mother, any more than God can divest Himself of His Godhead. Nor is this maternity a thing of figure or shadow; it is genuine and true, and unquestionable; it is a maternity in the sense in which the world at large is wont to apply the term: saving only that it involves a more absolute and engrossing title than that which the relation of mother usually implies towards the fruit of her womb: inasmuch as Mary, to her Son, is the one only source of human life and of bodily substance; and representing in her own person the claims of father and mother at once. Yes! not a particle that goes towards the building up of His human frame, but He chooses to owe to Mary. I say chooses; for this is no thing of chance; no random arrangement; no measure adopted upon sudden impulse; it is predetermined as long as the Incarnation itself; it is an essential element in the Eternal decree which was to make God man. Well; let it be conceded that Mary is the Mother of Jesus; that admission is forced upon the mind by the facts of the case; and in the Sacred Scriptures she is spoken of as the mother of Jesus; when St. John says: "There was a wedding feast at Cana of Galilee, and the mother of Jesus was there. That admission (say some persons) must not carry us too far; you Catholics call her the mother of God—not merely the mother of Jesus; and that doctrine is untrue, nay more, implies an impossibility; conveys an idea which is really blasphemous. For God has no beginning; else He would not be God at all. The Son of God, the Second Person of the Blessed Trinity, is, indeed, begotten of the Father; but by an eternal generation; a generation altogether unlike any birth in time. You cannot therefore say that Mary is the mother of God, without saying in the same breath that God had a beginning, that there was a time when He was not, and that Mary ushered Him into existence, and started Him on His career. Such are the objections of many non-Catholics who have imperfectly fathomed the meaning of the Incarnation and its necessary consequences. Let us see how far the objection has any pith or substance, and how far it justifies the charge brought against us as Catholics of raising Mary to a level with the Godhead, at least, and making her a sharer in the worship which reason and religion reserve to God alone.

Now let me ask you a question. Are you right in speaking of your mother—of her who gave you birth—*as* your mother? The question seems silly. The whole world answers, "of course, it is right." But remember: you are a composite being. You have a body and a soul. Your body, indeed, you owe to your parents: but how about your soul? They did not beget that; that was given to you by the great Creator—life and spirit, the faculties of the soul—these come expressly from His hand, and are joined by Him to matter to constitute the rational man. How then can you speak of the mother or father of any man? Why not limit yourself to the assertion of their parentship over the body, seeing that the soul is not derived from them, not of their giving? It is for a very good reason. It is because body and soul are knit together into one being; for a man is not a mere company, or a firm consisting of two independent and equally responsible partners; he is one person; one *ego*; and to this personality are rightly referred the acts and conditions of both the spiritual and the corporal substance which combine in him. He has two *natures*—the material and the spiritual; but only one *person*; and that person is the man, who speaks of the members of his body and the powers of his soul as equally alike himself. If his limbs or organs ache, it is himself that suffers; if his feelings are stirred, or his intellect or will is exercised, it is equally himself who feels, and thinks, and wills. Such is the mystery of a personal union between two natures. The two natures make but one self, one person; and father and mother are progenitors of the unity of the one man—not merely any one part of him; because, while life lasts, every part is associated in the one being. This is all very obvious, but it is important as furnishing the data upon which we are to judge whether Mary is or is not to receive the title of Mother of God. Who is Jesus? Is He man only? No: God forbid we should say so. First and foremost, He is God. He must be God, or the whole idea of an adequate atonement through a God-man falls to the ground. He is the very God-head, who, without putting off His divinity—which would be impossible and inconceivable—has taken upon Himself our humanity. How? Is it by merely associating these natures in an artificial grouping, as sticks are bound together by a rope? No. It is by the personal union, close beyond thought, such as I have described as existing in our humanity itself, and forming the principle of cohesion between soul and body. It is by a union which makes deity and manhood—which makes the divine essence, the human soul, and the human body, into one person, one *Ego*; who can as truly say with His human lips: "The Father and I are one"—as He can call Himself—the Son of Man, and the descendant of David; or say to His mother from the Cross: "Mother, behold thy Son." This union is called the *hypostatic* union; which is only using a word of Greek instead of Latin extraction in the sense of a personal union. It is because of this union that our Blessed Lord is found speaking of Himself sometimes as the Son of God, co-eternal and co-equal with His Father—"The Father and I are one," and sometimes as the Son of Man; the child of Adam, and in that character, inferior and subject to His Father; as when He says: "The Father is greater than I." But in all cases, it is the one Person that speaks, the one *Ego*; for Jesus is God as well as man; He is the divine Man; He is the Man-God.

Now Mary is the mother of this Man-God: not of the Man alone; just as an ordinary mother is the mother not of the body alone, but of the human being that results from the union of both natures. If we refuse to Mary the title of Mother of God, we refuse to Jesus, her Son, the honours of the divine Nature. If He is God, and all that He is, in body, soul, or God-head is equally divine, then hers is a divine maternity, and she is as truly Mother of God, as He is God. There is no second Being in question; she is either the Mother of God, or of no one; since there is no Jesus but the Eternal Begotten of the Father, essentially divine, though clothed in human nature.

And this is made clearer if we ponder on what is said by some theologians. Suppose Mary gave birth to her Son, a mere man; and that God united Himself to this man after his birth by a personal union; Mary would not then have been called Mother of God, because she had given birth to a mere man, who continued a mere man till that later event, with which she had no connexion.

But this was not so. The Son of God, made man, was Mary's child from the first instant of His conception. Isaias had recognised the mystery of light from afar: "Behold a Virgin shall be with child, and bring forth a son, and shall call His name Emmanuel which, being interpreted is, God with us. Ages rolled by, and the time came round; and the glorious Archangel proclaimed the same truth in the ears of the abashed maiden of prophecy. "Fear not, Mary, for thou hast found grace with God. Behold! thou shalt conceive in thy womb, and shalt bring forth a Son, and thou shalt call His name Jesus. He shall be great, and shall be called the Son of the most High; and the Lord God shall give to Him the throne of David His father; and He shall reign in the house of Jacob for ever; and of His kingdom there shall be no end."

All the endowments of Mary, beloved Brethren, which made her the most glorious by far of God's creatures, are only a corollary, a necessary consequence, of her maternity. That maternity placed her in a relation, and invested her with functions, with respect to the divinity, which required in her a sanctity that cannot be exaggerated, and every imaginable gift of soul in a degree surpassing all other creatures—even the most superb princes of the heavenly Court, if her character was to match her dignity. Suppose her less lavishly endowed, and you attribute to her divine Son a comparative indifference to spiritual beauty in those nearest and dearest to Him; seeing that He does not demand its highest development in her to whom He was united as she was, to Him, by infinitely closer ties than any other creature. Suppose her less lavishly endowed, and you represent Him as capable of establishing with one of His creatures the most intimate alliance conceivable in nature, while He makes another more pleasing in His sight, and more worthy of that alliance by the possession of a loftier range of virtues. Diminish her gifts, and you are free to picture Him, in His home at Nazareth, amid the tenderest outpourings of her maternal love, with His infant heart yearning, and His infant hands outstretched to receive the caresses of some other creature, dearer in His sight by the inward charms of the spirit, than she was whom He called Mother. Diminish her gifts, and you may suppose the mother and her Son, the King of Glory, separated in heaven by some other being, who has a right by higher merits, to a place nearer to His Sacred Heart than she, the mother, from whose flesh and blood He received all of humanity that was in Him. Away with such an anomaly! The thought is intolerable; it is to ascribe caprice and inconsistency to the all-perfect God who is essentially firm and constant, and who judges just judgment. It stands to reason that He made her best, because He wished her to be nearest. She could not be His mother, unless she was unapproachably perfect; she would not have been unapproachably perfect, if she had not been selected as His mother. When it was announced to our Blessed Lord, on a certain occasion, that His mother and brethren stood without, seeking to speak with Him, what did He say?—"Whosoever shall do the will of My Father, who is in heaven, he is My brother, and sister, and mother." This answer meant that the foremost requisite for an intimate union with Him, even on the part of His own mother, was superior virtue and spiritual excellence. That was before kinship, and the very first condition of the divine maternity. And again, when the woman in the crowd shouted out: "Blessed is the womb that bore Thee, and the breasts that gave Thee suck": "Yea, rather," was His comment, "Blessed are they who hear the word of God, and keep it." Yes; kinship could not please, unless previously adorned by that divine charity which implies every virtue besides; and constitutes the bond or clasp which embraces all perfections. This matchless charity, by which God drew Mary's soul to Himself, must pave the way for that miraculous maternity which drew God into her Virgin womb. Such is the order of thought in the Archangel's first message: "Hail, Mary, full of grace; Fear not, Mary, for thou hast found grace with God":—Then: "Behold thou shalt conceive." Yes, she must be a supremely worthy mother; for in His generosity He would accept the secondary laws of human nature; He would of set purpose conform to the influence of heredity, which is so strong in the blood; and while He made Himself strikingly like in outward feature and bearing, to her who was His only earthly parent, He had so perfected her inwardly by grace, that He could bear to inherit and reproduce the very lineaments and traits of her character—a character most carefully moulded beforehand to the ideal of human integrity, and goodness and purity, compassion and gentleness, supreme horror for sin, and self-sacrifice to death for the sinner. Again I say: She was so perfect, because she was His mother; she was His mother because she was so perfect. Thou art all fair, my love, my dove, and there is no spot in thee. Fair in the instant of thy conception; for the Most High sanctified His tabernacle. Fair and spotless in life, as none besides; confirmed in grace; preserved from the least stain of venial sin or semi-deliberate imperfection. And with thy spiritual beauty, vested with a species of omnipotence, because He, thy Son, cannot resist thy pleading; but must fain listen to thy voice, which was the spell of His infancy and childhood, and which never ceases to thrill Him with a strange joy and delight, because He has never ceased to be thy Son; the best and most fond and loving that ever has appeared amongst men.

O, Mary, Mother of God!

THE PRESENTATION OF OUR BLESSED LADY.

Mary the Type of the Cloistered Life.

THE Church, beloved Brethren, with her characteristic wisdom, avails herself of the multiplied examples of holiness which her history presents, for the purpose of filling our imaginations with ideals of virtue, which, though ever so exalted and supernatural, are none the less real and substantial. Almost every day in the year, therefore, she gathers her children at her knee, and, as the mother of the Gracchi was wont to tell with pride of the deeds of her noble sons, who perished in their efforts to serve a fickle and ungrateful people, she tells them the story of some heroic brother or sister, now sleeping in the Lord, whose life was a brave struggle against the enemies of their salvation, and whose death, far from being an incident of sorrow, was but a proclamation of their victory. Thus she stores our minds with pictures of heroism, which teach us our duty more effectually, because they are not abstract lessons addressed to the understanding alone, but living and breathing exhibitions of virtue. The Queen of Saints, as might have been expected, is often brought before our minds in the various scenes of her life; for as we view her in connexion with this or that event, new perfections are revealed in her character; and she is found to centre within herself the graces of all the heavenly hosts. She is like some rare diamond, so charged and instinct with light, that it never can be moved without darting new rays, and astonishing the eye by the dazzling variety of its lustre. Her conception, her birth, her presentation in the temple, her purity, her maternity, her sorrows, her assumption, and all the mysteries of our Lord's life, with which the thought of Mary is inseparably intertwined—what an array of merits do they record, what incentives to virtue do they present! The contemplation of these gifts, with which God has adorned His mother, cannot fail to inspire us with a deeper reverence for Him, whose divine holiness made it necessary that she who bore Him should be so unspeakably holy. Thus the Christian, in the words of the Psalmist, "in His heart hath disposed to ascend by steps," because by considering the endowments of the Mother, he attains to a more perfect knowledge of the Son.

Not the least interesting in the group of festivals connected with the name of Mary, is that which we celebrate to-day—her Presentation in the Temple. This feast recalls to our thoughts an epoch in her career which must be dear to all her children; when, in the first springtide of her days, she consecrated to God her whole life, with its every season, and all the fruit and blossoms it should produce. It is refreshing to dwell upon the details of the charming picture which unfolds itself to-day to our memories. Her holy parents, St. Joachim and St. Anne, have determined to gratify the pressing desire of their little daughter, by offering her to the Lord, in accordance with the vow they had made before her birth. Willingly do they make the sacrifice; although doubtless they feel many a pang of parental affection; and as they gaze upon that innocent angelic face, which had been to their humble household what the sun is to the heavens, an agency to brighten and to cheer it, the features of their child grow blurred and dim through the gathering tears. At last the day arrives, and Mary bids farewell to the home where her infancy has been nurtured; the home she has made sacred to the angels by her infantine piety. Has she no sorrow in her heart at the parting? Yes; but it is a sorrow which has no mingling of selfishness; a sorrow to see others grieve; a sentiment; a sorrow most acceptable and dear in the sight of God. Forth, like a bride, walks the little maiden, grave but joyous, towards the well-known domes and turrets that overshadow the sacred city, towards the temple where God has His home. Costlier than that temple's costliest ornaments, than the plates of thrice-refined gold that flash on its walls and its cornices, more precious than the gold and silver that adorn it, is the treasure she is about to deposit there—as a tribute to the living God—the priceless treasure of her heart. What painter could ever delineate the sweetness, the absorption, the calm yet rapturous resolve, that shines upon her face, and brightens from beneath her scarce-lifted eyelid, as she walks through the busy streets towards her destination? Onwards she passes, not noting, not noticed, by mansion, booth, or counting house; she hears not the hum of business; she hears not shout, nor jest, nor laughter; there is but one sound in her ears, the soft voice of her Beloved murmuring to her:—"Arise, my love, my dove, my beautiful one, and come!" And ever, as the tender invitation thrills through her being, her heart offers itself, for life or for death: "My Beloved to me, and I to my Beloved, who feeds among the lilies, till the day break, and the shadows retire." Such is the burthen of that still interior canticle which Mary sings with the Spouse of her Soul.

The little party have reached the temple gates; silently, thoughtfully, they traverse its echoing cloisters; the word of farewell has been spoken; the farewell kiss imprinted with quivering lips by the fond parents upon their daughter's brow; and a sacrifice is registered in heaven more welcome a thousand-fold to God than all the smoke that ever curled upwards from the immemorial holocaust, than all the blood of victims that gushed from beneath the sacrificial knife through all the ages. No tumults of public joy mark the great event. The world is as dead to that little maid, upon whom its destinies hang, as she is dead to the world. What is she that the world should regard her? She is not on the list of its great ones; all her glory is within. Let Sulla, Pompey, or Cæsar, slaughter a nation, and desolate its cities; and then what shouts of acclamation will rend the skies! What swarming multitudes will follow the victor's blood-stained car! How many brains will set to work, how many furnaces will roar, how many chisels shall be busy, recording the wholesale massacre in marble or in bronze! Nay, let a gladiator but plant a dexterous blow in his adversary's breast, and there is a greater stir and flutter in the world, than attends the Presentation of Mary, though this is the greatest act ever performed by mortal since the birth of mankind. But she has as little influence upon the vast world—upon its interests and its passions—as some great unpriced pearl, that lies motionless under the deep, has upon the unfathomed waters that roar above it. The world has as little influence upon her, as the elements of wind and water have upon the star that shines in its distant sphere as steadily, whether they are at peace or in stormy strife. Yet, if there is joy in heaven, before the sight of the angels of

God over one sinner doing penance, shall not the powers of heaven be moved, to behold the nuptials of the child Mary with her only Love? Yea. The three Persons of the ever-blessed Trinity take part in this pageant which eyes of flesh cannot see. The Eternal Father hangs with fondest affection over that pure child upon whom He has so clearly stamped His divine image, and blesses her with a new blessing, in return for her self-immolation. God the Son smiles lovingly upon her, and accepts her by anticipation as His worthy mother. The Holy Ghost caresses her, His Bride, chosen among thousands, arrays her in a nuptial garment that outshines the robes of the Angels, and brings forth from His treasury of grace every costliest gem to adorn her; until all the heavenly courts are dazzled at the sight, and make the pillars of heaven tremble with their hosannas. Even the demons who wander about the earth, and hover round the confines of heaven, have reason to quake to-day at the shadows of coming trouble, for well they know the prediction, which forewarned them that the seed of the woman would crush the serpent's head. Often have they listened with awe and horror to the inspired words of the prophets, who caught glimpses through the mist of the half-revealed future, of the light of the world, the expectation of the nations, the Saviour of mankind, the Conqueror of sin and hell.

So Mary is now an inmate of the temple; dedicated to one employment, the praise and service of God. How soothing is the sacred quiet and hallowed seclusion of its walls to a heart that thirsts for God alone! Now her only desire is acomplished, her one longing satisfied. For often and often—child as she is—she has cried out with an ardour and intensity beyond that of the Psalmist: "Oh how lovely are Thy tabernacles, Lord of Hosts! My soul longeth and fainteth after the courts of the Lord! My heart and flesh have throbbed after the living God. For better is one day in Thy courts than a thousand." "As the heart panteth after the fountains of water, so my soul panteth after Thee, O God!"

Some there are, doubtless, beloved Brethren, who, as they view that little recluse, kneeling in her chamber motionless in an ecstasy of prayer, or busying herself in such pious offices as are suited to her tender years, would exclaim, with the bitterness of long-rooted prejudice:—Out upon the fanaticism which withdraws so useful a member from society, and deprives her fellow-creatures of the benefits of her example, and the thousand services she would delight in rendering them. It is to deify selfishness, thus to isolate a soul adorned by so many virtues, from all contact with her fellow-beings, and pen her up in perpetual self-examination and self-communing, as if she had been made without any obligations or duties to society, or rather, as if she had been a criminal with whom all intercourse was infamy. God desires no such separation from home and family. Is it not God who has consecrated the family bond? Who without desecration shall unfasten it? What He has joined together, we have no right to put asunder. It cannot be that God approves of burying a child alive in the gloom of this conventual sepulchre. Let her go into the world, and marry, and rear a family of good children, as she would well know how, that her virtues may live after her in the souls she has moulded. Or if she will not marry, why not find vent for her charity in philanthropic works? Are there no sick to nurse, no poor to succour, no ignorant to teach? Nay, for that matter, her own father and mother are not so young, nor so strong, nor so blessed with worldly advantages, that she can leave them without well-grounded motives for solicitude.

Thus, beloved Brethren, with their own sharp tongues would many men censure such a life, and scout such a vocation. Yet in forming opinions upon questions of so much consequence, it is well surely to proceed with caution. For it would by no means be wild to assert, abstracting from God's known dominion over the universe, that if any little committee of worldlings, were appointed to revise and criticize the scheme of Providence in all its many details, a large proportion of its ordinances unfavourable to human liberty, would be rejected as harsh and cruel, or as unfair in the distribution of advantages and burthens, or as incongruous in the design, like architecture of no fixed order. Yet this itch for freely measuring all things, even the things of God, by the standard of what is called "Common Sense," is hazardous in the extreme, in the face of some of the dicta which we find in the inspired writers. What does St. Paul say? "Oh the depth of the wisdom and of the knowledge of God! How incomprehensible are His judgments, and how unsearchable His ways! For who hath known the mind of the Lord, and who hath been His Counsellor?" A startling and bewildering statement! St. Paul was eminently versed in the mysteries of God; a man familiar with visions and revelations; who, as he tells us himself, was caught up into Paradise, and heard sweet words which it is not given to man to utter; yet to him God's ways bring nothing but awe, perplexity, and astonishment. Perhaps then these unkind critics I speak of, who so sweepingly and mercilessly condemn the life of the cloister, and who doubtless are sincerely anxious not to differ from the judgment of the All Wise, would for one moment be timid of their own convictions, and open to lights higher than their common sense, if such shine in the firmament. They would find themselves, in their self-sufficiency, pronouncing the judgments of God quite comprehensible, and His ways anything but unsearchable; they would see that in effect they assume that they do know the mind of the Lord, and act with the air and manner of Counsellors, who can better His designs and purposes.

Let us then have recourse to sacred writ. The Old Law, beloved Brethren, had its own system of religious life, imperfect, indeed, and rudimentary, like other institutions of the Jewish dispensation, when compared with the maturer forms of the law of grace, but still unmistakeable. Who were the Nazarites? They were men and women, who, under God's sanction, and at God's prompting, made a vow to lead a life of special sanctity, and placed themselves, in pursuance of their vow, under a rule involving certain restrictions, which are laid down minutely in the Book of Numbers by God Himself. "And the Lord spoke to Moses, saying, 'speak to the children of Israel, and thou shalt say to them: when man or woman shall make a vow to be sanctified, and will consecrate themselves to the Lord, they shall abstain from wine and everything that can make a man drunk.'" He went on to lay down further restrictions besides certain ceremonial liabilities. From their dietary they were to exclude vinegar of all sorts, raisins and grapes, and the whole produce of the vineyard. And to mark them off as vowed to His service by a badge analagous to the shaven crown of the modern religious amongst their oriental brethren, they were bound to let the hair grow untrimmed, and no razor was to pass over their heads during the term of their consecration. This surely is a sufficiently distinct foreshadowing of the Christian monk and nun. It is the monastic system in the germ. Again, how often does God decree that the darling of a family, its star, its pride, and its hope should be snatched from its midst by an early death, and should leave in the bosom of its surviving members a void which no after friendship can fill. How then can it be inconsistent with the attributes of that same God that He should sometimes require a separation almost as cruel, by giving to some beloved one a special vocation to His exclusive service? Was it not God's will that little Samuel should be separated unto Him, and placed in the temple, there to live removed from home and friends, who often sent their yearning thoughts after the amiable and beloved boy. It is God that gives, it is God that takes away: equally blessed in either case in His name, equally holy and unimpeachable His decree. But you cannot think with patience of the unkempt solitaries, who haunted the deserts in the early ages, and whom the Catholic Church regards with unqualified favour. Let us again have recourse to the Holy Scriptures. At the threshold of the New Testament we are startled by a strange unearthly figure, that points with lean finger towards the Lamb of Prophecy, who taketh away the sins of the world. Who is this wild apparition that starts out of the rocks like a shaft of their own rugged stone? It is St. John the Baptist, the Precursor of Christ, who has prepared himself for his high office by living in the desert since he was a child. He, with his coat of camel's hair, and the leather girdle about his loins, would have made quite as wild, uncouth and eccentric a figure as they in the banquet-halls and state-chambers of the great. His diet was as light and as unsatisfactory to the natural man as theirs; if they lived on dates and figs, he lived on locusts and wild honey. He, like them, assuaged his thirst from the springs of the desert. To him, as to them, the great plain of the wilderness was the floor of God's temple, the towering rocks its buttresses and pillars, the vast-spreading canopy of the sky its variegated roof. He, like them, wore his knees hard and horny by praying incessantly, with no hassock but the bare stone. In one word, St. John is as great a defaulter, when tested by this thing called "Common Sense," as ever the hermits were, and assuredly if the hermits were to be condemned for their manner of life, St. John ought to share their condemnation in all consistency. Yet has our Blessed Lord left behind Him a single expression of disapproval with reference to St. John, or St. John's choice of self-persecution and solitude? Did He ever caution his disciples to beware of his austerities, as mere extravagances and vagaries unacceptable to God? Did He ever exhort him to give up his wild life, and mix in society, and marry a wife, and rear a family, and do good by his example? No, on the contrary, taking him just as a strange unsocial eremite, our Blessed Lord extolled to the skies the sanctity of that sun-burnt, half-starved, skin-clad, desert-roving ascetic, the model of solitaries then un-born, and by his surpassing eulogium tempered the censure of the world for the poor nun and monk of modern times :—"I say to you, there hath not risen among them, that are born of women, a greater than John the Baptist."

But clearly, beloved Brethren, as the example of St. John the Baptist proves with what favour God regards a life of retirement and severe self-denying asceticism, our Blessed Lord's own history is a more conclusive refutation still of all adverse criticisms upon such a life; because if these criticisms apply to monk or nun, they apply to Him with tenfold emphasis. When God became man, it is no mere conceit to say that this entire world was but a cell and hermitage to Him, the Great and Infinite God. Yet this world was all too large for His humility and His love of retirement, hardship, and contempt. Except for the interval in which He was lost to view among the teeming population of Egypt, He was of His own free will confined, I may say cloistered, in an unimportant province, in an insignificant village, in a tradesman's cot, and for how long? For thirty years of His life! Thirty years in a life of thirty-three! Stupendous truth! That He to whom all power is given in heaven and on earth; for whom the prophets have been crying—O that Thou wouldst rend the skies and come down; for whom the sick and miserable race have been crying louder still, by the stress and stormy horror of its daily sins: that He who has come at last to seek the lost sheep, to destroy the kingdom of vice, to build up amongst mankind an empire of justice and righteousness, to place His divine compassion for His fellow-men beyond all doubt or controversy, and to win us, as the Scripture says, "by the cords of Adam, by the bonds of love," that, nevertheless, when He has come at last, He should lie nine whole months in His mother's womb, and after His birth should bury Himself in hovels unknown and unnoticed; and should crown the whole anomaly by giving to His public ministry not one tithe of the time He spent upon earth! Yet day by day, during those thirty years, the tide of sin roars to heaven, and dashes the stars with its foul spray; the cries of poor men for relief, of sick men for healing, of cripples for the use of their limbs, rise day and night over the valley of tears: and where the while is He who alone can allay the sin, and find remedies for every ill that flesh is heir to? There are demoniacs amongst the hills, there are the victims of palsy in the cities. The long stricken friendless sufferer waits in vain by the healing fountain's brink, while his more favoured companions in affliction are helped by eager loving hands down the descent. Blind men pine in their darkness, longing for the light. Widows mourn over the living props of their age torn from their sides; lepers sun their loathsome bodies outside the gates of the sacred city, their eyes fixed wistfully upon their native towers now doubly dear to them, because they can visit them no more; the poor are dying the spiritual death, for want of the Gospel which is to be preached to them; and still the Great Healer tarries? Where is He? Lisping at His mother's knee, planing, sawing, cutting timber, in a lonely vault of Galilee! Is it for this He has all power given to Him in heaven and on earth? Where is His active benevolence? Why does He not, at the call of men like our critics, go out into the world, and mingle with mankind, and preach to them, and teach them wisdom, and heal their festering maladies? Why does He not take His stand in the capital of the world, denouncing the wrong, and proclaiming the right? Why does He not gather the philosophers around Him, and take their systems asunder, and trace for them the silver thread of truth in the tawdry web of error? Why bury Himself alive? Why seclude Himself from mankind, whom He came to benefit? Beloved Brethren, we must say with St. Paul: O the depth of the wisdom and of the knowledge of God. This long seclusion of His was no whim; but the most clear, unmistakeable, and solemn counsel of a life of religious retirement, and an exhortation to fly from all notice, esteem and popularity. And if the poor monk is accused of being a drone, the waster of gifts, an unnatural being, self-exiled from his fellows, self-contained and oblivious of the claims of society; lo! the prototype and model: no other than Jesus Christ Himself.

There are some, however, beloved Brethren, who would incline to regard Mary, the little nun, as she knelt in her lonesome chapel to pray, or paced the cold and hollow-sounding cloisters, with more of amiable pity than fierce disapproval. She would seem to their fancy as a flower, transplanted but to wither, away from the broad sunshine, and the free airs of heaven: or a caged bird sitting disconsolate, with drooped head, and motionless plumage! They could not conceive of her except as pale and care worn, wasted with melancholy as much as with pious vigils. Such is the delusion of those who would fain institute a crusade for the purpose of rescuing the pining nun from her cloister, as if she were in sad and unwilling captivity. But they forget the adage, first spoken by a great observer. There is nothing good or bad but thinking makes it so. All have not the same taste, nor the same ideal of happiness. The sportsman loves the moors, and the clear bracing air; the student will sit for ever in his study, the smell of musty volumes sweeter in his nostrils than dainties to the senses of the epicure. Others again are restless and unhappy until they are on ship-board, and the anchor is weighed, and a voyage is before them over the wide main. So we are like trees; we do not all flourish in the same kind of soil. Now what ideal of happiness has that little maiden, whom we left in the chambers attached to the temple?

God prepared Mary to be a worthy mother, of whom, when He took flesh, He should not be ashamed. Hence there was no endowment that could ennoble her character which He refused her. Her heart was the most consummate instrument and organ of love which the Divine Artificer ever placed in the breast of a mere creature. It enabled her to love God more ardently, more perfectly, with a more complete absorption of every faculty and aspiration than the Cherubim and Seraphim could love Him, although their pure ethereal essence is free from all the trammels of the flesh. How could it be otherwise? Is it to be supposed that God, the Incarnate, could allow any being a right to sit nearer to Him, or to be more closely united to Him; could give any being a higher claim upon His love, or a higher title to His rewards, than the mother who conceived and bore Him, and gave Him birth, and nurtured Him with her own substance? In her, then, human nature saw itself more elevated, glorious and admirable, than in the persons of our first parents, while yet they walked in innocence among the beauties of Paradise. Her intellect was clearer than theirs, saw the sovereign Good with keener vision; and more fully apprehended the relations of created goodness and beauty to the fountain of all that is beautiful and good. Her feelings and emotions were more than theirs, the handmaids of reason, and the auxiliaries of virtue. She knew no desire that could cause her a moment's hesitation in obeying God's will. She had no experience of that unhealthy thirst after evil that belongs to the fallen race of man, and the baffling of which constitutes the struggle of life. Her will too obeyed the electric touch of conscience, which is the luminous handwriting of God, with inconceivable exactness, promptitude, and fidelity. In fine, her physical organisation was so wrought, that far from being an obstacle to the love of God, or an element of distraction, it furnished a perpetual stimulus to good. Her very senses, I say her very nerves, her virginal flesh and blood, instead of retarding, and weighing her down, rather buoyed her spirit up as a stream, and bore it more swiftly onwards towards the ocean of all sanctity. Every faculty, then, of soul and body conspired to make Mary love God. This will be better understood, perhaps, if we take the liberty of illustrating sacred things by profane. You know how happily men's temperaments are sometimes adapted to some particular walk of art. One of the greatest of departed musicians will at once occur to the mind, in connexion with this subject. It was not merely that he had a great genius for music; but the very nerves and tissues and humours of his body were so delicately combined and balanced for the purpose of the musical art, that from an infant harmonies were to him rapture and ecstasy, discord torture, and physical agony. Even the harsh sound of a trumpet would, when he was a child, throw him into convultions. Perhaps from this example, beloved Brethren, you can better understand what I mean, when I say that Mary's entire conststituion and temperament, bodily and mental, made the love of God not merely a delight but a necessity. The hunger and thirst of her whole being, then, was for God. "My heart and my flesh cry out for God.—*Ps.* 84. 2. My flesh longeth for Thee in a dry thirsty land.—*Ps.* 63. 1. As the hart panteth after the fountains of water, so my soul panteth after Thee, O God." What cares she for all that this world can offer for its pleasures or its ambitions— "One thing have I asked of the Lord, this will I seek after, that I may dwell in the house of the Lord all the days of my life."— *Ps.* 26. 4. "This is my rest, here will I dwell, for I have chosen it.—*Ps.* 131. How misplaced and delusive then is the compassion of worldlings for the life of seclusion to which Mary, and the imitators of Mary, have devoted themselves at the call of God. If you pity the nun, first shed a tear of condolence for the Angels, who are singing day and night their unceasing hymn, Holy! Holy! Holy! If souls love God—they love to be alone with God—they care only to be with God. Let Martha then busy herself with much serving. Mary sits in a trance of attention at the feet of our Blessed Lord; and though her hands are idle, and show no result to the eye, yet "hath she chosen the better part which shall not be taken from her."

"THE ASSUMPTION."

TO-DAY, beloved Brethren, we are invited by Holy Mother the Church to direct our thoughts to the glorious closing of a unique career, when the Mother of the World's Redeemer received the reward of her virtues, and her unexampled self-immolation in the kingdom of her Son.

There are few spectacles that so stir the feelings, and enkindle the enthusiasm of our natures, as the triumphant return of some great commander from a campaign in which his genius has rescued his imperilled country from outrage or ruin. What swarming multitudes follow his chariot, what deafening applause, thunderlike, roars to heaven, as he bows his acknowledgements to his grateful admirers; how every bosom in the unnumbered throng dilates with pride at the sight of the hero, as if it were raised to a nobler elevation by the merits of this great compatriot! But all the grandeur and impressions of such a pageant fade away, as the stars fade before the dawn, when compared with the spiritual ovation—invisible to human eyes—which Mary received in her assumption. To that triumph—the greatest, save the Ascension, that any child of Adam ever received, she walked, indeed, through the portals of death—that was inevitable: for that solemn sentence, "It is appointed to all men once to die," is the written doom of every child of Adam, even of Him who overcame death, disarming it of its sting, and robbing it of its victory.

Mary must die, therefore, but her death should be no tearful parting with a life of luxury and ease, that had enthralled the heart, nor the despairing finale to a career of sin; it should have no ingredient of bitterness in its chalice for the pale lips on which the last breath quivered. It should be a benediction and a grace a dissolving in the tenderness of a tide of love, such as nature could no longer support, nor the overwrought heart contain! It should be a new birth from the womb of a darksome and feeble life straitened by many conditions, to an existence of light, and freedom, and empire, and boundless joy, and never-ending fulness of satisfaction. It should be a substitution of elastic youth for the stiffness and weariness and weakness of sixty winters. It should be the revelation of a pinnacle of honour and glory, which Mary's humble dreams had never shadowed forth. In short, the coming of death to Mary, soft as the falling of a cloud upon the green hills, was a signal to the whole court of heaven to come forth in their glittering myriads, order by order, and to greet with most heartfelt acclamations of welcome, with pealing hymns and canticles of joy, their mistress and queen, the heroine of the world's history, the woman of prophecy, the glory of Jerusalem, the pearl of humanity, the Mother of the Incarnate God. From the heights of the highest heaven, through all the grades of its nobility, where Cherubim and Seraphim are embosomed in the light of God's presence, reflecting the clearness of His knowledge and the glow of His love, all the eyes of God's princes are fixed upon the form of this revered and beloved creature, as she rises from the earth, upborne triumphantly by privileged spirits, to the throne prepared for her beside her Divine Son. How beautiful does she seem in their sight, this sweet maiden, in whom are centred all the combined graces of virginity and motherhood, and all the perfections of every class of saints. "Who is she that goeth up by the desert as a pillar of smoke, of aromatical spices of myrrh and frankincense, and of all the powders of the perfumer."—*Canticles* iii. 6. Severally the orders of the Angels, and the various classes of saints, reflect mainly some one aspect or attribute of God's perfections; but they see in Mary all their manifold characteristics, which give them their individual beauty, and majesty, and charm, marvellously united. Angels and Archangels, swift ministers of the Divine will; the Thrones on whose outspread wings the Sovereign judge executes justice; Principalities who direct the heavenly hosts in carrying out the decrees of God; the Denominations with their subject legions, ready to move at their beck; the Virtues, by whose agency miracles, and signs, and wonders, astound mankind; the Powers, who hold in check every malign influence, and overawe the armies of hell: all these, with God's nearest ministers, the Cherubim and Seraphim, behold in Mary, more gloriously exhibited, the qualities which make their special attraction, and are the source of their grandeur and loveliness : all bow down their heads in willing homage before the imperial and surpassing endowments of this fairest creature of God's hand.

And so too, with feelings of pride and exultation, all the sons of Adam, who have won their way by their appointed paths to this celestial kingdom, all hail her with transport as their own flesh and blood, raised by her unequalled perfections to an excellence far beyond the highest of the unbodied spirits of heaven, and showing transcendently in her own person the very virtues which ennobled themselves. The Patriarchs, whose memories are embalmed in Holy Writ, hail in her the God-like simplicity, and the maturity of wisdom and prudence, which had shone in their own lives. The Prophets wonder to think how deeply she has penetrated into the mysterious chambers of God's mind, and how matchlessly she has been endowed with every supernatural faculty and power. The Apostles admire that ardent and consuming zeal for man's salvation, kindled from the flame of the most intense charity, which made her a holocaust, pierced, and mystically slain, and burnt to ashes, along with the great Victim upon the altar of Redemption. The Martyrs wave their palms, won by the ordeal of fire or sword, swiftly dealt destruction, or lingering pain, at the sight of her whose martyrdom of the spirit had been incalculably more terrible than the worst of their trials. The Confessors welcome her as the Queen of Confessors, whose every breath, from her birth to her death, had been a proclamation of God's sovereign rights, and of man's duty of absolute subjection. The Virgins point to her with delight, as the virgin of virgins, who, by her spotless and unsullied integrity of maidenhood, had won the privilege of claiming the Incarnate God for the fruit of her womb.

Thus every Saint, and every Angel in that unimaginable multitude, has some special insight into her gifts and virtues, which enhances his admiration, stimulates his enthusiasm, in this magnificent pageant of welcome, fans the flame of his devotion, and draws more closely the bond of his loyalty.

Unite your hearts and voices to-day, beloved Brethren, with those of the blessed in Heaven on this great anniversary, in thanking and blessing God for all that He has done, through Mary, for the human race, for all the virtues with which He has adorned her, and the height of glory to which He has raised her.

If we strive to honour Mary on each of her other festivals, we ought to redouble our efforts to-day; for, as holy writers tell us, this is the greatest of her festivals, commemorating as it does the consummation of her life's work, and her translation to eternal bliss.

And while you offer her your praises and congratulations, beseech her to procure for you the graces of which you stand most in need : for the power of her intercession is commensurate with her unparalleled dignity as Queen of Heaven. Be not afraid to ask her for even temporal blessings; such as health and strength, success in business, or rescue from besetting troubles; for if you ask aright, God will give you these blessings in such measure as will not be pernicious to your souls, or obstructive to your salvation. But above all, ask her to obtain for you the spiritual blessings, in which you are deficient, a share in her spirit of humility, the foundation of all the virtues; in her love of God and of all mankind in God, which is the bond of perfection, and in her spotless purity. Ask her particularly to enable you by her prayers to overcome the passion most dangerous to you.

In conclusion, beloved Brethren, let me correct a misconception which is not uncommon amongst our people.

The existence of this festival of the Assumption does not imply that we are under a strict obligation to believe that the body of our Blessed Lady was transported to Heaven after her death, as well as her soul. This, the Church has never taught in the same manner in which she has taught the Infallibility of the Pope, or the exemption of our Blessed Lady from the taint of original sin. It is not "of faith," though as an inference from the dogmas of faith, it is so certain that it would be at least rash to deny it. For it is repugnant to our ideas that the sinless flesh of Mary, which clothed the Son of God made man in the garb of his humanity, that her frame, which had been the shrine of all purity and seraphic love, should be allowed by her Divine Son to go through the noisome and hideous transformations of the grave, which are the fitting lot of our sinful bodies.

MARY.

(Month of May).

IT would not be fitting, beloved Brethren, to let the May pass by without saying a few words in praise of that peerless Maid and Mother, to whose honour the month of fresh leaves and opening flowers is consecrated by the Church.

Our belief is, beloved Brethren, that God in His munificence has given us many aids to salvation. Not only have we His law written upon our hearts; not only have we peace and self-approval when we do our duty, and the sting of remorse punishing our departure from the path of virtue; but outside us too, we have countless helpers and countless influences, which draw us, as with many cords, upwards towards the Kingdom of Heaven. We have the example of our good neighbours, their kind wishes, and earnest prayers, and meritorious works, in the blessings of which we are sharers by virtue of the Communion of Saints. There are our friends in Heaven, whose hands, that once blessed us, are withering in the grave, but whose true hearts and fond memories cling to us in a better land. There are the legions of saints, canonized and uncanonized, who pray for us incessantly, that we may have strength to fight the good fight to the end, and to earn the reward which eye hath not seen, which ear hath not heard, which it hath not entered into the heart of man to conceive. There is our Good Angel, ever walking the paths of the world along with us, our sleepless sentinel in the hours of darkness, our guardian and protector through the busy day, sympathising with us in our sorrows, and partaking in our joys, and mourning over us and praying for us in our infirmities and falls. But there is One, who in love and devotion to our welfare, in tenderness and compassion, yea, and in power too, stands all alone; our Blessed Mother Mary. There is no love like the Mother's love; and she is truly our Mother.

Bitter were the pangs of her child bearing, when, at the foot of the Cross, she bore the race of sinners, whose eldest brother was dying that he might give them life, and was suffering ignomy that He might win them honour. "Mother, behold thy Son," said He; "look not to me now, in whom your heart has had its treasure, I go to the Father; but you have another Son, yea, a family of children, to whom you are bound henceforth by the ties of motherhood." "Son," said he to St. John, "behold thy Mother." and from that time the disciple took her to his own. Nothing is said of her feeling to him, her maternal devotion, her ardent love. But oh! how burning, how tender it must have been.

When God called her to be the universal mother, the new Eve, he gave her the mother's heart towards us all. His way is, to fit His instruments for the work they have to do. And so, I repeat, having given her this great family of mankind, he gave her a heart large as the object it was to embrace, deep as the ocean, universal as the air. Mother of God she had been; now she became mother of sinners. A strange mixed race it was, to which her maternity bound her; many a leper was among them, many a cripple, many a victim of hideous disease. Some were wild and wayward, proud, passionate and rebellious; treacherous, overreaching, griping, miserly; intemperate, corrupt of heart, foul of tongue; impure of action; all disorders were there, stamped upon that strange race of brothers, making the earth a lazar-house of sin, whose stench rose to heaven. Yet, all these types of iniquity—in flesh and blood—all belonged to her by a title God Himself had created; all had a right to call her mother.

And what are her feelings towards the poor wretches who fill with their noisome lives this hospital of the world? Would you realize her feelings, or rather would you faintly guess at them? Then turn to the poor earthly mother, from the number of whose little flock one is stricken down with some repulsive malady. The stranger shrinks from touching the poor little sufferer, nay, with difficulty allows his eyes to rest upon the sore-seamed, raw, and defaced countenance, which seems but so much moving and animated corruption. But the worse it is, the more disfigured it is, the more the mother's heart-strings tighten around it. She turns night into day, watching beside the sick bed, soothing the pains of her little one, and ministering to its every want. This, beloved Brethren, is a poor shadow of the love of Mary towards her brood of ailing and sinful children. She feels most for the most wretched; she prays for them incessantly; she pleads their cause, when the anger of God blazes out against them; she follows them through all the mazes of their sins, waiting for them with holy suggestions, virtuous impulses, providential mishaps maybe, at every turn of their careers; and, in how many cases God alone knows, winning back her lost child perhaps at the very moment when hell had gathered its fiends to close around him. If an earthly mother keeps a warm place in her heart for the scapegrace of the family, whose extravagance may have ruined his friends, and his disorderly life covered them with disgrace; if she hopes in him, when all hope seems vain; if she weeps in her solitude over his treasured portrait; which recalls to her memory the days of his innocence and the season of his promise; if from his crushed and heart-broken father, who has cursed the day that brought him into the world, she succeeds, by her importunate entreaties, and her tears, in begging a small pittance, sufficient to keep the life in the breast of her wanderer—oh! how much more will our mother in heaven cling to us while life remains, hoping against hope, struggling to rescue us in spite of ourselves from the misery we are bringing upon our own heads, and begging grace after grace from our offended and angry Maker, to save us from eternal ruin.

Such are her feelings; now what is her power? There is a sufficient indication of it in the Gospel. St. John tells the story.

"There was a marriage in Cana of Galilee," says he, "and the mother of Jesus was there. And Jesus also was invited, and His disciples, to the marriage." In the midst of the feast, Our Lady's eye, quickened by her charity, perceived that the wine was failing. This was an accident, which she knew would bring deep pain and embarrassment upon the young couple. Her kind heart could not brook the thought of their confusion: she whispered to her Son, "They have no wine." And Jesus saith to her: "Woman, what is it to Me and to thee? My hour has not yet come," as much as to say: This is scarcely an occasion important enough to call for a miracle; it is not for us to see that the guests have sufficient wine. And in any case, the term at which I was desirous of beginning to exhibit My power over nature by working miracles has not yet arrived. Here were two strong objections to Our Lady's petition; nay, the answer might seem almost to imply a refusal. Does she understand it so? No! She did not judge Him by His words alone; she knew His heart; she could interpret His look, His tone of voice, His manner; she knew He meant not to repulse her. What then does she do? She saith to the waiters: "Whatsoever He shall say to you, do ye." Now there were set there six water-pots of stone, according to the manner of the purifying of the Jews, containing two or three measures a piece Jesus saith to them: "Fill the water-pots with water." And they filled them up to the brim. And Jesus saith to them: "Draw out now, and carry to the chief steward of the feast." And they carried it. And when the chief steward had tasted the water, made wine, and knew not whence it was, but the waiters knew who had drawn the water; the chief steward calleth the bridegroom and saith to him: "Every man at first setteth forth good wine and when men have all well drunk, then that which is worse. But thou has kept the good wine until now." This beginning of miracles did Jesus in Cana of Galilee: and manifested His glory, and His disciples believed in Him.

Here you have a stupendous testimony of Our Lady's influence with her Divine Son. He puts forth His power over the elements, in a marvellous manner, at her request, before the time when He had purposed to begin working miracles; and that, too, when the occasion was from one point of view insignificant and unworthy; simply to gratify His mother's kindness, which could not bear to see the young people put to the blush before the assembled guests.

With such a mother, beloved Brethren, to watch over us, how can we despair? It is for this reason precisely that God gave her to us, that we might look upon her, and hope. Jesus Christ is compared to the sun, she to the moon; and justly. For all her glory is borrowed from Him; her smile is but a reflection of His beauty; her sweetness is a testimony to His winning splendour. But then, we can rest our gaze upon the moon, when the sun's blaze would dazzle and scorch us. And so also, when the Sun of Justice, our future judge, whom we have offended, is terrible to our thoughts, by reason of its brightness and majesty, and all-searching light; we may, without fear, in the night and darkness of our sins and sorrows, look to her for guidance and reconciliation, until the daylight of grace is restored to us. Nor is she thus set up as a rival, but a helper and handmaid of her Son. All the praise we give her is so much incense offered to Him who made her, and adorned her. When we turn to her with confidence, we are but glorifying the mercy of God, imaged in the person of this creature, who never thought unkindly of any one, and whom God intended in His mercy, by the influence of her unfailing gentleness, to be our helper in our earthly pilgrimage, and our sweet guide to our happy home. May she pray for us now and at the hour of our death. May she obtain for us the grace to cherish a love for her, and a solid devotion to her; for there could not be a greater pledge of deliverance from evil habits, or strong passions; there could not be a greater sign of predestination to eternal life, than a constant and persevering desire to do her honour. Remember what she said to one of her servants: "Quidquid modicum, modo sit constans: I care not how short your prayer may be, provided it be persevering." A few "Hail Marys" said every day without fail, would go far towards saving you, if you only said them with a longing desire to be rescued from your sins, and to acquire the love of God.

THE INFLUENCE OF MARY ON MODERN CIVILIZATION.

CIVILIZATION, beloved Brethren, owes an incalculable debt to the ideal of virtue fostered in the Christian world in the person of the Mother of God. From the earliest times it was a maxim with the children of the Church that God prepared every one, by the operation of His providence, to fill with credit and honour the sphere allotted to him in the pre-ordained system of the world. Be he prophet, or priest, or judge, if God has called him to any great work, His bounty has provided him with overflowing graces and superabundant aids, has endowed him with a constitution of soul, and disciplined him by the circumstances and events of his life, for the adequate performance of the commission with which he has been entrusted.

Grounded on this safe principle as a foundation, Christians have logically and securely filled in the scanty outline of Mary's character as it is painted in the Holy Scriptures, and by a constant tradition coming down to us from the Apostolic age, have venerated and loved the cherished image of Mary, the mother of Jesus, as that of the all-perfect woman, the loveliest copy of the Divine Attributes, embodied in a mere creature, that has ever shone upon the world. To our enemies this amplification of the Scriptural portrait seems altogether gratuitous. But it is far from being so. All the virtues we ascribe to that paragon of virgins and model of mothers, as the stem, branches and leaves of the oak are embossomed in the acorn, are included in the one proposition: she conceived and gave birth to the Son of God. There, is the patent of her nobility! There, is the all-sufficient guarantee of her pre-eminence in grace! The Son of God predestined her from all eternity to be His own dear mother, nay, His mother and father in one; He would receive the flesh and blood that united him to the race of Adam, only from her chaste womb ; He would accept from her the mould of His features, and the likeness of her soul, as the child re-produces the mother in face, and form, and disposition—for to these human laws did He conform Himself ; He would be to her a Son unmatched for filial love, as she should be a mother, supreme in maternal tenderness and devotion ; that thus they might form the bright examplar of that unique relationship through time and eternity. What follows from this ? Surely and certainly that He made her worthy of her position ; that He created her full of grace, and full of the virtues of which grace is the seed ; that He adorned her like some delicious garden, with every flower and fruit that could delight His soul ; so that the sight of her might be refreshment to Him in this weary world, and the thought of her like a lingering perfume. "My sister, my spouse is a garden enclosed, a fountain sealed up. Thy plants are a paradise of pomegranates, with the fruits of the orchard. Cyprus with spikenard. Spikenard and saffron, sweet cane and cinnamon, with all the trees of Libanus, myrrh and aloes, with all the chief perfumes." Tell me the gift He shall grudge her. Show me what adornment she can dispense with, to be a mother, not unworthy of such a Son. Ah ! beloved Brethren, He will not cling in her embrace with all the fond abandonment of the babe, to whom the mother is above all in the whole world, without first pouring upon her in unstinted and divine profusion every attribute of s ul, which forms the attraction of His saints. He will not give any other daughter of Eve such superior fascinations of virtue as to divert Him from His chosen mother ; or to demand in justice a higher place in His kingdom, in return for higher merit or a warmer place in His heart.

Thus reasoning, beloved Brethren, the faithful have in all ages held Mary to be non-pareil, the unequalled type, of all that is perfect in human nature. And this unshared supremacy and queenliness of virtue, far from eclipsing the brightness of her beloved Son, has only enhanced His sun-like splendour and majesty of character ; for all the embellishments she owns are of His bestowing, and a necessary result of His incomprehensible perfections, which would give its highest sanction to holiness in the person of His mother ; and, therefore, all her brilliance and beauty proclaim His supreme brightness and glory, because it is all but a borrowed and reflected light.

And this ideal of a delicate, fragile, modest and retiring lady, overtopping in her grandeur the sons of men, yet retaining supereminently a woman's heart, has done more towards banishing the barbarism, allying the brutality, softening the hardness, developing the humanity of the native disposition bequeathed to Adam's children, than all the teachings of philosophers, and all the projects and devices of statesmen and sages. To that ideal we owe the emancipation of woman, slowly but steadily, through all the ramifications of society; until she has come to occupy a position which the womankind of pagan ages past, and of pagan countries now, might well contemplate with envy. It is the veneration and love of Mary that has raised her sex out of the dust where she was the slave of man's will, and the instrument of his pleasure; and filled every manly breast with deepest respect and tenderest courtesy towards these his sisters, whose weakness appeals to his strength, and whose gentleness of nature is a study for his imitation. The knights indeed of mediæval days have passed in their gleaming armour, with nodding plume and twinkling lance-head, into the shadows of the melancholy past; but that sworn courtesy to the weaker sex, that sweet simplicity of heart, in doing them honour; that self-forgetful devotion to the cause of the oppressed and the helpless, that vowed reverence and affection for Mary's name, which reigned in their hearts and dictated all their duties and functions of honour, kindliness and true knighthood did not die with them, but fructified through the ages, the same essential spirit in other outward forms.

Yes, beloved Brethren, the love of Mary, the study of Mary's character and the imitation of her virtues, is no debasing influence, as her enemies pretend, rather it is a stimulus to every good quality that owns a root in the soil of our nature. She is the woman, who (according to the first recorded prophecy), was marked out in the designs of God to crush the serpent's head. And in the breasts of her faithful children and votaries, her heel is upon that malignant crest, and the poisonous tongue of Satan plays vainly in his jaws. His heads are many as Hydra's, all venomous, all threatening, all watchful. He has many shapes, which no heel can crush but hers. Here is the serpent of pride, with its asp-brood of boastful speech, arrogant presumption, the simulation of absent virtues; obstinate adherence to error, unbrotherly wrangling, an unaccommodating and perverse disposition, reluctance to obey. In another soul

Satan takes the form of the greedy dragon of avarice, gaping for his prey. Here it is, the green-eyed monster envy. Here his eyes flash and his mouth foams; and his hissings tell you his name is Anger. Here, again, he lies surfeited and bloated, breathing the fumes of strong drink, and you recognize the vice of gluttony, with sloth beside it, lying relaxed and helpless, its torpid offspring. And last of this hideous den of dragons is the monster lust, vomiting its horrors, and making the air unbearable with its stench: while it cowers out of sight and turns away its hateful eyes from the light, as that chaste maiden mother comes at the invocation of her child to drive the invader forth. Oh, how many are the temptations to which life exposes us! Let us thank God that He has given us so potent a protector and guardian. Let us bless Jesus for bestowing upon us this mother, our Lady of Perpetual Succour, to cast sin out of our souls, to stave off eternal death, to crush the deadly serpent in all his forms and disguises. Let us never fail to invoke her in time of trial and temptation; crying with all the undoubting trustfulness of a little child: " Mother, help me. Mary, oh Mary, come to my aid." Let it not be merely prayer of the lips, when day by day we cry out to her: " Pray for us sinners now, and at the hour of our death." For death approaches, beloved Brethren, step by step, stealthily but surely; and we know not how soon the clock may strike our last hour, and send us forth into the dark way where none may go with us, save Mary our mother, to shelter us from the wiles and snares, the re-doubled wrath and violence of our adversary, who lies in wait, and employs his whole force at that last scene of our life's campaign, knowing that his time is short.

HELP OF CHRISTIANS.

MARY is our help, because she is the Mother of God and our mother also. This humble maiden was, by His eternal decree, raised to a dignity, which, while it elevated her high above the highest spirits that minister at the Divine throne, required in her a sanctity most God-like and unparalleled, to fit her for her unique office. And so moulded into a perfection of grace which set her apart in her beauty and lustre, as the clear full moon stands alone amongst the lights that rule the night, she received in due time the message of God conveyed by the lips of the Archangel Gabriel; and bowing her head to the will of her Maker, forthwith conceived within her womb the Incarnate Word.

Without exaggeration it may be said that it was Mary's virtues that won us a Redeemer. Not that redemption could be earned on any title of strict justice, by any creature whatever; it was God's free and spontaneous gift. But Providence had so arranged that Mary's virtues should, in the fitness of things, receive its reward in making her the Mother of God, the Great Deliverer. It would have been incongruous, unsymmetrical, and foreign to God's methods, if Mary had been made so towering and gigantic in the stature of her sanctity, amid a world, including the angels, which was composed of pigmies in comparison with her, if she had not been destined to so intimate an alliance with the Divinity. Or, to put the same truth in other words: God the Son having decreed to become man, had adorned His destined mother so ravishingly with all supernatural endowments, that He was fain to stretch forth His hands as it were, from the bosom of His Eternal Father, to ask this unrivalled creature for a share of her virginal flesh and blood to furnish forth His human body.

"Thou art all fair, O, my love, and there is no spot in thee:—One is my dove, my perfect one is but one; she is the only one of her mother, the chosen one of her that bore her—Open to Me, my sister, my love, my dove, my undefiled."

Thus it came to pass that this gentle maid, all unknown to the world, but yet the glory of our race, the delight of the angels, the terror of hell, bore about in her blessed womb, for nine months, the very God that made her. What a Magnificat did she sing, through all the period of ecstasy, as she pondered that the Creator of the World had made her His own, own Mother, in a far stricter sense than belongs to ordinary maternity, for every particle of that human frame, in which the Person of the God-man was enshrined, was derived from her sinless flesh exclusively, and owed nothing to a human father. And then, in the ripeness of time, she brought forth that Son, not with the throes of anguish, to which the sin of Adam condemned his infected daughters, but in a painless, joyous, and most sacred delivery.

But another kind of delivery was in store for her, when she became the mother of that sinful race, which her Son had come from heaven to save. It was when she stood beside the blood-stained tree, under the shadow of Him whom her soul loved, and counted the moans and the gasps of the great Victim that hung between earth and heaven. He fixed His failing eyes upon the face of His mother, who stood pale and cold as marble amid the sea of tossing forms and faces, and said to her: "Woman, behold thy Son"; and then, turning to St. John: "Son," said He, "behold thy mother." Thus by the Omnipotent Word, by which all things are made that are made, Mary became the mother of all that mass of sin-tainted creatures, of whom the apostle—a frail man liable to sin—was representative, and for whom her eldest-born was sacrificing His life. Dire were the throes of that child-bearing, and heavily did she feel the effects of that sentence which, in the dawn of the world's history, was passed upon the mothers of a sinful seed:—"In sorrow shalt thou bring forth children."

At that word of power, which fell from the lips of her dying Son, a change came over the heart of Mary. Already that heart was an ever-flowing fountain of tenderness and compassion. But the affection of a mother differs from every other form of affection, not in degree only, but in kind also. Thenceforth Mary was constituted the new Eve, the mother of the living. Thenceforth, by the imperious dictate of her nature, she was forced to love all the brethren of her Crucified Son, no matter how unamiable, how repulsive they might be, with the fond, passionate, patient, all-hoping, all-enduring love of a mother. And with her new functions, she became aware of the birth in her bosom of new joys and sorrows, new sympathies, and hopes and fears, which she had not known before.

This then is the reason why she is addressed as Help of Christians. She, by virtue of the maternity thus bestowed upon her, is urged by an insatiable craving to struggle perpetually for our welfare, both here and hereafter; while we, on our part, though unworthy children, have a claim upon her devotion, and a right to her services; and are prompted by a heaven-born instinct to turn to her for succour in all our needs; even as an infant, in every access of hunger and thirst, every throbbing of pain, every fit of uneasiness and alarm, flies to its mother's bosom, and seeks safety and healing in its mother's arms.

And as the earthly mother is furnished by a kind Providence with all that is necessary for the sustenance of the child at her breast, even so is Mary in possession of all the means of salvation. She is the spiritual vessel which was declared by the Archangel to be full of grace, and from which we draw the waters of eternal life. She is the Mother of Grace, because she has a mother's rights over Him who is the Author of Grace.

And think, beloved Brethren, how gracious is this dispensation of an all-loving and indulgent God, by which He gives us a spiritual mother, bound to us by the most sacred ties of a divinely-appointed maternity. It was not enough that the Son of God should himself take the form of man, and make Himself our brother, to disarm our fears by appearing amongst us in the same humanity as ourselves, and to win our confidence by the amiability, the gentleness, and kindleness of His character. It was not enough that He should bring home to us the mercy of the Godhead by a thousand acts and traits of compassion. Call up in your imaginations that beneficent figure. How tenderly He bends over the couch of the sick! How fondly He raises His healing hand to banish disease from helpless paralytics, from the victims of fever and every deadly ailment: from the possessed one whose body is smeared with the blood shed by the struggling demon from within; from the loathsome and dread lepers, whose presence taints the air. Behold him, as He stands at the mouth of the tomb in which lies his friend Lazarus, already yielding to that law which links corruption to death. How passionately does He weep over that supreme type of human sorrow and woe, begotten of man's rebellion, till the spectators are constrained to cry:—" Behold how He loved him." What a world of regretful memories, thwarted desires, and fruitless efforts, foiled compassion in the tears which He shed over the doomed city of His love, and in the plaintive never-surpassed elegy which He utters over the vision of her squandered opportunities and prostrate greatness: "Jerusalem, Jerusalem, thou that stonest the prophets, and slayest them that are sent to thee, how often would I have gathered thy children as the hen gathers her chickens under her wings, and thou wouldst not."

And as bodily pain, in its most repellent guise, has no power to blunt His sympathies, neither does His gentle heart shrink from contact with the most polluted and hateful sinner. Rather does He court such company, proclaiming it to all the world that He came not to call the just, but sinners, to repentance. When respectability is ruffled and decorously indignant at the sight of that poor public sinner, who obtrudes herself upon the banquet of the godly, and whose odorous ointment poured upon His feet, recalled only her own notorious scandals, what does He do? Instead of spurning her from Him, He makes Himself her unabashed herald and eulogist, to trumpet through all the echoing vista of the coming ages the depth of her sorrow, and the intensity of her love. " Many sins are forgiven her because she has loved much." Well was it said of him of old: " He is not the man to break the bruised reed, nor to quench the smoking flax."

Still, beloved Brethren, man could scarcely forget that Jesus had a twofold function, that He was destined to be not only our Redeemer, but our Judge, that he was raised up, according to the prophecy of holy Simeon, for the ruin, as well as the salvation, of many in Israel. That hand that healed the sick, and traced on the ground the unexpected sentence of acquittal for the poor woman taken in sin, did also beyond a doubt overturn the tables of the money-changers at the vestibule of the temple, and laid stripes upon the backs of their owners in fulfilment of the saying: " The zeal of thy house hath eaten me up," The self-same lips that prayed in the death agony for the forgiveness of His ruthless and barbarous enemies:—"Father, forgive them, for they know not what they do"—must one day send thrilling through the heavens and the earth, the terrific condemnation of the impenitent: Depart from me, ye cursed, into everlasting fire! Oh, no wonder that the writer of the great hymn of compunction should writhe with terror at this thought, and address the Meek and Humble of Heart under this aspect with the words: Just Judge of vengeance, grant me pardon of my sins before the day of reckoning! No wonder that men should tremble at the thought of this King of tremendous majesty.

This fear, beloved Brethren, so far as I have described it, is rational, and salutary, and falls within the purposes of Providence as an initiation to wisdom. But God would find us a mediator even with this Mediator; a being whom we could approach without diffidence or timidity, whose office should be severed from, as her character should be alien to, every ministration of sternness or severity; who should be privileged to control in our behalf all the machinery of grace, and every agency of compassion and love. When our cowering and timorous hearts, conscious of their guilt, shrink from the presence of our future Judge, when we fear to look upon the face of Him whom we have pierced and outraged, God sends us this sweet womanly form, the envoy of His kindness, to inspire us with hope, and to reconcile us to the Sovereign, whose recreant defaulting vassals we have been. Her suit He cannot reject, for she is His own most beloved Mother, pleading for the unworthy children whom heaven has given her in charge; and pleading, too, with all the vehemence and ardour of a mother.

In raising up for us, beloved Brethren, not only a Redeemer, but also this incorporation of God-like tenderness and pity, the great Father of all did but act in harmony with His own character, as He is revealed to us in both the natural and the supernatural order. Nowhere can we turn through the whole vast round of creation, without being amazed at the prodigality with which He has scattered abroad the riches of his inexhaustible nature. He has cast economy aside; and has made the universe a museum and storehouse of wonders. "The heavens and the earth are full of the majesty of His glory." Earth, air, fire, and water, the chemical elements interwoven in the fabric of the world, the varied surface and lining of the globe, its living furniture of plants and animals; the untiring march of stream and river; the pulsation of the mighty ocean; the fretwork of the starlit sky, and the mystery of the ever moving clouds. What are these but a myriad voices silently proclaiming the illimitable profusion and affluence of the Divine bounty. We scarcely realize how far the Creator differs from the creature, till we view him as our charioteer, who holds in His hands the reins of this uncounted and prodigious team, and guards and directs all, without the smallest exertion of mind or apprehension of disaster.

So also, beloved Brethren, in the supernatural order, lavish expenditure is His great characteristic. With Him, indeed, there is plentiful redemption. When He might have saved us with one ejaculation of praise uttered by His human lips, one upraising of His blessed hands to heaven, He must suffer all the ills of human life—obscure and despised—and finally die a hideous death amid unexampled torture and shame, and shed the last drop of blood in His body. When He might have paid our ransom in pence, He purchased it with treasures of gold and heaps of precious stones.

Again, beloved Brethren, you know that He has not contented Himself with watching over our safety in person, and surrounding us with all the benign and effectual safeguards of His providence. And yet His guardianship surely needed no supplementing. No matter who may be our guard and our protector, it is only under the shadow of His wings that we can breathe in hope and confidence. Yet what has He done? He has assigned each one of us at birth a spirit to accompany us through the journey of life, and to ward off the dangers that beset our path. "He has given His angels charge over thee, to keep thee in all thy ways." And why? Is it that He, the Creator, may take His ease, having deputed trusty ministers to do His work? No. Every act of the kind Sentinel that stands by our side requires the Divine co-operation. It is a characteristic dispensation of His exuberant bounty thus to multiply our helps and our helpers, and to hold out a thousand friendly hands to draw us to salvation.

Thus then He has given us, in Mary, the Queen of Angels, our supreme helper under His own divine Son. At baptism when we were admitted into the household of the Faith, we received the right to cry Abba! Father! to the most High; to be united by a true kinship with Jesus, our first-born Brother: and to call Mary—

without hyperbole or fanciful figure of speech—the mother and the help of Christians. Nor does this office of Mary's detract from the merits of her divine Son, the Redeemer of the world; rather it does but reveal more amply and explicitly the significance and value of His work. For to the virtue of His precious blood we owe not only our title to eternal salvation, but all the tender, consoling, and helpful relations which belong to this maternity—all the hope it infuses, all the gratitude it inspires. Mary's love for us, therefore, and the help she is empowered to grant us, is only the outcome and fruit of redemption, as the love of earthly father or mother is but an evidence and an effect of the love borne us by our Father who is in heaven.

Great need have we, beloved Brethren, of her help in this world of frailty, temptation and sorrow; and many are the offices in which Mary's position, as our mother and our help, involves her. Soul and body we are exposed in this fallen state to many dangers, diseases, and miseries; nay, to temporal and eternal death. We are individually of small account in the sum total of the human race; we are less than a drop in the ocean, or a sand on the seashore; but to each one of us how momentous are our lives, how all important is our destiny. Every Christian, believing as he does in an immortality beyond the grave, must tremble when he asks himself the question: after all shall I be saved or shall I be lost? When I bid adieu to this world, will death's grim figure transform itself into an angel to welcome me to a land where there is no more peril, nor labour, nor weariness; no sin, nor sickness, nor care; but all-sufficing joy for evermore? Or will it darken into the hideous lineaments of the demon that throws open the gates of the everlasting prison, where no ray of hope or solace is to enter through all eternity? That is the great problem. If we are safe on that head, the mischances and troubles of this transitory career would have little sting to wound us, and no poison to leave in the wound. But oh! the uncertainty of our fate! the many considerations that complicate that awful problem; the many dangers that threaten us; the many passions that are watchful to betray us; the many bad habits that so early begin to rule us; the sweep of the world's wicked current, which it is so hard to breast; the subtlety and strength of so many unseen foes who lie in wait for our destruction. Where, amid all these bewildering perils are we to turn for security? Where is the anchor of our hope? It is

Mary, the Help of Christians, on whom we are to fix our eyes, whenever this dreadful calculation of our final destiny scares, and haunts, and terrifies us. She is our anchor, she is the star of our sea, our security is in the thought that she cannot, without acting an unnatural thought, without denying her motherly instincts, and turning her back upon the duties which her Maker has imposed upon her, cease for a moment to exert all the influence and power she possesses, to rescue us from our foes and win us the prize of salvation. So long, therefore, as there is life, there is hope for every Christian; for with such an advocate to plead for the sinner, he has but to implore her from his heart to break the chains of his captivity, and to bring him to the freedom of the children of God; and she can no more turn a deaf ear to our prayers than He will flout her petitions.

And as Mary cheers us with the hope of final happiness, so does she watch over us at every period of our lives; and if we do not obstinately and wilfully resist, bears us safely in her arms through every danger. She stands by the font when the child of Adam receives the new birth by water and the Holy Ghost; and imprints upon the brow of the newly born infant a mother's loving kiss. Nor does she allow the occasion to pass without anxiously forecasting the difficulties which her child must encounter in the stormy voyage of life, and begging some special favour from her eldest-born to prepare it for its after-trials. She is more assiduous than any earthly mother in her services and her endearments. Through all the sweet season of its innocence she caresses it with an affection similar to that which she bestowed upon her own darling— the child of her womb—during the days of His infancy; and lives over again, in her relations with the Christian babe, that life of delight and ecstasy, which she experienced in nursing the Infant Saviour of the world. We may be assured that no birthday goes by for the little one, which is not signalized by some gift or adornment procured by the prayers of this ever-mindful mother.

Many an obstacle to its pious training is removed by her heartfelt prayer. As his mind gradually opens she labours to bring his soul into harmony with his duties, she observes the earliest indications of his character; she notes the first evidence of any evil bias which his nature may present; and prays more earnestly than before that sin may never deface that baptismal beauty which has made him so like her divine Son. As he grows up she visits him with many captivating and potent influences, that soften his heart, lie like balm on his memory, and never loose their hold upon his imagination. She speaks to him in the modest face, downcast eyes, and crossed hands of her image : from her own nook in the quiet Church she holds out to him the infant Jesus in her arms to call forth his love and to win him to goodness. While delighting his childish fancy, she rains down benedictions upon him, when he puts on her medal, or learns to recite her Rosary, or has himself invested in the livery of her Scapular, or reverentially cherishes some pictured episode in her life. She brings him under the magic of many a sweet hymn which is warbled into his enraptured ear, and which links words of child-like tenderness and trust to delicious and never-to-be-forgotten melody. When for the first time he presents himself timidly at the tribunal of penance, she prays with him and for him, adds vividness to his sense of the horror of sin, and intensity to his contrition, and rejoices to see the blemishes of his soul removed, and the light of grace shining forth again in undimmed lustre.

But if, alas! he is unfortnnate enough to receive a mortal thrust in the dread encounter, and to lose the grace of God, she quits not the battle-field; but raises beside his festering corpse the prayer of a bereaved and desolate mother; and calls with a loud and powerful cry to her divine Son, who died to save the sinner, to restore her lost child to life and to her. If the sinner be not obdurate —for it is his own fault if he continues in death—she clasps him again to her bosom more fondly and thankfully than the widow in the Gospel, when she received back her child from the jaws of the grave. And if there be joy before the angels of God over his conversion, surely tenfold rapture must throb in the mother's heart. And even though he should for years wander away, like the prodigal from his father's house, and waste his substance in riotous living, she follows him, tearful, but not hopeless, through all the scenes of his misguided career, as St. Monica followed her son; shielding him from many a temporal disaster, keeping the angel of death at bay, repeatedly turning back justice, as it advanced with fiery bolts in its hand, to execute the vengeance they have provoked. Well for him, then, if he clings to any little record of his early attachment to Mary, if he reverentially cherishes any emblem of her affection, or keeps up any trifling devotion in her honour. For sooner or later, if he be not absolutely oblivious of her, and steeled against grace, her perseverance will conquer; and one happy day or other, the recollection of some long-forgotten hymn, consecrated to his heavenly mother, and fragrant with associations connected with the spring of life; the words of some book or some preacher, insignificant enough in themselves; some worldly calamity or loss; the example or the death of some friend; will be turned by her prayer into an instrument of grace, will unexpectedly touch the hidden springs of feeling; and bid the healing tears of contrition to flow.

Then, beloved Brethren, her inspirations and whisperings fill her children's hearts with reverence, as they receive the different sacraments belonging to their state of life, or called for by the needs of the passing hour. When they approach the altar to partake of the banquet of love, she joins her thanksgiving to theirs; and, mother-like, outpours her gratitude for the favour granted to her children; and their feeble supplications are enforced by her words of more than seraphic ardour. She assists at the rite of confirmation, in which her boyish warrior is introduced to the stern conflict of life, and raises her hand to bless him, ere he mingles with the throng of veterans, over whose heads flutter the pennons of the great Captain. If he is called to the apostleship of the priesthood, she, the Queen of the Apostles, extinguishes in his breast the love of the world, obtains for him the spirit of supreme self-sacrifice, and fires his breast with zeal for God's honour and glory, and for the coming of His kingdom. If her children enter upon a wedded life, she blesses the nuptials by her unseen presence; and prays that God may make the union of the two hearts a source of mutual happiness and merit, an instrument of sanctification, and an omen of eternal joy. In the breasts of the elected spouses of Christ, she fosters an undying love for the angelic virtue of chastity, as well by her prayers as by the luminous ideal of maidenly modesty and self-denial, which her own life on earth presents, and by the fascination of her example. Her picture or image cannot be contemplated without banishing or abashing the demon of uncleanness, and her name is a spell to drive away evil thoughts. Her form, clothed in the radiance of its chastity, with the light of the stars around her head, and the silver moon beneath her feet, rises up before the All-Holy God, and shuts out as it were from His sight the reeking abyss of the world, and averts from the herd of sinners many an appalling catastrophe.

Pride of intellect and spiritual pride—the companions—the forerunners of immodesty—when they develop into heresy and schism, find in her a tower of David, a Tower of Ivory, upon which their paroxysms of anger and rebellion are spent in vain; and sooner or later perish under the power of her prayers. "Thou alone," says the Church, addressing her, "hast given its death-blow to every heresy throughout the world." It was thus that her Rosary, taught by her to her beloved son Dominic, and through Dominic to the whole body of the faithful, succeeded in the course of time, by inculcating meditation on the mystery of the Incarnation of her Divine Son, in uprooting one of the most malignant heresies that ever threatened the peace of society. True wisdom, on the other hand, finds in her, who is the seat of Wisdom, and the Spouse of the Holy Ghost, a most powerful patron and director in its studies; and turns in all its difficulties to the Mother of the Incarnate Word, to whom the Church applies the saying: "I, Wisdom, dwell in counsel, and am present in learned thoughts." It is to this Lady of Good Counsel that the most illiterate Christian addresses himself by an instinct of his spiritual nature, to be guided aright in every embarrassment, doubt, and perplexity; nor does he seek her counsel in vain. Nay, there is no limit to the aid which she is commissioned to give. Her prayers have set aside the laws of nature themselves, as the upraised hands of Joshua stayed the setting sun, till the cry of victory sounded in His ears. Many a portrait of Mary, without pretentions to art, and black with the grime of ages, has been, and still is, the goal of pious pilgrimages, undertaken by her children beneath the pressure of disorders pronounced by medical men incurable, congenital defects of the system, or bodily deformities that made life burthensome, and unserviceable. And through every successive generation the growth of votive tablets, and emblems of disease and deformity, hung up as memorials around that miraculous shrine, has been an ever-accumulating evidence, against an unbelieving age, of Mary's power and Mary's love. How many spots over the length and breadth of Christendom have been made holy by her apparition in seasons of impending calamity? How many forests, and groves, and wells, villages and solitary mountain-passes, has she wrested from the demons who roam the world vainly searching for rest, and consecrated by her sweet image against all evil influence? This very land was once her dowry and her choice domain. On how many tempestous headlands and dangerous rocks, has the lamp of some little sanctuary dedicated to her honour, and standing lonely amid the roar and foam of the ocean, been as a star of safety to the storm-tossed mariner; because it whispered to him, amid the hurly-burly of the elements, that he had a mother all-powerful over the most threatening sea, who was ready and anxious to save her child from destruction.

Nor is it only in such tempests that Mary is our help. Often when the haughty conqueror, flushed with triumph upon triumph, has doomed her children to death or captivity and her shrines to desecration; when already the thunders of their advancing legions were deafening the ear and terrifying the heart, have her prayers rolled back the advancing tide, and whelmed in mid-career the Pharoah who persecuted her people. Then did the awe-stricken world realize for a season that union of beauty and irresistible might ascribed to Mary in the Canticle of Canticles: "Who is she that cometh forth as the morning, rising fair as the moon, bright as the sun, terrible as an army in battle-array?"

In conclusion then, lest the seed should fall upon unfruitful ground, let one and all of you, on this feast of your Holy Patroness, dedicate yourselves afresh, soul and body to be henceforth her devoted servants and loving children. I would ask you one question. Have you ever thought seriously of all that Mary has done for you? Have you ever pondered at length upon all the interest she has taken in you, all the love she has outpoured upon you, all the temptations in which she has shielded you, all the dangers from which she has rescued you, all the graces she has procured for you by her intercession? Have you ever made her an adequate return for all her services? But why do I speak of an adequate return, which is a thing impossible and inconceivable? If we were to vow ourselves henceforth to be Mary's slaves, and to spend our days and nights in doing Mary's bidding, it would all be as nothing in comparison with what we owe to her.

How then are we to show that we are not unmindful of her claims? Let us make a distinct resolution that we will never allow a day to pass, between this and the day of our death, in which we will not do something to honour Mary. Let us resolve furthermore that whenever the opportunity presents itself we will labour to kindle a similar devotion in the hearts of those who come under our influence. But let not this be the limit of our resolve. Let us show our sincerity, and prove the sterling and solid worth of our protestations, by making real sacrifices, in the token of the high admiration with which we regard our heavenly Queen and Mother, and of our longing desire to be enrolled amongst the number of her accepted servants. Remember that without self-sacrifice, all religious emotion, all enthusiasm of the feelings, is very deceptive: it is like sun-lit vapour, beautiful indeed, but passing, ineffectual, and barren. Let no appeal to our charity, such as is made to you to-day, be made fruitlessly in the name of Mary. When the opportunity is offered by God, and a clear call comes from Him for some good work, especially in support of Catholic education, or for extending the succours of religion to those who are spiritually destitute, let the desire of proving the sincerity of our love and devotion to His Blessed Mother, conquer the suggestions of worldly prudence, which only too often is mere selfishness under the thinnest disguise. Perhaps our obedience to a truer inspiration and a nobler impulse, may be the condition fixed by Providence for the bestowal of some spiritual grace, or temporal blessing for ourselves, or those we hold dear, for which we have hitherto sighed in vain. Perhaps it may be the long-expected remedy that will bring back harmony to troubled households, prosperity after an unbroken period of distress, joy after much sorrow, peace of conscience after many trials and falls. Perchance, even as I speak, our Good Angel, and the great adversary, descry upon the horizon, a little speck of darkness, which, by and by, will expand into a cloud and tempest of misfortune. If on occasions like this we give generously, in obedience to the inspiration with which God is good enough to visit us, we make the surest preparation against disaster, and in the day of trouble we shall realize the truth of the epithets applied to Mary by the Church:—Comfort of the Afflicted! Refuge of Sinners! Help of Christians!

OUR PREDOMINANT PASSION.

WHILE you are engaged, beloved Brethren, upon the work of self-examination that belongs to this time of penitence, it is fitting that you should find out, and take pains to chain up, if not to kill, that master-passion, which has been the occasion of your principal sins and disorders in the past. For, with most of us, if not all, there is one passion to which we specially incline, with which we are oftenest in conflict, or under whose tyranny we mainly groan. This vice, which is called by Spiritual writers, the predominant passion, it is most important that you should discover and understand; that you may be able to detect it under its different disguises—for often it has as many masks as a play-actor—and that you may furthermore prepare against it the special weapons and methods of attack and defence which it is least able to withstand. If you give your chief attention to the destruction or disabling of this passion, all else will be comparatively easy. No master of the spiritual life will advise you to go attacking here and there, and beating about the bush; all your energies should be centred upon this arch-enemy; upon him you must fling all your forces; knowing well that if you cut the leader down, the general rout of petty vices will scatter, powerless and incapable of inflicting a grievous blow. Let me then say a few words this morning to help you on this subject.

Examine yourselves then, as to whether Pride be not the Captain of these adverse legions; the ruler of your lives; the likely agent in your final overthrow. Have you been accustomed from childhood upwards to exact from those around you a consideration, respect and attention, which you do not give them in turn? Do you fire up at the least breath of disparagement, and vent your resentment in haughty words and looks, and malicious acts of revenge? Are you eager to mix a little of the bitter powder of dispraise and unfriendly criticism with every sweet draught of commendation prepared for a neighbour; are you practised in the art of finding spots in the sun, flaws in every virtue, except what you attribute to yourself? Do you speak of yourselves and your doings oftener than you would suffer your neighbour to speak of theirs; with the secret feeling that of course you, and all that concerns you, must have a greater interest in the eyes of all sensible folks, than anything relating to your neighbours. Perhaps you are too shrewd to boast and brag, and so put a pretty dress of modesty upon your pride, as travelling mountebanks put lace and scarlet upon their ugly monkies; hoping that your self-depreciation will bring praise from the company. This is an odious hypocrisy. Remember the words of a profane poet, after giving an example of this kind of masked pride: "and the devil did grin, for his darling sin is the pride that apes humility."

Or perhaps it is more vanity than pride that rules you, the difference being, that a proud man despises the world, but the vain man courts it and lives in its good opinion. Possibly you are perpetually fishing for admiration; perpetually showing off your imagined excellences of soul or body; your talents, your wit, your cunning, your strength of sinew, your swiftness of foot, your nimbleness, your dexterity, your good looks; nay, it may be you go so far as to take a peacock's pride in your finery, your clothes, hats, ribbons, or coloured gew-gaws, which possibly occupy your imagination even during Mass or Benediction. Oh! surely, if this be so, you realize the saying of Scripture: "Man when he was held in honour did not understand it, but was likened to senseless beasts." The Eternal Victim is raised up between heaven and earth, to call down mercy and grace upon you by His sacrifice of propitiation; and you—your mind is all the time roving about among your odds and ends of dress, extracting pleasure and satisfaction from them, as the bee draws honey from the flower, contrasting them with your neighbour's, and revelling in your own superiority of taste or judgment, or in your ampler means.

But perhaps your chief thirst is for money. This love of money, beloved brethren, is a very insidious vice; and if you are not in earnest in your search, if you are not seriously bent on finding out the evil that lurks in your heart, you may pass it without notice, or even approve of it under the false name of prudence, economy, worldly wisdom. And while this vice has such a power of hiding itself away, or putting on a deceptive mask, and going by another name than its own—for under the name of Avarice, who would harbour it?—it is all the time a most destructive and deadly passion. The Scripture says: "There is no greater vice than the love of money. For such a one putteth even his own soul to sale." Be not hoodwinked therefore; if you are too fond of money, be determined to find it out, and put an end to it. Otherwise you are sleeping with a serpent under your bed, that by and by will unwind his coils and fascinate you with his dreadful eye, and fill your veins with a mortal poison which no antidote can extract from them. Ask yourselves then, are you too eager to acquire money; are you willing to slave and toil for every petty gain, while you are slothful in all that concerns the service of God? Perhaps you like to hoard up your savings, and often find yourselves turning over in your mind the amount you have laid by, and surprise yourselves in anxious calculations as to how you may increase your store; and all this with feverish hopes and fears, while you never spend a sigh upon your sins, never think of laying up merit for the next life. You are loth to part with your money, even in the payment of your just debts; you defer it; you exercise your cunning in finding shifts to shirk the payment, or to lessen it. As for acts of generosity, they are out of the question. You brand generosity as extravagance and rail at it; or else you are apt to think yourselves highly generous for giving what you are bound to give. Neither God's appeal nor man's, neither the cause of religion, nor the cause of suffering humanity can pierce the iron with which your heart is plated. Oh! the meanness, the degradation, the folly of this vice! A day will come, when you must leave your money behind you and go before God, who made you the steward of his gifts, and render an account of the talents He has committed to you. Woe to you on that day, if you be found to have buried your talents in the earth, to have done no good with your money. There will be only one sentence for you: "The unprofitable servant cast ye into exterior darkness; there shall be weeping and gnashing of teeth."

But perhaps your ruling fault is a proneness to sensuality and self-indulgence. If so, you need very little assistance in discovering the fact. A man who eats or drinks to excess, or who indulges in immodesty, can scarcely hide it from himself. This is matter rather for sighs and tears, humble and earnest supplications, thoughts of death and the rigorous judgment that will follow death, than for careful investigation.

To drunkards, or even moderate tipplers, I would say one word. Let them remember that they are accountable for every sin which they foresee they may likely commit when under the influence of intoxicating drink. Your drunken quarrels, blows and taunts, the revelations of matters which should be kept secret; your curses, oaths and blasphemies; in fine, the acts of impurity dictated by the demon drink; these are not lost, but put down to your account, against the final reckoning-day. Again, if you foresee that your habit of intemperance will shorten your life—as it does in most cases—you are already as much self-murderers, as the poor wretch who has drunk poison, and who lies helplessly awaiting his doom. Moreover, if you are fathers or mothers, you are accountable to God for the diseased and morbid bodies you bequeath to your children; you have upon your heads the curse of the misdeeds, to which their bodily disposition, inherited from you, gives them a dreadful bias. When your frames, pampered and soaked with drink, shall lie rotting in the earth, their sins, their wild and insatiable thirst for self-gratification will cry to heaven against you. Beware then, ere it is too late, for you stand on the brink of an abyss of evils, the depth of which no eye can fathom but God's.

And when, beloved Brethren, you have laid your finger upon the predominant passion, ask yourselves one question more. What have you done so far, through your twenty, forty, sixty years of life, to subdue it? Have you prayed againt it, as the Psalmist did: "Let not any injustice hold rule over me." Have you thought of it with as much interest and anxiety, as you have of even your temporal affairs? If you discerned the first symptoms of cancer in your flesh, how soon you would fly to the doctor, to be saved from the ravages of that hideous disease. But here is a far more frightful cancer—a cancer of the soul—that angels shudder at, that God averts His face from; and yet you eat, drink, and make merry, regardless of it. Rouse yourselves now at last from your dangerous lethargy, lest delay should ruin you, and you should fulfil the awful saying of Job:—"His bones shall be filled with the vices of his youth, and they shall sleep with him in the dust." Say with holy David, "I will confess against myself mine injustices to the Lord"; and it will not be long before you can add, with him: "And the Lord hath forgiven the wickedness of my sin."

COVETOUSNESS.

AT this season of the year, beloved brethren, when mingled with the kind wishes and heart-felt remembrance of friends the post brings us also its periodic sheaf of bills, and the phantom ghost of past expenditure rises up to trouble us, when we are busy reviewing the condition of our funds and too many of us are trembling at the meagreness of our purses, it seems to me opportune to say a few words on the inordinate love of money, and of those objects that money can purchase.

You know that the unchecked and unmortified love of money is ranked amongst the seven capital sins, because like its six bad associates it is the mother of many sins besides. As St. Paul says writing to his disciple Timothy, "They that will become rich fall into temptation, and into the snare of the devil and into many unprofitable and hurtful desires, which drown men into destruction and perdition. For the desire of money is the root of all evils; which some coveting have erred from the faith and have entangled themselves in many sorrows. But thou, O Man of God, fly these things, and pursue justice, godliness, faith, charity, patience, mildness.—I. *Tim.* 9-11.

Like its six fellow vices also, covetousness is entitled to the name of deadly, because though every act which it prompts is not necessarily deadly in its guilt and malice, nevertheless it is capable of producing mortal sins of its own inherent badness, without borrowing malice from any other sins. It is especially odious in the sight of God because it withdraws the heart from its allegiance, and sets up an idol in His shrine, an idol, too, all material and gross. Hence St. Paul denounces it as a species of idolatry which suffices to exclude its victim from the Kingdom of Heaven. "Be not deceived" says he, "neither fornicators nor covetous shall possess the Kingdom of God."—I. *Cor.* vi. 9. And again "Know ye this and understand that no fornicator, nor unclean, nor covetous person which is a serving of idols hath inheritance in the Kingdom of Christ and of God." It seeks an object outside God to live for, to love, to pant for. It ignores the precept, "Seek ye first the Kingdom of God and His justice," and practically distrusts the promises attached to its fulfilment. "All other things shall be added to you." It ignores the wisdom of the wise man, and scouts the counsels of the experienced who know that the love ot money is an insatiable thirst, which every draught of prosperity only aggravates. "I heaped together for myself," says the inspired sage, "silver and gold and the wealth of kings and provinces. I made me singing men and singing women, and the delights of the sons of men, cups and vessels to serve to pour out wine. And I surpasssed in riches all that were before me in Jerusalem, my wisdom also remained with me. And whatsoever my eyes desired I refused them not, and I withheld not my heart from enjoying every pleasure and delighting itself in the things which I had prepared, and esteemed this my portion to make use of my own labour. And when I turned myself to all the works wherein I had laboured in vain, I saw in all things vanity and vexation of mind, and that nothing was lasting under the sun."— *Ecclesiastes* ii. 8-11.

It seeks contentment and the satisfaction of the heart's deep cravings from objects which can never satiate the appetite, for says St. Augustine, "Thou hast made us, O God, for Thyself, and our hearts are restless till they find their rest in Thee." In short, it is a vice which, as it slights God's love and spurns His commandment, so it sets aside the dictates of reason and common sense, and the testimony of experience. But, alas, to many of those who are held under the bondage of this vice, their folly will never be brought home, until death rudely awakens them from their dreams of covetous longing, miserly economy, screwing and scraping, usury, trickery, and fraud, and they recognise in their own personal history the truth of the saying of the Psalmist—"The men of riches have slept out their short sleep and have found nothing in their hands."

Such being the nature of this vice, beloved Brethren, it will not surprise us to find it inveighed against in the sacred writers with an energy and vehemence that make us tremble. Listen to the prophet Amos—"I saw the Lord standing upon the altar, and He said—'Strike the hinges, and let the lintels be shook, for there is covetousness in the head of them all, and I will slay the last of them with the sword; there shall be no flight for them, they shall flee, and he that shall flee of them shall not be delivered. Though they go down even to hell, thence shall My hand bring them out; and though they climb up to heaven, thence will I bring them down. And though they be hid in the top of Carmel, I will search and take them away from thence; and though they hide themselves from My eyes in the depth of the sea, there will I command the serpent, and he shall bite them.'"

And St. James thus addresses the rich men whose hour has come at last and whose eyes have been opened too late to their poverty—"Go now ye rich men, weep, howl in the miseries which shall come upon you, your riches are corrupted, your garments are moth-eaten, your gold and silver is cankered; and the rust of them shall be for a testimony against you, and shall eat your flesh like fire."—*James* v. 1. If the words of a human voice outpouring its indignation upon covetousness be so terrible, what think you will be the bellowing thunders of the Divine wrath, shaking the heavens themselves, when he who has sold his salvation for gold and silver stands shivering at the eternal bar to receive the sentence which his iniquity has earned him.

Of course, beloved Brethren, these awful bursts of wrathful menace are provoked by deadly sins of covetousness, particularly by a grievous habit of that vice, but they show besides God's hatred of the sin in all its manifestations both great and small. It cannot exist in the soul without either extinguishing the fire of charity altogether, or impairing its fervour, and its beauty and brilliancy, and threatening sooner or later to quench it fatally. It is not always easy to detect, for it wears masks, and is skilful at disguises, and calls itself by false names. It generally puts on the guise, and assumes the title of prudence, fortifies itself with sounding maxims and worldly wisdom, talks of laying up against a rainy day, insists on the duty of avoiding extravagance, of looking to the main chance, of taking care of the penny and leaving the pound to take care of itself, of providing for sons and daughters, their education and settlement in life, it employs ever so many such discreet texts and specious pleas. It often professes, with a dry, hard jocularity, to stand in terror of the workhouse. This is its outward aspect, and the disguise often deceives even acquaintances, who do observe that the man is somewhat near, but little suspect how tightly the heart is coiled round and contracted, and stifled by the vile adder of covetousness. As for the victim himself, as a rule he does not believe himself a victim; and if there be an avaricious man here to-day, I am assured that he is rather applying my words to his neighbour than to himself. And this it is that makes the vice of covetousness so subtle and so treacherous. If you are addicted to drink, you cannot conceal the fact from your own knowledge, the sot is most frank in stuttering out the confession of his weakness to every one whom he can buttonhole. But the avaricious man knows not his malady, and a few years render his blindness almost incurable. Another unfortunate circumstance in connection with this vice is, that while other passions often yield to the wear and tear of life, and decay with the decay of the frame, avarice is the most powerful in the oldest bones, and burns fiercely in frames almost undermined with the weakness and infirmities of age, and will light up the feeble eyeballs, and quicken the failing pulse to the last gasp. It was thus with the poor wretch whom the saintly Curé of Ars mentions in his instructions. Much time had been spent in bringing this man to a sense of his position, and as it appeared to the good priest not without success. Life was fast ebbing away, and the sweat of death was breaking out upon the pale, care-worn, and emaciated face. No time was to be lost, the legions of hell, like bloodhounds, bared their fangs at the prey. With solemn and touching words of exhortation, the Curé raised the sign of redemption before the eyes of the dying man, it was a crucifix of silver, beautifully wrought, but instead of inspiring him with sorrow, and hope, and love, of which it was the symbol, the sight of the precious metal revived in his heart the demon of avarice. Gathering unexpected strength he darted forward, clutched it eagerly, and crying out that it was worth so many gold pieces, fell backwards on his pillow a corpse. And thus he died: avarice had been his daily companion through life, and was not to be thrust from his death-bed. Now how may a covetous man recognize his failing? First, if he is not prepared to do God's will, and to obey the commands of the Church owing to his thirst for worldly gain, no matter how he may search the dictionary for euphonious names to disguise his passion, he is guilty in God's sight of covetousness. If he finds that where his salvation, and the means to attain it on the one side, are in conflict with worldly interest on the other, and he gives the advantage to the latter, he is guilty in God's sight of covetousness. So also if his mind is perpetually occupied, even in prayer time, with anxious thoughts about his business difficulties, and his prospects, going through mental calculations, as to the money he has, the money he wishes to have, and the best means to attain the object of his desires. He is covetous, if, for the sake of vile lucre, he neglects the public worship of God, and stays away from Mass or from Benediction on Sundays or holidays that he may add to his worldly store. He is covetous if he seeks to improve his position by trickery or fraud. He is covetous if, possessing riches, he takes an overweening pride in, and places an undue confidence in them, arrogantly fancying that his money has made him semi-omnipotent, and that everything should yield to his will, his less wealthy fellows should be cringing and subserveint in his presence, because forsooth, he is a moneyed man. "Charge the rich of this world," says St. Paul to Timothy, "not to be high-minded nor to trust in the uncertainty of riches, but in the living God."

He is covetous if, being endowed with sufficient means, he is too penurious to expend them in procuring the necessaries of life for himself or his family, or in providing them with proper food in health, or with skilful professional aid, medicine, and the needful delicacies in time of illness; or again, if he does not dress his wife and his children decently according to his station of life. The spectacle of that miserly old man, who was found the other day stark dead of starvation, although he had, strapped to his waist, a bag containing upwards of 80 sovereigns, was enough to make the demons jibe if their contempt did not overpower their ridicule. He is covetous if he is hard to the poor, giving them crusty advice instead of half-pence, or treating them to injurious words, which add a sting to their poverty. "He that hath the substance of the world," says the disciple of love, "and shall see his brother in need, and shall shut up his bowels from him, how doth the charity of God abide in him." He is covetous if he find it excessively painful to part with his money, even where justice demands the forfeit, if he defers payment of his debts as long as he possibly can. It is little wonder if the covetous should feel as if the heart were being torn out of their bosom when they are forced to disburse; for where a man's treasure is, there will his heart be also.

Examine yourselves then, beloved Brethren, carefully and sincerely in the sight of God, and if you find the smallest seed of avarice in your heart, rest not till it be cast out. Remember you are but stewards of your riches; God is the owner, and to him you must one day give an account how you have administered his property, and what you have done with His talents. If they are almost all spent upon yourselves, upon your comforts, and diversions, while Churches are burdened with debt, schools are crippled for want of support, widows and orphans are crying for food and clothing, and a hideous famine is laying waste a land of christians and of brothers—God knows, as you should know, you are not doing your duty. The badness of the times are as a trumpet call to the wealthy, to outpour all that they can spare for the relief of the distressed. You will not lose by giving—not even in this life. Ponder well the quaint words written upon an old tombstone, and purporting to come from the lips of the dead —"What I kept I lost, what I gave I have." Yes, you will but be banking in heaven the money you devote to deeds of charity and mercy; and you shall have your own hereafter with usury. But if you harden your hearts to the call of distress and misery, beware lest avarice grow upon you unawares, darken your path, and lead you to perdition. Resist the beginning, or you know not where you may end. Judas was once a darling of God, filled with the fruits and gifts of the Holy Ghost, and chosen among men to be the Ambassador of God to His fellows. Little did he think when he began to love money, that his passion would so blind him, that he would become a thief, a hypocrite, professing falsely to care for the poor, a man of sacrilege, eating and drinking judgment to himself, and last of all a treacherous deicide, betraying his Lord with a kiss, for the price of a runaway slave. Did the picture of his self-strangled corpse, hanging in the wind with bowels protruding, and the stamp of despair upon his scowling visage, ever present itself to his youthful mind, as the termination and goal of all his hopes and yearnings, and the crowning of a boyhood of virtue and promise.

ANGER.

THE passion of anger was, in the state of unfallen nature, subject to reason. Adam, before his sin, suffered no inconvenience from its assaults. But his disobediance brought upon the race he betrayed, together with other calamities, revolt, disorder, confusion, and chaos, among the feelings and passions. Desires and apprehensions, joys and sorrows, hopes and fears, which had once submitted to the yoke of reason, became wild, wayward, and unruly; and oftentimes, singly or in mutual combination, tyrannized over the whole man. Affections broke away from the traces, like maddened horses; and followed their bent in a gallop, trailing in the mire the dignity and sobriety of man's rational nature. Anger, like the rest, wrenched itself loose from control; and, from time to time, seized upon its victim, as a demon might, and for an interval transformed him into a madman. The ancients had a legend, that to the composition of man, different animals had contributed qualities characteristic of their kind; and that anger was nothing else but the working up and seething in our clay of the fiery element contributed by the raging lion. Certainly, by anger man is changed into a brute. But man's fury is culpable, because it is capable of restraint, whereas the poor beast cannot do otherwise than rage under provocation. The bull in the arena must roar, and stamp, and foam at the flaunting of the red flag. Man need never play the wild beast.

Now there are different temperaments, some more strongly prone to, and swayed by anger than others. Physiologists speak of the sanguine or full-blooded temperament, which is noted for quickness, vivacity, and unsteadiness; and they class the *Choleric* disposition under this head. However, no matter what be their classification, there are some naturally more hot and excitable than their fellow-men. Oftentimes, they are those who, in their childhood and youth, were overfed and over-indulged, particularly with flesh meat. Parents who foolishly pamper their children in this manner must abide by the consequences: they are but feeding the wild beast in them.

Those who are conscious of a very irritable temper, what are they to do? Are they to regard themselves as unfairly treated by their Maker? No! God has given them that passion of anger for their good, and, if they behave like men, their passion will work for them nothing but good. Men are sometimes placed in charge of gunpowder magazines. Is that a crime or injustice on the part of those who give them the commission? No! They are well aware what precautions will secure them from risk. The black dust, in which the thunder and lightning lie asleep, in whose bosom lurks the force of earthquakes, will slumber on as harmless as a babe, unless the fire be applied to it. But a single spark, so minute that dropping on the sensitive surface of the body its faint smart is scarcely felt before it is extinguished, were it to fall among that torpid mass, calls forth hideous explosion, deafening crash of thunder, and wide-spread wreck and ruin. Anger then is this dangerous magazine of explosive material given to us to watch over. We are abundantly cautioned as to the safeguards we should employ against its ravages. Nor are we left to ourselves to deal with it. If we be only in earnest, we have God's help to secure us against its dreadful out-burst. But, to put aside figures of speech, it is no plea for your passionate temper, that nature gave it to you. If you were born with some bodily disease upon you, would you not strive to get it healed? Though the remedy should be slow and lingering, unquestionably you would adopt it, if it only promised an eventual cure. So with anger. You may have begun life as the most passionate of infants, kicking, scratching, biting, screaming, and going into convulsions of ill-temper. But under judicious parents, who combine sweetness with firmness, who avoid all exhibitions of fickleness and caprice, who themselves set an example of gentleness by their uniform demeanour, and who take care to keep your tender minds as happy as possible, without, at the same time, allowing you any unbecoming or injurious indulgence—something will have been done to give you a command over your temper, before you have begun even to realize the battle that is before you. Suppose, further, that you are taught from the first to pray earnestly and perseveringly, not alone for grace in general, but in a special manner for the grace to gain the mastery over your angry passions, you have made the second step towards ultimate victory. Few, indeed, take to heart the question of temper as St. Philip Neri did. Once, as a little child, he was reciting, with his usual recollection, some portion of the office, when he was interrupted by his sister, who sought to draw his attention to something else. The little Saint, being a child of Adam, resented this interruption, which appeared so untimely and so profane; and pushed her rather roughly away. For this trifling outburst of anger—anger too, which to many would seem justifiable—St. Philip wept tears of contrition through all the years of his youth; it furnished tears to his manhood; and in his old age, with the wreaths of many a triumph, and many an heroic act, upon his brow, this boyish offence gave him ample motives for humiliation, self-distrust, and sorrow.

If you are in earnest in praying against the tyranny of anger, your efforts will not end with prayer. You will adopt the measures usually prescribed as preventive or medicinal with respect to this passion. For example, you will forecast the seasons and circumstances in which your temper is likely to be tried; and you will fortify yourself against surprise, by dwelling upon the motives of meekness, the fruitlessness of anger, the unseemliness of its transports, the serious nature of its consequences; and by praying that the God of Peace, who alone can keep the heavens clear, will prevent the threatening tempest: "From anger, hatred and all ill-will, deliver me, O Lord." You will follow the purport and spirit, if not the literal bearing, of the counsel laid down by some of the heathen philosophers—never to speak under an impulse of anger, till you have counted a hundred. And then, when you do speak, you will keep out of your words all appearance of the fire that glows within you, and aim at speaking even more mildly than your wont, mindful of the wise man's dictum: "A soft answer turneth away wrath, but a harsh word stirreth up fury."—*Prov.* xv. 1. Should you become aware that, through some unexpected and uncalculated occurrence, some slight, or provocation, flashed upon you suddenly, your temper has already swept you away, and hurried you into expressions of impatience, resentment, defiance, contumely, contumely, or haughty vexation; you will there and then make the best amends you can, by subduing your spirit, bending yourself to utter words of gentleness, and apologizing for the excess into which your bad temper has betrayed you. This is the least to be expected from men, who are commanded: "If one strike you on the right cheek, turn to him the other also." You will, moreover, follow the advice of ascetic writers, who recommend that we should form an alliance with the imagination in our warfare against pride and anger, by conjuring up in the fancy circumstances apt to provoke us to irritation, by calling before our minds the bearings, the air, the tones, the attitudes, of those whom we are disposed to dislike, and whose presence is apt to fret, and harass, and exasperate us ; by dwelling upon imagined insults, wrongs, detractions, calumnies, rash judgments, false interpretations of word or action, of which we are the victims ; and thus goading ourselves into the first feelings that belong to anger and malignity; then dropping on our knees, beseech God to help us to overcome ourselves, and never to fail in patience, which alone hath a perfect work. This is part of the drill recommended to hasty and irritable tempers. Of course, such a method would be out of place in other equally dangerous and even more deadly forms of temptation; and that for very obvious reasons. Nor will the earnest man forget to review at night the result of his day's struggle, with a view to annul the effects of his frailty, and to nerve himself against the struggle of the following day. Moreover, in his perpetual consciousness of rash and inconsiderate disposition, which may, without his distinct knowledge, be producing frequent petty acts of anger, and throwing off sparks, as it were, unnoticed, he will always take care to avail himself of the virtue of that water, which, from the blessing the Church has imparted to it, is justly called holy, and which, as a Sacramental, has power to blot out the guilt of indeliberate venial sin. He will, therefore, gladly sprinkle himself with that salutary dew, whenever it is at hand, whether in the Church, or at home, or in the house of a friend; saying from his heart—"Sprinkle me, O Lord, with hyssop, and I shall be cleansed; wash me and I shall become whiter than snow."— *Ps.* L. 9.

Ah! Beloved Brethren, if passionate men and women went to all this trouble to acquire the virtue of meekness, the world would not be such a bear-garden as it is. We should not hear, as we passed by the houses of our people, shrieks and curses blent, as from the suddenly-opening door of pandemonium. Our poor little children would not have their ears assailed, from morning till night, with a hideous litany of oaths and curses, such as resound n many Catholic houses, through all the hours of daylight, and which make the still night a blessed time. Husbands would not give way to a brutish harshness and boorish sullenness with the partners of their lives, whom they have chosen in God's sight for better or for worse, not as paragons of all virtues, but as mixed compositions of good and bad; and whom they know to be the weaker and the more delicate vessel. Wives would not exercise that feminine talent of finding out the sorest places in their husband's susceptibilities; of saying malicious things with an air of innocence, when they are crossed; of looking the injured martyr; of indulging in untimely silence; of taking a covert revenge for some fancied lack of attention in a thousand ingenious ways, which make no great noise or ado, but draw blood as surely as their needles. How different from the spirit of the sweet St. Frances of Rome, who lived for forty years with her husband in unbroken peace, the only strife and contention between them being who should be the kinder and the tenderer. Though she was ardently devoted to prayer and contemplation, she never took it amiss, when her husband interrupted these delicious occupations; unlike some of our devotees, whose faces, beaming a moment ago with seraphic enjoyment, gather a look of vindictiveness and grim severity, when they are disturbed. "A married woman," she used to say, "must, when called upon, quit her devotions to God at the altar, to find Him in her household affairs." And there is a beautiful legend connected with this subject. On one occasion, while reciting the office of Our Lady, she was called away four times in beginning a psalm; and her patience and obedience were rewarded, by finding when she returned the fifth time, that the words of the verse were written in letters of gold.

Towards the close of the third century, there were two friends living at Antioch, one a priest named Sapricius, and the other a layman, named Nicephorus. After many years spent in the nninterrupted intercourse of genuine friendship, one unhappy day an unfortunate breach occurred, which severed their hearts, and embittered their feelings. For a long time each avoided the other's presence, or, if they met in the street by accident, passed by with a silent scowl. But Nicephorus had a placable heart which at last got the better of his resentment. The memory of the vanished days of friendship, peace, and happiness, contrasted sadly with the consciousness of his late tempestuous, angry, and resentful mood; and for God's sake, and for the sake of his long-rooted affection, he sent a messenger to crave forgiveness from the man he had parted with in passion. But Sapricius, priest as he was, forgot the example of his meek master, the prince of peace, and returned a sullen answer. Again, messengers were sent upon the same errand; and alas! with the same result. A third time, Nicephorus humbled himself to beseech pardon by the intervention of their common friends; but as an anvil is hardened by the strokes of the hammer, so did the heart of the unworthy priest grow more stiff and relentless under these repeated solicitations. Nicephorus, however, was not discouraged; with streaming eyes, he went in person, subdued and sorrowful, to his old friend's house, trusting that the spectacle of his sincere penitence and keen regret would have the effect of kindling again the embers of their former friendship. He threw himself down upon his knees, and by all solemn adjurations prayed for the forgiveness of his fault. But pride was stronger than the impulses of old kindness; and he went away sad and unforgiven.

Meantime a storm of persecution broke over the Christian world; and the priest Sapricius was one of the first arrested for the crime of belonging to the forbidden sect. Undismayed, he confronted the terrors of the pagan governor's court, and the sight of his assembled satellites, athirst for Christian blood. Boldly he acknowledged himself a Christian, proudly he proclaimed himself a priest. His body was compressed in a powerful engine, that shot agony through every limb; but his voice rose in the midst of the executioners:—"My body is in your hands; but my soul is my Saviour's: that you cannot reach." Pain seemed incapable of subduing his fortitude; it appeared but labour lost to torture this priest of the unknown God. His sentence therefore was read—"His head was to be severed from his body, for contemning the decree of the Emperors."

With a cheerful face, Sapricius stepped forth amidst his guards, the crown, as it were, already in his grasp, and on his lips the words of St. Paul: "I have fought the good fight." But lo! amidst the hurrying crowd that throng to see the victim, the sad and tearful

countenance of his former friend. Now was the time. With a throbbing heart, bursting with revived fondness and admiration, Nicephorus threw himself on his knees and cried aloud: "Martyr of Jesus Christ, forgive me the wrong I have done you." No answer came from the lips that had but now made so glorious a confession. Pride and resentment had sealed them tight. On wended the procession; and at another turn in the road, his eyes red and swollen with weeping, Nicephorus meets him again. Again he flings himself at his feet, and in a voice choking with emotion repeats his humble petition. But the devil of proud anger once admitted is not easily expelled. Sapricius turns his hard face aside, and deigns not even to look upon the supplicant. Scoffed at and jeered as an idiot, the poor man continues to pour forth his fruitless entreaties. But the block is reached; the axe gleams in the executioner's hand; the soldiers form around in regular array. It is then that God's slow-creeping vengeance upon anger and resentment makes itself felt. The heart of a proud man is no acceptable sacrifice upon the altar of the Lord.—"If I should distribute all my goods to feed the poor, and if I should deliver my body to be burnt, and have not charity, it profiteth me nothing."—I. *Cor.* xiii. 3. The unforgiving priest quails and trembles: "Stay, my friends," he cries out, with quivering hands outstretched and eyeballs strained with terror, "Stay; do not put me to death. I am ready to do whatever you desire. Lead me to the altar; put the smoking censer into my hands." Shame and amazement were painted upon the face of Nicephorus; he rebuked the fallen priest with his foul apostasy, and turning to the guards, he exclaimed, in the courageous voice of a soldier of Jesus Christ, "*I* am a Christian: my faith is in Jesus Christ, whom this wretch has forsaken. I will die in his stead." And thus in reward for his humility, meekness and charity, the sacrifice of the good Nicephorus was accepted; while the proud, arrogant, angry, revengeful and unforgiving disposition of the priest Sapricius invited his eternal ruin. As long as resentment even smoulders in our breast, no petition of ours can be heard, no offering can be acceptable to Him who has bidden us imitate first His meekness; who has warned us that when we approach the altar, if we remember we have anything against our brethren, we must leave our gift before the altar and first be reconciled to him, and then come and offer our gift.—*Matt.* v. 23-24.

GLUTTONY.

THE sin of gluttony may be committed by either eating or drinking to excess. Both excessive eating and excessive drinking are deadly sins; that is to say, need no borrowed or external malice to separate us eternally from God. They belong to the number of those seven poisoned darts of the devil, which if they completely enter the soul, must needs produce death They are both opposed to the Cardinal virtue of Temperance, whose function is to exercise a rational restraint upon every faculty virtue, thought, word, and action.

When Temperance deals with eating and drinking, it is called Sobriety. This virtue of sobriety is an indispensable condition of salvation. It is needful, to enable us to avoid the crafty strategy and long-practised wiles of our old adversary the devil: "Be ye sober and watch, for your enemy, the devil, like a lion, goeth about seeking whom he may devour." It is needful too as a foundation for our hopes of ultimate happiness: "Wherefore having the loins of your mind girt up, be sober, trust perfectly in the grace which is offered you."—I. *Pet.* i. 13.

And while it is a condition absolutely required for salvation hereafter, and for a Christian confidence here, it is also a preservative of health and a guarantee of long life, and on that account also incumbent upon us, since we are bound to maintain and cherish the life God has given to us. "He that is temperate shall prolong life."—*Eccles.* xxxvii. 34. First, let me speak on the subject of gluttony proper, or the vice of eating irrationally.

It consists, beloved Brethren, in an ill-regulated attachment to the pleasure of eating. This attachment shows itself in many different ways. Sometimes in eating too much, and thus oppressing the engergies of mind and body instead of refreshing them, according to the saying of a well-known Pagan writer. Sometimes it shows itself in an inordinate nicety as to the quality or the preparation of our food. So that, as French people say, it is a vice ruling alike in the *gourmand* and the *gourmet*, in the man who overloads his stomach, and the man who aims at gratifying his palate with dainties. Again, gluttony is committed when a man gives way to voracity or greedy rapidity; when he eats at unbecoming times and seasons, anticipating hunger, instead of waiting for its signal; and lastly, when he frequently dwells in conversation with a keen and silly relish, and as it were a smacking of the lips, upon the subject of agreeable meats and drinks. In all three ways, man may degrade his intellectual and spiritual nature, wallow in the mire of his own carnal appetites, commit the sacrilege of turning God's image into the image of a swine, and as St. Paul says, become one of the "enemies of the Cross of Christ, whose end is destruction, whose god is their belly, and whose glory is their shame."—*Phil.* iii. 18.

Now, beloved Brethren, if you would know something of the mischief this vice of gluttony has wrought in the world, you must go back to the very opening of the annals of our race. It figures in the first page. Eve saw the forbidden fruit and that it was fair; and duped into believing that it would be in effect as beneficial as it was in appearance delicious—she ate it; and prevailed upon her obsequious lord to eat it also. There was the sin that broke up the fences, uprooted the leafy trees, and devastated the flower-beds of Paradise. Thenceforth happiness, like that smiling Eden, was guarded from the approach of man as by a seraph with flaming brand. Labour and unrest; decay, disease, and death; strife, and mortal feud; the bondage of the flesh, the tyranny of the passions; all these followed swift upon that sin, and were its just and equitable punishment. What was it that turned a world, teeming with beauties, and crowned with the smile of God, into a valley of tears, darkened with the shadow of death? Answer with truth. It was not the blasting breath of demons, whose baneful agency shook down the halls and barns of Job, slew his sons, scattered his flocks and herds, and covered his flesh with sores. It was the sin of pride, along with the sin of the *Gourmet*—gluttony.

And every here and there in the Scripture narrative, Gluttony shows its hateful head, bringing disaster in its train. It robbed

Esau of his birthright, and sewed deadly dissension between himself and his brother. It brought down heavy woes upon the children of God in the wilderness:—As yet their meat was in their mouth: and the wrath of God came upon them. And he slew the fat ones amongst them, and brought down the chosen men of Israel."—*Psalm* lxxvii. 30. It helped to fetter the soul of the miserable Dives, in the prison of hunger and thirst: so that he who fared sumptuously every day, placing all his joy in his viands instead of his duty, moaned piteously for a drop of cold water to quench his thirst, and all in vain. It was a portion of the sin that ruined Sodom: "Behold," says the Almighty God, "this was the sin of Sodom, pride, fulness of bread and abundance, and the idleness of her and of her daughters."—*Ezech.* xvi. 49.

And now, beloved Brethren, to pass from the historic scourges it has inflicted to the every-day maladies and disorders that follow it.

It sows manifold disease in the body. I have heard a medical man of large experience say that over-eating contributes more to the death rate than over-drinking. This sounds paradoxical; but the reason is, because it is not often the direct agent in inflicting death, but generally does its deadly work through some form of disease; whereas excessive drinking is more dreaded, and generally considered more destructive, because sudden death is so often traceable to its direct operation. But whether excess in eating works directly or indirectly in destroying the system, what matter does that make? The tyrannical Roman emperors did not often smite their victims with their own hands; but were they less to be dreaded, did they cause less destruction, because they called in their executioners to perform the bloody task?

Of all the forms of gluttony, the most pernicious to body and soul alike is the excessive consumption of flesh meat. Man was not intended to be a carnivorous animal. The make of his teeth, and the nature of his digestive apparatus show that he was intended to live neither on vegetables solely, nor on flesh solely; and the wholesomest diet is that which embraces a fair proportion of both. Unfortunately in these days, the baker is being driven out of the field by the butcher; and cereals or vegetables have little chance against flesh. Side by side with this increase in the consumption of flesh, there is a strange multiplication of that hideous and terrible disease—cancer, which like a demon takes possession of the flesh, and penetrates into the organs with a hundred claws, that every day become more tenacious, until at last neither the power of medicine nor the edge of the knife can dislodge them; and death follows, oftentimes amid tortures that language cannot describe. The spread of this awful complaint is due, in all probability, to excess in the use of flesh meat.

But if this species of intemperance works evil in the body, how much more lamentable are its effects upon the soul. We sometimes speak of the voluptuous temperament of the natives of sunnier climes; and contrast with their sensual ardour and thirst for self-indulgence the more cold, correct, and balanced dispositions of the Northern races. But it is to be feared that any advantage our more rigorous and chilly climate may give us, the inordinate appetite for flesh-meat is likely to destroy. It imbrutes the nature, and makes soul and body gross and carnal. It boils like a fever in the system. And our newspapers from time to time reveal black deeds of Satanic immorality perpetrated by natives of these countries, such as rival the worst abominations which the annals of Southern crime even could produce. Of a very similar character, so far as its consequences are concerned, is the consumption of dainty meats, spiced and curiously prepared, to stimulate the appetite and delight the palate. A reasonable variety of dishes is absolutely recommended, as the system thrives better with a change of diet. But this is very different from that endless diversity of delicacies for which sea and land are ransacked, and which are wrought up with practised art into piquant entrées, that give a galvanic life to the over-wrought and languishing appetite. No wonder that the history of the Roman empire should have been defaced with so many horrors of iniquity and foulness, considering the prevalence of this vice of gluttony in every form. Their professed epicures often accepted three invitations to dinner the same day; and being perplexed to find admission for the manifold delicacies set before them, actually provoked a vomit between their meals, to prepare themselves for the banquets yet to come. Sometimes they took a bath to restore their fainting relish, and reinvigorate their deadened energies; and horrible to relate, their pampered forms were found lifeless in the water which had been intended to renew their life. No wonder, I repeat, that the flesh, so flattered and deified, should tyrannize over the whole man, and should run riot in all manner of immodesty; until even the better

Pagans themselves shuddered, invoking darkness as a cloak; and looked to the heavens in half expectation of seeing the immortal gods—themselves no models—coming down in wrath and in might to pour out destruction over the world.

Other faults are also consequences of this vice of gluttony, both over-eating and over-drinking, which it will be more convenient for me to treat at once. They are an ugly surrounding, a vile herd. First, foolish jollity. It is a sight to make the wise man weep, when warmed with gluttony the roysterer cracks his jokes, with peal on peal of boisterous laughter, outweighing a hundred-fold the wit of his effusions. Look at him next morning— cadaverous, red-eyed, imbecile, crapulous, despondent, world-weary;—a limp and shrunken specimen: it is a big price to pay for a few hours of vanishing laughter and forced merriment. Second, scurrility: or the effort to rouse course fun by ridiculing others, by buffoonery, odd undignified mimicry, absurd anecdotes, farcical fictions, and unmeasured banter. Third, a proneness to unchecked, unguarded, restless talk. "In multiloquio non deerit peccatum"; says the Book of Proverbs. "In much talking, there will be no lack of sin." If this is true of the sober man, how about him who is burdened with meats, and steeped in strong drink? "Truth will out in wine." All kinds of untimely truths will then be revealed, and seals of secrecy recklessly broken. Nothing will be sacred to the eyes of the drunkard. But even apart from the violation of confidences, there is such a flux of folly discharged from the glutton's mouth, as ought to shame any witness of it into an utter renunciation of the vice. It is an old story that the Spartans were wont to deter their young men from drunkenness by exhibiting a helot in the midst of them with this artificial idiotcy upon him, the effect of intoxicating beverages; as the very appearance, the bleared eye, the thick and inarticulate speech, the foolish utterances, the staggering gait, and imbecile gesture and bearing of the drunkard appeared to them to be the very best sermon against excess. Fourth, there is a diseased development, for the time being, of two dreadful vices under the influence of gluttony, whether by eating or drinking—viz: impurity and anger. Of this I have sufficiently spoken already. Fifth, an abiding consequence of pampering the body by food or drink taken to excess, is the decay of the mental powers. "A sound mind in a sound body" has in every age been proposed as the best object to aim at through the medium of education. And if the body be very unsound, as it comes to be when it is day after day, week after week, made the channel of poisonous beverages, or the flesh-pot of pernicious meats, it almost invariably happens that disease communicates itself also to the mind, and rots away the faculties; paralyzing the memory, troubling the imagination and rendering it unruly, and blunting the edge of the intellect. It is thus that often the finest minds are hopelessly clouded, by the time they should be attaining their prime. Not without reason does a boon-companion (in one of our great dramatist's comedies) who becomes suspicious of the pungency of his own wit, remark to himself: "Methinks sometimes that I have no more wit than a Christian or an ordinary man has: but I am a great eater of beef, and I believe that does harm to my wit."

ON SLOTH.

I will speak to-night, beloved Brethren, of the vice of Spiritual Sloth. It consists in a carelessness for the things of God, and a disposition, from an apprehension of difficulty, to neglect the means of salvation. The word used for sloth in the Latin language signifies heedlessness; our Saxon word sloth is connected with the adjective slow, and means a heaviness and an absence of activity in the spiritual life. This vice is directly opposed to the objects for which God placed us in the world. We were born to labour, because to us descended the primal curse: "You shall earn your bread with the sweat of your brow." Without painstaking and trouble, most of us cannot earn the means of subsistence, and none of us procure that supersubstantial daily bread, the grace of God, for which Our Blessed Lord taught us to have recourse to our Heavenly Father. A life without labour, a life of ease and listlessness is a grand mistake; it is an arrow shot wide of the mark; it is a precious beverage outpoured on the thirsty sand. For life is but as the workday which by and by will come to a close, and usher in the eternal rest. No work, no wages is our motto. Our Blessed Lord compares himself to a householder who invited the labourer into his vineyard; and when evening was come said to the steward: "Call the labourers and pay them their hire, beginning from the last even to the first."—*Matt.* xx. 8.

And again, He likens himself to a man going into a far country, "who called his servants and delivered to them his goods; to one five talents, to another two, and to another one; to every one according to his proper ability, intending them to trade in his absence upon the money entrusted to them. Two of them carried out his wishes, and were rewarded for their exertions by seeing their capital doubled." But "he that had received the one talent, going his way digged into the earth and hid his Lord's money." And when the day of reckoning came, the Master praised the diligence of the two servants who had profited by their opportunities, and advanced them to offices of dignity and trust. But he that had received the one talent came and said: "Lord, I know that thou art a hard man; thou reapest where thou hast not sown, and gatherest where thou hast not strewed. And being afraid, I went and hid thy talent in the earth; behold, here thou hast that which is thine." And his lord answering said to him: Wicked and slothful servant, thou knowest that I reap where I sow not, and gather where I have not strewed: thou oughtest therefore to have committed my money to the bankers, and at my coming I should have received my own with usury. Take ye away therefore the talent from him, and give it to him that hath ten talents. For to every one that hath shall be given and he shall abound; but from him that hath not, that also which he seemeth to have shall be taken away. And the unprofitable servant cast ye out into the exterior darkness. There shall be weeping and gnashing of teeth.—*Matt.* xxv. 14, &c.

Behold the end of the listless man, beloved Brethren, who was sent into this world with faculties of soul and capabilities of body, that would have enabled him had he been diligent, to add to the sum of God's glory, and to have achieved for himself an eternity of joy and happiness. His days pass idly away; his talents are buried in the earth; one by one, the graces which God decreed before the birth of time to give him are flung aside and squandered; day by day the stupor grows upon him, until his condition becomes hopeless; his intellect cannot settle patiently upon the thought of God, or balance the dread chances of salvation or ultimate shipwreck; his memory has no room for those awful mementoes of God's wrath, which roar like thunder, and flash like lightning in the Scriptures; his passions swarm upon him, like vermin on the beggar that is too lazy to cleanse himself; his will is confirmed in its feebleness, until its purposes and resolves are untrustworthy and variable as the tides; for as the Scripture says: "The sluggard willeth and willeth not."—*Prov.* xiii. 4. In fine, he is like a man floating down a smooth current towards a brawling cataract that leaps into dark and fathomless gulfs below: the sunshine warms and cheers him; the fresh odour of the forest trees that rise from the margin comes wafted to his nostrils more grateful than incense;

the song of birds falls dreamily upon his ear; his brain is lulled into a sweet lethargy; his apprehensions are laid asleep; and all the while, inch by inch, he is being borne to the brink of that abyss. Nearer and nearer he floats, still wrapt in this fatal trance, until at last the distance is traversed, and the doom comes swift and sure. One shriek of awakening consciousness, one wild tossing of the arms to heaven, and amid the monotonous thunders of the waterfall, he plunges into darkness and death.

Such is the fate of the sluggard: a smooth and easy life ending in hideous catastrophe. Or again, if I may be excused for trying to paint the folly of the sluggard by a second illustration: he is like the poor drunkard, who has tossed glass after glass of his favourite beverage, until oblivion has stolen over his brain and numbness settled on the limbs; he lies at last without feeling or thought, relaxed and helpless. Meantime, some accident has set fire to the house in which he lies: the flame spreads along the walls, climbs the staircase, wraps the furniture, soars out of the windows, waves its red flag over roof and chimney, and when its fury is spent, a few charred bones lying by the hearth are the only relic of the drunkard. The sluggard's destiny is the same: long draughts of ease, comfort and pleasure; helplessness and lethargy; eternal fire. And alas! beloved Brethren, in spite of the fatal influence and the terrific punishment of this vice, how common it is!

How many are there, who have not the courage and the manliness to lay their hand to the plough, though the day of life is waning, and the field that Providence has alloted them to work lies rough and unfurrowed before them! How many seem to say by their conduct: Oh! if it were no trouble, I would do my duty! Quite forgetting that toil is a necessary condition of goodness; and that man's life is a warfare on earth. If we have no burthen, if we are making no effort in life, we are no followers of Christ, for He has said: " If any man will come after me, let him deny himself and take up his cross daily and follow me."—*St. Luke* ix. 23.

Look around you, beloved Brethren, and see how the world abounds with men who profess to follow Christ, and yet bear no cross on their shoulders. One man knows that the fatal passion for intoxicating drink is daily growing upon him. His conscience tells him, his true friends warn him, his director (if he has one) dins it into his ears that he must change his life, or he is a lost man. The time has come when he must either give up strong drink altogether, or restrict himself to a certain fixed quantity in the twenty-four hours. He is cautioned not to enter a public-house, because it is a dangerous occasion of sin. Or he must renounce certain companions who are luring him to his ruin. But every counsel and cautious warning is lost upon him. He is too slothful to extricate himself from his danger. He has not resolution enough even to take the first step. And thus he lies cumbering the ground till the day of doom arrives, and he is cast into the fire.

Then there are others who have sunk into the slough of uncleanness, and are too apprehensive of the difficulty and painful effort required for their deliverance, to call for help, or to raise a finger to secure it. A wicked friendship, to misapply a noble name, has made all their faculties captive. Their inmost being sighs for release; their spirit often groans at the bondage, but they are weighed down as by paralysis; they will not renounce the person, they will not abstain from visiting the place; they will feed the flames of concupiscence by the exchange of gifts and letters, and by a sort of fatality—the fatality of sloth—they spend their days and nights in forging the chains they are to wear, and writing out, letter by letter, the sentence of their own eternal reprobation.

Others again are too slothful, too fond of their own ease and comfort, to keep the precepts of the Church. They will not abstain on the Fridays, they must have their meat They will not fast, though well able to do so. Oh, the day will come when a raging hunger and thirst shall consume their pampered frames, and when their palates shall be strangers to every gratification.

Or, perhaps, they find some excuse on the Sunday morning for lying in bed, with the full sunshine streaming into their chambers, when the august Sacrifice of the Mass is being offered in the temple of God, and answer the summons of their Father and Benefactor by groaning their reluctance drowsily and turning on the other side; thus, in their sloth, making deliberate choice of death rather than life.

Perhaps they are parents who neglect the education of their children. They are aware that the little ones depend upon them for their goodness and regularity in after life; and that neglect of their training is sure to be followed by self-will, a forward and disobedient spirit, impatience of control, self-indulgence, and to sum up all in one frightful word—irreligion Brought up by bad fathers and bad mothers, it follows, as a natural law, that if they unfortunately live so long, these poor children will become bad fathers and mothers themselves, and will keep alive the vices of their parents long after they have erected the lying tombstone to mark their last bed. Yet, knowing this, the parents are too incapable of a decided step, too torpid from sloth, too unaccustomed to effort of any kind to begin the performance of that all-important duty; they make now and then perhaps a show of sending them to school, but they have not zeal enough, energy enough to wrestle with the difficulties that beset the work; the boy's own grumbling and disinclination are enough to weary them in the contest, and their desire for the well-being of their child ends in a few curses hurled at the truant, and an appeal to heaven to witness how much they have to endure. Sunday school and Benediction many of them never think of: it is too much trouble to send their children, who are left to scamper about the streets with bad companions, and to contract all the vices they witness, while their ignorance remains unvisited by a single ray of light to guide them to better things. Is it any wonder that these parents should live to find their children a thorn in their sides, and at death should learn, to their dismay, that their sloth in dealing with them is the one bar to their salvation, and is of itself enough to bury them fathoms deep in the eternal pit.

So far, beloved Brethren, I have spoken of sloth as disabling in our primary and essential duties; when it is always a mortal sin. But the languor of sloth unfortunately oftentimes oppresses even those who are in the grace of God. They know for example that they are under a habit of venial sin, and that they are not troubling themselves much, perhaps not at all, to destroy this habit. They think, because no number of venial sins can amount to a mortal sin, they may indulge such habits with impunity. They forget that every venial sin they commit is diminishing their supply of grace, and so paving the way for a grievous fall. They do not adopt the remedies that would heal these disorders which impair their beauty in the sight of God. When they kneel down to pray, they never think of begging for special graces to overcome the predominant faults. They do not dream of going to Confession and receiving Holy Communion for the direct purpose of obtaining a cure. They are quite oblivious of the power they might wield against the besetting sin by means of novenas, or by procuring the prayers of God's servants here, in purgatory, or in heaven. Is it any wonder that such as these should over and over again learn to their shame, sorrow, and amazement, to what a degree of feebleness they have been reduced by their sloth, when temptation comes strong upon them, and that at last they should recognise with sadness the truth of Our Lord's terrible saying, "I would thou wert cold or hot. But because thou art lukewarm, and neither hot nor cold, I will begin to vomit thee out of my mouth."—*Apoc.* iii. 15-16.

Whatever, therefore, be your condition before God, beloved Brethren, you have need to bestir yourselves and shake off sloth. If you are in sin, be warned in good time. The Confessional is always at hand inviting you to be cleansed, and to stand prepared for death, which will come like a thief in the night. Many a one has let such warning go in at one ear and out at the other, until at last he has heard the stern accents of his master addressing him: "Give an account of thy stewardship, for now thou canst be steward no longer."

And you, beloved Brethren, who frequent Confession and Holy Communion, you who think you stand, beware lest you fall. Watch and pray that you enter not into temptation. Be diligent in your duties: "for cursed is he that doth the work of God negligently." Cultivate a holy industry: lay up to yourselves treasures in heaven. If you are loath to do any good work, well, take the first step, the rest will surely follow. And always remember the motto, as a stimulus to your energy: "Non progredi regredi est"—"not to go forward, is to go backward.'

ON LYING.

GOD, beloved Brethren, has enriched us with the faculty of speech, to the end, that we may communicate our feelings, thoughts, and desires to one another, as occasion may require. The most imperative quality of speech therefore is manifestly truthfulness; if that be wanting, the very object for which we received this wonderful power of speech is perverted; and God is outraged by the abuse of His gift. There are indeed times and seasons when prudence bids us check the tongue—that dangerous and restless organ—and refrain from speaking, lest we should betray some interest of charity or justice. There is a time for speaking and a time for silence. Nay, we may occasionally find ourselves in circumstances in which impertinent curiosity may be foiled, danger to life or limb averted, a reputation rescued from ruin, an important secret preserved inviolate, by the use of a form of words in which truth is respected, but from which a meaning may be drawn by our neighbour that will mislead and baffle him in his untimely or unjustifiable enquiries. Such was the answer given by St. Athanasius to his pursuers, when they hailed him from their bark and asked him if he had seen Athanasius pass that way. "Yes," said he, "you are coming very near him." But in no instance is it lawful to tell a lie, that is, to speak contrary to what one thinks. If you could empty hell, if you could restore the wrecked hieraches of heaven to their pristine dignity and splendid and bliss; if you could raise up out of the fiery flood the evil generations immersed there; if you could undo the decree that binds the lost in the eternal chains, kill the everlasting worm and quench the fire that is never to be extinguished, by telling one little fib, you must not do it. All the good you would thus effect would not compensate for the one lie. And why? Because a lie is essentially an offence against God; whilst these are benefits procured for creatures; and no circumstance, however grave, no object, however exalted or important, no consequence, however desirable, can change its character. A lie it is, and a lie it always must remain; a violation of the primary purposes of speech; a rebellion against the dictate of conscience; an object of everlasting hatred to the God of truth. The soul which is stained with this vice is of the devil, the father of lies; it is stamped with his foul image and superscription, and belongs to his treasury. Heaven knows it not, and will not receive it. For not merely is God truthful: He is truth itself. His nature and essence is truth. So that every lie is a blow struck direct at His being; is an act of mutiny against His person. God then could no more permit a lie, than He could abdicate the throne of His Eternity, or strip Himself of His divine nature.

No wonder then, beloved Brethren, that the liar is denounced as an enemy of God, and an adherent of Satan, the great adversary, and the first of liars. No wonder that his lot is cast with his father in eternal darkness and horror. In the Book of the Apocalypse, when the voice came from the great presence, Alpha and Omega, the beginning and the end, sitting upon the throne, and proclamation was made that the glories of the new Jerusalem were reserved for the faithful "that shall overcome," there is an addition of these awful words:—But the fearful and unbelieving, and the abominable, and murderers, and whoremongers, and sorcerers, and idolaters, and all liars, they shall have their portion in the pool burning with fire and brimstone, which is the second death."—*Apoc.* xxi. 6-7-8. "Thou wilt destroy all that speak a lie."—*Ps.* v. 7. "Lying lips," says the Book of Proverbs, "are an abomination to the Lord."—xii. 22. The vice of lying is inconsistent with the life of grace: for "the mouth that belieth, killeth the soul."—*Wis.* i. 11.

From these passages, beloved Brethren, it is manifest how grievous is the error of those who hold that in case of urgent need it is lawful to lie. This doctrine was one of the great watch-words of a certain sect in Spain, about the middle of the fourth century, called Priscillianists, after the name of their founder. They held a number of anti-christian and anti-social theories, such for example as the unlawfulness of marriage; and to conceal their true character, their motto among themselves was: "You may swear and perjure yourself to preserve your secret." Such folly is strange enough in anyone, but it must needs surprise us to find among the number of those who defend the lawfulness of lying in critical emergencies, such names as those of Origen, Cassian, and Theodoret. Cicero's opinion was that lying was like poison—a deadly thing, but that it can be used sparingly, like hellebore for medicinal purposes: for example, by a king, or civil ruler in defence of the community whose interests he is called upon to guard.

St. Augustine and others divide lies into three kinds: jocose, officious, and pernicious. Jocose lies, as the name itself indicates, are those lies which are told in jest. Officious lies are those that are intended to benefit someone, while they are capable of injuring none. Those lies are called pernicious, which can do no one any good, and which are calculated to injure either soul or body, position or character. Under this head are included all perversions of the doctrines of faith, and all untruths that promote immorality. To this list may be added lies of excuse, which are officious lies in our own favour. Of course, some of these lies are gravely injurious to our neighbours, and therefore hateful to God, and sufficient to sever the soul from His friendship for ever; and it is of these lies that we are to understand the fearful denunciations and the torrents of menace outpoured upon the vice of lying in the different parts of Scripture. But if a lie does no harm to a neighbour and no special dishonour to God, it is not indeed removed from the category of sin, but it ceases to be mortal. No matter how trifling a fib may appear, it cannot be otherwise than an irregularity and a deviation from the rule of right reason : and therefore a slight upon that God, who provides us with reason as a guide and ruler in all our actions. As we are constituted rational animals, we cannot degrade ourselves by a single act of unreason, consciously indulged, without thereby offending the gracious framer of our being. But it would be absurd to suppose that God would punish, say, a jocose lie, by a sentence of eternal separation from Him. If so, then God would condemn a man to hell for stealing a farthing. One may, however, be too rigorously scrupulous in the matter of jocose lies. When it is perfectly clear from gesture, grimace, tone of voice, or surrounding circumstances, that our expressions are not intended in the literal sense, and that the untruth or exaggeration contained in them is not employed for the purpose of deceiving, but only to create a little timely merriment, such deviations from the formal exactitude are to be reckoned amongst the graces of conversation. To find fault in a puritanical spirit with these freaks of speech would be of a piece with condemning a man as a liar who took the liberty of calling a soldier a lion, an elder a Solomon, a stalwart man a Hercules, a cunning man a fox, a meek man a lamb, or an amiable man or woman an angel.

Still, parents who are anxious to bring up their children in the healthiest tone would do well to avoid all those silly exaggerations, distortions, oddities, and fables with which it is the custom to entertain, allure, and tranquillize the infant mind. We certainly show an appearance of kinship with the apes in our faculty for imitation—a faculty which exhibits itself in the earliest stage of life; and in our dependence upon imitation for our enjoyment of the comforts, and our performance of the duties which belong to us as men. If it were not for the universal instinct for imitation, every career would be an experiment, uninfluenced by past experience, and we should have none of that agreeable uniformity which serves as oil to the wheels of life. Every one of us would have to invent his own system of diet; and knives and forks might be rejected by minds of less original and more primitive turn. Now, what I am aiming at is this: if your children, in their milkiest and most innocent epoch, come to conjecture that you cajole and deceive them; that you take pleasure in filling their minds with false notions, and in raising their wonder by chimeras transparent in themselves, but not at first transparent to their young minds, and exaggerations that lend themselves to the expediency of the moment, they will very soon conceive the idea, that it is a mark of maturity and a desirable accomplishment of great value in the affairs of the world, to be able to make a dextrous use of this faculty for deceiving; and, as monkeys are said to have taken a fancy to smoking from observing men smoke, you may expect your children, ere long, to emulate you in the science of deception, and to become wonderful adepts at that objectionable game.

Machiavelli, a statesman who lived at the end of the fifteenth and the beginning of the sixteenth century, whose name has become a proverb for craft and duplicity, wrote a book called "The Prince," in which he laid down a system of rules, to aid a civil ruler in the successful discharge of his office: and, among other things, he states that a prince has a right to employ deceit and treachery against his foes, and to break faith with those to whom he has plighted himself, as soon as changing circumstances open out some new path of interest, and an old policy ceases to be advantageous. But he did not escape the watchful vigilance of the Church, whose place it is to keep her flock from the poisonous pasture of false doctrine. Clement VIII., pronounced a solemn condemnation upon the specious defence of falsehood, bad faith, and diplomatic hypocrisy contained in that dangerous work.

Before I conclude, beloved Brethren, I must say a word about the sin of Calumny, that is, falsehood injurious to a neighbour's character. Even detraction, or the revelation of real failings, vices, or disgraceful deeds, is a most heinous sin in the sight of God. It will not shelter the detractor from the shafts of divine vengeance to say:—"I only told the truth. You have no right to sacrifice a neighbour's character in the ordinary circumstances of daily life, unless there be some very grave and urgent reason constraining you to do so. Till he has publicly and notoriously foreited his good name, you may not meddle with it. Bad though he may be, that God is the jealous defender of his honourable repute, who tolerates the sinner, and makes him the recipient of many a worldly gift; that God who maketh His sun to shine on the good, and raineth on the just and the unjust."

But how much more tolerable will it be for the detractor than the slanderer, who, by a falsehood, blasts his neighbour's good name! Surely a rigorous judgment awaits that man, who, with one blow, stabs at the God of truth, and grievously wounds the reputation of his innocent neighbour.

To sacrifice another's good name is worse than to rob him of his money: "for a good name," says the wise man, "is better than much riches." And restitution is more obligatory after the sin of slander than after the sin of theft, inasmuch as reparation is more valuable. The calumniator is bound openly to retract his falsehood, and if his mere retractation is not enough, he must even affirm on oath, or appeal to witnesses to confirm his statement. He must take all necessary trouble that his withdrawal of the charge may reach, not only those to whom he communicated the slander, but those to whom it would be likely to spread. He must make the retractation as public as his false accusation. And whilst, of course, he is not bound to brand himself as a malignant liar, supposing he can repair the injury by simply stating that he finds he has made an unfounded charge against one quite innocent, which he bitterly regrets; still, if there is any risk to be run, the slanderer must run it; on his reputation, rather than on that of his victim, must suspicion rest, if shadow of suspicion there be left; if one of the two must suffer, surely justice requires that it should be the guilty rather than the innocent.

ON RASH JUDGMENT.

"JUDGE not, that you may not be judged. For with what judgment you judge, you shall be judged : and with what measure you mete, it shall be measured to you again."—*St. Matt.* vii. 12.

These are the solemn words, beloved Brethren, in which Our Blessed Lord denounced the vice of rashly judging our fellow men, and believing them guilty of sin without sufficient reason. He who summons his fellow creatures before his own secret tribunal, scans their words or actions, and pronounces upon their hidden thoughts and purposes is an usurper and an impostor, who pretends to a place that belongs not to him, but to God, the judge of all ; and in his turn he shall stand before a higher court, and be treated as mercilessly as he treated others. This is the vengeance that shall overtake him ; his own malice shall be made the standard for his own requital ; there shall be " justice without mercy to him that hath not done mercy." The prospect of such a termination to a life of rash judgments ought of itself to deter us from that vice. It is harrowing enough to think of that day when we shall be severed from all earthly companionship and sympathy, and when tremblingly conscious of our guilt we shall be thrust into the awful judgment hall of heaven, to answer for our works done in the flesh to Him who searcheth the reins and the hearts. But that day of wrath acquires ten-fold terrors to our imagination, if we have reason to think that the Judge who is to weigh us in the balance shall have been biassed against us, predisposed to the utmost severity, and pledged to visit our presumption upon our heads in sternest scrutiny and most unsparing rigour. Then will the sinner who yielded to rash judgments in life be pierced with anguish, finding that he has increased the chances of an unfavourable judgment by his lack of charity, and that his trial begins with a fearful likelihood of a tragic issue. If he could only undo the past, how complete would be his repentance; how anxious would he be to sift his own thoughts concerning his neighbour, that he might be spared the hideous penalty of confronting a Judge who, already before the process of examination begins, shows in his frowning visage the anticipation of the culprit's doom and rejection. Ah! he would be most careful, most circumspect now, if he could on any plea get back to earth from that awful tribunal. How scrupulously would he confine himself in his judgment to the sphere of his own actions and words, and to the examination of the heart from which they came; thus securing beforehand the leniency of the Eternal Judge, and softening down as far as might be the appalling features of that scene!

Yet, beloved Brethren, from want of thought, the great majority of Christians do not realize the force of Our Lord's threat as to the peculiar vengeance which will overtake those who judge rashly. However small may be the circle in which you move, it is not venturing too much to say, that you must have observed in some one or other of your neighbours a tendency to this vice; an ambition to sit in the chair of judgment, and to deal out hard sentences to all whom they cite before them. Nay, in your own hearts may you not soon discern, if you only take pains to examine, a strong bent to this vice: a propensity to turn over in your thoughts the bearings of your neighbour's words and actions, and to take it for certain, upon insufficient grounds, that there is evil at the bottom of them? Your own hearts, I say, if you question them, will bear this testimony. Happy are you if your memory be not loaded with instances of outspoken rash judgments, such as poison the minds and jaundice the sight of your less malicious neighbours, and infect the very air you breathe.

The causes of this universal tendency of mankind to think evil rather than good of their fellow creatures are numerous. Some of them are enunciated by St. Francis of Sales. Certain dispositions are naturally bitter and sour, communicating this bitterness to everything that enters their thoughts. Others think evil of their neighbours through pride, fancying their own merit is enhanced if their neighbour's is lowered. Some, again, find pleasure in dwelling upon their neighbour's supposed drawbacks and failings, because these give a sweeter flavour to their own good qualities. Others, knowing the wickedness of their own hearts, are elated to discover that they are companioned, not solitary in their vices. Others love to scrutinize their neighbours' lives in a sinister spirit, merely to give occupation to their wit, sagacity, ingenuity; and grow bolder and bolder if events should now and then seem to confirm their conjectures. Others are so swayed by love and hatred that they always judge their friends tenderly; and deal out invariable harshness to those whom they dislike; except in cases of *jealousy*, where the more the friend is beloved, the greater is the disposition to gather tokens of vice from the most innocent actions. And lastly, fear, ambition, and other passions often lead to rash judgments in those who are subject to them.

Then again, rash judgments not only differ in their origin but also in their operation. You may misjudge a person from external tokens which are fallible; as when Socrates was pronounced drunk, because his face was more rubicund than usual. It was thus that Totila, king of the Ostrogoths, misjudged St. Cassius. For seeing his face flushed, he said to himself: "This is not the man he is reputed: manifestly he is an habitual wine-bibber." He had scarcely conceived the thought, when the devil entered into his armour bearer, and the convulsions and frenzy of the possessed man could not be stilled or arrested till St. Cassius laid his blessed hand upon him. Then Totila confessed his rash judgment and acknowledged the sanctity of God's servant, thus miraculously revealed. Or you may put a bad construction upon an action which in itself is neither good nor bad; or the action may to all appearance be virtuous, and you may judge it vicious, as when Our Blessed Lord was presumed to have wrought His miracles of charity by the agency of the devil; or when Heli believed Anna the mother of Samuel to be under the influence of wine because when in the fervour of her prayers in the temple her lips moved with unusual excitement; or you may recognise an action as good and refuse to give it its full credit; on seeing a man commit a sin you may fly to the conclusion that he is enslaved to the habit; or lastly, you may form a censorious estimate of a whole community or class, as addicted to a particular sin, because you have found out that some of its members have committed it. These are the chief varieties of the vice; the bad branches of a bad tree.

Now, beloved Brethren, there is one fact connected with rash judgments that ought to make them particularly odious to a frank and manly soul. It is that we *do* know real evil of ourselves, becuase we know that we have had light to see the good path and the bad, and grace to follow the right one, and that with full deliberation we disobey God's will. But we are not sufficiently master of our neighbour's thoughts; we are too ignorant of the light and grace vouchsafed them; too much strangers to the conditions of their misdeeds to be able safely to say what degree of guilt they have contracted in breaking the law of God. The very condemned felon who lies in gaol waiting the execution of the death sentence for some deed of blood—with his sullen, repulsive frown, his brutal passiveness and insensibility to all promptings of remorse, the diabolical halo which his villainous career seems to throw over his rugged form—even he, the outcast of society, the type of crime to the eye, may have been less guilty in the sight of God, even as he savagely smote his enemy with the fatal blow, than we, when without incurring any public censure or social retribution we have indulged a spiteful and malignant spirit, and by our detractions and calumnies sacrificed a neighbour's reputation and killed his peace.

For we may have sinned in full knowledge, and with perfect deliberation; the murderer in gross ignorance of all law, human and divine, and in the headlong frenzy of passion; we may by our act have been a thousand times more unfaithful to God because we have resisted the blessed influences of a long and careful training, the example of virtuous parents and well-conducted friends, the accumulated obligations and daily increasing strength which have resulted from the Sacraments, the multiplying bonds of divine tenderness, the memory of divine whisperings and caresses; all these I say may have deepened the hue of our guilt beyond imagination, while the murderer's crime may be correspondingly mitigated by his forlornness and neglect in boyhood and youth, the wretched surroundings of his whole career, the habit of evil formed before it was well understood, and the absence of all reclaiming influences. Ah! God does not judge as man. And therefore should man beware of trusting his own judgment. "Do not judge according to appearance, but judge just judgment." "Who art thou?" cries out St. Paul—*Rom.* xiv. 4.—"that judgest another man's servant. To his own lord, he standeth or falleth." Leave him to God, and attend to yourself. One venial sin is so heinous in the sight of the holy, holy, holy Lord God of Sabaoth, that if you knew you had, by God's special grace, committed only one in your life, you never could sufficiently bewail your misfortune, condemn your ingratitude, and loathe your baseness. Your occupation from the moment you committed such a sin should be to sorrow over it, and your motto should be with the Psalmist, "Against Thee only have I sinned and done evil in Thy sight."—"My sin is always before me."—"Every night I will water my couch with my tears."

But how if you have committed grievous sin, not once but many times; how if one period of your life has been disfigured by a repeated habit of mortal sin, which has made you the enemy of God, the child of Satan; how if your whole life has been but a miserable series of relapses, in which you seem to have kissed the Son of Man over and over again in the banquet of peace and love, in order that you might, Judas-like, betray Him to his foes? Alas! beloved Brethren, is it for such men to sit in judgment upon their neighbours:—to pretend to weigh the secrets of other hearts when they know not their own—to assume the office of deciding upon inward and unseen motives, by certain outward appearances, which are oftentimes as much unreliable a token of the heart, as a single brick or stone is an inadequate representation of the building it comes from—above all, to condemn with an acrimony and rigour, to exercise unsparing severity in sentencing your poor fellow creature, as though you were Apostles with a deep insight into the consciences of others, and a commission to smite the guilty, as St. Peter smote the scheming Ananias and Sapphira; being instead of this, "wretched, and miserable, and poor, and blind, and naked?"—*Apoc.* iii. 17. "Why seest thou," says Our Lord, "the mote that is in thy brother's eye; and seest not the beam that is in thy own eye? Or how sayest thou to thy brother: Let me cast the mote out of thy eye; and behold a beam is in thy own eye? Thou hypocrite, cast out first the beam out of thy own eye, and then shalt thou see to cast out the mote out of thy brother's eye."—*Matt* vii. 3-4-5.

In fine, beloved Brethren, let those who are disposed to judge their neighbour guilty of sin upon frivolous presumptions, remember that they are themselves rendered by that very fact more liable to fall into the sins they suspect in others. This is one of the mysterious dispensations of God's providence. There was a certain Abbot, named Machetes, who used to caution his disciples repeatedly against rash judgments, bidding them to judge themselves and not their neighbours. And he confessed that his motive for this constant admonition was, that on three occasions in his life he had made bold to judge and censure his neighbour, and that shortly after, on all three occasions, he had fallen precisely into the sins of which he had supposed his neighbour guilty.

We ought, then, beloved Brethren, to resolve never to merit that covert but most scathing rebuke which Our Lord bestowed upon the Jews who were crowding around the poor sinful woman, intent upon shedding her blood according to the law: " Let him who is without sin amongst you cast the first stone." As we are not blameless in the sight of God, let us never take it upon ourselves to blame others, unless our office as minister of God, as guardian of the public peace, as parent or master, impose upon us the unwelcome task. On the contrary, let the faults of our neighbours, where they are most publicly blazoned and universally decried, only draw from us the exclamation of the good monk who, whenever he heard of another's fall, was only reminded of his own extreme frailty; and cried out in his humility of heart: "It is your turn to-day, it may be mine to-morrow."

ON CALCULATING THE CHANCES OF SALVATION.

PRIOR to the recent elections, beloved Brethren, there was much anxious speculation as to the relative prospects of success that offered themselves to the rival candidates.

You know that as the day of election drew near, the partizans on either side left no means untried to discover their real strength, and to forecast the fortunes of their favourites. It was carefully computed how many votes Lord Ramsey would gain or lose by his declaration of policy with reference to Home Rule; and Mr. Whiteley's attitude towards the question of Sunday closing added an element of interest and anxiety to the calculation. It was a subject of anxious consideration to the friends of both, what bodies of voters could be relied upon as staunch and trustworthy. In short, every man would fain have raised the veil that curtained the future, and read the evening papers announcing the result of the polls a few days beforehand.

I do not purpose to preach you a political sermon. I am no admirer of pulpit utterances on political subjects. The priest's arena is religion, not politics, and it is his duty to leave the members of his flock free to choose which party in the state they will, except in cases where religion is imperilled, and statesmen tread on holy ground that belongs not to their domain. I have in view a higher object than the advancement of my political predilictions, if I have any. It is this. I would ask you this morning to give a little anxious thought to the calculation of your chances of success in the great trial of life. Come now, put to yourselves, each of you, the question: What are the probabilities of my being saved or lost? So far as the present enables us to conjecture the future, so far as my character, disposition, habits, tone of thought, companionship, temptations, past history, give me data for estimating, will the day of doom, the hour of death, the fixed and fatal moment when I shall breathe forth my soul, find me a friend or an enemy of God; and open to me the gate of repose, or drag me down into the regions of eternal torture and unrest? Ah, beloved Brethren, this is the great problem of problems. Parties may go see-sawing through intervals of success and of failure, all the interests of the world may fluctuate, and ebb and flow, your worldly prospects may be bright or cloudy; all this may inspire uncertainty and a vague dread of coming evil, but how vain, fleeting, vapoury, and insignificant, are all these subjects of interest and concern, in comparison with that one problem: when my course is run, will it be well with me, or not? Will it bring a fresh voice into the heavenly courts, to swell the choirs of the blessed, or will it be another soul shipwrecked with its rich freight of unavailing grace. When the sods fall with their dull thud upon our coffins, will it be the angels or the devils that shall rejoice? When the pathetic words are read in sad and solemn tones by the officiating priest: Assist him, all ye saints of God; meet him, all ye angels of the Lord, receiving his soul, offering it in the sight of the Most High:—Will the prayer be heard above, and the glorious welcome accorded to the stranger; or will the Angel Guardian, that struggled and interceded for us, mount uncompanioned and melancholy to the throne of God?

I will not insist, beloved Brethren, while helping you in this momentous calculation with reference to what is truly the main chance, upon the fearful odds which your very nature brings against a prosperous issue to your career. You know well that the majority of mankind do not display upon their characters a stamp sufficiently God-like to deserve a place among the children of the Most High, either on this or the far side of the grave. You know that the world, as a world, is corrupt and bad, and tending downwards, nay, shooting into the gulf, like a cataract that has begun its leap. "Woe to the torrent of human custom," cries out St. Augustine, a man that knew mankind well. Everywhere vice —everywhere the concupiscence of the flesh, the concupiscence of the eyes, and the pride of life. Everywhere men loving evil rather than good. So that the most we can say of any man, as a rule, is that he struggles against himself, and that with so many trips and failures that he cannot claim, in justice, to be classed otherwise than among the herd of sinners. Such being, without exaggeration, the condition of the world, we are not surprised to hear the Word of Truth declare : " Many are called, but few are chosen." First, then, ask yourselves this question ; are you so unlike your neighbour, in disposition and in habits, as to bear upon your foreheads, so to speak, tokens of God's special choice and of God's justification? On the face of it, are you clearly unlike the world at large? Is there any strong presumption furnished by your course of thought, your aims, and your conduct, that you do not belong to what St. Augustine has called the "Mass of Perdition." Or are you conscious that you are weak, that you are full of sinister and wicked promptings, liable to temptations, subject to falls, easily moulded by evil influences, slow to do good, reluctant to thwart your will, indulgent to your appetites, and forgetful of spiritual things, and generally careless of interests connected with the unseen world ?

Surely, beloved Brethren, we must all allow that we feel the old Adam very strong within us, and that our enemies, the enemies who threaten to make our lives in the end a fiasco and a tragedy, are those of our own household.

But now look, beloved Brethren, more particularly into your own lives, as distinguished from those of your neighbours, and ponder well what prospect your individual histories and characters afford of final success, or of final catastrophe. Look back to your early years ; and ask yourselves how far you were biassed towards good, and advanced towards the hope of a blissful eternity by your early training. If your parents were both, or either of them, unfaithful to their duties as members of the Church of Christ, if they were neglectful of prayer, unfamiliar with the salutary workings of the Sacrament, unscrupulous in missing Mass on Sundays and holidays; if they were brawlers or backbiters, if they were slaves to drunkenness, or captives to licentious habits, or even if without these grosser vices, they were worldly in their whole tone, conversation, views, ambitions, and predilictions : alas ! you must mark down their influence as something against your chances of salvation. They have left you an evil inheritance in the mere memory and secret poison of their lives ; and God alone can wring out of your hearts, often at the expense of much torture and anguish, the venom in which their failings and sins will likely have steeped you in your tender years. Ah! beloved Brethren, good parents are amongst God's most powerful graces to sow the seeds of virtue in the soul, and to make the path of mature life smooth and prosperous. But the influences of wicked or negligent parents track the poor child, like the malice of a demon shaping his evil course, for years and years, and often giving its colour and hue to the shadows of a miserable deathbed. Then, beloved Brethren, question yourselves as to the further surroundings of your childhood. Did you begin early to take pleasure in the company of young boys who had initiated themselves prematurely in vice and graduated with a ruinous precocity in the school of evil. Did you drink in their tales of corruption; did you allow your imagination to embrace the images their conversation suggested; did you make it a point of ambition to become like them? Did the badness of the heart expand into deed as well as word, and defile the temple of your consecrated bodies, which had been washed with the waters of baptism and anointed with blessed oil? If so, score it down a black point against the probabilities of your salvation. There is another companionship which is of its nature more insidious and destructive, namely, communion with depraved authors through the medium of their books. If the authors are bad, depend upon it their books contain the very distillation and essence of their depravity, and that in a form that fascinates the mind, and of a subtlety that searches the inmost depths of man's nature. If you have allowed yourselves to revel in such banquets of baneful sweets, for any considerable period of your life, you have reason to fear that you have not yet discharged the virus from your system, but that it awaits only the occasion to develop into a mortal distemper, which will rob you at last of the life of your soul, and cheat you of a happy immortality. Then again, beloved Brethren, examine your conscience as to the sins you have occasioned in others, and the souls you have seduced by your persuasions, incitements or example from the path of virtue, if it were only for an hour. Ah! scandal is a sin that makes us not merely into rebels, but arch-rebels, and leaders of revolt, and which, while it provokes the anger of God, stirs up the prayers of the angels against us. "He that shall scandalize one of these little ones that believe in Me," says the Lord, "it were better for him that a millstone should be hanged about his neck, and that he should be drowned in the depths of the sea. "Woe to the world," He continues, "because of scandals."

Awful words, beloved Brethren, especially as proceeding from the mouth of our gentle and merciful saviour. Have you in your past history any episode that brings your life under this hideous ban. Is the curse upon you? Are your hands red with the blood of your neighbour's murdered soul? "Where is thy brother Abel, said the Lord to Cain?" And he answered, "I know not, am I my brother's keeper?" And He said to him, "What hast thou done? The voice of thy brother's blood crieth to Me from the earth. Now, therefore, cursed shalt thou be upon the earth, which hath opened her mouth and received the blood of thy brother at thy hand."

The life of the soul is more precious a thousand-fold than the life of the body, and the voice of our murderous and deadly scandal rises up from the earth, pierces the clouds, and rings through the heavens, clamouring for vengeance in the ear of God. Scan your lives well, beloved Brethren, and indulge in no false assurance that you have not at least as much reason as the Psalmist for praying—"From the sins of others deliver me, O Lord." Until reparation has been made, and repentance has cleansed your forehead, you go about the world a worse murderer than Cain, and though you may sit in high places, and wear an outward appearance of blamelessness, the angels, as they pass, see upon your brow the sign of blood, and shudder. If the sin of scandal be another adverse element in our calculation as to our ultimate welfare, how blessed an omen is it, to have helped others forward to heaven by word or by work; and to have specially interested the souls of the just in our salvation. Yes! You have a powerful auxiliary towards the attainment of your last end in every virtuous action, which has enlisted the prayers and wishes of your fellow-creature in your behalf, and in looking through the darkness of the past, your eyes may well brighten, and your hearts beat with hope, if you discover such charitable deeds, shining like lamps, whose oil is never consumed, and never will be for all eternity.

Once more, beloved Brethren, have you ever, during any part of your life, been scornful or careless of the gift of faith, of the treasures to which faith admits you, and the advantages which it places at your disposal? Have you, out of human respect to please others, or from a silly self-conceit and ignorance combined, affected to view the sentiments of the faithful, and the doctrines, practices, and precepts of the Church from a sort of vantage ground, as though you were above such pettiness, and beyond the reach of such superstition? Have you made light of that which the Church approved or inculcated, and which all ages of Christianity have sanctioned by their belief and by their adoption —works, such as the utility of fasting, the necessity of mortification, the true wisdom of the austerities practised by the Saints, the veneration which the Saints merit, the respect due to holy persons still living, or holy things, the hallowed character of the priestly office, the sanctity and beauty of the monastic life, the sacredness of vows, the importance and the beneficial affects of frequent Confession and Communion, the spiritual virtue or efficacy for good, which the blessing of the Church imparts to water, and oil, and wax, and other materials used in her service? The jibes of the scoffer, or the indifference of a weak and unmatured faith, if indulged for a considerable period of your life, must be reckoned as among the things which make your salvation problematical.

And now, beloved Brethren, for one moment turn your eyes inward upon your tconscience, and tell me what prognostic is there of your ultimate triumph over your mischances of life. What if the parable were literally fulfilled in your case, that death shall come like a thief in the night, either smiting you unawares, or making your whole soul quake with turbulent alarms, and bewildering fears for some short half hour, and then hauling you before your Judge? Are you habitually in a state of grace? If you are not, if, on the contrary, you are accustomed to go to your rest and rise to your labour with the consciousness that you are no friend of God, what a fearful omen of an ill-provided death!

The consequences will not be temporary trouble, hardship, or torture, but everlasting doom. Yet worse than this consciousness of guilt, a thousand times worse as an omen of perdition, is the hardness of heart which has grown callous to all the agitations and pains of remorse. Your last hope has left you, if you find that you can go on in your sins from day to day without adverting to your danger, or being sensible of the wretched plight in which you live, when your ear has grown deaf to the clanking of your chains, and the passing scenes of life are able to banish every thought of the unseen, and to quench the higher aspirations of your nature. It will take a miracle to convert a sinner who has no remorse.

Nor are they far from this hopeless condition who, being conscious of sin, abandon prayer almost entirely. There is always a chance for a man who prays, and sometimes the tiny thread of a few "Hail Marys" said daily during a life of sin, has been sufficient to draw back the poor ship-wrecked sinner sooner or later from the boiling sea that had all but threatened to engulf him. But bear in mind, beloved Brethren, that the longer you have been absent from the sacraments, the more you have increased the odds against your salvation. Every month you have put off reconciliation with God has added to the probabilities of your eventual discomfiture. After a time it would be as easy to shift a pyramid as to rise up from under the accumulated weight and obstacles which your delay has heaped upon you. And this applies with double force to those who have contracted a habit of grievous sin, and who, day after day, are swelling the contents of the cup of vengeance, till by and by it must brim and overflow. Are you a drunkard enslaved to drink, who has indulged so much in your past that your whole system is vitiated, and every vein in your body, when the fit is on you, is raging with thirst for the poison? If so, let each week of your folly be marked against your hopes of eternal life. Are you licentious and impure, with imagination defiled, understanding enthralled and enervated, will enfeebled and yoked in bondage, memory a hell of seething recollections, passions all enlisted in the one wild pursuit, and dashing, like hounds, pell-mell after the one quarry, the whole being, with all its finest faculties, lying pig-like in the miry sty of sensuality. If this picture of an extreme case even reminds you of lines in your own character, you have reason to tremble at the prospect of the day of reckoning. That devil of impurity is not easily cast out, though nothing is impossible to God. The passion often glows even in the dying eyes of the aged sinner, and feeds the last flickering taper in the lamp of life. "Thou wilt consume me," says holy Job, "for the sins of my youth."—*Job.* xiii. 26. He cannot lightly put off as a garment, a passion that has infected the blood, a habit that has blended completely with his nature. "His bones shall be filled with the vices of his youth, and they shall sleep with him in the dust."—*Job* xx. 11.

But alas! how hopeless it is, if some complication involves you in the same meshes with some unfortunate partner of guilt, whose life, whose every breath and pulsation, seems a prophecy of ruin to you both.

Do not think, beloved Brethren, that I wish to scare or discourage you, I speak in view of the dread saying of our Blessed Lord, "Many are called, but few are chosen," and I would fain urge upon you to make, as the Apostle says, "your calling and election sure." There is no reason for discouragement. Heaven and earth are full of motives for hope and trustfulness. Look up to heaven, and there you see a Father who loves you, the Father who has created you, and whose handiwork you are, however defaced and disfigured by your own misdeeds, whom you have a right (the right conferred by baptism) to call by the name of Abba Father, and at every period of life to address in the words of the ancient penitent: "Qui plas masti me, miserere mei—Do thou who hast fashioned me have mercy on me."

Look up to heaven, and there you will see the Queen of All Saints, whose standing title is an exhortation to you not to despair, for she is called, and she really is, the Advocate of Sinners. Remember that, however unworthy you are, you have been admitted by Baptism to the Communion of Saints, and that, in consequence of that high privilege, you have a share in the prayers of the Saints, and of the Angels, who sing their eternal hymns before the throne of God, and that you are a partaker of the merits and the good works of the faithful upon earth. The tribunal of penance is an exhortation to you to hope. There is the abiding pool of cleansing which has received the blessing of Christ for the restoration of the sinner. There is the pool of cleansing, which awaits no hours or seasons of salutary stirring, and into which you need no hand to let you down.

It is a motive of hope, confidence, and courage, that you have not to tell your tale of sin and sorrow to angels, but to men, men of flesh and blood like yourselves, men full of weakness, and, as the Apostle says, encompassed with infirmity, who have need to offer sacrifice first for their own sins and then for your sins. They would belie their own past history, they would belie the possibilities, the guilt that they must recognize in themselves, if they treated you in your prostration and sorrow scornfully, or cruelly, or harshly. And while you pursue this calculation, each with the reference to your own past history, personal surroundings, and peculiar circumstances, beloved Brethren, remember that it is only serious reflection that will rescue your souls from sin and danger, "With desolation is the whole world made desolate because there is no one who thinketh in his heart." You would do well from time to time to recur to the saying of the saintly author of the "Following of Christ":—"It is better to live a good life than stand in dread of death."

THE PARTICULAR JUDGMENT.

FAITH, belovéd Brethren, tells us that we were born to work, and not to idle. We came into this world to earn by our labours a right and title to a better world than this. We have not our fixed abode here; we are only on our trial for a time, and our term of probation is sooner or later to end; and, when the end comes, our bodies will be laid in the bosom of the earth, to waste and crumble; but our souls must go forward into the presence of a Judge, all knowing, who judges just judgment, and who will exact a rigorous account of our lives. Oh, what a scrutiny, what an examination that will be!

Think, beloved Brethren, what horrors meet the sight oftentimes, when some neglected room, shuttered and hid from the day, is suddenly thrown open to the searching rays of the sun, and in that clear light, the filth it harboured, the disgusting and loathsome forms of existence it concealed, are laid open to the view! But what shall it be, when the chamber of a godless heart, where iniquity has been stored, where devils have had their lurking place, is illumined by the gaze of the All-seeing God! What treasures of forgotten sin, what a heap of evil thoughts, desires, and deeds are laid open before the throne of All Sanctity! What will be the wrath of the Holy One, to see the defilement of that soul which in baptism He had sealed as his own, which He had claimed as his choice and hallowed sanctuary.

Such, beloved Brethren, will be the result of that examination in too many cases—a spoiled life, disappointment to God, despair to the poor self-ruined sinner.

Time has been given us in which to labour, and we have idled the time away. Night surprises us before we have done the task allotted to us; nay, often before we have seriously started it. We dream out our short dream, intent only upon gratifying our whims and passions, and lo! Death calls out our name; we awake from the sleep of our folly, and are hurried before the great Master— with nothing in our hands. Where are the good thoughts, the charitable words, the prayers, the deeds of mortification, the fasts, the penances, the alms, the well-performed duties of our state of life, which we ought to be able to show, as the sheaves we have gathered, to the Lord of the harvest?

But perhaps we have lived a pretty respectable life, as things go. We have been to Mass on the Sundays and Holidays, when we have been lucky enough not to drink to excess the night before: we have turned up for our Confessions and approached Holy Communion, once or twice or oftener in the year, because it was the custom for the respectable folks in the neighbourhood to do so: we have dropped a mite occasionally into the poor-box, or given a helping hand to a failing neighbour, but always with prudence enough not to pinch ourselves in the least, not to deny ourselves the slightest luxury we are used to, in the performance of these cheap charities. We have not disgraced ourselves by public drunkenness, or by haunting the bars of noted public houses; but we have had our own little drinkings in private, we have hankered after the bottle, and fingered it to our heart's content, when no one's eye—no human eye—was upon us. We have shunned the tumult and confusion of quarrelling; but we have given scope enough to our malice, by talking ill of our neighbours; by praising them in a half-hearted way, to provoke censure from the company; by sneering at them; distorting their words and actions to their disadvantage; revealing their faults or misdeeds and enjoying their unpopularity. We have not risked the health of our bodies, or endangered our good name by open immodesty; but we have defiled the conscience with foul imaginations, wicked desires, recollections or anticipations of sin, corrupt conversations, words of double meaning, the secret perusal of newspaper scandals; nay, perhaps with actions too, which no eye can see save God and our good Angel. We have given our children a good schooling, and brought them up creditably; but we have never cared to watch over our words and to be guarded in our actions before them, so as to prevent their tender minds from getting a wrong bent, and inclining to evil rather than good; much less have we striven by our own religious lives and edifying behaviour, to make the path of virtue easy to them. Behold, these are the best virtues we can offer to our Maker, as the fruit of a long life, perhaps of manifold advantages, of sacraments, of graces beyond number. Like the barren fig tree in the Gospel, we have borne nothing but leaves, and like that tree, we have earned but the curse—for our time is over now—"may you bear nothing more for ever."

Yet in truth, He had deserved better at our hands He had deserved that we should work for Him, since He first worked for us. "What is there which he ought to have done for His vineyard that He has not done?" He came down from heaven to live with us, to enlighten, comfort and lead us. He bore hardships and contempt for us; He toiled with his hands at a poor man's craft—for us; He prayed, preached, fasted—all for our advantage; finally, He shed His blood to redeem us from sin, and to leave us in that blood, a fountain of graces suited to every need. Has He deserved such half-service, such dawdling, such coldness, as we offer Him at the best? Are the fruits of this lavish redemption, this precious outpoured blood, to be nothing but a careless life, prayers without heart or fervour, religious services and exercises evaded, or gone hrought without a pulse of devotion; distracted Masses, Confessions that bring no change for the better; Communions cold and perfunctory? Such a return is contrary to nature. Put a seed in the ground: gather the earth about it; let the dews and rains soak it; and the warmth of the sun penetrate it; and by and by, it comes up, lifting its head out of the mould, a fragrant, brilliant flower, or ripe, nutritious grain. But here are our souls, made most fruitful by the Holy Ghost, planted in the soil of the Church, fed with the dews of the precious blood that fall in the Sacraments; fostered by the warm breath of an all-loving God; and yet the season passes, and all goes for nothing. It is a miracle of hardness and insensibility to thwart so many good influences, and to render unprofitable the passion and death of the Son of God. Nothing can equal the miracle of our hardness, except the miracle of God's patience and tenderness.

Perhaps, beloved Brethren, I have already said enough to direct you in that work of self-examination which you should perform at this holy season, when God cries aloud: "Let the impious man forsake his way, and the wicked man his thoughts, and return to the Lord, and He will have mercy on him. . . He wills not the death of the sinner, but that he be converted and live." You were but a short time ago reminded of your mortality by the solemn imposition of the blessed ashes upon your forehead, accompanied by the impressive words of the Church : " Remember, man, that thou are dust, and into dust thou shalt return." Let not that warning be lost upon you ; make your preparation in good time for your departure hence, by judging yourselves severely now, that your judgment may be lightened hereafter. And if you are apt to think too well of yourselves, ask yourselves only one question.— Do you love God with your whole heart and soul, with all your strength and with all your mind, and your neighbour as yourself. If you cannot say with St. Peter, " Lord, thou knowest all things ; thou knowest that I love thee," then tremble lest the curse uttered by the Apostle be your inheritance. " If anyone love not Our Lord Jesus Christ, let him be anathema."

Ah ! it is to be feared that very few indeed are truly labouring in earnest to acquire that love; that few indeed make this their chief business—according to the injunction: " Seek ye first the kingdom of God and his justice, and all other things will be added unto you." If, beloved Brethren, you feel that you are to be classed among the number of the remiss, then resolve without delay to cast off your sloth. Put not off your conversion till to-morrow, for "to-morrow is an uncertain day." In fine, let me address you in the words of the Apostle : " Brethren, we exhort you not to receive the grace of God in vain," for he says : " In the acceptable time I have heard you, and in the day of salvation I have assisted you. Behold, now is the acceptable time ; behold, now is the day of salvation."

DIVINE HOPE.

I PROPOSE to-night, beloved Brethren, giving a short instruction on the Virtue of Hope. It is, as you know, one of that beautiful trio of virtues which are termed theological, because they have direct and immediate reference to God. Faith enables us to accept God's revelation upon the testimony of the Church. Hope enables us to put our trust in God as the all-powerful, all-merciful, the all-faithful, who has promised us eternal life if we obey his laws, and Charity unites us to God, the all-beautiful by the bonds of affection. These three virtues then like true attendants at the throne of God, always keep their eyes fixed upon his face. The rest have reference to God more indirectly and are not admitted so near His Divine person, for example, the Cardinal virtues of Prudence, Justice, Fortitude, and Temperance, the office of which is to contribute to the healthy action of other virtues. Of course, the time will come when every veil of mystery being rent asunder, the supernatural world and the truths connected with it, which now are hidden from the sight, will be brought home to our consciousness with such force, vividness, and certainty, that Faith will be no longer needed, and like an Angel that has guided our path to the gates of death, will vanish when we reach the bourne of our journey. Hope, also our bright and genial comrade in this valley of tears, who has cheered our intervals of despondency, and held us by the hand through all the rough ways, as a mother does her child, will not accompany us into the next world, for there is no occasion for its services, when all that we longed for is in our grasp, and joy is ours for evermore. Of all the three, Charity alone will follow us, the companion of our immortality.

To come, then, more particularly to Hope, it is defined to be a theological virtue infused into our hearts by Almighty God, like every gift not included in the scope of our human nature, by which we expect, with fullest confidence, both eternal happiness and the means necessary to attain it, on account of God's faithful adherence to His promise.

You see, then, beloved Brethren, that theological hope is not a vague and wavering forecast, half desire, half anticipation, but a clear and pronounced expectation of the glory to come. For it is founded upon God, the only stable groundwork of our confidence, who has no prompting within to urge him to capricious change of purpose, and no power without which can disturb his counsels or thwart his designs. It is then at the best with some degree of doubt, apprehension, and misgiving that we hope for success in life, for abounding wealth, for social respect or eminence, for this or that promotion, for commanding attainments or the continued enjoyment of bodily health; since all our efforts to attain these objects, however determined and however sustained, may end, as they often do end, in failure and disappointment. Hence the saying, founded upon the experience of actual life. "The race is not always to the swift, nor the battle to the strong." Unforeseen factors and influences may enter into the problem, and may thwart all our calculations and baffle the very men who seemed by their qualifications bound to succeed. But in the spiritual order, it is different. Try and you are not merely likely to succeed, you are absolutely certain. "My children," says the book of Ecclesiasticus, "behold the generations of men, and know ye that no one hath hoped in the Lord and hath been confounded. For who hath continued in his commandment and hath been forsaken? Or who hath called upon Him, and He despised him? For God is compassionate, and merciful; He is a protector to all who seek Him in truth."— *Eccles.* ii. 11.

You may sow your seeds in the ground, and they may for a time be favoured by the dews and the rains, and the warm fostering sunshine, but in spite of all your care, the frost may suddenly nip the growth, or some unpropitious influence make itself felt, and the fruits you expected be lost to you. But in the spiritual world, if you only do your share towards rearing the plant of virtue, there will be no lack of vivifying dews, nor timely rains, and the smile of the all-gracious God shall be to it a fruitful and unfailing sunshine. In the spiritual world, I say there is no uncertainty; success and merit are exactly commensurate with our heaven directed labours. There shall be no disappointment, no failure, no loss. "Blessed is the man," says the Psalmist, "who hath not walked in the counsel of the ungodly, nor stood in the way of sinners, nor sat in the chair of pestilence. But his will is in the law of the Lord, and in His law he shall meditate day and night. And he shall be like a tree planted near the running waters, which shall bring forth its fruit in due season. And his leaf shall not fall off and all whatsoever he shall do shall prosper."—*Ps.* i. 1-4.

Now, beloved Brethren, these considerations ought to arrest the attention, not merely of those who are leading a good life, but even more of those who are fettered by habits of sin. They may be at present as reckless, worldly, ungodly as you please. They may be in pride the counterpart of Lucifer. They may be furies in their anger. They may be Nero's in merciless and wanton cruelty. They may drink strong drink like Scandinavians of old, and be saturated in every vein and vessel with intoxicating poison. They may be more hideously polluted than Tiberius Cæsar, or any other foul occupant of the throne of that disgraced, imperial Rome. They may be as usurious and miserly as the worst type of Jew in real life, or portrayed in fiction. And yet, granted only that they avail themselves of God's grace, that they begin to work against themselves, it follows, as light follows the sun, that they will be redeemed from the bondage of their nefarious habits, and crowned by the grace of final perseverance, will reign with Abraham, Isaac, and Jacob, with the Prophets, and the Apostles, with the Confessors, and Virgins, and Martyrs, and shine like stars for all eternity.

The change is incredible save to the apprehension of faith, which knows that to God nothing is impossible. By the sound of his voice, our Blessed Lord called forth Lazarus from the dead, when his sojourn of four days in the tomb had gone far towards dissolving the frail flesh upon his bones, and reducing it to unsightly putrefaction. When in the dread words of Isaias: "Under him the moth was strewed, and worms had become his covering," when the cere-cloth was soiled with the hideous decomposition within, when the features had begun to grow not only ghastly but undistinguishable, and the eyesockets were but as vessels of uncleanness, even then the dread work of the grave was arrested, and the tide of decay rolled back, the instant that word of power vibrated in the air: "Lazarus, come forth!" He came with sinews firm, with skin glossy and sound, with organs playing in healthy activity once more, with face redeemed from the horror of death, and eyes radiant with the joy of recovered life. And thus will the sinner be brought back from the noisomeness and impurity of his sinful habits, from the dead and oppressive mould, from the moth and the worm to the free air, the joyous alertness and elasticity, and the bright sunshine of a Christian life, if he only turn to the all-powerful, all-merciful God, and humbly and sorrowfully have recourse to Him in the Sacrament of Revival, the Sacrament of Penance. "Thou hast prostituted thyself to many lovers." God declares by the mouth of the prophet Jeremias, "Nevertheless return to me," saith the Lord. "and I will receive thee."—*Jer.* iii. 1. "Let the wicked forsake his way and the unjust man his thoughts, and let him return to the Lord, and He will have mercy on him, and to our God for He is bountiful to forgive."—*Is.* lxv. 7.

These are the promises of the God of Truth, who can neither deceive nor be deceived. "Amen," said Our Blessed Lord, "Heaven and earth shall pass away, but My word shall not pass away." O that we had a voice of iron and a hundred tongues, to noise and trumpet it through the world, till every nook of sin re-echoed it. Do not despair. Pray, pray, pray, and you shall be saved. "Ask and you shall receive, seek and you shall find, knock and it shall be open to you." What you cannot do, God will do by you. However feeble you are, however crusted with sin, however hopeless and gone, seize the plank, go to Confession, beg pardon and you shall be forgiven. If you fall again, confess again, and again you shall be restored to favour. How many times does Our Blessed Lord tell us to forgive our enemies? "Not seven times, but seventy times seven times," that is to say, as often as he offend. Will God fall short of the standard which He appoints for men. "The Lord is merciful, and with Him is plentiful redemption." Listen to the words of devout Blosius— "No matter how numerous and grievous your sins may be, never despair of obtaining pardon. Have you fallen? Then rise and address yourself to the Physician of your soul. Have you fallen again, again rise, lament your frailty, call upon your Saviour and His mercy will lift you up. Have you fallen a second, a third, a fourth time, nay oftener still? Rise once more, weep and sigh for better things, humble yourself and God will not abandon you. He has never yet despised, nor will He despise a contrite heart. He has never yet rejected, nor will He reject those who have recourse to Him with true repentance. If you never tire of rising after your sin, He will never tire of forgiving you. If you should fall a hundred or a thousand times in the space of one short hour, rise again, and with a holy confidence of pardon, rise as often as you fall, and give thanks to God He has not suffered you to sink lower, or to remain longer in the slough of sin. Even if you should deny your God, which God himself forbid, after receiving from His hand innumerable graces and favours, humbly acknowledge your guilt, detest your sin, resolve never to offend Him again, determine to lead a better life, and be assured of pardon—God is Almighty, it is as easy for Him to forgive countless myriads of crimes in a moment of time as one peccadillo. Let not, then, the recollection of past sins disturb you, but ponder on the consoling words of the Apostle—'Such some of you were, but you are washed, but you are sanctified, but you are justified in the name of Our Lord Jesus Christ and the spirit of Our God.'"

This passage, beloved Brethren, is from the pen of a man illumined to an unusual degree by the spirit of God.

You remember the story of the young man who was turned by St. Philip Neri from a sinner into a saint. He was entangled in habits of impurity, which crippled him from all good and wasted his whole life, all his energies and powers of mind and body. Hearing of St. Philip's fame, he was seized with curiosity to speak with him, and went to the confessional where the saint spent so much of his time. St. Philip at once perceived his wretched plight, and his heart was wrung with pity. Did he scold him? Did he upbraid him with his misdeeds? Did he threaten him with the judgments of a long-suffering God? No; he made him promise to return to confession every time he sinned, and on receiving the promise, absolved him. The young man was not long before he fell again, ; but, faithful to his pledge, he returned to his director, and received absolution. Repeatedly he fell, and was absolved as often as he confessed, for the saint saw that he was striving and struggling against the violence of his passion. At last the remedy began to take visible effect. The vicious company in which he had moved became by degrees distasteful to him, till at length he shunned it as he would a troop of demons; the evil ties he had contracted one by one were broken; the dangerous occasions of sin were no longer frequented; sensual diversions became objects of dread and horror; and books calculated to re-kindle the fever of lust in his veins were for ever cast aside. In one word, he became a most devout Christian, a subject of edification and an an agent of good wherever he went.

Take courage, then, one and all, whatever be the condition of your souls. This is a season when God seems to raise the voice of comfort and encouragement louder than ever, and when the words of holy Zachary find an echo in our souls: "Blessed be the Lord God of Israel, because he hath visited and wrought the redemption of his people." Yes, as the prophet said, "The Lord of Hosts hath visited his flock."—*Zach.* x. 13.

Mingle with the rude shepherds, men like yourselves, with their own history of sin and care, their own recollections of lost opportunities and squandered graces, who nevertheless have been blessed with the vision of angels, and have heard the joyous minstrelsy of heaven. "Let us go over to Betlehem, let us see this word which has come to pass, which the Lord hath showed to us." There gaze your fill at the incarnate goodness of God, shrunk into the shell of an infant frame, most sweet, gentle, and approachable, with a smile of brotherly love upon His lips, and the light of divine kindness in his eyes. There ponder on the generosity which dictated such a transformation. You cannot ponder long before hope shall kindle up in your soul, as you come to understand that this advent of His in the guise of a sweet child is only the pledge of a love which will remove every barrier to your salvation, if you will not cross and thwart it. The force of the inspired words will distil its balm of refreshment and peace into your heart: "He that spared not even his own Son, but delivered him up for us all; how hath he not also with him given us all things."—*Rom.* viii. 32.

THE KINGDOM OF CHRIST DOOMED TO THE HATRED OF THE WORLD.

OUR Lord, beloved Brethren, was yearned for by the prophets through centuries of trouble and degradation, as the great King who was destined to restore the glories of the House of Israel, and to give peace to the dark, fretful, and tumultuous world. "For Sion's sake," cries out Isaias, "I will not hold my peace, and for the sake of Jerusalem, I will not rest, till her just one come forth as brightness, and her saviour be lighted as a lamp."—lxii. 1. "The Gentiles shall walk in thy light, and kings in the brightness of thy rising."—lx. 3. "Iniquity shall no more be heard in thy land, wasting nor destruction in thy borders, and salvation shall possess thy walls, and praise thy gates. Thou shalt no more have the sun for thy light by day, neither shall the brightness of the moon enlighten thee: but the Lord shall be unto thee for an everlasting light, ... and the days of thy mourning shall be ended."—lx. 18, 19, 20.

And who is this mighty Conqueror? The same prophet paints his portrait as the heir of the promises and the darling of God: "A child is born to us," and a son is given to us, and the government is upon his shoulder: and his name shall be called Wonderful, Counsellor, God the Mighty, the Father of the World to come, the Prince of Peace."—ix. 6.

How strangely, beloved Brethren, was this prediction fulfilled to the mind of the Jews! Lo, the day dawns, and the promised light appears. What! Can it be true? This Almighty Messiah turns out to be only a poor woman's child; His reputed father an aged mechanic, living from hand to mouth; His lot among the dregs of the people; His private life a life of sordid labour and unaspiring retirement; His public career, to the eyes of the world, a failure so absolute, and ignominious, and linked with so tragic a close, as to justify, humanly speaking, the contempt and neglect, inspired by His humble origin, and His isolation from the learned and the great. And yet this is the very King whose advent was heralded by the trumpet-voiced procession of prophets echoing through the centuries. "My kingdom," said He to Pilate, "is not of this world. If my kingdom were of this world, my servants would certainly strive that I should not be delivered to the Jews: but my kingdom is not from hence. Pilate therefore said to him: Art thou a King then? Jesus answered: Thou sayest that I am a King. For this was I born, and for this came I into the world; that I should give testimony to the truth. Every one that is of the truth, heareth my voice."—*St. John*, xviii. 36, 37. And if His kingdom was to be a spiritual one, spiritual too were to be the glories of His reign; spiritual His achievements, His triumphs, and His crowns; spiritual the light and the peace He was to diffuse over the earth. "Peace I give you," said the Prince of Peace, "My peace I leave you: not as the world giveth, do I give unto you."—*St. John*, xiv. 27. This was His bequest to His beloved ones at His last supper, when He bade them farewell. It was from a worldly point of view, no visible heritage; it was not a lot of comfort, ease, or good fellowship with men; much less of popularity, honour, civic homage, favourable repute, abounding wealth, luxurious living; it was to be a struggle within and without. Rigorous self-discipline and unrelaxing labour, prayer, watching and fasting—these were to be the spirit's perpetual home-occupation: without, she had to suffer suspicion, misunderstanding, calumny, social estrangement; nay, rancorous hostility, persecution, chains, racks and death. Such was the last legacy of the Prince of Peace; treasured by His children as a joy and an honour; as St. Paul cries out in his own burning style, "God forbid that I should glory, save in the Cross of our Lord Jesus Christ; by whom the world is crucified to me, and I to the world."—*Gal.* v. 14. Long ago, Our Lord had said: "Blessed are you when men persecute you for the sake of the Son of Man."—*St. Luke*, vi. 26.

And on the other hand, had He not denounced all peace with the world as a misery and a curse: "Woe to you," said He, "when men bless you; for in this, according to these things did their fathers to the false prophets of old."—*St. Luke*, vi. 26. Falsehood the world could tolerate; but truth, which He, the Living Truth, came to teach, they hated, defamed and hunted down alike in the master and in His disciples. If He was reviled and hounded to death, so should they be. "The Spirit of Truth the world cannot receive."—*St. John*, xiv. 17. "If the world hate you, know you that it hath hated me before you. If you had been of the world, the world would love its own; but because you are not of the world, but I have chosen you out of the world, therefore the world hateth you. Remember my word that I said to you: "The servant is not greater than his master; if they have persecuted me, they will also persecute you."—*St. John*, xv. 18, 19, 20.

Such is the future of clouds and storms which Christ sketches out for His church; a future whose troubles were to be compensated by the inward joy of that Paraclete, who was to abide with them for ever, "the Spirit of Truth whom the world cannot receive, because it seeth Him not, nor knoweth Him; but you shall know Him; because He shall abide with you, and shall be in you."—*St. John* xiv. 17. And He himself was to be a comforter, whispering joy into the ears of His suffering members; as He promised in the memorable words preserved by *St. John* xvi. 33: "These things I have spoken to you, that in Me you may have peace. In the world you shall have distress: but have confidence, I have overcome the world."

Yes! the victory of the Church was to be as strange and as signal as that of her master, and consummated amidst unexampled disgrace and shame. She was to be strong in her utmost weakness; in the pangs of death exhibiting her immortality; ruling from the gibbet; never so much honoured as in the garb of scorn and mockery; making treasures of her wounds and scars; turning ill-omened crosses into relics of veneration; making iron fetters more precious than gold.

You see, beloved Brethren, our Lord does not hint that these trials and persecutions are to be the lot of His Apostles alone; but of His kingdom. His Church, as opposed to the world; *i.e* those who refuse to receive the testimonies handed down by the Apostles. Indeed, it is not for one moment to be supposed that as long as the descendants of the Apostles continued to preach the truth of Christ, the world would ever abate its hatred or relax its opposition. In a certain sense, the world is as firm, consistent, and unshaken as the Church can hope to be; since as long as truth is truth, the unerring instinct of the world is to hate it.

MARTYRDOM,
A MARK OF THE CHURCH.

PART I.

OUR LORD, beloved Brethren, was foretold by the prophets under the title of the King of Peace. It was difficult to root out of the minds of the Jews, the notion that this and similar titles, by which the Messiah was foreshown, indicated an earthly King who should rule mightily over the world, putting an end to wars and bloodshed, and subduing the savage instincts of men. It is no wonder that the words of the prophet Isaias, sounding in their carnal ears, should produce such an impression. "In the last days," says he, "there will be prepared the mountain of the house of the Lord upon the top of mountains, and it shall be lifted above the hills, and all nations shall flock to it. And many peoples shall go, and shall say: "Come and let us ascend to the mountain of the Lord and to the house of the God of Jacob, and he will teach us his ways, and we shall walk in his paths; because the law shall go forth from Sion, and the word of the Lord from Jerusalem. And he shall be judge over the Gentiles, and shall bring home conviction to many peoples. And he shall melt down their swords to make ploughshares, and their spears to make reaping-hooks; nation shall not raise the sword against nation, nor shall they be disciplined any more for battles."—*Isaias* ii. 3. And in another memorable passage, the prophet repeats the same prediction with circumstances most striking and beautiful, and in a strain as remarkable for its poetic inspiration as for its spiritual fervour and strength. "The wolf," said he, " shall dwell with the lamb: and the leopard shall lie down with the kid: the calf and the lion, and the sheep shall abide together, and a little child shall lead them. The calf and the bear shall feed; their young ones shall rest together: and the lion shall eat straw like the ox. And the suckling child shall play at the hole of the asp: and the weaned child shall thrust his hand into the den of the Basilisk. They shall not hurt, nor shall they kill in all my holy mountains, because the earth is filled with the knowledge of the Lord, as the covering waters of the sea."—*Isaias* xi. 6. And this expectation of the Jews that a great Saviour would come and bring peace to the troubled world was shared by Pagans even, about the time of Our Lord.

The most famous of the Roman poets has left us a piece in which he sings in rapturous strains of the approaching period, when the earth shall be renewed with a worthier race; and a new golden age begin; when wickedness and fear shall be banished; when the soil shall pour forth sweetest flowers without culture; when the herds shall stand no more in dread of the lion; when serpents shall perish, and poisonous herbs wither and die.

And how, beloved Brethren, were these predictions fulfilled? Very strangely, indeed, to the mind of the Jew. Their mighty ruler turned out to be a poor man, whose name was unknown outside his own little corner of the world; one held in contempt, as sprung from the lower orders of the people: "Is this not the Carpenter's son?" one regarded by the Scribes and Pharisees at first with astonishment and wrath as an upstart, at last with mortal hatred and jealousy, as capable by word and work of moving the people, speaking as one having authority and performing wondrous cures. This was the Prince of Peace. And a prince he was in his very mien and presence, as the soldiers and rabble felt when they were about to apprehend him in the garden, and when his word and look smote them to the ground. But peaceful too; gentle, winning, dove-eyed; not apt to crush the bruised reed nor to extinguish the smoking flax. Full of all merciful and tender ways; finding means in his infinite wisdom, of rescuing the poor woman taken in sin; pouring floods of compassion into the broken heart of the Magdalen, and soothing her with praise; beaming love into the soul of poor, impetuous, self-trusting Peter, and recalling him as with an embrace from the midst of his treason. Behold the Prince of Peace. He came not to battle for earthly crowns. "Put back thy sword into thy scabbard," said he to Peter, "they who take the sword shall perish by the sword." What to him were the weapons of earthly warfare, when, at his prayer, his Heavenly Father could send him legions of Angels, whose fiery falchions could mow down armies like grass, and tumble together the solidest bastions like card-castles. Nay, without invoking the aid of the heavenly Spirits, could he not call upon the elements of creation to battle in his cause: "Fire, hail, snow, ice, stormy winds that fulfil his word." Did he not show his power over the elements when he bade the winds and the sea, and presently there came a great calm. And in the presence of his dead body, you remember how an earthquake tore the earth, and rent the veil of the temple, and the dead rose from their graves, and appeared to many in the Holy City. But through persecution and enmity, the Prince of Peace, was content to evade the wiles of His foes, instead of punishing them. He did not care to contend with them. He came indeed to found a kingdom, and taught his disciples to pray that this kingdom might flourish: "Thy kingdom come," but "My kingdom," said he to Pilate, "is not of this world." So all the promised blessings that were to come with Him were not temporal, but spiritual. His peace was to be spiritual peace—the peace of a good conscience. Listen to Him as He discourses at the Last Supper on this subject: "Peace I leave you, my peace I give you; not as the world giveth, do I give to you." No; this peace was a bequest not of comfort, of ease, and good fellowship with men; but of hardship, mortification, self-contempt, suspicion, misunderstanding and calumny from the world, social isolation, nay, rancorous hostility, persecution, chains, racks, and death. This was the bequest he left his disciples and his Church at the Last Supper. He intended to give them a blessing in the gift; and he did. For had he not said at the very outset of his career: "Blessed are you when men hate and persecute you, for the sake of the Son of Man."—*Luke*, vi. 22.

Here then is the heritage of Christ's Church: the benediction that links heavenly peace with earthly trials, that ensures us sorrows, but recompenses us with the joy of the Holy Spirit.

The Church of Christ must be a Spouse of blood; thorn-crowned for her nuptials, her garment purple as of those that tread the wine-press. There is no other sign that can make up for the want of this. She must not be on good terms with the world. "Woe to you," said Our Lord, "when men bless you; for in this way they acted to the false prophets of old." If he was reviled and persecuted, so must she be: "the disciple is not above his master." The sons of the Church were to stand in opposition to the world, even to the coming of the Judgment-day, as much as the Apostles themselves. And why not? What the Apostles preached, their successors were to preach also. And if there was to be no change in doctrine, if the Church of Christ was ever to stand up, as Christ did, for obedience to authority, for due submission of the reason and the will, for self-denial, for the evangelical virtues; the world be assured, would scoff and jeer, slander and persecute her to the end. In this respect the world would be as stable and unwavering as the Church itself. If the Church always struggled manfully in behalf of truth, and denounced ungodliness, the world, with its own steady instinct, would hate her, would snarl at her perpetually, and bite when it could. This, then, was the commission of the Apostles: "The harvest indeed is great," said Our Lord, "but the labourers are few. Pray ye, therefore, the Lord of the harvest, that he send labourers into his harvest. . . Go forth: behold I send you as lambs into the midst of wolves." They were to prepare themselves for this fate; to be the prey, for which carnal men would thirst, as ravening wolves for the blood of the flock. All the forces of the world were to be arrayed against them. Worldly science was to regard her as an intruder and a usurper of territory not her own. Worldly art was to decry her purity as coldness and demureness. Worldly politics would pen her up in some small cage, and deny her an interest in questions affecting flesh and blood. Worldly society would condemn her precepts as impracticable, fanatical, and silly. Thus to the end of time she was to walk the world with swords and lances at her throat. Hatred of her was to turn even the sweet springs of natural relationship sour, and snap the bonds of blood and marriage that knit us to each other. "Think ye," said Our Lord, "that I am come to give peace on earth? I tell you no; but separation. For there shall be from henceforth five in one house, divided; three against two, and two against three. The father shall be divided against the son, and the son against his father; the mother against the daughter, and the daughter against the mother; the mother-in-law against the daughter-in-law, and the daughter against her mother-in-law."—*Luke* xii. 51.

Now, which of the great bodies, calling themselves Christian, stands this test of its divine origin? Which of them has the evidence of persecution in its favour? Look around you. Can you doubt for one moment? The Catholic Church is the great bugbear of the world; the great eyesore; the one nuisance that all other creeds would willingly join in burying fathoms under the earth. She alone finds it impossible to please the world. The cosy little national Churches, however they may wrangle at times, have their seasons of mutual compliment, when they exchange smiles and kindly speeches, and bury past unpleasantness, and shake hands with a sort of after-dinner warmth. But that Catholic Church, she is warned outside the pale of such fraternity. The whole press of Europe is down upon her. Her whole system is the subject of daily misrepresentation. Her doctrines and practices, after being explained a thousand times over, are coolly tortured as of yore into superstition, and idolatry, and what not, as though man had a right to turn a deaf ear to her explanations. And the haters of all religion, the infidels, concentrate their hate upon her; and, when occasion offers, burn her churches and butcher her members. Nor has she lost her old fame as a missionary Church. Within your day and mine, she has gathered in sacred vials the yet warm blood of her martyred children in far savage lands. And what she is to-day, she has ever been. Her history has been a history of persecution, trouble, disaster, but never failing strength and energy Look upon her face; it is stamped with many a scar that bears witness to combats past and gone; yet there is no token of age there; she is still young, without blemish or wrinkle. She looks now upon her persecutors, in their hour of triumph, with the same fearless eye with which she once confronted tyrannic dynasties and barbarous hosts, long since swept into the land of shadows, and sunk into the oblivion of the tomb. And her very enemies, in the midst of their song of joy, tremble lest their victory should again out of their hands.

MARTYRDOM
A MARK OF THE CHURCH.

PART II.

THE first meaning of the word Martyr is Witness. A martyr, in the Christian sense, witnesses to two things: first to the firmness of his convictions; secondly, to a wonderful power and efficacy in truth itself to keep his will unshaken amidst danger and death. A martyr sacrifices his life rather than give up his creed. Surely then, he must be set down as eminently a sincere man. When it comes to that last test of sincerity, who shall stand it? Will men die for what they do not believe, or what they do not care for? Will they suffer the loss of all worldly goods, nay, of dear life itself, for some hobby, some crotchet, some opinion or view, in which their very heart is not enlisted? No. The fool stops short of that. The fool is cautious before the rack and the wheel of torture, the hungry fire, the axe, and the disembowelling knife. However obstinate a man may be in his opinions, he is not accustomed to preach them from the scaffold, unless he credits them and feels them all-important. When therefore the Church of God unfolds her long catalogue of martyrs to the world, she reminds them in the first place, that she has had thousands of children, who have proved their unfeigned and absolute belief in her teaching, by that most unquestionable testimony, the willing sacrifice of their lives, rather than part with it.

It is not to be supposed but that in the Church established by Christ, there would be found a singular and superhuman constancy on the part of its members in clinging to the doctrines committed to them by their divine founder. In all ages, it might have been with certainty calculated, that the stamp of most earnest conviction would distinguish the true Church from false imitations. And sure enough, the Catholic Church is most singular and conspicuous, even in the claim it asserts to the multitudinous, blood-stained army of witnesses. No other Communion, calling itself Christian, can pretend to rival her in this respect. And this is not because they undervalue such testimony. On the contrary, they are all anxious to produce some specimens of the martyr; they are all of them glad to find a blood-stain on their annals; nay, they have gone the length of swelling their paltry list by the addition of characters, whom they profess to revere as martyrs, but whose lives were disgraced by the most violent passions—pride, hypocrisy, factiousness, deceit, and debauchery. Of these I may have more to say by and by. I am now only insisting, that the members of all Christian Communions must, in reason, be very glad to be able to point to any co-religionist, who appears to have parted with life and its blessings, rather than relinquish his creed. For such a heroism seems to argue that other professors of the same creed are not impostors, but men ready to follow the same path in the same cause. Yet, with all their willingness to show up as many martyrs as possible, with all their efforts to extend the title of martyr to political and social offenders, and men engaged in semi-religious faction struggles, they must admit themselves very far behind us in the multitude of their witnesses. I may sum up, therefore, by saying that the Catholic Church has upon it sure tokens of a divine origin, because its children have always been ready to prove the sincerity of their belief, by forfeiting, not only their wealth and their liberty, but their very lives, rather than deny their faith.

But, beloved Brethren, if we examine the question more closely, we shall find that martyrdom witnesses to something more than the sincerity of the martyr's belief.

If, in the course of generations and centuries, we observe a particular Christian Communion perpetually and uniformly producing martyrs, men who have not hesitated to give the extremest proof of their absolute belief in its teaching, we are forced to attribute this extraordinary fact to some cause above human nature; in other words, to regard it as a miracle in the moral order. When I see the sun, at man's bidding, stand still, till the battle-storm is over in the valley, I say, God, the Author of Nature, has departed from the routine course he has himself established, or, as men put it, has suspended one of the laws of nature; in other words, has worked a miracle in the physical order. So, when I see this wondrous succession of martyrs, reddening every new page of the Church's history that I turn over; when I see their fond mother, with whose milk they drank in fortitude, ever engaged in the sweet sad task of gathering and enshrining their bones; I am obliged to confess that there is something in the action of faith itself, that raises nature above its normal powers; I am forced to infer the existence of a supernatural aid; I bow down before a miracle of a higher kind than the arresting of the sun in its career, and the unwonted lengthening of the day. If I do not admit that God works this wonder, I cannot explain it at all. For remember, martyrs do not sacrifice themselves only in times of political or religious ferment, when men's blood boils in their veins, stimulating them to deeds of daring, and nerving their courage to a pitch of heroic endurance. It is not under the influence of a fanatical frenzy, that they give themselves to death, like the poor Hindoos who, when their idol, Juggernaut, is passing in procession, borne upon its massive and ponderous car, fling themselves in wild enthusiasm under the grinding wheels. They have suffered in cold blood; after long and wearisome imprisonment; fully aware of all they were losing, urged by no passion but the love of truth and of the Master of Truth, who had said: "If any man will deny Me before men, I will deny him before my Father, who is in heaven."

Again, it was not strong men, with robust frames, alone that showed this courage. The tender maiden, St. Agnes, suffered as willingly as the martial St. Sebastian. Neither was the courage of the martyr evinced in the case of nations proverbial for their constancy in suffering. The victims have been recruited from races of all kinds, delicate and hardy. Nor have they suffered with the proud object of triumphing publicly over pain, and thus robbing their enemies of a cruel satisfaction, like the American warriors, who have sung songs at the stake, in the midst of a ring of torturers. They have had no prompting of personal hatred to steel them against suffering, like those who perish in the heat of party strife; for they have been men overflowing with charity, full of forgiveness, whose last gasp has been a prayer for their persecutors. The spirit of the martyr is independent of age as well as sex. It strengthens the heart of infants, as when the little Theresa and her brother set out for Morocco, that they might die for the faith, and earn the martyr's crown, until their aspirations were rudely checked by their guardian, who gave chase to the runaways, and overtook them in their journey. It is a spirit which, without hardening the heart or blunting the affections, despises the secondary ties of earth, and looks for a deathless union in a happier sphere.

Thus animated, Symphorosa, in the reign of Adrian, led her seven sons to martyrdom; and by her example spurned them on to die bravely here, that they might enjoy eternal life in their common home hereafter. It was thus that Saint Rufina lived through the dread ordeal of seeing her seven children butchered before her eyes in the reign of Marcus Aurelias; seeing one beaten to death with lead-weighted scourges; two others with heavy clubs; another hurled into eternity from a beetling eminence; and the remaining three beheaded. She saw it, and lived through it; nay, while they underwent their sentences, that mother who loved them, as only a good mother can, raised her voice of encouragement and exhortation; and blessed them as they died. For four months after, the fiendish persecutors left her to await her own death, and to ponder in her loneliness upon that vision of horror.

I repeat then, beloved Brethren, there is no human strength of nerve, or constitutional courage, no exceptional robustness, no aim of pride or vanity, no stimulus of hate, no desperate fanaticism, no fire of political animosity that will reasonably account for martyrdoms, undergone by persons of both sexes, of all ages, of every race and country, learned and ignorant, gentle and simple, rich and poor, influential and of no social mark. If our witnesses were not so absolutely diverse in their histories and the conditions of their martyrdoms, there might be some rational suspicion of merely human causes producing such instances of heroic endurance. But, the very diversity of their circumstances baffles the philosopher, who would not attempt to refer their courage to influences merely human. So that the effect produced upon us, when we look back on the history of martyrs, is just the same as was produced so often upon Pagan crowds, who were converted by being spectators of the cruelty of the persecutor on the one hand, and the gentleness and patience of the victims on the other; we recognize, like them, the presence of a heavenly Sustainer and Strengthener, who keeps the heart from fainting, though the flesh shrinks and quivers, and who raises up the weak that He may confound the strong.

FAITH A DISSOLVING VIEW IN NON-CATHOLIC ENGLAND.

NON-CATHOLIC England is a dissolving view, in which creeds are daily vanishing, changing colour, putting on new forms, blending into one another, intermixing chaotically, and perplexing the thinking mind by a wild confusion of movement, which, far from being indications of vitality, are only the throes of a diseased system advancing towards final dissolution. Already the condemnation of Colenso for discrediting the Pentateuch seems like the act of a mediæval tribunal in its remoteness and strangeness. German criticism of the whole texture of the Bible, old and new, has eaten like some potent acid into the minds of many cultured men. It is becoming more and more fashionable to regard Sacred Writ as a piebald thing of shreds and patches; the sacred writers, recognised by past generations, as mythical; the events detailed, as impossible or allegorical, where they are not ludicrous; the dates assigned to those events, hitherto unchallenged, as out of joint with ascertained history.

We see a Regius Professor of Hebrew at the University of Oxford, and the head of Pusey house in the same University, and many other eminent Protestant divines, labouring to propagate the destructive criticism of the German school, which a few years ago would have been regarded by the mass of Protestants as rank infidelity. And yet this book, the authorship of which they are so industrious in overthrowing, is to them the one guide to religion and morals, the sole oracle of Christian life, the ultimate referee in all dogmatic controversy. It matters not that this oracle of the Bible, speaking through its stereotyped lines and columns, has dictated scores upon scores of discreditable creeds to different minds; and that before the death of the Arch-Reformer, who elevated the dead letter into a living Rabbi who hath the words of eternal life, there were fully fifty sects that based their diverged tenets upon its text, and fought for their several views, not merely with pens of gall and wormwood, but with sword and firearms, and the torch of the incendiary. Notwithstanding all this, "the open Bible," the Bible without note or comment, the Bible interpreted by private judgment, was accepted as the sole teacher to whom all must bow. Now, their Bishops skulk from this new field of battle, and watch the mêlée in silence from afar. A number of orthodox believers in the Establishment, issue a protest against the new opinions; but no Bishop's name is on the document to give it an air of authority. The Bishops stare helpless at the ferment and decomposition that is going forward.

Another section of the National Church, feeling the timbers giving way beneath their feet, are straining every nerve to establish a connection with the great ark of salvation. They *will* be true Catholics; they will be identified with the early English Church; they shovel aside clumsily the objection, that they bear not the remotest resemblance to that creed of monks and nuns, of Mass and Indulgences, of Papal Supremacy and Jurisdiction, but like lunatics who are subject to an illusion as to their identity, playing parts of all kinds, from kings and queens to cart wheels, they fill the public ear with their clamouring claims to be considered true Anglo-Saxon Catholics, the co-religionists of Adrian and of Wilfrid. And so they shape their outward worship to suit their contention; and we have travesties of Mass and Confession, of fasting and abstinence, pretty episodes of celibacy, mock-monasticism, with the shaven head, and picturesque convent costumes: all strangely eyed by a public, whose open-mouthed stare says plainly, we know you not. In vain does another sect rave at these extravagancies, as they deem them; the slow and rusty machine of Ecclesiastical Jurisprudence is set in motion amidst much outcry on both sides; sittings are held; learned ambiguity frames the judgment; and the old-fashioned Protestant sees all his efforts at purgation in the Establishment frustrated. So the boundary line widens, and sectaries camp in different parts of the same field, as estranged in feeling and sundered in doctrinal conviction as Mahomedan and Jew. To make up for the discord reigning within, there are many cries of fraternity addressed to the long despised Nonconformists outside. When these dissentients hold conference, the Protestant Bishop condescends to greet them with the most brotherly salutations. Revival meetings tend to the obliteration of dogmatic landmarks, and on the same platform, joining in hymn and prayer, are the representatives of the Church of England, and of all the sects that have broken from their allegiance to her: all are there save the Catholics, against whom now, as in all ages, the censure of uncharitableness and bigotry is levelled. The American Evangelists have left behind them a motto, that serves as a rallying cry of the new dogmatic indifferentism: we have been trying for a long time how far we can differ; let us now see how far we can agree.

A grotesque parody of Christianity with male and female officers, professing to aim at the regeneration of the slums, startles the day of rest with shrill outcry of hymns, and blatent sermonettes in the open air, and the loud din of drum and trumpet. Its professed mission to the poorest of the masses, and its works of charity, set forth by a leader, who has not his match for successful advertising, since Barnum died, has given a shock to the luxurious, at whose door Lazarous lies festering with sores and fainting with hunger. And thousands upon thousands of pounds have been placed at his disposal, to help to rouse the wretched denizens of court and alley from the mire and misery in which they lie. This union of the benevolent and conscience-stricken in the work of humanity, notwithstanding differences of creed, has been a fresh incentive to the growing indifference to dogma: and now all religion and morality resolve themselves into active benevolence. Now all creeds are good and very good, if they are not all equally good. The Thibetian politeness is spreading, which makes it incumbent in every man to praise the religion of his neighbour. Christianity has its merits forsooth, recognized by those who reject the Divinity of its founder; and who, unwilling to sever themselves from the grand results of Christian civilization, whose advantages they enjoy, accept the mere manhood, in its obvious amiability, and heroism, and compassionate tenderness, as the central figure of a new worship, which they place on a level in the West, with Buddhism, and Mahometanism, and Brahminism, in the East, that is as equally suited for the elevation of the races who come under its influence. And in the last few weeks, the Protestant Archbishop of Canterbury, at a meeting of the Society for the Propagation of the Gospel in foreign parts, has ventured to eulogize the creeds, which they send their missionaries to supplant. He denies that they are wicked; he says that they are great, embodying the best aspirations and thoughts of many men; and why? Because noble characters are formed under their influence, men of piety, justice and truth. He instanced Mahometanism in particular, as proving itself a good tree by the good fruit it produces. "Let no Christian believe," says he, solemnly, "that any great religion, which God has permitted to grow up, ministered in itself to pride, and lust, and cruelty. It would be just as reasonable to attribute to Christianity the sins of London: and the mission which proceeded in such a belief would not succeed."

Here then, Buddhism, Brahminism, and Mahometanism, in short, every form of belief which God has permitted to grow up, is thereby in itself holy and fertile in holiness. And if so, what need of Christianity? Paganism was a holy system, if judged by the criteria of the oracle of the Protestant Church. What words could be more encouraging to your artificers of new creeds? Set to work couragously: shape a new worship, which seems to you more suited to modern thought and modern needs, than those handed down: have no misgivings; if God allow it to grow up, it will be a "good" creed; for all you know, it is destined to expand: time only can tell whether success will prove it a good creed or not. Therefore take up your tools and begin the work. You will be a benefactor to mankind, if you can invent another machine for the manufacture of good, just, and pious men, equal to the system of Buddha, or Mahomet.

Is it any wonder that at such a pronouncement from one of the mitred leaders of the Church of England, Theosophism should make a bid for the favour of the cultured minds of this island? Is there any reason to find fault with the proclamation of Theosophism, that no creed (except Catholicity), is an obstacle to membership in that mystic brotherhood? Yes! ye long-haired lions of the drawing-room who affect a reputation for profound thought, for audacious and unchecked speculation, for superiority to the trammels of hereditary beliefs, go ye into that temple of fathomless wisdom, where ye shall be as gods—one with the impersonal deity who is nature: be ye Mahatmas; wield ye the wand of a half creative power, which compels the elements of nature—your brother—to your will: it is thus you will accomplish the destiny marked out for you; and it is thus you will have the finger of wonder, and the eye of awestruck admiration directed to your thoughtful visages by the frivolous ladies of a frivolous age.

And is it any wonder, on the other hand, that Agnosticism should grow less timid of the light of day, and bolder in its self-avowal! With such a phantasmagoria before their eyes of melting and vanishing dogma, with the vision of a discredited oracle in the tattered Bible, why should they be shy of expressing their contempt impartially for all this rout of creeds, that fought bitterly a while ago, and now are engaged in mutual compliments, warmer in proportion to the growing conviction that one creed is as good as another; what wonder is it that they should defiantly declare that all this ferment is vanity of vanities; and that God has not given his creatures the means of knowing who or what He is. Why should they not scout this tumult where camps are breaking up, and old enemies are fraternising, respecting the tenets for which their forefathers suffered disability and persecution, and the cry is going round—"It's of no consequence." Yes, the time is coming when these effete systems will give multitudes of recruits to the ranks of a dogmatic indifferentism whose one tenet is, let self be your one care, we know not God, we know not His nature, we have no reason to believe that the religions which trace their origin to Him are anything but myths—in many cases, grotesque myths; we have no reason to believe in the supernatural; we have no reason to believe in a hereafter. If all these things be true they are not made plain to the thoughtful mind; and no responsibility can rest upon those who reject them.

Such is the goal towards which men of culture are tending in this land of Protestantism, and towards which they are being helped forward by the action of the Established Church and the sects. Yet the Agnostics are not justified by the confusion which they observe in the lives of these motley-hued believers. Their whole ground is irrational. If they deny the existence of a Divine, supernatural revelation, or its possibility; if they deny the cogency of the arguments in favour of the Jewish and the Christian dispensation—the type and the fulfilment of God's great scheme of Redemption—at any rate the marvellous record connected with that history is so momentous, that it must needs be accepted by any thinking man as a challenge to a sincere enquiry and patient investigation. How many are there in these busy times who answer the challenge as they should? How many are there who try to find leisure, amidst their own chosen pursuits and studies to read the defence of that Revelation, and the facts it embraces? How many are there who go no further than the perusal of the authors whose professed aim is to dismantle the edifice of ancient beliefs, and to shatter its battlements and towers?

John Stuart Mill must have often been arrested by the lofty claims of Christianity, and by the acceptance of those claims on the part of so many thousands of deep thinkers, and by the influence it had acquired and the effects it had produced amongst millions upon millions of men; yet in the list of authors which he gives as the sole sources of his information, and the teachers who formed his mind, there is none that could serve as a fitting interpreter, or a powerful defender of the systems established under a Divine Revelation. And as it was with Mill, so is it with hundreds of others. They forget the motto: "Audi alteram partern"—"Hear the other side." They are a jury who listen attentively to the charges preferred against a prisoner, and decide his case off-hand without hearing his defence. This is not honest—and I repeat (considering the importance of the issue), it is irrational. Yet such is the growing custom. Men are content with their Strauss, their Renan, but have they read any of the learned authors who have exposed their pretentions, and shown the extravagant demands they make upon our credulity, in trying to prove the Gospel a legend or a myth. And surely they are aware that many attacks have been made upon Christianily, which have failed signally and are now forgotten; whilst their frustration, and the triumph of the cause they assailed, are driven out of the mind by a renewal of the assault from other points, and with fresh weapons.

Geology, or rather perverse professors of geology, have attacked Revelation: yet to-day that controversy is no more. Christians accept all the conclusions of that science, which are really established, and are no less Christian than before. The defence of the Bible by eminent critics, and thinkers—men not to be blinded by the glamour of tradition—is itself a proof that no attack has been decisive. The records of history, which unbelievers hoped to make their witnesses and supports, cannot, by the judgments of experts, be strained to a time so remote, as to contradict the facts of Holy Writ; though great were the efforts made to carry the genesis of races back, far beyond the Biblical limits. When the long-buried monuments of the Assyrian and Babylonian empires were opened out to the eye, and the mystic inscriptions on their basaltic and alabaster slabs and obelisks, and winged bulls deciphered, the world held its breath, and infidels hoped the time had come at last to prove the records of the inspired writers to be fictions.

But, lo! They rose like trumpet-tongued witnesses to the truth of those narratives, which they were expected to convict of falsehood. There the Scriptural Sargon stood forth, not only as a real monarch, but a distinguished man : there was corroboration, of the Scriptural account of the tribute-paying kings of Israel and Judah, of the usurping Jehu, of the conquests of Tiglath-pilesar ; of Salmanazer ; of the eclipse of the glory of Sennacherib ; of the Babylonian captivity ; of the strange history of Nebuchadnezzar ; confirmations of the most minute and curious description. The effect was like an explosion, stunning the mind and clearing the air. It was a resurrection of generations of dead men, to bear their testimony to the truth of the inspired chronicles. And now new ground is taken : the Divine books are cut up into their component parts, distinguished by differences of style, of circumstance, of evidence of character in the writers of the times discribed, of literary ability, of radical purpose and scope ; all with a view to show that it is a mere cento of scraps from various hands, with no more title to inspiration than the miscellaneous ballads tacked together by the ballad-monger, and with no earthly possibility of an origin such as is ascribed to them, by ecclesiastical writers. But note this. These destructive critics all differ from one-another in their opinions as to the division of these scraps ; they all demolish one-another's theories ; they agree only in one thing—their determination of destroying the divine claims of the Bible by any means in their power.

Go back over this great history of the assaults made upon Revelation and its organs through all the ages ; and the conclusion to which, inevitably a sober-minded man is driven, is—that as previous attacks have failed, so are the attacks of the present generation destined to fail also. Yet, we have not to deal with sensible men, nor fair-minded men. We have to deal with sciolists, who, from their own little section of knowledge, affect to judge all things ; who are, from the first, prone to scoff at

Religion, and to rebel against the yoke of moral discipline; who take no trouble to question the past, nor to weigh the evidences in the balance of truth; but who think themselves quite safe in falling in with the fashion, and raising the laugh of the scorner against the whole system of Revelation.

So much for the evidences of revealed religion. But what is to be said about those who deny that they can discern in themselves, or in the natural world around them any urgent dictate to believe in a personal God? They are characterised in the Scriptures: "dixit insipiens in corde suo; non est Deus." The fool has said in his heart: "There is no God." He is certainly a fool who denies that on the face of the universe, and in his own microcosm, or small version of the universe, there is the clear signature of a Creator, full of wisdom, of power, of beneficence. Let no such unbeliever attempt to awe us by the brilliancy of his parts, or the extent of his attainments in any domain of science, or literature, or art—I care not what. He is a fool; because he refuses to admit what is obvious. If he says it is not obvious to him, he is either duping himself or wishful to dupe others: each a silly role.

Am I saying this from the impetus of my personal zeal, or the vehemence of my personal passion. Is it rhetoric? No! It is the measured pronouncement of St. Paul.

There were philosophers and would-be philosophers in his day, and long before, who against the light of reason denied the existence of an omnipotent Creator, or held gross and debasing opinions as to His nature and attributes, and this is what the inspired Apostle says of them. "As they liked not to have God in their knowledge, God delivered them up to a reprobate sense to do those things that are unbecoming: being filled with all iniquity, detractors, hateful to God, contumelious, proud, haughty, inventors of evil things, foolish, dissolute, without affection, without fidelity, without mercy."—*Romans* i. 28-32.

"For the wrath of God is revealed from heaven against all ungodliness and injustice of those men that detain the truth of God in injustice. Because that which is known of God is manifest unto them. For the invisible things of Him, from the creatures of the world are clearly seen, being understood by the things that are made, His eternal power also and divinity: so that they are inexcusable. Because when they knew God, they have not glorified Him as God, or given thanks, but became vain in their thoughts, and their foolish heart was darkened. And they changed the glory of the incorruptible God into the likeness of the image of a corruptible man. Wherefore God gave them up to the desire of their hearts, unto uncleanness. Who changed the truth of God into a lie ; and worshipped and served the creature rather than the Creator, who is blessed for ever." Amen.—*Romans* i. 18-25.

ON MIXED MARRIAGES.

"WHAT doth it profit a man if he gain the whole world, and suffer the loss of his own soul; or what exchange shall a man give for his soul?"—*Matt.* xvi. 26.

This, beloved Brethren, is the weighty and momentous question the frequent repetition of which, by St. Ignatious, then a student of Theology in Paris, so wrought upon the vain and ambitious spirit of Francis Xavier, who was at that time teaching Philosophy with great applause, that it lifted the veil of delusion from earthly honours and earthly gratifications, and penetrated his heart so deeply with the fear of God and the longing for salvation, that he renounced the world once and for all, and gave himself body and soul to be the thrall and bondsman of Jesus Christ.

It is that same question we ought to ask ourselves, beloved Brethren, whenever worldly purposes and projects, with their agreeable glamour, are weaving their spells around us, and whenever we are in danger of being fatally blinded and engrossed by the transitory interests of life. Seek not, we shall say, seek not the honours that end in the winding-sheet and the dust of the grave: seek not the pleasures which are but the prelude to corruption; seek not the treasures of gold and silver, broad lands and lordly mansions, to absorb my thoughts or to lure the affections. One thing only is necessary, that I should save my soul. The alternative is ruin, without hope or alleviation; absolute and eternal. "What doth it profit a man if he gain the whole world and suffer the loss of his own soul?"

Well would it be, beloved Brethren, for those young men or women who turn their thoughts to marriage, if, in taking a step so important and irretrievable, they were guided by the purport o the awful admonition implied in this solemn maxim. If ever there is a turning point in life, where God's light should illumine the mind, and God's grace strengthen the heart, it surely is when a young man resolves to unite his lot with a partner for life, who shall be nearer and dearer to him than his own natural kith and kin, and shall be so intimately his own, as to be flesh of his flesh and bone of his bone. What tremendous consequences hang upon his choice! What a responsibility rests upon him as he sits down to decide into whose hands he shall commit so large a share in his future! Where is the young maiden so good, so trustworthy, so faultless, so helpful, so deeply sympathetic, responding so faithfully and tenderly to every thrill of his human heart's fibre, entering so fully into his inmost hopes and aspirations, and so thoroughly understanding them, withal so patiently gentle under difficulties and so persevering in her devotion, that her plighted faith shall be a pledge of continued happiness, till death cut the sweet knot asunder? But more than that, where is the girl whose life shall be so full of Christian virtue, so instinct with vivid faith, so ruled by the maxims of the Christian religion, that her influence, her sovereignty over the young man's soul, instead of adding hazard and difficulty to the problem of his eternal salvation, shall be a fresh safeguard, a lifelong exhortation and encouragement, and an assurance of eventual bliss.

O, beloved Brethren, how few young men there are who deliberate thus soberly in the choice of their future companion, or who seem to imagine that there is anything to consider or to weigh, except the fancy of the hour, the vanity of an enviable match, or the immediate tribute they would offer to the impulse of their affection. Yet as they so gaily clinch their resolution, what various after-careers are they preparing for themselves. How many after-events—some, perhaps, sad, some deplorable and heartrending, some hideously tragic, do they hold like threads in their hands, and play with so light-heartedly? No apprehension lingers over them shadow-like to warn them of what is before them, or to bid them pause ere it be too late, and take God into counsel and ponder upon the old question, "What doth it profit a man if he *gain* the whole world and suffer the loss of his soul." The image of the creature shuts out the Creator; the eyes of the man's mind are rivetted upon the girl's good looks, her accomplishments, her musical laugh and fascinating manners, the piquancy of her conversation, the amiability of her temper—even the elegance of her dress and the good taste of her toilet. The eyes of the girl are fixed upon similar superficial attractions in the young man.

These, then, are the chief factors in their resolutions—I had almost said, the only ones. And yet all the time perhaps there is one thing forgotten—and by far the most important thing of all—the religion of that person upon whom the choice of marriage has fallen. She has many qualities to win admiration, but there is one blank, one dificiency, for which all these good qualities cannot compensate, the want of the gift of faith. This misfortune, this flaw, is almost overlooked, it occurs to the mind last of all. It counts as nothing against personal graces and gifts. And yet, good God! what does such a marriage mean? It means two hearts indissolubly linked that can never thoroughly comprehend each other. It means distance, coldness, and incapacity for sympathy on the subject of Religion—a subject whose influence should pervade every action, intertwine itself with the very tissue of the thoughts, and mould and model the whole character—a subject which, as life lengthens out through successive years, and the judgment approaches, ought to assume to the well-constituted mind, a greater and greater magnitude and importance. It means mysteries and puzzles, found by each of the couple in countless habitual actions, performed by the partner, and unexplained by an intelligent appreciation of early training. It means, accordingly, a mutual distrust at the best; and an uneasy sense that complete harmony can never be, since the two lovers are pitched in different keys. It means that where each should be, in all respects, a support and a source of fortitude to the other, they are each left to pursue, in the region of religious thought and feeling, their own path, alone and unfriended by the other—perhaps without even a breathing of good-will, nay, with positive repugnance and aversion. No matter, then, under what happy auspices a mixed marriage may be celebrated, in general such a union justifies the words of the poet:

> "It is the little rift within the lute,
> That by and bye will make the music mute,
> And, ever widening, slowly silence all."

What a world of misery would be saved, beloved Brethren, if men and women did but recognise the truth that marriage is a most sacred contract, that it should be approached with feelings of reverence and piety, and not treated as something profane or indifferent, a speculation or a source of excitement; that to it the maxim should apply "Sancta sancte tractanda," "Holy things should receive holy treatment"; that it belongs to God's providence to order matrimony for the eternal welfare of those who contract it; that it therefore behoves those who contemplate marriage to do what in them lies to make that union pleasing and acceptable in the sight of God, lest it should be a bar, and not an aid, to sanctification. How diametrically opposed to this rational and Christian conduct is the practice, unfortunately so common, of drifting into matrimonial engagements with non-Catholics, as if religion had nothing to do with marriage; and awaking to the fact that the Church disapproves of such alliances, only when the hour approaches which is fixed for the fulfilment of the promise. No director is consulted until it becomes agony for the parties to burst the fetters which they have forged link by link. The advice of parents or of prudent friends is not asked till it is too late. Perhaps—God forgive them—if the parents *were* asked, they would be too blinded by questions of worldly interest and domestic convenience to interpose the barrier of their authority between their child and a guilty match. And yet oftentimes (I say it solemnly in God's presence) it would be better for those parents to see the murderer's knife plunged into the breast of the child, and to be dabbled with the heart's blood of the dying victim, than to follow his steps, or hers, to a union that fate was to link with lifelong suffering, persecution, and sorrow.

Yes, beloved Brethren, disguise it not from yourselves, be you the contracting parties in such marriages, or be you their unhappy parents, in many cases God has tied up the punishment with the act, and retribution follows this neglect of the question of religion in marriage as day follows night. I venture to say that if a Catholic, on the eve of marrying a non-Catholic, were to see the days of married life unfolded in some magic mirror, which had the power of imaging forth the future, in countless cases, notwithstanding the lateness of the warning and the fascination of the time, they would start back in horror at the sight, and abjure as they would the fellowship of asps and dragons the contemplated union. For what would they see? Witness if I lie, the tears, and sighs, and pining misery of many and many a Catholic within the circuit of this motley city, yea, within the limits of this small parish. What would they see? They would see the love of their non-Catholic partner, for whom they had slighted their God and made little of their faith, grow gradually, perhaps abruptly, cold, until scarce the embers of the old fondness remained; they would see the peremptory gesture that forbade attendance at the Sunday's Mass and Benediction; they would see the look of hatred that was called up by the sight of Crucifix or rosary beads; they would be horrified at the brutal and ribald jest that greeted the mention of monk or nun or priest; they would witness the outburst of scorn and rage with which the laws of abstinence were scouted from the house, the gibing word or blasphemous oath that hailed morning or evening prayers when opened and closed with the Sign of the Cross. Worse than this. They would see the hand of that lover, now so gentle and smiling, and lavish of endearments and full of promises, raised to strike her to whom he had made show of giving his heart and pledging his undying devotion, because she persisted in the practice of the faith which he had solemnly promised to respect.

The mother would see the little ones, that ought to have formed a new link between husband and wife, made instruments of cruel severance and disunion by being taught to execrate her religion, as idolatry and superstition; and as the gulf expands between them and her, she offers her life for them in vain. They are gone from her! Lost to her and to heaven for evermore! Or, if the man be the Catholic, he sees in this mystic glass, that foreshadows the future, how, in his unavoidable absence from home, his own children are alienated by slow degrees and withdrawn by insidious devices from the faith that he reveres, and that he would fain root in their heart of hearts; he sees his little ones taught most cunningly to deceive him as to what is going on; he recognizes that the principle attributed to so many Catholics by their enemies—to do evil, "good may come of it"—is practised most shamelessly by the demure evangelical; for his own children play the hypocrite to his face, and by most unblushing lies, mislead him, until the work of the proselytizing demon is done—and the souls of his offspring are lost for ever to the faith of their fathers.

Think not, beloved Brethren, that I am inventing, or even exaggerating. The identical case is under my own cognizance.

It has occurred not two miles from this spot, with aggravations of treachery and faithlessness, too uninviting to dwell upon.

But you will say, beloved Brethren, that these are extreme types. Would to God they were impossible, would to God they were even uncommon. It is the priest alone who knows in how many cases the Catholic woman, who has taken a non-Catholic partner, has chosen, not a husband, but a tyrant; in how many cases she has taken upon her not so much the yoke of marriage, as a persecution; in how many cases her home becomes a realm, where the penal laws rage again, because of religion, though mutilation and summary death are not included in the code. Many is the household in this city, where the picture of God's Mother must be hidden away; where the Rosary—the blessed medal, the Agnus Die, must be kept carefully out of sight, lest it should be the signal for blasphemies and perhaps blows; where the ejaculation of prayer must be smothered on the lips, or given to the air in inaudible whispers; where a mother's yearning benediction is breathed timidly over her child, lest, perversely taught as it is, it should maliciously report the crime to the brutal bigot, who rules the house with a rod of iron. And this, alas, is the sequel to a courtship in which the man's soul went forth a thousand times to that poor woman in warm impassioned vows, and tender promises, that made distrust or misgiving seem to her an enormity, as she turned to scorn every warning hinted to her by discreet and well-meaning friends. The tears flow amain, as she thinks of that period of fond delusion and short-lived folly; and the prospect of death itself seems fairer than that retrospect of betrayal and falsehood.

Yet, beloved Brethren, sad as this picture is, that magic mirror would reveal to some a more melancholy sequel still. Terrible is that picture of domestic tyranny, of isolated suffering and persecution, endured for justice sake; but far worse, far more awful, is the picture of a household in which religion is cast off like an ill-fitting garment. Mass and the Sacraments are abjured for the sake of a fatal and accursed harmony; the conscience of the Catholic is drugged and drowned until in its lethargy it feels no more the stings of remorse; this numbness and insensibility gradually lead to a settled callousness that no grace can penetrate; and the end of all is a reckless glorying in the comforts and diversions and joys of this life, and that delusive happiness that says "Peace! peace! when there is no peace."

Oh, most hideous fate in the sight of God and His holy angels! more appalling a thousand times than the scenes of violence and brutality, persecution and even bloodshed that leave the sense of religion unimpaired in the breast of the Catholic and his conscience alive to the dictates of duty; or, rather, that preserve and strengthen the gift of faith in the soul of the erring one, and fill it with the penitential sorrow that blots out past sin. Hideous picture! I say, but more hideous still when its remote consequences are contemplated; children growing up either indifferent to religion or attached to a false creed; unchecked, unguided by word or work on the part of the Catholic parent, and deriving from that parent's example only lessons of unmitigated worldliness, a passion for this fleeting life, and a complete oblivion of the estimate of things beyond the grave. And so the scene moves swift, age comes, and death; as the tree leans it falls; and the summing up is this: Give that sinful body to the slime of the earth; bury that renegade Catholic without hope; he is of the earth, earthy. Their whole career cannot be better described than in the inspired words of holy Job:—"Why do the wicked live, why are they advanced and strengthened with riches, their seed continueth before them, a multitude of kinsmen and of children's children in their sight, their houses are secure and peaceable, and the rod of God is not upon them, their little ones go out like a flock and their children dance and play. They take the timbrel and the harp and rejoice at the sound of the organ. They spend their days in wealth, and in a moment they go down into hell."—*Job* xxi. 7-13.

THE LEAFY MONTH OF JUNE.

WE have now reached that interesting period of the year, beloved Brethren, when Nature, at the call of her Master, rises, as it were, from her bier, with every function and every grace of life restored to her. Many months she lay, grim and death-like, rigid, still, and cold; the wild blasts of winter singing dirges over her grave. But He has spoken the word of might, who said: "I am the Resurrection and the Life," and once again the earth reveals the fulness of her teeming energies, and throbs with the pulsations of a fresh youth. We have just entered on the "leafy month of June," as a poet, who loved nature, happily designated it; a month which the Church has dedicated to the Sacred Heart of our Blessed Lord, the source of every goodly leaf, and flower, and fruit that adorns the souls of men. As we grow older, I suppose that the changes of the year, with all their shifting pomp and pride and circumstance, possess for many of us a greater and greater fascination, are awaited with livelier expectation, and elicit from us a warmer sympathy than in our earlier days. But be we ever so young, sentiments of joy, and of thankfulness to the bounteous Creator of the world, must spring up within us as we behold the earth, which seemed dead, revive into such exuberant bright and tumultuous life again; as if once more our Blessed Lord had said: "She is not dead, but sleepeth." We must all, I say, young or old, feel our share of the universal gladness. When our eyes rest upon the vivid green of the new-clothed trees in their prime; when we see the thousand quaint and beauteous grasses, flowers, and shrubs lifting themselves out of unsightly nooks, which we little suspected, perhaps, of harbouring such treasures; when we mark the blue of the sky, splendid as a new-woven and unworn garment; when we behold the sweep of the fertilizing showers amongst the new vegetation, or listen to the lark as it soars away in ecstasy skyward, like the soul of the good man released from the trammels of the body—we must be indeed insensible if we do not feel ourselves part and parcel of a glorious system, in every wheel of which there is evidence of a loving Artificer, who has bent fondly over His work, and has left the touch of a master hand upon all its parts. We must recognise everywhere—in the heavens and on the earth, on hill and in hollow, in the swift, hurrying stream, and on the palpitating sea—the generosity and love of that heart which has planned it all for our gratification and behoof, and as a type and promise of more bewitching scenes to come. Yes! to the thoughtful mind of the man of faith, every bud and leaf and blossom, every reach of azure above his head, every dark procession of rain-charged clouds, which do but frown in sport upon the land they foster, as a loving nurse makes faces at a babe—all the myriads of fair things that compose the visible world—are as so many tongues giving praise to their Maker, and inviting us to join in the chorus of gratitude. To our lips—as we cast our eyes around—come instinctively the words of the Psalmist, who in his own day felt intensely what I now strive feebly to express, "Let all Thy works, O Lord, praise Thee, and let Thy saints bless Thee. Sing ye to the Lord with praise, sing to our God with the harp. Who covereth the heaven with clouds, and prepareth rain for the earth. Who maketh grass to grow on the mountains, and herbs for the service of men." All these things are not servants of man alone—created to minister to his wants and to delight his senses—but they are servants of God also, who day and night seem to upbraid us for our thanklessness and our forgetfulness of our Benefactor, though He has enriched us with gifts far transcending theirs. Well might the good old monk, in his solitary walk, strike with his staff the little flowers which bordered his path, and which lifted their brilliant heads in the sunshine, and from their scented cups, as from so many thuribles, poured forth the incense of their worship to the sky: "Be silent," said he, playfully, as he smote them one after another, "be silent, ye pretty little children of God. I know you are chiding me for my callousness and my want of gratitude to our common Creator. Too well do I deserve your rebuke. May He who made me teach me to be thankful as you."

Now consider, beloved Brethren, the vast and unfathomed wisdom, the all-comprehensive grasp of intellect, and the unsleeping vigilance which are called into operation in the reconstruction, year by year, in their unnumbered species—without mistake, flaw, or omission—of all the leaves and blossoms which go to form the beauty of each successive summer. Look at the marvel from an arithmetical point of view. Which of you will count the lines that are engraven, or the veins that are embossed, upon a single leaf, let alone the leaves of a whole track of forest? Which of you will reckon up the blades of grass upon a single meadow, let alone the herbage of the unmeasured mountain? But how if we stretch our imaginations from a hillside to a county, from a county to a province, from a province to a whole country, from a country to a continent, from a continent to the entire acreage of the earth! Yet bear this in mind. Unlike the sands of the seashore, whose multitudinous array staggers and bewilders the fancy, every leaf and every blossom, though it be not endowed with reason, is, nevertheless, a living thing. Like man himself, every leaf and every blossom has, by God's eternal decree, its conception and its birth, its infancy and its prime, its decay and its death. Every leaf and every blossom is planned with as much forethought and care, is launched into existence with as much deliberation, is fed as daintily from the sap of the parent trunk, is enriched as sedulously by shower and dew and sunshine, as if it were the only object of its kind which had been produced by the hand of God, and had a title to His attention. Every leaf and every flower is as truly distinctive in its features, as truly individual in its fashioning, as any given man is distinct and recognisable among all the members of the race who have gone before him, and all who are to follow him to the end of time.

What inexhaustible fertility of design does this variety in nature's plan attest? Look at the artist—be he poet or painter or sculptor. If he does but produce some well-discriminated types of character before he begins to repeat himself and to degenerate into mannerism, he is lauded to the skies; his creations, as they are called, are the wonder of his fellow creatures. But now turn your thoughts from the human intellect—which, however richly endowed, is, nevertheless, limited and circumscribed—to the Eternal, the infinite mind of God! Behold how it multiplies its endless billions of varied creations in every region of life, so that, like the elaborate pages of some illuminated manuscript upon which the artist toiled to vary his design from page to page, the diversity of its creations defies every effort of human ingenuity to detect a single instance which shows identity of design or barrenness of invention. And what shall we say of that all-seeing, all-arranging, all-mastering Providence, which watches over every humble blade of grass, every insignificant flower of the field, with a care as concentrated as if it were absolutely exclusive? What shall I say of that Providence which spreads so prodigally, not only in spots frequented by man, but even in sequestered hollows among the wild mountains which have never found their way into a map, the mantle of its verdure and the fairy network of its floral decoration? Even as I speak, amid far seas, upon lonely islands, whose shores have seldom felt the indentation of a keel or echoed to the tones of a human voice; in sunny solitudes, whose silence is broken only by the cries of unknown sea birds, or the sound of gurgling waves, or the tumult of an occasional tempest, the kind and benignant work of the Creator is being carried on as elaborately, as ceaselessly, as indefatigably, from season to season, as in the most favoured bowers and gardens, which court the admiring eyes of the civilised and cultured world.

No wonder then, beloved Brethren, that in all ages, the world of leaves and flowers has been regarded with warm sympathy by mankind, because it furnished forth a reflection and an image of his own transitory destiny. The oldest and the greatest of heathen poets has drawn out the comparison between man and the leaf upon the tree, in his own sweet and powerful manner, when he says by the mouth of one of his heroes: "As is the race of leaves, so is the race of man. Some leaves the blast strews upon the earth, while others again the blooming wood produces. So with the race of men; one generation of men passes away, and another springs up to take its place." And the same thought is expressed even more powerfully by the Psalmist:—"Man's days are as grass," says he; "as the flower of the field, so shall he flourish. For thy spirit shall pass in him, and he shall not be, and his place shall know him no more."

Thus, beloved Brethren, every leaf and flower whispers its own "memento mori." Every leaf and flower says to us: "Remember, man, that thou art dust, and into dust thou shalt return." And by an easy transition, it carries our thoughts forward to that day when the whole universe will be sunk in ruin; and in the depths of our souls, the Psalmist's solemn and sublime words echo plaintively: "In the beginning, O Lord, Thou foundedst the earth, and the heavens are the works of Thine hands. These shall pass, but Thou remainest; and all of them shall grow old as a garment. And as a vesture Thou shalt change them, and they shall be changed; but Thou art always the self-same, and Thy years shall not fail."

In the sermon on the Mount, beloved Brethren, which you will find in St. Matthew's Gospel, Our Blessed Lord exhorts the multitudes, who have gathered around Him, to trust in the Providence of God; and beautifully enforces His lesson by calling our attention to the care which is bestowed upon the birds of the air, and the flowers of the field—creatures infinitely less valuable in the sight of God. Man, He says, has two principal wants to supply. He requires food, and he requires clothing. About these things he ought not to be too anxious; because, if he is faithful in the performance of his duty to God, God will not fail to supply these necessities. If God's Providence feeds the birds, is it likely to allow man to perish? Does not the Divine power watch over your growth to maturity through all the stages of helpless infancy and dependent youth, when you are absolutely unable, by any contrivance of your own, to maintain that growth? And will Providence neglect to provide vesture for man, His own immortal child, when He clothes the flowers of the field in such radiant, delicate, and many-hued garments? But listen, beloved Brethren, to Our Blessed Lord's own words:—

"Be not solicitous for your life, what you shall eat, nor for your body, what you shall put on. Is not the life more than the meat, and the body more than the raiment? Behold! the birds of the air. For they neither sow, nor do they reap, nor gather into barns, and your heavenly Father feedeth them. Are not you of much more value than they? And which of you, by taking thought, can add to his stature one cubit? And for raiment, why are ye solicitous? Consider the lilies of the field, how they grow; they labour not, neither do they spin. But I say to you that not even Solomon, in all his glory, was arrayed as one of these. And if the grass of the field, which is to-day, and to-morrow is cast into the oven, God doth so clothe, how much more you, O ye of little faith? Be not solicitous, therefore saying, what shall we eat, or what shall we drink, or wherewith shall we be clothed. For after all these things do the heathens seek. For your Father knoweth that you have need of these things. Seek ye, therefore, first, the kingdom of God, and all these things shall be added unto you."

To this lesson, which is inculcated by Our Blessed Lord, beloved Brethren, I will venture to add another. You know it oftentimes happens that Christians are discouraged and despondent, because they find that, although they make serious efforts to amend their lives, their faults, and shortcomings, and vices, cling to them. They lose heart because week after week, or month after month, they present themselves at the tribunal of penance with the self-same catalogue of sins.

Now even this absence of visible progress ought not to make us too nervous. It is better for us to fix our eyes upon our present duties, and to strive to perform them diligently, than to be too intent upon scanning our past life, and forecasting our future dangers. Perhaps this very deficiency in sensible advancement, is one of the means provided by your kind Maker to prevent your falling back; because you would be likely, perhaps, to put down too much to your own merits; and so, losing humility, you would lose all. While, therefore, a reasonable attention to past, and a reasonable anticipation of the difficulties of the future is commendable, our best course is to devote ourselves with great diligence to the means of salvation, and to leave the rest to God. These means are—first, the avoidance of all occasions of sin; secondly, perseverance in prayer; and thirdly, the frequentation of the Sacraments. He who adopts these means will be in the position of the man whose will is in the law of the Lord, and of whom the Psalmist says: "He shall be like a tree, which is planted near the running waters, which shall bring forth its fruit in due season. And his leaf shall not fall off, and all whatsoever he shall do, shall prosper."

"COELI ENARRANT GLORIAM DEI."

("The Heavens show forth the Glory of the Lord.")
18th Psalm.

AS every touch, beloved Brethren, in the composition of a masterly picture witnesses to the excellence of the painter's hand, so does every object in creation, from the greatest to the least, exhibit the impress of God's wisdom and God's power. The vast array of burning orbs, that stud the firmament on a clear night, are recognized from age to age as a proclamation, which pierces to the extremity of the universe, of the majesty and glory of Him who lit them and fixed them in their places, marks out their several paths, and superintends without effort their regular and harmonius action. With the Psalmist, every wise man, who lifts his eyes to that star-glittering canopy, must cry out, in the depth of his admiration and awe: "The heavens show forth the glory of God, and the firmament declareth the work of His hands. Day to day uttereth speech, and night to night showeth knowledge"; that is, when one day dies, another takes up the hymn of God's praise, and every night that darkens over the earth brings fresh evidence of God's matchless being. "There are no speeches nor languages where their voices are not heard; their sound hath gone forth unto all the earth, and their words unto the end of the world."

It was the silent but convincing language uttered by the stars, and so beautifully described in this passage of the inspired writer, that made the great heathen orator and thinker, Cicero, exclaim: "Who can scan the heavens, and be guilty of such folly as to deny that there is a God?"

But, beloved Brethren, while the imagination is so deeply impressed by the stupendous fields of space which are traversed by those worlds, that shine in such hushed and orderly array above and around us, while we are absorbed in speechless wonder at the power that hung them, thus huge, in moving myriads over the length and breadth of the great vault of heaven, we are apt to forget that the smallest insect that buzzes in the air is an important addition to the great orchestra that sounds forth the praises of God, the Author and Ruler of the Universe. Every tiniest insect, indeed, inasmuch as it possesses within its atom-like frame the breath of living sense and the spring of living motion, is even a more marvellous specimen of the divine skill and omnipotence than all those billions of inanimate spheres that spangle the firmament. Even the animalcules, whose bodies are so microscopic that battalions of them can stream on the current of the air through the eye of a needle, are witnessing, in the swarming of their unimaginable multitude and the lightning-like rapidity of their birth and extinction, to the fertility of the Supreme Mind, the type and donor of all life, with an eloquence actually surpassing the majestic harmonies of the spheres. In the kindling of the brief consciousness that links them for the fraction of a second with the generations of their kind, past and to come, they are a better image and representation, than the stars themselves, of the living perfections of that Being, who described himself to Moses, as Jehovah, which signifies— "I am who am."

But the visible creation, beloved Brethren, has its crowning glory in man, and in man's nature God's being finds its noblest reflection and its worthiest exponent. Man's twofold constitution, the material and the spiritual, are masterpieces of the creative mind. Mixed as he is of earthly elements, he is a flower that opens out its perfections and develops its beauties before it sinks again into the mould from which it borrowed its substance. But that visible nobility and grace is joined to an unseen spirit, which within it speaks and moves and acts, and raises the whole creature into a new order of being to which no flower can claim kindred. Behold, a union so delicate yet so strong, so intimate and yet so free from confusion, as to bespeak a power beyond limit in accomplishing it. The body alone, with its senses, all so like in the substance of their organs, yet so different in the effect they produce —for sight is a different world from hearing, and hearing from smell—the body, with its multitudinous swathing of nerves and sinews, its blent composition of solids and liquids, and tissues variously endowed for the work of life, its free and unembarrassed exercise of a thousand unobserved forces put in motion by every act, and almost in every breath—is itself a nobler work than all the system of the heavenly bodies, the poising of their weights, the adjustments of their courses, and the beauty of their changeless illumination. But, admirable as is the mechanism of the body, the soul, which is not open to the blade of the dissecting-knife, is a thousand times more subtle and intricate, and more worthy of the hand that made it. Unlike the body, it defies, instead of inviting, the agencies of corruption, because its substance is one and spiritual, and therefore not resolvable into parts nor amenable to destruction, save by the withdrawal of God's support, which would be as an edict of annihilation. It wields a vast panoply of powers, that makes it little less than the angels, and raise their owner into the category of a god, as the scripture says: "You are gods, and all of you sons of the Most High." With its perception and intellect it can penetrate beneath the outer shell and surface of the world, and pierce deep into the inmost meanings and purposes and causes of things. It is consumed in its depths with an insatiable passion for the truly good and the truly beautiful, which all the blind groping and mistaken ambitions of a fallen nature cannot obliterate, nay, to which they all point. Above all, that soul, with its glimpses of the undimmed reason of the Creator as its beacon-light, and its disappointed longing after perfection in the midst of the shortcomings and harassing discomfitures, and the weary clanking of the chain of evil habit, has the God-like faculty of the will, by which it can turn itself hither and thither at pleasure, choose this course or that, as best squares with its sense or its inclination, and is thus in a position to offer to its Maker what no other work of His hand less than man can offer Him, the homage of a sentient, intelligent, loving, free and unshackled nature.

And this is why, beloved Brethren, from amidst the flames of the great furnace, the Hebrew children, in their noble canticle, called upon all creation to give glory to God, beginning with things inanimate, and rising through the various grades of living things till they reach humanity—the acme of created life in this visible world. "Bless the Lord, ye heavens; bless the Lord, ye sun and moon; bless the Lord, ye stars of heaven; fire, hail, snow, ice, stormy winds that fulfil His word, beasts and all cattle, serpents and feathered fowls, every shower and dew and breath of the Lord, fire and heat and cold, frost and snow, night and day, light and darkness, lightnings and clouds ; let the earth bless the Lord, let it praise and exalt Him above all for ever. Bless the Lord, ye mountains and hills ; all things that grow on the earth ; the fountains, the seas and rivers ; whales and all creatures that move in the waters ; the birds of the air, beasts and cattle ; and, last of all, ye sons of the Lord bless the Lord, let Israel bless the Lord, let it praise Him and exalt Him above all for ever."

Willingly or unwillingly then, beloved Brethren, man, as a piece of matchless handiwork, must give glory to God, as testifying to His matchless mind, just as the flower does that lives through its stages of unconscious beauty and fragrance. But when man rules all the movements of his body and all the acts of his soul in accordance with the law of his Maker, then indeed his being is precious in the sight of God, and the sacrifice he offers of the fruits of his noble gifts is most acceptable to Him who gave them. The high value of such tribute paid to our Creator it would be most criminal to depreciate. Perhaps we should strive more earnestly to make the powers of soul and body minister to God's honour, if we thought more frequently how high is the price He sets upon the homage of our nature, and how much He longs to receive it Grievous is the wrong we do Him in squandering the gifts which that nature includes, for we rob Him of the fruits of that highest gift amongst them—our free affection and our free will. It is, I say, a monstrous robbery, the plunder of a property most highly esteemed by its owner. Let not the sinner think that in throwing himself away, he who inflicts the ruin is the only one to lose by it. However he may undervalue that being which he abuses, there is One, its Framer, Who cannot regard it as otherwise than most precious and valuable. "The works of Thy hands, O Lord, Thou wilt never despise."

To walk thus blamelessly in the sight of God, and to control from day to day the manifold machinery of our being according to the dictates of reason and of religion, is a grander exhibition of the divine power, working through frail elements and devious forces, than all the order and splendour of the heavenly bodies. Let us not then imagine that we are offering a trifling gift to the Almighty, if we offer him the thoughts, words, and actions of the most ordinary, commonplace, and undistinguished life : provided only we are struggling at all times to live in conformity with his commandments. We are offering him his own work, a work which cannot be less than divine. So that we ought to take courage, and say with the Psalmist: Bless the Lord, my soul, and let all things that are in me praise the name of the Lord."

Let such be the morning consecration, by which we dedicate to Him all the movements of our whole being during the day.

But such is the perverse, downward tendency of our corrupt nature, beloved Brethren, that unless we frequently turn our to God, and solicit His aid, something will surely go away in the intricate machinery of soul and body, of which we are appointed overseers. Though we should do our best, there will be some imperfection; but this will be readily forgiven on the score of our good will by our merciful Creator, " who knows," says the Scripture, "what is in us." And such imperfections will weigh the lighter against us, if we from time to time make to God an oblation of every thought, word and action, which we perform, and even of the mechanical and involuntary movements of soul and body; dedicating to His service, as far as in us lies, every outcome of the nature He has bestowed upon us, and making His, by an act of our will, everything He has given, even to the breath we draw. To this end, we ought never to omit our morning and evening prayers, with the consecration to God of our whole being, which those prayers should include. This consecration will make holy whatever you do during the day or the night; it will be as the portion of frankincense which is sprinkled in the burning bowl of the censor, which will continue, even when our thoughts are otherwise engrossed, to mount up in fragrant wreaths to heaven. It will stamp every act, from the greatest to the least, with the seal of prayer, and make it efficacious in God's sight for our welfare, and for the advantage of our brethren, who are united to us in the communion of saints. It will enable us, without effort, to comply with the precept of the Apostle: " Whether you eat or drink, or whatever else you do, do all for the glory of God." It will be a fulfilment of his exhortation to the Thessalonians: " Pray always." It will be a ceaseless communing with God, and a preparation for a holy death. Was it not because this method of self-consecration to God was habitual with him, that St. Charles Burrowmeo, when playing a game of chess with a friend, on being asked what he would do if he knew that he was presently to die, answered without hesitation: "I would finish the game. I began it for God's honour; and for God's honour I would complete it." Thus reasonable recreation, undertaken for the refreshment of the mind, or from a motive of charitable complaisance, is made, by this practice of constant self-oblation, an action so holy and so pleasing to God, that we need no more fitting prelude to immediate death.

But if, beloved Brethren, we are drawn to God by the bonds of pure love, we shall not be content with our morning and evening prayer, and their accompanying acts of dedication. A lover is not satisfied with occasional and formal calls upon the object of his devotion. And so, if we love God, God will often be in our thoughts; our hearts will often turn to Him in the midst of our most absorbing occupations. He is kind enough to leave His door open to us; so that at any moment we may place ourselves in His presence. In His kindness He allows us an interview at any moment we claim it; instead of wearying, we delight Him, by our importunity. Remember the effect of pure love upon St. Ignatius, when, in his thirty-third year, he began the study of grammar, to prepare himself for his high vocation. The thought of God was so inextricably wrought into the texture of his mind, that it obtruded itself in all his studies, and made him for a time incapable of remembering his lessons; so that in conjugating the Latin verb, "Amo," (for example) he would find himself repeating: "I love God, I am loved by God."

And thus we have good reason to suspect ourselves of coldness, if we do not recall God to mind occasionally during the day. For this purpose we should adopt some ejaculation which calls forth our feelings of devotion and fervour. "Jesus, Mary, Joseph, I offer you my heart and my soul," &c., or, "O sacred heart of Jesus, I implore," &c.; these are amongst the golden aspirations which are constantly going up to heaven from many a Christian heart, out of the workshop and the office, from the college and the school, from the kitchen and the nursery, from the docks and the barracks, and away upon the heaving sea, amidst rough winds and dangerous breakers. With the old solitaries that peopled the sands of Egypt we are told that the favourite ejaculation was: "Incline unto my aid, O God; O Lord, make haste to help me." No more pithy, beautiful, or effective petition could be framed than that which formed the sole prayer, day and night, of the rock-entombed Penitent in former days: "Qui plasmasti me, miserere mei! O Thou who didst make and mould me take pity on me." The more these brief petitions are uttered the more is our life sanctified, the more copious is the influx of grace, the greater is the tribute which our being pays to its Creator—as a tree beside the running waters—the higher is the eminence, the nobler the dignity, the more stupendous the reward to which we raise ourselves for all eternity.

Oh, beloved Brethren, if we did but understand this, our lips would be constantly moving in prayer like a good Redemptorist Father whom I remember from my boyhood. He was then preparing for the priesthood, after a youth more remarkable for innocent mischief than for thoughtful piety, for he was not at the time conscious that God would call him to minister at the altar. He was almost suddenly seized with a spirit of gravity, of solid virtue, of unostentatious self-denial, of studious application, which transformed him into a model for the ecclesiastics of the house. And well I remember how we boys used to watch him as he ushered us into the study hall, dangling his keys in an absent manner, and his lips perpetually moving in prayer, while his eyes were quite blind to the things about him. The result was that he maintained order less by his vigilance and severity than by our respect for his sanctity. God rest his soul! He joined the Congregation of St. Liguori, and after edifying all who had the happiness to know him, went contented and happy to an early grave, and now doubtless is praying in heaven for the college that educated him and the order that gave him to God.

If we had this spirit of prayer, beloved Brethren, we should seize with avidity every opportunity of praising God directly and indirectly; frequently inweaving in our conversation, where we could do it without seeming affected, "God be praised," "Thanks be to God," "God grant"; or recalling the dead, "God be with them," or "God rest their souls." Parents would take every opportunity of saying to their children, "God bless you! God reward you! God guide you!"

CARE OF ORPHANS.

An Appeal in Aid of a Charitable Institute.

WE are made, beloved Brethren, in God's image and likeness: and our whole duty on earth may be summed up in one precept, viz.—to preserve and perfect that image and likeness to the utmost of our power, and according to the measure of our grace. God must imprint himself upon us so that men shall involuntarily say, in the words of Holy Scripture, "I have said: you are Gods, and all of you the sons of the Most High."—*Ps.* lxxxi. 6. Now there is no characteristic of God more conspicuous than His mercy; His mercy is over all His works.—*Ps.* cxliv. 9. And among the evidences of His mercy, there are few more striking than His love and tenderness towards the widow and the orphan. It was impossible for the Jews, with the commands and counsels of their Sacred Books before them, ever to forget the duty of comforting, succouring, and providing for the fatherless and the widow.

In the 145th Psalm, describing God as the sole foundation of all hope and confidence, the inspired writer says of Him: "The Lord keepeth the strangers, He will support the fatherless and the widow." In another Psalm, He is called the "Father of the orphan, and the Judge of widows." He puts Himself forward in all his heavenly might and majesty as their special champion, and the avenger of their wrongs. "You shall not," says He, in the Book of Exodus—xxii. 22—"hurt a widow or an orphan. If you hurt them, they will cry out to me, and I will hear their cry. And my rage shall be enkindled, and I will strike you with the sword, and your wives shall be widows; and your children fatherless." Nor is He content with placing the barrier and bulwark of His word between them and all ill-usage or outrage: He goes further. He bids His people to befriend and cherish them. In the book of Deuteronomy, when Almighty God lays down the time and manner of the celebration of the Feast of Weeks, and again of the Feast of Tabernacles—two of the three great annual solemnities with the Jews—He orders, amongst other things, that the fatherless, and the widow within their gates, shall be admitted to the gaieties, enjoyments, and banquets of the festive season.—xvi. xiv. 11. And again, God's compassion for His forlorn and destitute creatures comes out in other instructions given in the same book. He orders that any forgotten sheaf on their cornfield, after reaping, shall be left "for the fatherless and the widow to take away."—xxiv. 9. And in like manner that the remnants of fruit on the olive tree, after the time of gathering, and the remaining clusters of their vineyards, at the time of vintage, shall be their perquisite and consecrated portion.—xxiv. xx. 21. And to the fulfilment of this command He attaches a most desirable promise—that He himself will bless those who obey "in all the works of their hands."—xxiv. 19.

In the book of Isaias, again, after expressing in tones of awful indignation the disgust and nausea inspired by their carnal and heartless rites and oblations, "Offer sacrifice no more in vain; incense is an abomination to Me. My soul hateth your new moons, and your solemnities."—i. xiii. 14. He goes on to lay down the conditions on which His erring and guilty people shall be forgiven; and among them is the duty of charitable deeds to His destitute children: "Judge," says He, "for the fatherless, defend the widow."—i. 17. And He pledges Himself that if they do so, though their sins should be red as scarlet, they shall be made as white as "snow"; and if they be red as crimson, they shall be white as "wool."—i. 18.

These clear and definite directions in behalf of the widow and the orphan acquire ten times more emphasis and importance, because of all the duties of life compassion for the destitute seems the least likely to be forgotten and the most powerfully inculcated by the dictates of our nature. One might think that God had so richly endowed our heart with pity for the needy and desolate that He might have afforded to leave the performance of our duty in this regard to our own humane impulses.

Men who might forget or evade the obligation of giving to God that public and private worship which is due to Him, as the Creator of the individual man, and the Artificer of the framework of society into which he is incorporate, would not be likely so soon to lose this sense of the kindness due to such objects of compassion. Yet Almighty God was not content with planting humanity in our hearts. He intensified our instinct of compassion by the explicitness of His commands, disentangled the precept of charity from all possible web of self-interest that might have obscured and smothered it, and added the tremendous sanction of His threatened vengeance, as well as the gracious pledges of remuneration and reward, to enforce His merciful designs.

And we, beloved Brethren, have to direct us not merely our reason, the dictate of our conscience, and the pulses of benevolence and pity which are common to all the seed of Adam; we have not only the will of God as contained in the Old Testament for our enlightenment and direction; but the words and example of the all-bountiful, the incarnate God. You know, beloved Brethren, our Lord bade us to love our neighbours as ourselves, and Himself set us the sublimest example of charity, by laying down His life, not for friends merely, but for the most rancorous and deadly enemies. But he made the standard precepts of charity more attractive, by impressing it upon, us that whatever kindness we do to His younger brethren in the flesh, and to the inferior members of His body, He would account as done to Himself in person. "He that receiveth you receiveth Me, and he that receiveth Me receiveth Him that sent Me."—(*St. Matt.* x. 40. "This is My commandment, that you love one another as I have loved you."—*St. John* xv. 12. "All the law is fulfilled in one word, 'Thou shalt love thy neighbour as thyself.'"—*Gal.* v. 14. "If any man say I love God, and hateth his brother; he is a liar."—I. *St. John* iv. 20. "We ought to imitate the charity of God, who came to give us life, not in return for love, but having first loved us."—1 *Ep. St. John* iv. 8, etc. And what He did He commands us to imitate.

Behold, then, the inducement and the recompense held out by our blessed Lord for your works of charity, tenderness, and pity; we place God Himself under obligation, make Him our debtor who is faithful to repay, and know that every act of bounty and compassion that proceeds from our hands finds its way to the Lover of our Souls, to Whom we owe so large a debt of gratitude, and soothes and delights Him amid the trials, slights, and injuries which He daily receives from His ungrateful brethren of the earth. What a wonderful stimulus is this to works of mercy and benignity! How powerful a motive does it furnish in particular for kindness to the orphan! For as surely as we take them by the hand, wipe the tears from their eyes, clothe their nakedness, assuage their hunger, quench their thirst, give them the shelter of a friendly roof, and place them in an asylum of security against the harassing wants of the body; so surely is it proclaimed to the heavenly hosts that you have succoured and sheltered the Babe of Bethlehem, and found Him in your hearts a refuge and a home. This idea, beloved Brethren, for all its beauty and grandeur, bears no tinge of false romance. It is Jesus Christ himself Who has expressly stated it. Listen to His own description of the last judgment. "Then shall the King say to them that shall be on His right hand: Come, ye blessed of My Father, possess you the kingdom prepared for you from the foundation of the world. For I was hungry and you gave Me to eat; I was thirsty and you gave Me to drink; I was a stranger and you took Me in; naked, and you covered Me; sick, and you visited Me; I was in prison and you came to Me. Then shall the just answer Him, saying: Lord, when did we see Thee hungry, and fed Thee; thirsty, and gave Thee drink? And when did we see Thee a stranger, and took Thee in; or naked, and covered Thee? or when did we see Thee sick or in prison, and came to Thee? And the King answering, shall say to them: Amen, I say to you as long as you did it to one of these, my least brethren, you did it to Me."—*St. Matt.* xxv. 34, etc.

Now, beloved Brethren, by contributing liberally towards the Orphanages which the Bishop and his clergy, with the co-operation of a pious and generous laity, have established to receive the poor orphans of our great towns, you are by one act performing all the works of mercy, spiritual as well as corporal. You are saving many a poor little helpless creature from the pangs of starvation and the fierce fever of thirst; you are lifting their weak and shivering frames out of the gutter, and placing them, comfortably clad, smiling and joyous, in homes of light and cleanliness; far from the drenching shower and biting wintry blast. Nay, more: you are ransoming the captive; for what was left to the poor creature you have rescued, but bondage to ignorance, passions and vice; the heavy chains of corrupt influence weighing them down beyond the power to rise; a life of infamy, perhaps, and a death of shame and despair.

And oh! beloved Brethren, if you should be still callous or indifferent to the calls of humanity, turn to the alternative picture which the dreary world presents, and the daily records of the country exhibit. Conjure up in your imagination the vision—alas, no empty dream—of the young ruined girl who, after her brief sum of illusions, after a few short draughts of pleasure—bitter-sweet God knows, and leaving heart-sickness behind, goes forth at last, with reeling brain and maddened pulse, and the inward hellfire of blasted hopes and affections she would fain forget, under the calm and silent stars of God. Onwards she hurries, with streaming hair, towards the dark and rushing river. Pausing a moment on the bridge, like an ebon monument, with scarce a prayer for mercy, reckless and frantic, she hurls herself into the cold wave, whose lapping sound, as it washes the piers of the bridge, is her only dirge and requiem. Nor say that this is an extreme picture. Would it were more exceptional. Perhaps the little neglected one—whom a rich man's spare coppers might save: yea, the money he spends on his cigars or his superfluous beverages—grows up amid the dregs and the refuse of our cities, with no one to take an interest in her, save that interest which selfishness inspires, with little or no schooling or instruction; how can she fail to come to maturity confirmed in evil habits, at best, but one degree above public disgrace—utterly undisciplined—a curser and swearer; a violent and irreclaimable virago; and a drunkard, whose evil end is foreshadowed in the very lines and hues of her dissipated face.

Ah, beloved Brethren, at the best, if you follow up the probable destiny of the neglected orphan, you will be led into tragedies and horrors which will make you bow your head with shame.

Think again, beloved Brethren, how many of the spiritual works of mercy you include in that one donation towards these refuges for the orphan! You instruct the ignorant; not merely in those secular branches of knowledge, and in those industrial employments which will promote their worldly interests in after life, but also in the truths and the practices of religion, which will form their safest anchor amid the tempests of the world, their best omen of success, and their greatest solace in failure. You not merely counsel the doubtful, but, through the medium of a Christian education, give them the source of life-long prudence and discretion. You comfort the sorrowful by placing the friendless and lonely in a sympathetic and sisterly relationship with good companions of her own age, by healing the wounds of grief and bereavement. What a grand complication of charitable deeds! Truly a seed cast into the ground that will bear fruit a hundredfold! Go into any orphanage of the town, and I venture to say you will be delighted to see the healthy faces and cheerful looks of the poor little ones, to whom God has been a father, and whom he has gathered, by the agency of the charitable, under the shadow of His wings, during the period of their helpless infancy and youthful peril. Look at their playrooms; inspect their workrooms; visit their sweet little chapel, that echoes to the orphans' grateful hymn; explore their clean and orderly dormitories; converse with the consecrated virgins who have given their lives to the good work; and you cannot but be gratified and deeply moved; you will be made of stone if you refuse your aid towards the support and development of so noble and so touching a charity.

You visit them in sickness and provide them with remedies towards their recovery or afford consolation, the ministrations of friendly hands, and the sound of friendly voices to soothe them in the hour of their departure. You perform the last offices of Christian piety to their inanimate clay, and lay them decently to rest in the shrine of a consecrated grave. "My son, shed tears over the dead and neglect not his burial."—*Eccles.* xxxviii. 16.

THE NATIVITY.

NOW that Christmas is at hand, beloved Brethren, it behoves us to consider what fruits we may reap from a due preparation for that great festival. The coming of the incarnate God into the world is a spectacle which cannot fail to increase every supernatural grace in the hearts in which God will reign. "Drop down your dews, ye heavens," cries the prophet, "and let the clouds rain the Just One." Yes! the coming of the Just One is as a heavenly dew that will freshen the thirsty earth, and make the desert places of our souls to blossom like the rose.

Consider then, with me this evening, how meditation upon the mystery of our Lord's birth must, if we are well disposed, intensify our faith, animate our hope, kindle our charity, and move us to the deepest contrition for our sins.

And first, this mystery must needs, by exercising our faith, develop and strengthen it. What is faith but believing without seeing? Blessed, said our Lord, are those who believe and do not see. Part of our regular trial in this life—a trial which the grace of God makes light for us—is that we cannot see the truth without surroundings of difficulty, without circumstances which in an evil and self-sufficient mind might lead to the triumph of doubt and unbelief. Wisely did God ordain it so, for as man fell by indulging the unhealthy yearnings of the intellect and humouring his curiosity in objects forbidden to him, so part of the allotted penalty entailed by his fault consists in our being forced to bend down our intellects into a posture of unquestioning submission and lowliest homage. The trial then derives its character from the fault of which it is the punishment. And the humility which is implied in faith is an act of reparation to our Creator for the offence of Adam in presumptuously seeking to raise himself to a knowledge beyond his sphere. Blessed, then, truly are those who do not see and yet believe, for they help to restore the glory of God impaired by the ambition of our first parents, and they consult their own eternal interests, by combating in their own souls the very vice which effected the downfall of the children of God, and ushered misery and death into the world.

Come, beloved Brethren, along with me, to the spot where your Saviour has but now been born; and let us see this mystery of faith, to which we have to bow down our intellects. It is the coldest season of the year in Judea; a season in which the day is often dark and squally, and marked with frequent rain and sleet, as in our own climate, and in which the nights are bitterly chill at the best, and often severe with nipping frosts. Hanging above us, on the ridge of a mountain-range that stretches towards the Northern Star, is that little city, of which the prophet fondly said that it was not the least among the princes of Judea; the city of Bethlehem, where David's eyes first saw the light, and where now a greater than David is born. In those fields, the minstrel-king began his chequered career by tending his father's flocks. We mount the rocky ascent, traced in lighter tint upon the whiteness of the surrounding cliff (for the stone all round is white); and enter the streets of the city. These, like the streets of most oriental towns, are narrow and somewhat irregular; but less so than those of more pretentious cities. As the winter blast sweeps round the corners and past the deep gateways, and storms round the cupolas, which rear their ghostly heads above us, the intense cold is enough to remind us that on this rocky platform, we stand two thousand five hundred feet above the sea. As it approaches midnight, notwithstanding the inclemency of the night air, and the lateness of the hour, the city still echoes to the feet of bustling slaves, whose masters have arrived during the day to register their names upon the census-list of the city of their origin; and twinkling lights, and the occasional sound of merry voices, show that a sheltering roof and well-lit hearth, on such a night, are apt to lengthen out the hours of watching. By degrees all sounds are hushed; and darkness and the whistling wind are our companions. If we turn our steps eastwards, and descend the brow of the rock, where now a fortress convent lifts itself defiantly into the air, as if challenging the prowling Arabs of the plain below, we see another light, dim and red and flickering, that issues from the mouth of a rude cavern, such as in the rocky regions of Judea are often utilized as stables. We stand at the unguarded doorway, and view that strange scene, which for all the long series of centuries, till the Saviour of the world comes as its judge, will haunt the imaginations of men, as a revelation of God's love, humility, gentleness, and compassion. By the glare of a wretched lantern, we trace the form of an elderly man, with silvered hair, bowed down in a posture of profound reverence; and a maiden, girlish, and modest, hanging in breathless admiration and rapture over an infant that lies wrapt in swadling clothes upon the straw-piled manger. In a mysterious light, that suffuses the little face, and faintly illumines the entranced features of the mother, we see a countenance which has something unearthly and fascinating, beyond the beauty of infancy itself. It is God made man. Here, in this crevice of the rock, where the ox and the ass house themselves from the bleakness of the seasons, He has of His own free will chosen to be born, having by His Providence arranged that the caravansary of the town should be full of guests, and every inn and lodging should be engaged. He came unto His own, and His own received Him not. At door after door, footsore and weary, that saintly man and his virgin charge had knocked in vain through the hours of the dying day, and far into the night: but there was no place found for the Creator; and David would have wondered to see Him, whom he called in spirit Lord, the rod which, according to the prophet Isaiah, was to come forth out of the root of (his father) Jesse, the flower that was to rise up out of his root—the deliverer, the Saviour, given to the world in so mean a place. But self-humiliation is the first and the last lesson of that Saviour's life; an outcast He is born; in a rock-hewn miserable stable borrowed for that august nativity; and an outcast will He die, in nakedness, upon the tree of shame; having been cast forth as an accursed thing, whose presence polluted the sacred city. He came into His own, and His own received Him not.

What say you then to this humble incarnation? Do not blink its difficulties. He who never had a beginning, consubstantial with the Father, begotten not made, by Whom all things are made that are made, was born a few moments ago into His own world. The Creator has become a creature, and has borrowed the flesh in which He clothes Himself from an earthly maiden, the work of

His own hands. Those swaddling-clothes fitted the Eternal Word. Those tiny hands, that show no larger than the pink rosebuds born amidst the first blushes of the year, are stronger than lightning or earthquake—they shaped the world, measured the abysses, and separated the ocean from the dry land. Through those eyes beams the everlasting wisdom of God.

Do these stupendous facts stagger our faith? No. God is truth, and truth has said it. The Word was made flesh. We bow our heads and humble our proud souls and cry out: We believe, O Lord, thanks be to Thee, through whom we believe; the Giver of all good gifts. Thanks be to Thee for ever, because Thou hast given us an opportunity of showing our submission to Thy truth by believing the word Thou hast uttered, though as yet our eyes are sealed to the overwhelming glory of Thy Son, which is now hidden beneath the veil of humanity, but which will one day be the reward of Thine elect in that kingdom where the Lamb is the only lamp that shines.

And what is the effect of the nativity upon the virtue of hope? Ah! what motives for hope does not that sight present? Come hither, ye whose courage flags and whose heart fails in the wearisome battle of life. Darkness no longer reigns. The sun has risen, the Orient from on high hath visited us. It is the signal for joy. The heavens ring with angelic hymns. Earth is illuminated not by the stars of night alone, nor by the red glare of the shepherds' watch fires, but by the radiant presence of multitudes of the heavenly spirits. And what is the hymn? Is it some awful chant that tells of fear and prostrate worship, a sound as of many waters that thrills the heart with a vague fear of that far land of holiness from which it comes! No, it is meant to cheer us, to fill us with confidence. It is a promise of reward for the perfect, for those who persecute the flesh like the Anchorites of old, young martyrs who die in torment; in short, for high and heroic virtue. It is a hymn intended for the ears of the meanest amongst us—the struggling, the weak, the wayworn, the despondent. It promises all good things; it promises the peace that passeth all understanding to those who are wishful and earnest, if feeble yet striving; if less ardent lovers of the Cross than might be, yet never losing the habit of mortification; if not all heavenly and all detached, yet weaned from an inveterate attachment to sin. "Glory to God on high, and on earth peace to men of good will."

Look at this mystery, in fine, beloved Brethren, in its relation to the virtue of charity The incarnation and birth of our Blessed Lord has been to the saints a source of unceasing admiration, and a neverfailing stimulus of love. And how could it be otherwise? It is not in human nature to look coldly upon those who have made great sacrifices for our welfare. Now what sacrifice can match this which our Lord makes in placing himself upon a level with us worms; in descending from heaven that he may raise us up to heaven; in assuming our nature with every thorn that surrounds it, save the sting of sin; in making himself our brother, flesh of our flesh, bone of our bone. It is logically impossible that such a sacrifice could ever be made except by God, because none but God can overstep the chasm which separates the finite from the infinite. "Greater love than this no man hath," said our Lord, "than that he should lay down his life for his friend." True indeed of human friends. But our Lord knew that He Himself had gone further still; for, urged by purest love, He had in a sense divested Himself of his Godhead, so far as He could do so without losing it, and shrunk His infinity into the shell of a human frame, "being in habit," says the Scripture, "found as a man." Let romancers spin their pretty fictions; no romancer's brain could imagine love like this, a love which brought, not some earthly monarch, with his train, to lay his all at the feet of a poor maid who hid her raggedness in a peasant's hovel; but a love which brought down the King of Kings and the Lord of Lords to share their infirmities with the poor, wretched, guilty, and perishing race of man, the unworthy and self-marred production of His hand. He humbled Himself, taking the form of a servant.

But even supposing the incarnation, beloved Brethren, it did not follow that our Lord should be born amidst such circumstances of humiliation as are revealed to us in his nativity. One miracle was not enough for Him, He heaps miracle on miracle, that He may overwhelm our incredulity and warm our cold hearts. Deep calls upon, deep truly, until even we, with our giddiness and our lukewarmness, our darkness of mind and callousness of heart, wonder at the gulfs and abysses into which His love bears Him. He might have sprung upon the earth full-formed and a marvel of human perfection; but no! He must assume the form of a helpless infant. And why? All from winsome affection, for He knows well the charm of infancy to soften the hardest natures with its innocent smiles. If the Lord of Hosts, then, comes as our little Prince of Peace, surely He will come in the bosom of some august and great old family, amidst imperial surroundings suited to His royal origin. Draw aside the veil, and behold the answer to your surmise, written upon the heartless straw-littered floor, written upon that strange cradle upon which His form reclines, written upon the mean swathing bands that enwrap Him; written upon the poor garb of His young mother; written upon the care-worn brow of the poor mechanic, His foster-father; proclaimed, in fine, by the presence of the two dumb animals, His only train of attendants. Why this absence of pomp and splendour, this poverty, this cheerlessness in every external circumstance? All from love, once more. All from that instinct which calls the rough, rude shepherds round His crib before the kings from the East, with their attendants and their train of camels, and their presents of spices and gold. All from love of the poor, the outcast, and the miserable, who chiefly need consolation; for this was the very sign that our Lord gave to St. John of his own divine mission. "The blind see, the lame walk, the lepers are cleansed, the deaf hear, the dead rise again, the poor have the Gospel preached to them. And blessed is he that shall not be scandalized in Me."—*Matt.* xi. 5-8.

THE EPIPHANY.

STRANGE, Brethren, is the vision which to-day's retrospect opens out to the mind's eye. The Holy City, the city of Jerusalem, presents an appearance of unwonted excitement, and the streets are filled with eager crowds, some of whom gather into knots in the squares and at the corners of the streets, while others, goaded by curiosity, hurry forwards in a noisy stream in one direction. If we join the moving throng we find ourselves at the gates of Herod's stately palace—one of the many sumptuous edifices with which the usurper from Idumaea has adorned the city of his adoption—and there behold the spectacle which has occasioned all this commotion. A magnificent cortege of mingled camels and mules, with gorgeously attired slaves controlling and guiding them, is coming to a halt near the entrance to the palace. Great is the bustle of the attendants, loud the neighing and snorting of the animals, which paw the ground impatiently under their variegated housings as the crowds of sightseers gather around them. Amidst this glittering cavalcade our eyes are rivetted upon three forms more commanding in their mein than the rest: one a venerable man with a flowing white beard and straggling locks of snowy hair escaping from his jewelled turban; then with him is a man in the prime of life, attired as regally as his elder companion, and commanding equal respect from the motley troop; and a dark-hued man, with sable beard, wearing the aspect of the race which, wherever it came from, is called by the popular name of Ethiopian. As these noble figures ascend to the hall of Herod a few of the rabble, moved by the novelty of the sight, raise a shout of applause, but these are soon hushed with angry scowls and words of contempt by the doctors of the law, the priests, and the pharisees.

Who are these strangers? Whence do they come? And on what errand are they bound? They are the three sages from the East, whose names shall live in tradition to the remotest times as Melchior, Gaspar, and Balthaser.

Eastwards from Jerusalem is their home; thirteen days journey from the sacred city, at the rate of travelling, which such an elaborate cortege would permit; probably (although it is controverted) from the rich lands of Arabia, whence the Queen of Sheba came to offer her tribute of admiration to King Solomon; and whence the Psalmist predicted that princes should come to adore the living Word of Wisdom, born of the Father, and incarnate in the world :—" The Kings of Tharsis, and the islands, shall offer presents, the Kings, Arabians, and of Saba shall bring gifts."— *Ps.* lxxi. 10. Balthaser, whose complexion is dark, as he shall in future times be depicted by painters, would seem to come from the selfsame shores of Arabia, from which sprang the queen who conferred with Solomon : and who, in the book of Kings, is styled Ethiop. All three are from a region not far, at any rate, from that Arabian region of Moab, in which Balaam predicted the great King and Deliverer, whose coming should kindle a new star in the sky :— "I shall see Him," cried this prophet, in his raptures, "I shall see Him, but not now; and shall behold Him, but not near."

A star shall rise out of Jacob, and a sceptre shall spring up from Israel—"Out of Jacob shall He come, and shall rule."

More than fourteen hundred years before, had that prophecy been uttered; and all that time, as year followed year, the eyes of the Orientals of those parts had scanned the heavens for the sign of the Great King, and as watchmen had been posted from generation to generation upon a lofty eminence to report to the people the appearance of the welcome glare. At last it had flashed upon the eye of the watcher; the self-same night when the shepherds were summoned by angels to see the new-born Prince of Peace, the infant Saviour of the world.

These sages felt the call of God, though it spoke to them not by angelic voices, but by the dumb invitation of that burning light, which was born that night a stranger among the constellations of heaven. They delayed not to obey; they sought no excuse for tarrying; they listened to no counsel that suggested motives for apprehension. The pressing duties which belonged to their position as the princes, guides, advisers, judges, and priests of their people (for so manifold was the character of the Magi); the dreary length of that journey westward to the land of prophecy; the many dangers which beset their path both going and coming; the unpropitious season, with its days of rain or snow or sleet, and nights of darkness and benumbing cold, which would cover the whole period of their journey; all these difficulties, which to the remiss and lukewarm nature would appear ample justification for inactivity, did but kindle the ardour of these holy men, who knew that obedience derives its best lustre from the obstacles it overcomes. And God visibly rewarded their virtue. For as their procession began its march, immediately the star moved also, and went slowly forwards across the lights of heaven, like the torch of some unseen angel appointed to guide them. When they reached the Holy City, however, it disappeared. Now, doubtless, it was needed no more, for all the country of Judea must be in a ferment of joy at the birth of the new-born King whom God had so long ago promised. But in the streets of Jerusalem there was no unwonted stir—nothing but the humdrum round of business, interrupted awhile by the appearance of the strangers. There were no bonfires on the hills; the valleys sent back no echo of gladness to the acclamations of a thankful people. There was no noise of psaltery or harp, of timbrel or choir, of strings or organs, or high-sounding cymbals. Amazed at such inexplicable calmness or stolidity in men who had so many motives for rejoicing, the Magi enquired of the crowd where was He born King of the Jews? We have seen His star in the East and are come to adore Him. But their questions were met with looks of blank surprise and answers that attempted no solution of the enigma. What was to be done? The star had disappeared and the attitude of the people was a puzzle. Apparently there was no further direction from God or man. Were they therefore to abandon their search, and to return home without accomplishing their purpose?

Again, in such a conjecture, a listless spirit would have found reason enough for desisting from a laborious, perhaps a dangerous, enterprise. But the resolution of the sages evinced their disciplined virtue, and the habit of perseverance in the midst of obstacles. They would seek the ruler of Judea, and would question him as to this heaven-promised suzerain, whose vassal he would doubtless be. Accordingly, to the gates of Herod's palace they were led by the people, who now gathered thick and fast from every part of the city. Herod received them blandly, affecting deep interest in the object of their journey. But Herod's smiling face was but the mask to a troubled heart; for the Scripture tells us that he was troubled, and all Jerusalem with him. And good reason had he for alarm. For thirty-six years, as a probable reckoning represents, he had occupied the throne of a usurper, which he had maintained with all the cunning of a fox, and all the cruelty of a tiger. An Idumœan by birth, he had adopted the religion of Judea; and he had determined to make the national creed an instrument for the furtherance of his ambition, as the first Napoleon sought to make the re-establishment of Catholicity a ladder to permament power. It was by the aid of the Romans that he assumed the sceptre of Judea, and took possession of Jerusalem. Not one man or woman who stood in his way, that he had not butchered. His blow had fallen in turn, whether by secret assassination or open violence, upon the legitimate heir to royalty, the priest Hyrcanus; upon the nephew of Hyrcanus, the priest Aristobulus; upon the daughter of Hyrcanus, his own wife, Mariamne; upon Mariamne's mother; upon his wife's mother, Alexandra; upon his own two sons by her, Alexander and Aristobulus, and upon Antipater, his son by another wife. Thus the constant fear of being dethroned had haunted him day and night, and as love of power had been his passion, the dread of rivalry had been his scourge; and had filled his brain with schemes of bloodshed, and steeled his heart against pity. Well did he know that the Jews were expecting a heaven-sent deliverer and King, who should raise them from dishonour and subjection, and extend his rule to the ends of the earth. And while he trembled lest this expectation should be realized, he was not slow in seizing the opportunity it offered of keeping himself before the public's eye, as a champion of the Jewish creed, and a benefactor of the Jewish race, thus tacitly claiming to fulfil the conditions of the Messias promised to the fathers of the nation. It was to this end that he had embellished Jerusalem with many noble buildings, and above all had restored the temple upon such a scale of magnificence, that is was reckoned amongst the wonders of the world. In spite of his success, old age was creeping upon him, and he was already, according to one account, in the first stages of a loathsome malady, the consequence of his sinful habits, and the final agent of his death. But though he felt that his doom was not far off, the old passions burned as fiercely as ever in his breast; and while the advent of the Magi upon their strange pilgrimage brought deadly terror to his heart, it fixed him in the immovable resolution, that come what might, he would find out this babe that threatened the short remnant of his reign, and ruthlessly put him to the sword; a resolution which led to the wholesale slaughter of the innocents.

Meantime he called together all the chief priests and scribes of the people and inquired of them where Christ should be born. There was no doubt, no uncertainty, in their response. In Bethlehem of Juda, said they, thus distinguishing our Blessed Lord's birthplace from the other Bethlehem in Galilee. "For so," they continued, "it is written by the prophet. And thou, Bethlehem, the land of Juda, art not the least among the princes of Juda; for out of thee shall come forth the captain that shall rule my people Israel."—*Micheas* v. 2. Now mark the duplicity of the old dissembler, Herod. "Privately calling the wise men he learnt diligently of them the time of the star which appeared to them"—trusting that so he might ascertain the age of the child whom he feared as a rival—"and sending them into Bethlehem, said: 'Go, and diligently enquire after the child, and when you have found Him bring me word again, that I also may come and adore Him.'" Thus he crowned the hypocrisy of his life by a most daring blasphemy in concealing his deadly purpose against the Messiah, under the mask of religious zeal and devotion to his heaven-appointed sovereign, the Christ of God.

With thankful hearts, the Magi set out again, and turned their faces towards the city of David. "And behold," says St. Matthew, "the star which they had seen in the East went before them until it came and stood over where the child lay. It was a journey of about six miles through undulating valleys; and the distance gave the sages abundance of time to reflect on the strange circumstances, which ushered them into the presence of the long-promised Captain of Israel. He, then, the new Solomon, the expectation of the nations, whose coming was looked for, at this time, by every people under the sun, had chosen to come into life, unknown to the very race whose sovereign He was by right of birth, and whose renown He was destined to spread throughout the universe. Mysterious, indeed, was this arrangement of Divine

Providence; but to minds like theirs, accustomed to meditate on God's ways, and to search for Him as a hidden God; to minds, that knew how little God loves the pomp of this world, how little He is a favourer of persons, how kindly He regards the poor and the lowly, it brought fresh motives for contempt of earth, and fresh incentives to that virtue of self-concealment and self-abasement, shrinking from the hollow honours that man can bestow, which must have been characteristic of their unworldly and docile natures.

At length, the least and the greatest of cities, Bethlehem, the city of Bread, as the name implies, the city of the heavenly manna, with its airy heights and romantic pinnacles of stone forming a diadem on the rocks, was seen against the sky. How the hearts of the Magi beat, at feeling themselves so near their destination! How deeply they admired the humility of the Incarnate God, who chose for His birthplace, not the famous city of Jerusalem, but this old-fashioned place, so remote from the splendour and pageants of the world. But all their anticipations were as nothing, to the circumstances of humiliation with which the new-born King had surrounded His nativity. The star that guided them rested not upon the dome of a goodly house that bespoke at least mediocre respectability; rested not upon the comfortable inn of the city; rested not upon the humblest hut or cabin in the meanest quarter; but, going steadily onwards, descended the hill a little and came to its destination, over a wretched cave in the rock, open to the bleak air, and to the whistling wind, and the rattling shower, where the littered floor bespoke it as a shelter for the lower animals that aid the labours of man. While their attendants stared and wondered, convinced that their sage masters were at fault, the Magi reverently bent to the ground, at the entrance to the cave; and prostrated themselves before the Emmanuel, God amongst us; and remained for a while motionless in adoration and thanksgiving. At the remote end of the cave, dimly lit by the scant daylight, is the object of their wonder and their worship. A little smiling babe, lying in the straw, voiceless, helpless, crownless, sceptreless, without a palace, without a home, without a courtier or adherent, save the gentle maid that kisses Him, and the venerable bareheaded elderly man that bows before Him; yet this is He, the King of Kings, and the Lord of Lords, whose name is called Wonderful, Counsellor, God the Mighty, and the Father of the world to come, the Prince of Peace, the Light unto the revelation of the Gentiles, and the Glory of God's people Israel. And while they offered in fervent prayer the treasures of their overflowing hearts, they produced also the material gifts which their country furnished them, according to the usage of Eastern peoples, to be the tribute of their lifelong servitude, and to be the symbols of His manifold character, and of their own dispositions. Out of their coffers they brought forth ingots of glittering gold, the precious metal which the author of the book of Proverbs likens to Wisdom, "My fruit is better than gold," for they would thus signify that He was the second Solomon, and the wisest of all wise kings that were ever to wear a crown. They presented Him with frankincense, symbol of sacrifice, as a token that they recognised in Him, on the one side, the twofold character of God the Supreme, to whom alone it is lawful to offer sacrifice; and on the other, the man of all men who had been chosen as High Priest to offer to heaven an acceptable oblation. And lastly, they presented Him with myrrh, a gum used for the purpose of embalming and preserving the dead, to show that they believed Him to possess a body like our own, liable to death, though by virtue of His divinity it should be saved from ever seeing corruption. "As their God," says St. Leo, "He is presented with incense; as man, with myrrh; as a king, with gold"; for thus the wise men would fain venerate the union of the divine with the human, and make their gifts an emblem of their belief. And lastly, by a secondary symbolism, these presents betokened their dispositions of soul: gold stood for their charity, the most precious of virtues; incense, the fragrance of their ceaseless prayer; and myrrh, that mortification of the flesh which preserves our fallen nature from corruption.

THE HOLY NAME OF JESUS.

TO-DAY, beloved Brethren, we are called upon by the Church to celebrate the greatest name that stands written in human annals—the name Jesus.

In honouring a name we honour all that the name implies. We give no undue, no superstitious importance to the mere sounds that make it up, as if they held some charm or spell apart from their meaning. But in the same manner as when we kiss the Crucifix, our thoughts are borne away from the bleeding, writhing form to the mighty mystery of Redemption, so when we bow the head at the name "Jesus," we are paying our homage to the Saviour, the Redeemer who wrought our deliverance.

Two names there are that stand out prominently among all the holy names which are our heirloom and property from early times—Jehovah and Jesus. When God spoke to Moses out of the burning bush He bade him tell the Children of Israel, whom he was sent to deliver from the bondage of Egypt—"*I am*," or "*Jehovah*, hath sent me unto you." This name of Jehovah was the symbol of God's matchless being. It meant the Being of beings, the fountain of all life, the Being who depended for existence upon no one, the Being upon whom all beings depended, without whom all would have been loneliness and vacuity, the eternal, the infinite God. This, then, was the name by which God chose to reveal Himself to the Jews, a name of awe and majesty. And so deep was the veneration in which it was held that no lip was allowed to shape it, save that of the High Priest, and his only once in the year. All others were fain to refer to it by a conventional substitute, which rendered it unnecessary to use the name itself. This cautious and distant reverence was of a piece with all the history and institutions of the Old Law, where God appeared as the God mighty and powerful, visiting the sins of parents upon their children to the third and fourth generations; the God of hosts, before whom the pillars of heaven tremble; the God of justice, who drowned the earth with a deluge of waters, rained fire upon the wicked cities of the plain, and visited the Egyptians with terrific plagues, and scourged His people with hideous chastisements following close upon their sins. This was the aspect God chose to wear in the Old Law; He was a father indeed, and a merciful father, but one whose hand was familiar with the lash, one whose wrath was sweet and amiable to those that feared Him, but terrible to His enemies. But there was another period in store. He, whose very nature in its mysterious depth was all justice, and yet all mercy and love, prepared for us from the first a season of boundless love, prodigal grace, unspeakable indulgence. That was the New Law. And with the new revelation came a new name by which God was known to His people; the name of our Emmanuel, or God amongst us—the sweet, inspiring, hopeful name Jesus or Saviour.

Oh! my Brethren, what worlds of kindness there are in that name, Jesus. In it we read the whole story of our Redemption. And what a story! No tragedy could be so laden with guilt, misery, horror, catastrophe, as that of the race that God placed upon the earth. He crowned them with glory and honour; He stamped His own image upon them; He made them little less than His angels; He raised them, creatures of clay as they were, to the dignity of His own companions and friends—for He was wont to walk and converse with Adam in the garden. But they sold Him for a wretched gratification; they stripped themselves of their robes of innocence; and took for their portion labour hardship, sin, disease, and death. Corruption grew with the advancing years, until at last all flesh had corrupted its way, and God, as He himself expresses it, absolutely repented that He had made man. Then came the flood, which cleansed the earth of its living breathing guilt, but did not purify the blood. The taint went on. Again sin was rampant, and flouted God under His own heavens. Why trace the deterioration of the world more closely? Suffice it to say, that all God's gifts were turned to His dishonour, and this beautiful world was the theatre of all abominations. In the intellects of men, the truths of the moral law became more and more obscure, until every vice was elevated into a god or goddess, and worshipped with bent knees, prescribed rites, bleeding victims, and streaming incense. Not barbarous nations only, but the most civilized empires of the ancient world disgraced themselves by such worship. The Egyptians could build pyramids, as durable as the earth they rest on; yet could fall down and worship a cow, a crocodile, an onion. The Greeks could leave masterpieces of sculpture and architecture, which are a model of beauty and genius, to all succeeding times; and yet could see nothing but pardonable weakness in fornication. The Romans were masters of statesmanship, military and engineering skill, and manifold mental refinement; yet could publicly honour a god of thieving, and a goddess of adultery. God looked down upon the earth, and saw it all; He saw how the law of right and wrong, which He had written upon the heart of man, was becoming well-nigh effaced; He saw how fathers were passing on their foul blood, and fouler teaching, traditions and example, to their sons; He saw how the flood of popular feeling, evil custom, national prescription and usage, was sweeping onwards the souls, even of thinking men, towards the abyss; and religion itself was leading them, to the sound of solemn music, towards their eternal ruin, and festooning the mouth of hell, as if it were the sacred porch of heaven; and all the while He was storing up His vengeance. What was this vengeance? It was a vengeance that awes, confounds, overwhelms us, not by its thunders and ravages, but by its sweetness, its tenderness, its compassion. He had sent His prophets, and they were stoned. He now decreed to send His only Begotten Son—saying, according to the parable, "They will reverence my Son." And as Lucifer and his angels had fallen through pride; as Adam and Eve had sinned through an inordinate ambition of attaining a knowledge forbidden them—pride again; so self-abjection, humility, and perfect obedience were to be the characteristics of the new revelation of God. "In the head of the Book it is written, that I should do Thy will," so "the Word was made flesh, and dwelt amongst us." The infinite God assumed our petty nature; the All-holy God became the kinsman of sinners; the Almighty laid down the bolts of His anger, and said:—"I will draw them with the cords of Adam, with the bonds of love." You have seen His coming, beloved Brethren, you have been witnesses of its lowliness and humility.

He came to us a trembling infant, appealing to us by His very helplessness. And so, almost unknown, He walked through the world; He endured all the hardships of life, as our true brother; and shrunk from no ill which we are called upon to suffer, though He had no share in meriting them. One breath of His would have saved us; one murmured prayer; and this condescension, had there been no more, would have claimed an eternal return of gratitude. But no. He must leave behind Him a picture to encourage and cheer us in all our woes, crosses, and troubles; the picture of a God-man willingly and patiently suffering the self-same afflictions, without earning them by His sins. Thus He lived: often hungry, often thirsty, often footsore, often houseless, often persecuted, nay, at last betrayed by a friend with whom He had exchanged the kiss of peace. And how did He die? He suffered a death, the prolonged anguish, the various torture of which has never been equalled. Alas! He did in truth come under the law of death, He did in truth taste its utmost bitterness: and with a palate most alive to the nauseousness of the draught: "Father," said He, "if it be possible, let this chalice pass from Me." Thus His human heart sickened at the sight of the proffered cup; but He remembered the brothers He came to save; and with head bowed in resignation, He added: "Yet not My will, but Thine be done." And the dregs of that chalice, the bitterness of its bitterness was when He felt himself as the scapegoat of sin, abandoned by His heavenly Father, and driven forth, as it were, into the wilderness, to die an outcast. Listen to His agonized cry, from the cross, as He saw the cloud of His Father's wrath darkening above, and hiding the light of His face—"My God, my God, why hast thou abandoned me?"

Thus laboriously Jesus lived, thus painfully He died, to pay the price of our Redemption, and to bring home to each of us the benefits of the great work. No human hero ever could compare with Him; not Curtius, the Roman, who is fabled upon his charger to have leaped into the gulf which had opened in the city, and which was not to close till it received the sacrifice of one of Rome's noblest citizens; not the Irish chieftain, who in the Danish wars, singled out during a naval engagement the most formidable of the enemy's generals, and sprang overboard with him into the sea, inextricably locked in fatal embrace. These sacrificed their lives for friends, man for man. But Jesus wrought the greatest of miracles, suffered the greatest of humiliations, in becoming man at all; and died not for His friends only, but for the worst of His enemies.

And what, beloved Brethren, has been the consequence of all this humiliation? His cross has become His throne, and He has ruled the world from that grim eminence. He who was reviled, has been raised up: and He Who humbled Himself has been exalted. Listen to St. Paul: "Christ became for us obedient unto death, even to the death of the cross. Therefore hath God exalted Him, and given Him a Name, that is above all names, that in the Name of Jesus every knee should bow, of those that are in heaven, on earth, and under the earth, and that every tongue should confess that the Lord Jesus Christ is in the glory of God the Father."—*Phil.* ii. 9, 10.

And if you would see as it were with your eyes, the virtue and the power of this Name which God has given to his Son, open the third chapter of the Acts of the Apostles.

Let us, then, beloved Brethren, do what we can to-day to honour that Name of grace, that Name of power. Remember that "there is no other name under heaven given to man, by which he may be saved." Be you saint or be you sinner, invoke with reverence the name Jesus: for if you are seekers of God, that Name will give you fresh light and strength; if you are ever so deeply sunk in guilt, remember He took that holy Name because He was to save His people from their sins." Make atonement for profanations: from the rising to the setting of the sun the Name of the Lord is worthy of praise.

CHARITY.

Quinquagesima Sunday.

WHILE we are examining our lives to find if they are consistent with the precepts of the Gospel, we must not, beloved Brethren, pass over one commandment which our Lord himself has laid down as one of the very first importance. He reduces the whole of our duties to two: love of God and love of our neighbour. "Thou shalt love the Lord thy God with thy whole heart, with thy whole soul, with all thy strength, and with all thy mind." And the second commandment is like to the first: "Thou shalt love thy neighbour as thyself."

This precept of loving our neighbours as ourselves, was never delivered with so much emphasis, was never raised to such importance, was never made so central a hinge of morality, till our Lord came to enlighten us. For this we have our Lord's own testimony: "A new commandment I give unto you, that you love one another as I have loved you." And it was indeed a new and a strange commandment, that we should measure our love for one another according to the tremendous, sublime, and passionate love which He bore to the human race. Thenceforth it became the duty of everyone professing to be His follower to love his neighbour after the fashion of our Lord Jesus Christ. The degree of love that Christ bore mankind—being infinite—could not indeed be ever matched by these cold hearts of ours. But the *kind* of love that He felt for His brethren of the earth could be imitated. What was the character of that love? It was just in giving every one his due, and in using the same weights and measures for our neighbours as for ourselves. It was generous in trying to secure that our neighbours should rather be indebted to us than we to them; for it is a more blessed thing to give than to receive. It was sympathetic—weeping with the mourner and rejoicing with those who are glad. It was active, not confining itself to mere gushes of feeling, but working and toiling, with hands and brain if necessary, for the benefit of others. It was universal, excluding from its circle no one whose veins inherited the blood of Adam; it was not earthly but heavenly, seeking the welfare of the soul rather than the body, and embracing all, from no fancy or predilection, but for the love of God. This is the kind of love we must have for our neighbours if we would resemble Christ: large, self-sacrificing, forgiving, taking in friend or foe." "If you love those who love you," said our Lord, "what reward shall you have. Do not the publicans do this?" So we must rise above this low standard and show the stamp of the charity of Christ. "By this shall all men know that you are My disciples." said He, "if you have love one for another." And, as in this life, the world is to recognise Christ in us by witnessing our mutual love, so, be assured, there will be no admission into heaven for those who show not this character. They are not like Christ and shall not be with Christ. They are of the goats, not of the sheep. If they wear not the wedding garment of brotherly love they shall go into the outer darkness. God is love; in His sight no hatred can live. No matter how shining your other merits may be, if you lack this you are not like the first-born, whose image is to be our passport to our heavenly home, our only title to our heavenly inheritance; and the sentence of the Father will be—"The charity of God is not in you. Amen, I know you not." Listen to the solemn words of St. Paul: "Brethren, if I speak with the tongues of men and of angels and have not charity, I am become as sounding brass or a tinkling cymbal. And if I should have prophecy, and should know all mysteries and all knowledge, and if I should have all faith so that I could remove mountains, and have not charity, I am nothing. And if I should distribute all my goods to feed the poor, and if I should deliver my body to be burned, and have not charity, it profiteth me nothing."—I *Cor.* xiii. 1.

Now, beloved Brethren, if you were suddenly called away to the judgment-seat of God, how would you answer an examination on this head?

Suppose your eternal sentence to hang upon this one question: Is your charity Christ-like? Do you love your neighbour as yourself? Have you any sort of confidence that your life would bear sifting, and that your trial would result in a favourable award? Have your thoughts, words, and actions been such, that you might expect to hear: "Well done, thou good and faithful servant."? Dare you look upon the face of Christ, as He stands at the right hand of God, with His brow crimsoned from the thorny crown, His side opened, His hands bearing the stigma of the cruel nails, —His whole body a record of the trials and triumphs of love— could you, I repeat, look Him in the face, and say: "I have loved my neigbour as myself? I have obeyed the Commandment —'Love one another as I have loved you.'"?

Turn your eyes inwards upon your thoughts and feelings. Is there no one to whom you bear a secret dislike, an antipathy? Do you trample down every blind shrinking and repugnance that rises within you towards the person or the character of your neighbour, or do you let your reason go captive to that foolish and disorderly feeling, by dwelling bitterly upon the qualities which occasion this dislike? Are you jealous or envious of his gifts or endowments, his success or his means? Do you take a pleasure in observing that he is overtaken by disappointment, loss, mishap, or mortification? Or, perhaps, you are ever on the alert to watch his actions in a sinister, spiteful, ill-natured spirit; presuming that their motive is unworthy or bad, and putting the worst construction upon them. Nay, do you not at times judge your neighbour rashly, and upon slender and insufficient grounds believe him guilty of sin? Then it may be that some slight or insult, or wrong, inflicted by a neighbour in pastime, is like a perpetual sore in your bosom; rankling and festering, and giving you no repose, keeping your mind constantly occupied in devising means to return the ill, dwelling with satisfaction upon the prospect of revenge, and gloating over the fancied humiliation you would occasion him. If you are conscious that you have harboured such feelings towards your neighbour, then think what sentence would be passed upon you by Him, who said:—"I say to you, love your enemies; do good to them that hate you; and pray for them that persecute and calumniate you."

Then what account could you give of your words and conversation to your Judge? Could you say to the meek and humble of heart:—"I have never spoken proudly and contemptuously to any creature, however lowly or degraded. I have never used abusive language, nor spoken malicious things to wound my neighbour, nor called him by opprobrious or stinging names."

Ah! beloved Brethren, if you will have to answer even for your idle words, your thoughtless and purposeless chat, how much more severely will you be judged for your uncharitable speeches! Think of the growing wrath of Jesus Christ, once your indulgent Saviour, now your Judge, when, in the presence of that tribunal from which there is no appeal, your wicked and malignant gossip is unfolded, with all the heart-burnings, misunderstandings, estrangements, enmities, ruined reputations, acts of revenge, which were the consequences of it? Then you will find what a long series of sins and sorrows often hangs upon one uncharitable word. As St. James expresses it: your tongue has been a little spark that has wrapt whole forests in ruinous conflagration. Strife and bad blood have followed your steps wherever you have gone. You have poisoned every neighbourhood you have visited, with your suspicious suggestions, your backbiting and criticism, your tattling and tale-bearing, your misinterpretations of fact, your diabolical faculty of torturing good into evil; for no contagion spreads so rapidly as the vice of uncharitableness. Thus your mission in the world has been to stir up rancour and discord; and your lot shall not be with the Prince of Peace.

Finally, beloved Brethren, think with yourselves, if your actions have borne the stamp of Christian charity. Can you say that you have never done your neighbour a bad turn? Have you never dealt unfairly, meanly, and ungenerously with him, when your interests have been involved? Have you taken a shabby advantage of his simplicity, candour, shortsightedness, and imprudence; as if you thought yourself placed in the world to overreach and dupe your fellows. Have you been guilty of striking or otherwise maltreating one whom God has made to His own image and likeness, and raised to the dignity of adopted son and heir, and nurtured with the bread of immortality?

But perhaps you have avoided such excesses. Even so, do not think your judgment ends there. You must show, not only that you have avoided injuring your neighbour, but that you have done him good. How far, then, have you exerted yourself to relieve the distress of others, to appease their hunger and thirst, to cover their nakedness, to find them a shelter from the inclemency of the season, to comfort them in their trials, hardships, and sorrows. How much have you done towards providing for their spiritual wants? Have you seen to the religious instruction and watched over the conduct of those under your charge? In short, have you regarded it as a privilege to serve your neighbour, to relieve and to console him, knowing that if you give a cup of cold water in the name of God, you shall not lose your reward?

Alas! beloved Brethren, there are too many of us, who have reason to tremble at the words of St. John :—"He that hath the substance of this world, and shall see his brother in need, and shall shut his heart against him ; how doth the charity of God abide in him?"

BLIND BARTIMEUS.

Quinquagesima Sunday.

WHEN our blessed Lord was at the height of His fame, and the name of Jesus, the prophet and wonder worker, was in the mouths of all the common people of Judea, He passed through the old town of Jericho in a sort of triumph, which was a foreshadowing of the jubilant welcome given Him in Jerusalem on the Palm Sunday following. From all the streets in the town, and from the scattered houses and hamlets in the neighbourhood, groups of excited men and women, their children open-eyed with amazement nestling in their breasts, or pattering by their side with unequal steps, hurried towards the gate of the city, where the noise of a multitude told of the presence of the great Healer and Rabbi of Israel. As the gathering crowds advanced, with the King of the Jews in their midst (so soon to be proclaimed as such with the derisive symbol of a thorny crown), the hum and the subdued acclamations of His joyful cortège are rudely interrupted by a loud cry, which comes from the direction of the city gate, and which is repeated again and again, in piercing and pathetic tones. "Jesus, son of David," cries the voice, in accents of agony, like those of ship-wrecked seamen on a crazy raft, when some vessel is sighted on the horizon, inspiring alternately wild hope and deadly fear, "Jesus, son of David, have mercy on me." It is some one, clearly, who is well acquainted with the pedigree of our blessed Redeemer, and who recognised Him as a descendant of the heaven-selected King, the pride of the Jewish people. It is one, moreover, who believes that this representative of David's line wields no ordinary power and is privileged to bestow valuable blessings. And so the voice bellows and roars, fast and furious, lest it should be swallowed up unheard in the general tumult:

"Jesus, son of David, have mercy on me." The crowd are scandalized at the indecorous uproar; they turn their eyes frowningly towards the spot from which it comes, and whom do they see?

There, beside the gate of Jericho, in his old familiar station, where for many a year he has sat or stood soliciting the alms of the passers-by, with face upturned all eagerness, with sightless eyeballs rolling, and with trembling hands outstretched, is old Bartimeus, the son of Timeus, the blind beggar of Jericho. Beside him, a companion in his occupation, as he is a sharer in his misfortune, is another blind man, not so well known to local fame.

The townsmen of the old beggar are annoyed at his unseasonable importunity. "Bartimeus," say many voices at once, in angry and chiding tones—"Hold thy peace. Disturb not the seemliness of this ovation which we bestow upon our Benefactor." But Bartimeus was bent upon one purpose, and from that he was not to be diverted by persuasion or by threat. He cried the louder: "Son of David, have mercy on me."

The gentle Being, whose sad, sweet face is the loadstone of all eyes, appears to be attracted by the cry. He stops, He signifies His desire to see this poor man, whose noisy invocation strikes with such a discord upon the joyous harmonies of the people's voices. The crowd halt, and some of the bystanders, taking the old man by the hand, murmur in his ear, "Be of good heart, Bartimeus; He calls thee."

"What wilt thou," said Jesus, when Bartimeus and his companion stood before Him with hands outstretched, and painful suspense and expectation printed upon every line of their weather-worn features. It is no common alms the old man sought, no dole of bronze or coin, such as he begged from the hands of his ordinary fellow citizens. A far higher boon is that to which he aspired. Through long and weary years he has groped in darkness along the streets and alleys of this city, sometimes helped forward by a friendly hand, sometimes guided by a faithful and sagacious dog, and, in all those years, he has never seen a human face, nor known the glories of the light of heaven, nor had any conception of the mysteries of form and colour, which make up a marvellous universe of themselves. Never did his soul light up at the sight of the azure sky, with its variegated clouds softly folded

in its bosom, or its stars scattered like a suspended rain of silver
over its depths; he had no cognizance of the pleasant green of
the earth, nor the changeful glitter of moving water. He knew not
the language of the human face, with its alphabet of brow and
eye, of colour and expression, scarcely yielding in significance to
the language of speech, with which he was familiar. In short, the
region of sight was to him a buried or a non-existent world. And
now, old as he was, he would fain look upon the visible creation
of God, which shows the impress of the Divine Artist in its every
lineament and hue, and which is worthy to be welcomed by the
Psalmist into the choir of God's servitors, who sing His praises.
" Let the earth bless the Lord ; let it praise and exalt Him above
all for ever." Perhaps this deep thirst, which makes poor Bartimeus
clamour for help to the Son of God, had its first prompting in the
strong and unappeasable longing that possesses him to see the
divine face of that Saviour whom all voices combine to extol,
whose miracles are the common topics of conversation among the
people, whose tenderness for the poor and needy is a subject of
universal praise, who has nothing but kindness and compassion for
the sinner in his humiliation. And so, to the question " What wilt
thou that I do to thee," which is addressed to Bartimeus by this
sweet, kind voice out of the darkness, the old man answers, without
hesitation or distrust : " Lord, that I may see." Jesus, the very God,
who in creation's infancy said " Let there be light, and there was
light," speaks the word now again, and instantaneously the little
world of that blind man's being, shrouded before in gloom, is
flooded with the beams of day, and made partaker of all the
delicious sensations which the living light awakens. Upon his
hitherto dead and withered eyeballs what a revelation of stationary
or moving forms and varied and intermingled tints of brilliant
foreground and softened distance, in one instant bursts! He
has suddenly felt himself transported into another sphere, in
which he had never previously set foot. All around him are
wondering and pitying faces, looks of sympathy that redouble
the effect of the murmurs of incoherent thanksgiving, amazement, and joy which sound upon his ear; but what rivets his
attention, amidst the novel sensations that possess him, is the
face of the Healer, the Son of David, to whose power and
compassion he had appealed, and not in vain. Who can speak
the unspeakable ? That face, divinely sweet, breathing the

very soul of compassion, smiling kindly upon the poor forlorn creature whom His word had delivered out of the womb of darkness—what a thrill it must have shot into the depths of Bartimeus' soul, what flowing sentiments of gratitude, what profound adoration of the almighty and bountiful Godhead, what ardent love and lifelong dedication of every sense and every mental power must that face have inspired!

We do not read of the after fate of the son of Timeus; but we cannot doubt that he followed Jesus to Jerusalem, and in the triumph of Palm Sunday was one of the witnesses, who bore testimony amid the joyous multitude to the divine power that worked by the arm of the Son of David. Neither have we any reason to doubt that the light thus poured upon the eyes of the blind man, and the flooding rays of the Divine Spirit, which at the same moment filled his soul, in reward for his undoubting faith, were the forerunners of a life, whose virtues bore constant testimony to the inward energy of the Son of God, as his eyesight was an outward monument to the divine power, which the Son of Man wielded over the human body.

Beloved Brethren, when we ponder upon that prayer, "Lord, that I may see," we ought to recall to mind the value and importance of that sense of sight, with which God has endowed us, and the vast scope of lawful gratifications and pure delights, which it has opened to us from day to day. If we have a spirit of faith, and recognize everything we possess as a gift from the liberal hand of our Creator, we ought to thank Him again and again, not simply for the aggregate of His endowments, but singly and specially for every bodily sense and every mental faculty and power of which we are the owners. It is a sad thought that multitudes go through life, and descend into the grave, without ever having expressed the slightest gratitude to the Giver of all good gifts for the noble being, so manifold in its attributes, which His goodness has bestowed upon them.

Again, beloved Brethren, when we repeat that simple, yet powerful prayer, which Bartimeus repeated with such importunity: "Lord, that I may see": we ought to remember that the eye of faith is even more necessary than the sight of the bodily organ; and we ought to call upon the Son of David, the Light of Lights, to make that eye of faith more sound, more keen, and more effective, for our guidance amidst the illusions and dangers of the world. The man, whose faith is feeble and deficient is, in the Spiritual life, more helpless and liable to disaster than, in this outer world, a man whose eyesight is dim and inadequate. It is the eye of faith that shows us the relative value of things temporal and eternal, and sets them each in their true light; it is by the eye of faith that we discover the vanity and criminal folly of sensual pleasures, with the terrible end that awaits them; it is by the eye of faith that we detect the hollowness of earthly honours and human fame, so soon to be wrapped in a worm-stained winding-sheet; it is by the eye of faith, that we estimate the true value of riches and wordly gear, which will leave their devotees, at last, as naked and empty-handed as they were on the day they first saw the light. Without this soundness of the Spiritual eyesight, without this vividness of faith, we shall never know, until it is too late, the full meaning of the words:—"What doth it profit a man to gain the whole world, and to suffer the loss of his own soul."

There is one other important suggestion or lesson, beloved Brethren, conveyed in the prayer of blind Bartimeus, which makes it especially appropriate as an introduction to the penitential exercises of Lent, and as a gospel ushering in the solemnity of Ash Wednesday. This season of Lent is intended to be a time of self-examination and of rigid scrutiny into the condition of our conscience. It is a time when opportunity is furnished us of judging ourselves with such severity, and making atonement for our offences with such earnestness and intensity of sorrow, as to disarm the rigours of that tribunal before which we must all one day stand to receive our sentence according to the works done in the body, be they good or evil. Let us ask the assistance of the Holy Ghost in instituting this examination, lest self-love should cloak our transgressions or conceal the dangerous tendencies and deplorable consequences of our passions. "Lord, that I may see," should be our frequent prayer in this season of penitential recollection. "Come, Holy Ghost, send down those beams which sweetly flow, in silent streams, from Thy bright throne above! O come, thou Father of the poor, thou bounteous source of all our store, come, fill our hearts with love." It is thus only, by invoking the illumination of God's Holy Spirit, and petitioning for the clear eyesight of faith, that we shall see the chamber of our soul as it really is in God's sight. In this light we shall see, perhaps, in holes and corners, heaps of filth or of rubbish that had escaped us ere our eyes of faith were opened; even the spots which we thought cleanest and brightest, alas! will be found too much tarnished and begrimed with worldly stains; the embellishments of virtue, upon which we prided ourselves, may discover to our gaze a tawdriness and unworthiness that will startle and scare us; and the very atmosphere of the soul will be found swarming with motes and particles, small besetting imperfections, the presence of which we had not, in our purblindness, suspected.

THE TEMPTATION IN THE DESERT.

IT is related of the great Julius Cæsar that when serving in the East, in his youthful days, he was always to be seen toiling onwards in advance of his men amidst the choking dust, with his head bared to the sun, although he was not blessed with a robust constitution. This superfluous exertion was formed upon a sound maxim. The personal example of a superior, in the performance of difficult and trying duties, has a sort of magic in it to awake the indolent, and to lend vigour to the languid. An officer who is self-sacrificing will have soldiers endued with a similar spirit.

It is for a like reason that our Blessed Lord, who was the eternal God, clothed in human flesh, disdained to lay down laws or impose burthens upon His followers, without Himself submitting to the precepts that regulated their lives, and sharing the yoke imposed upon them. And so we find that although He stood not in need of mortification as we do, He made himself a model of mortification, to encourage us in the unpalatable task. He was not one of those captains who, from a safe vantage ground, overlook the labour and sweat, the wounds and carnage of battle; but placing Himself in the van at the head of their columns, He cries, with a voice inspiriting as the martial clarion: "follow me! let my cross, borne on my own shoulders, be your standard in the strife. Keep your eyes on that ensign, and it will lead you to victory."

To-day we have presented to us in the Gospel a moving picture of our Lord's self-inflicted suffering, endured to stimulate and encourage us in taming our bodies by self-denial, and bracing our souls by self-discipline, and watching, and prayer. He had received the baptism of His Precursor St. John—the baptism of penance—prefiguring His own Sacramental baptism. The heavens had testified to His Divinity, by opening above Him, and revealing the Spirit of God descending upon Him as a dove; and the voice from heaven had spoken explicitly to the same purpose, "This is my beloved Son, in whom I am well pleased." The time was approaching when He should preach the good tidings of salvation to men, and exhibit Himself as the Divine and omnipotent healer of soul and body. And now He would prepare Himself for that exalted mission, as the ministers of the Church have ever since prepared themselves in imitation of Him, by a period of retirement, solitude, meditation, and prayer, that God, the Father, the giver of all good gifts, might bless the career marked out by heaven, and multiply the fruits of the ministry to which He was called.

Accordingly He was led by the Spirit, says St. Matthew, into the desert to be tempted by the devil; that is to say, the Holy Spirit, for our instruction and sanctification, urged Him into the wilderness that we might behold Him, and study His bearing under the assaults of the devil, and so learn ourselves by His example to repulse the adversary effectually. For a space of forty days—the mystic term adopted of old by Moses and imitated by Elias—for forty days, a period which, roughly speaking, constitutes a tithe or tenth part of the year—our Lord refused His sinless body the nourishment for which its shrinking tissues and fainting limbs and weakened brain were craving, and in spite of the feebleness and pain which these rigours occasioned, He consecrated each day and night of that first memorable Lent by penitential watching and fervent prayer. When repose could no longer be denied to His weary bones, He had no couch on which to recline in distress and heaviness of soul but the hard rock or the arid sand of the wild and far-stretching waste.

He had no companionship but the silent multitude of heaven's stars by night, and by day the onward-moving sun that typified His glory, or the prowling beast that haunted the solitude. There, remote from the habitation of man, He pondered your sins and mine, with the sadness of a loving brother that sorrowed over our perilous infatuation, and bemoaned our blindness and hardness of heart; and while the substance of His body wasted under His long-continued abstinence, and His poor frame had scarcely strength left to maintain the kneeling attitude of the penitent, He offered Himself for each one of us to His eternal Father, and begged that His self-abnegation might atone for our sinful indulgences, and might sooner or later stimulate each one of us to penance.

And so the weary days passed by, their painful series scrupulously counted, without a thought of shortening the ordeal, though human nature might faint and groan under the infliction, and the baked unmoistened lips and palate gape for a crust of bread or a drop of water.

At last He was well-nigh famished, for His fast had been no mountebank feat of abstinence from food protracted under safe conditions, with all bodily exertion carefully avoided, mineral and other draughts administered at intervals to cheer the hard-used system, and physicians, interested in the experiment, ready by the bed-side to carry it successfully through, but it was a stern and merciless denial to the body of the rest as well as of the sustenance that life demands; a self-persecution, under which the body would have sunk in death but for the support of Almighty power; and a mortification which was incalculably aggravated by His perpetual night-watching, by His prayer, and the deep emotions of love and sorrow that agitated His soul.

And all those forty days the great enemy has his evil eye fixed upon this strange mysterious man—a man whom he recognized as grander, more singularly holy than the prophets, yea, one proclaimed by that heavenly voice, which still sounded in the devil's ear, to be the Son of God. Who, or what can He be? The demon knows not, perhaps cannot conceive it as possible that this is no other than the eternal Word, whose Divine essence is united in one Personality with the nature inherited from that Adam whom his own wiles had overthrown. He longs to test Him, and to asertain what power He wields, and to match his own cunning against the virtue of that Saint whom heaven itself had praised.

The long and distressing abstention from all nourishment, the emaciation of frame, the haggardness of countenance, the feebleness of every movement, which Satan carefully marked in Our Blessed Lord after His fast, led him to suppose that his first efforts might advantageously turn upon the cravings of sense, which he doubtless calculated would be sharpened beyond endurance by such protracted thwarting of the appetite. The tempter therefore, coming, said to Him—"If Thou be the Son of God, command these stones to be made bread," to all appearance sympathizing with Our Blessed Lord in His exhaustion, and affecting to believe in His limitless power as Son of God. Satan recommended Him to save Hmself with all speed from the extremity of starvation by there and then working this miracle. He had of course but to speak the word, and the desert stones beneath His feet would assume the properties of food. But the wisdom of the Word made flesh was too great for the cunning of the devil. "Man liveth not," said Our Blessed Lord, "upon bread alone, but upon every word that proceedeth from the mouth of God." "You forget," He says in effect, "that God who makes bread His ordinary instrument for maintaining the life and renewing the strength of the body, may equally well use any other means He pleases to attain the same end; nay the very word of His mouth, without any material agency at all, is sufficient, if it be His will, to sustain the vital spark in our frames." Thus the tempter was routed by an act of confidence in the benign providence and Almighty power of God.

Repulsed in his attempt to goad our Blessed Saviour to sensuality, the devil changed his tactics. He took Him up into the holy city and set Him on a pinnacle of the temple. You see that our Lord placed Himself to some extent at the disposal of His adversary, that the discomfiture of the malignant spirit might be more signal, and the lessons prepared for our instruction rendered more complete. It is likely that He would but allow the devil on this occasion to exercise the natural power, which, if unrestrained by God's special decree, he possessed since his creation, by bearing Him up bodily and wafting Him through the air, as he lifted Simon Magus later; and thus setting Him upon one of the wings of the temple, which, with its flat roof and balustrade or parapet bounding it, furnished, like the generality of buildings in the east, a convenient and spacious promenade. Or, possibly, he led Him conversing the while by the ordinary route to the temple, and mounted to the roof along with him by the ordinary staircase.

Be that as it may, while as they stood overlooking the sheer descent to the court below, the devil opened his new battery. "If Thou be the Son of God," said he, "cast Thyself down, for it is written: He hath given His angels charge over Thee, and in their hands shall they bear Thee up, lest perhaps Thou dash Thy foot against a stone." But again the divine wisdom foiled his strategy and turned his machinations to his own confusion. He had urged our blessed Lord to perform a perfectly useless action, to throw Himself down from the summit of the temple for no object but wantonly to test the fidelity of God to His promise. He was urged to commit Himself to an act which, if the laws of nature were not arrested—laws established by the Creator of this world for its ordinary working—would have resulted in instant death and entailed the guilt of suicide, and that without a single adequate motive that could transform presumption into a laudable trust in the divine goodness. It would have been very different if He had been confronted with the enemies of Jehovah, the champions of idols, as Elias was confronted with the prophets of Baal; and inspired to call confidently upon the Almighty for an evidence of His power to confound the foes of truth, to cast down false gods from their usurped eminence, and to bring home to the weak and wavering the grandeur and glory and the omnipotent supremacy of the Lord of heaven. This second temptation—viz., to presumption—our blessed Lord met with an act of humility: " It is written again," said He, " thou shalt not tempt the Lord thy God." We may strive to picture to ourselves how proud Lucifer, the defeated rebel against the sovereignty of God, bore this stinging rebuff, and with what a grim countenance he saw his second attack frustrated by the humble submission of the man of God to the ordinary laws of the world in which His heavenly Father had placed Him.

A third temptation was still to be encountered, and this time the appetite upon which it turned was the craving of the human soul for ascendency and the delights of gratified ambition, the incense of flattery, the inflated sense of wealth and affluence, and a consciousness of arbitrary sway. It is a temptation that often sorely tries men of superior minds, who are able to master the more vulgar passions that take rise in the senses; it is a vicious craving, which on that account has been styled "the last infirmity of noble minds." To try our blessed Lord, Whom no meaner passion could allure, by this more spiritual and penetrating test of virtue, "the devil took Him," says St. Matthew, "up into a very high mountain and showed Him all the kingdoms of the world and the glory of them." It is manifest that the devil could not bring under the eye of our blessed Lord the whole round of the globe, with its mighty continents and vast mountain chains, its great dividing watercourses, and its endless distribution of tribes and peoples and nations; but he was able to fill the imagination partly through the hearing, partly through the sight, with an imposing tableau or glorious vision of all that the outspread world could offer to awaken the ambition or to excite the cupidity of man. He could, for example, have pointed out the directions in which lay the most important regions of the world, while he descanted upon the enviable destiny of him who held in each the reins of empire, and commanded the overflowing riches, the priceless minerals and precious metals, the various and inestimable produce, and the industrial and artistic treasures for which they were severally remarkable. Or he might have employed his power over the elements to conjure up in the air around them a phantom representation blazing with the purple and gold of brilliant sunsets; a resplendent panorama showing the characteristic features which distinguished the different quarters of the earth; and then by a magnificent illusion seek to stupify the judgment, to overpower the self-discipline, and to inflame the passions of his hearer. The lying promise with which the devil sought to dupe Jesus was bad; it was worthy of the father of lies. But worse still was to follow: he would actually make his false bargain conditional upon his receiving the honour due to God made man. "All these," said he, "will I give Thee if, falling down, Thou wilt adore me." But once again his efforts were futile, and he recoiled in shame and brought discomfiture upon his own head. "Begone, Satan," said our blessed Lord, addressing the demon by a name which signifies foe or adversary. "Begone, for it is written: The Lord thy God, shalt thou adore, and Him only shalt thou serve."

The terrible power of that word "Begone," coming from the meek lips of the Lamb of God, the self-same word which, as Judge of the world, He will address to the reprobate at the last day, and which will be the inauguration of their everlasting doom—the awful indignation concentrated in that word, and provoked by the blasphemous overtures of the evil one, in trying to secure to himself the worship reserved to the Godhead—completed the overthrow of the tempter; "the devil left Him," and, as he vanished, with pride mortified, teeth gnashing, and eyes flaming malignant fire, behold, angels came to Jesus, the King of Kings and Lord of Lords, arrayed in the lowly garment of a worn and wasted body, "and ministered to Him," till the warmth of renewed life coursed through His veins and lost vigour returned to His famished limbs.

WALK IN LOVE.

Third Sunday of Lent.

"Be ye, therefore, followers of God, as most dear children: and walk in love, as Christ also hath loved us, and hath delivered Himself for us, an oblation and a sacrifice to God, for an odour of sweetness—*Ephes* v. 1-2.

IN the epistle, beloved Brethren, which we read on the third Sunday of Lent, we are reminded by St. Paul of the great duty of love towards our neighbour, and have our attention directed to powerful motives for the discharge of this duty. How all-important is the virtue of charity, we have abundantly pointed out to us in the New Testament. The practise of that virtue, according to the oracle of Divine Wisdom, the new and greater Solomon Himself, is only another name for universal uprightness. What did Our Blessed Lord answer, when asked which was the greatest commandment of the Law? "Thou shalt love the Lord thy God," said He, "with thy whole heart, and with thy whole soul, and with thy whole mind, and with thy whole strength—this is the first commandment. And the second is like to it: thou shalt love thy neighbour as thyself. There is no other commandment greater than these." Love, then, in its twofold aspect, as it looks to God on the one side, and to man on the other, is the ideal of Christian perfection. It embraces every element that goes to make up perfection: for he who loves God ardently, and loves his neighbour for God's sake, will omit no duty, which he owes to earth or to heaven. Hence charity is styled the bond of perfection, as uniting in one soul all the constituents of the perfect man. How nobly does St. Paul dilate on this thought in his glowing panegyric on the queen of virtues! "Charity," says he, "is patient, is kind; charity envieth not, dealeth not perversely, is not puffed up, is not ambitious; seeketh not her own, is not provoked to anger, thinketh no evil; rejoiceth not in iniquity, but rejoiceth with the truth; beareth all things, believeth all things, hopeth all things." These manifold qualities indeed, so varied and so precious, are but the gifts and fruits of that Spirit of Love, that dwells in the soul of the charitable Christian.

They are the variously wrought and brilliant panoply of the full-armed Christian soldier; and like the joints, plates, rings, and scales of some mediæval coat of mail, present an impenetrable defence against the missiles of the devil, the world, and the flesh, which are ever hissing through the air. Thus encased, the Christian warrior passes unscathed through the warfare of life, and presents a stainless record to his great Captain, when the campaign is over, and the hour for recompense has succeeded the term of sweat and hardship.

And the best token, beloved Brethren, of the presence of Divine charity in the soul, the least fallacious and misleading, is a spirit of charity towards our neighbour. It is comparatively easy to persuade ourselves that we love God, if we are not outwardly irregular in our lives, if we say our morning and night prayers, and are careful to keep the precepts of the Church, and fail not at reasonable intervals to approach the Sacraments. But a scrupulous attention to all these observances may go hand-in-hand with many ill-regulated desires and unmortified passions. In fact, all these practices may be assiduously followed by persons almost entirely devoid of a spirit of self-denial, and therefore destitute of the first essential of a Christian life, which is expressed by our Blessed Lord in the words: "If anyone will come after Me, let him deny himself, and take up his cross daily, and follow Me." Further than this, the Pharisee, who was so gratified by the contemplation of his own outward acts of devotion, while all the time he was loathsome in the sight of God, from his pride and self-sufficiency and contempt for others, teaches us plainly that our very perserverance in the outward observances of religion may be perverted into a means of offending God, by ostentation becoming an incentive to vanity or to pride, or by breeding a spirit of overweening self-reliance and disdain for our neighbour; vices which are sure to provoke opposition from Him "who resists the proud and gives His grace to the humble." But test your love of God by your love of your neighbour, and you cannot easily make a mistake. Are you gentle, kind, forbearing, forgiving, beneficent, not to those only to whom you feel an attraction, but to all alike, for the love of God? Do you turn your eyes away from their shortcomings, blemishes, and defects of character, with a deep sense of your own unworthiness in the sight of your common Maker, with an intimate recognition of your own feebleness and frailty in the midst of the dangers that beset your soul, and with a constant remembrance of the blots and plague-spots in your own past history, which should dispose you to condemn no sinner more than yourself? If you stand this test, blessed are you! The Spirit of God, the spirit of love, rests upon you: the spirit of wisdom and understanding, the spirit of counsel and fortitude, the spirit of knowledge and godliness; and you are filled with the spirit of the fear of the Lord. On this side of the grave, short of a Divine revelation, you can have no surer indication that you are united to God in the bonds of charity. "He that loveth his neighbour," says St. Paul to the Romans, "hath fulfilled the law. For thou shalt not commit adultery, thou shalt not kill, thou shalt not steal, thou shalt not bear false witness, thou shalt not covet, and if there be any other commandment, it is comprised in this word: Thou shalt love thy neighbour as thyself. The love of our neighbour worketh no evil. Love, therefore, is the fulfilling of the law." The same thought is thus expressed by St. John, the disciple of the Sacred Heart. "If we love one another, God abideth in us, and His charity is perfected in us."

And now, beloved Brethren, let us turn to the words of the Epistle, which I quoted to you at the opening of this discourse. "Be ye therefore," says St. Paul, "followers of God, as most dear children." The word "therefore" shows that the subject is continued from the close of the previous chapter. That chapter is made up in great measure of exhortations to the Christians of Ephesus to live a life worthy of their membership in the mystic body of Christ, to "put off the old man" and to "put on the new, who is created in justice, and holiness of truth." Amongst other vices unworthy of their character he bids the members of Christ to put away "all bitterness and anger, and indignation, and clamour, and blasphemy, with all malice." He concludes with these words: "And be ye kind one to another, merciful, forgiving one another, even as God hath forgiven you in Christ." "Be ye therefore," he continues, "followers of God, as most dear children." Be mindful, he says, of the mercy of that God, who has forgiven you the many sins and transgressions of your life, through the passion and death of His own beloved Son; and be kind and forgiving to others, as He has been kind and forgiving to you. Let the gentleness and lenity He has shown to you be the measure of your gentleness and lenity to your neighbour. Play not the part of the unjust servant in the Gospel, who had scarcely been forgiven the debt of ten thousand talents which he owed to his master, when he throttled his fellow-servant who owed him the paltry sum of a hundred pence; and in spite of the very entreaties which had won the wicked man his lord's compassion, ruthlessly "cast his debtor into prison till he had paid the debt." Be ye, on the contrary, imitators of your heavenly Father. You know that by baptism you received the adoption of sons, by which you cry "Abba, Father!" Prove your adoption as His children by exhibiting similar traits of character. Those who would make good their claim to be His children must renounce all petty spite and rankling enmities—must cease to brood over wrongs or insults or slights; must abjure every prospect of retaliation and revenge. As children of the gracious and merciful Majesty of heaven, stamped, as it were, with His lineaments, conformed to the likeness of His eldest born, Jesus Christ, endowed with the attributes of a noble lineage, they must enlarge their hearts and open them wide to every heaven-sent inspiration of generosity. They must make their souls, not nests for the adder-brood of poisoned rancour and ill-will, but homes where peace and gentleness, forbearance and meekness, compassion and forgiveness, like a holy sisterhood, shall be sweetly cloistered. Thus shall they be most dear children indeed; for God will, as it were, recognize in them His own beautiful features, His own high bearing, His own noble spirit; and will hold them dear in proportion to the fidelity with which they reproduce the type and mould of His nature. "Ye are gods," says the Holy Scripture, to such as these, "and every one of you sons of the Most High."

"And walk in love," continues the Apostle, meaning thereby to intimate that we should not be content with the charity we have acquired, which, in spite of all our efforts, will fall short of perfection, but should labour to advance nearer and nearer to the standard of God's own love. And what sort of love is that? You may conjecture its might and fervour indeed from the bounteous hand, with which the divine Creator has enriched and beautified the world for man's abode, designed the glorious heavens, arranged the varying seasons of the year, made sunshine and rain our ministers, brought countless forms of sustenance out of the bosom of earth, called forth refreshing and strengthening draughts out of its veins to cheer the heart of man.

Still more clearly may you estimate His fondness for His poor creature by the stupendous elaboration evinced in man's being; in his body, with its multitudinous bones and joints, its divers organs so ingenious and varied in their structure, its senses so diversified and minute in their mechanism, each opening out a distinct and separate world of impressions, its million-woven system of nerves, each the channel of sensations, or the electric messenger of the will; its complicated, yet most orderly cordage of sinews and tendons, twined in thousands upon thousands through and through and round the bony skeleton; its admirable assortment of tissues, firm or soft, and of humours so varied in their constitution to suit their several situations; and lastly its marvellous system of blood-vessels, with the great central engine, the heart, propelling the stream of life through every minutest particle of the body, and repairing the constant wear and tear upon the whole structure. How lovingly is all this planned, how carefully and minutely is it carried out to the very last detail! No monastic illuminator, glowing with the passion for his art, ever laboured so affectionately over the minutiæ of his most cherished design, as God, our loving Creator, has laboured, so to speak, over this masterpiece of His wisdom and His power.

But the body, with all its wonders, is outdone by the soul. This impalpable essence, whose presence in the body is its only safeguard against collapse and dissolution—how marvellous is it in itself and in the powers it wields! Think of its various faculties: that imagination, which can reproduce the absent or the past in its own living shapes and hues; that intellect, which can analyze, compare, reason, and build up sciences; that memory, which is so capacious a store-house of facts, and fancies, and conclusions; that superb endowment of the will, which enables man to turn hither and thither, according to the impulse of his affections or the decisions of his judgment; the countless winged movements of the feelings, which wait on knowledge. How noble is this soul, which gives us a kinship with the Spirits of heaven, and with the infinite, indivisible Godhead! How great, how incomprehensible is the love, that planned its constitution, and set upon it the seal of the Divine image and likeness! It is perhaps only in disease or delirium that we can appreciate the multiplicity and grandeur of the soul's faculties; when we see them in their tottering whirl and wild confusion, like the towers of some noble castle in the convulsions of earthquake. Then only can we know how many voices go to make up the harmony of the entire soul when

> "We see that noble and most sovereign reason
> Like sweet bells jangled out of tune, and harsh."

But all these evidences of love are as nought to the mystery of man's redemption, and it is from this mainly that St. Paul draws his motive for charity to all men. "Walk in love," he says, "as Christ also hath loved us, and hath delivered Himself for us, an oblation and a sacrifice to God, for an odour of sweetness." If you would know how to love your neighbour look at your crucifix. Behold the victim of salvation, supported between guilty earth and offended heaven by His nail-pierced hands and feet. Look at those quivering limbs that tell of agony in every nerve, pale as the limbs of death, save for the incrustation of gore that clings around them. Look at that head, so drooped and heavy, clasped round with a cruel diadem, that crowns but to torture. Look at that face, so ghastly in its revelations of anguish, yet so full of gentleness and resignation and love for all mankind. There you read the love of the Father, Who spared not even His own Son, but delivered Him up for us all. There you read the love of that Son of God Who, though He thought it no robbery to be equal to His Father, yet emptied Himself, taking the form of man; came down from heaven and assumed our flesh, becoming a child of Adam and a scion of an attainted race; and then in the flower of His age delivered Himself up for us to God, an oblation and a sacrifice for an odour of sweetness. Ponder upon the love that urged Him to endure the most unheard of and inconceivable torments, not from necessity, but from deliberate choice. "Oblatus est quia ipse voluit." "He was offered up because He willed it." Ponder upon the spirit of forgiveness and compassion which filled the heart of Him who in His death agony pleaded for the pardon of His most bitter and implacable enemies: "Father forgive them, for they know not what they do." Thus, "greater love than this no man hath, that He laid down His life for His friend." And remember that this Saviour, Whose life you are pledged to imitate, and Whose maxims you are pledged to follow, has made that charity, which nailed Him to the cross, the badge and token of discipleship: "By this shall all men know that you are my disciples—if you have love one for another."

PASSION SUNDAY.

Affliction Transformed and Consecrated by the Sufferings of Jesus.

TO-DAY, beloved Brethren, our thoughts are directed by our holy mother, the Church, to the Passion of our blessed Lord. We are invited to meditate on the depths and intensity of his sufferings, and the mysterious motives of his voluntary and life-long pains, and his most tragic death. You know that sorrow and suffering, both mental and physical, are the offspring of sin. As the earth would not have burst into thorns and briars but for the blighting influence of the curse which it had provoked, neither would the body have become yoked to ceaseless labour, and oppressed with wearisome burthens, the victim of countless ailments, and a target for the unseen arrows of death; nor, on the other hand, would the soul have been the prey of so many fretful and feverish passions, so many agents of care and misery, if Adam had not failed in his trial, and forfeited for his descendants the privilege of a calm and well-ordered mind, and a body that harmonized with its spiritual guide and companion.

To Adam's rebellion, all earthly miseries are due. For God appointed, as he had every right to do, that our happiness on this side of the grave should depend on our first father's steadfastness and unwavering fidelity. Suffering and sorrow should come only at his invitation. In punishment of sin, God would consign the race of mankind to a temporal lot of hardship and manifold trouble. He would behold a spectacle he had not desired to witness; wretchedness and poverty, toil and sweat, sickness and deformity, death in many ghastly manifestations, rampant tyranny and groaning serfdom. His ear would be filled with cries of anguish and moans of despondency. His eyes would look through all the ages upon the creation he had made so fair transformed into a wilderness of thorns, a vale of tears.

But this vision of woe had another chapter not read by carnal eyes. It had its finale beyond the grave. There, in that land of retribution and justice, every inequality in man's lot in this world of April changes was compensated and balanced. Man's life was shown to be a brief prelude to his real destiny; and all his pains and griefs, however poignant and distressing to him once, seemed now as the unsubstantial shadows of the brain that scare the dreamer, or as the ailments of childhood that have left scarce a trace upon the memory. There the mystery of human affliction will be solved, and it will be shown that crosses and trials borne for God's sake were unspeakable blessings and graces, and ought to have been regarded as means and prognostics of a more fond and intimate union hereafter with the God of all delight and happiness. There it will be seen that earthly disadvantages and reverses were an unmixed evil, only for those whose depraved and disorderly lives made their lot in this world but the foreshadowing and warrant for worse pains and penalties in the world to come. To all but these, temporal afflictions were but God's angels, who, under a rough and unacceptable disguise, brought to our dwellings hours of spiritual plenty, and assurances of everlasting bliss.

But it must be observed, beloved Brethren, that in the old Law, the value of suffering in a spirit of patience and resignation to God's will was but dimly realized. For God, whose contact with the chosen people was more palpable and obvious to the senses than it became later, seems to have guaranteed his servants, in the ordinary course of His providence, against any overwhelming pressure or long-continued strain, if only they remained faithful to His inspirations, and corresponded with His grace. Frequently the children of Abraham were promised by the mouths of the prophets, that God would protect them from the wiles of their enemies, that in their straits He would draw nigh to them and open His ears to their petitions, and that He would gird them round with the serried phalanx of His unconquered angels. These promises were an evidence of His mercy, for they were made to an unspiritual and ungracious people, whose hearts were won most easily by earthly baits, as the strongest agency to steady their vacillating wills, and attract them to virtue, by coupling it with worldly prosperity. It was with this view that God recorded in the tablets of His Decalogue the promise that He would bless with a long life the children who should obey their parents.

And again, He stamped His image upon their souls as that of a jealous God, sworn to visit the sins of the parents upon their children to the third and fourth generation, and by this device frightened out of their evil habits many parents, who were less anxious to gratify their Maker than to shield their descendants from the scourge of vengeance. Hence, among the Jews, prosperity was regarded in the course of God's ordinary providence as the token and reward of merit, and adversity as the wages of sin.

The Jews had, indeed, before them the story of Holy Job, and knew how God was angered by the superficial and hollow speeches of his friends, who could not see him beaten to the ground by misfortune, his father's heart riven hopelessly by the sudden loss of his children, his body embossed and festering with loathsome sores, and lying helpless on a dung hill, without taking it for granted that these visitations were the consequences of his crimes. But even the story of Job's sorrows contained a sequal, which obscured its moral: for the holy man was elevated, after his term of trial, to more than the wealth and splendour of his former condition. To the minds of the Jews, therefore, nothing would be more natural than to ask our blessed Lord regarding the blind man. "Hath this man sinned, or his parents?" For they did not readily conceive of misfortune except as the direct outcome of guilt.

Such was the conviction deeply ingrained in their minds, that earthly happiness was the attendant of virtue, and that even on this side of the grave, misery, and overthrow awaited impiety. But with our blessed Lord a new era came; and hardships, pain and calamity, the offspring of sin, were consecrated, and hallowed, and rendered desirable guests by Him who was to redeem us from sin. Sinless himself, He would become the victim of sin's curse. In His own being, in the human soul and the human body which He assumed, and made divine, He would experience every distress, every care, every cross, that sin has given birth to, with the exception of sin itself. By a death most unparalleled for its accompaniments of torment of mind and body, and public disgrace and infamy, He would purchase us a title to life eternal and the glory of His kingdom; and by His voluntarily taking on himself every affliction of human nature, He would commend suffering for God's sake, as a sublime and enviable lot, and reconcile us to the troubles and trials involved in our existence. He would teach us by His example how to bear ourselves under the stroke of misfortune. He would give us a new motive for courageous endurance, viz. : the loving desire to be His comrade in the night of His sorrow, and a profound esteem of the privilege accorded to us, when He invites us by His heralds, pain and adversity, to watch one hour with Him, and share His dread agony in the garden. He would, in fine, urge us, as far as our frailty would admit, to long for contempt, and suffering, and hardship, as a proof that we seek to be no mere sunshine friends, who are apt to be profuse in their protestations of love amid the splendour of Thabor, and to absent themselves from the trials of Calvary. He would teach us to fix our thoughts on the Sabbath of everlasting rest and peace, which awaits the virtuous in the world to come; and to seek nothing in this life, which is under the ban of sin, except patience and resignation amidst the showers and wild tempests which, in spite of spells and glimpses of sunshine, are its normal and its merited portion. "I have given my body to the strikers, and my cheeks to them that plucked them; I have not turned my face from them that rebuked me and spit upon me."

With these kindly purposes in His mind, beloved Brethren, our dear Lord and Master came down amongst us. You know the outline of that life, you have some faint idea—for faint at best it needs must be—of the trials and the sorrows which this life entailed, He did not merely preach the beatitudes of willing poverty and griefs endured in a spirit of patience, He showed His esteem for the hard conditions of existence, by being Himself poor and pre-eminently the Man of Sorrows. "Blessed are the poor in spirit, for theirs is the kingdom of heaven: Blessed are they that mourn, for they shall be comforted"—these eternal truths, the only true source of consolation and fortitude, were not merely with Him the text of a discourse, but the motto of His whole career—its key and interpretation.

What a panorama does that career exhibit. The little hushed room at Nazareth that echoed the Archangel's message; the rock-hewn stable at Bethlehem, icy-cold with the rigours of a winter's midnight; the desert sands, tracked by the hurrying feet of His fugitive parents; the far-off land of Egypt, where He is lost amidst a teeming and idolatrous population, an atom in the mass of seething and struggling indigence; the workshop of Nazareth, where the hands that hung the lights of heaven in their places ply the carpenter's tools for a scanty and hard-earned livlihood; the daily task performed day in and day out; the monotonous routine from year's end to year's end till manhood's full maturity; the humble concomitants of His public mission, with the fame of which He might have filled the world; the instructions given on the lake shore or on the grassy hillside; the crowd of wretched and forlorn creatures that hang on His words, and gaze stupified at His miracles, and eagerly eat the bread which in His compassion He breaks to them; the malignant eyes of them that follow Him, and note His every act for malignant purposes; the weariness of His journeyings to and fro in search of the poor lost sheep of Israel; the coarse and scanty sustenance, often deferred beyond the demands of nature; the shelter of a roof offered to Him in charity; the stony couch among the mountains, under the canopy of heaven: the hall of judgment; the lying witnesses; the howling rabble; the fast-flowing gore gathering in one red pool beneath the whistling scourges; the agony of the mock coronation and the derisive homage; the cuffs and blows; the stumbling journey to Calvary; the last three hours of unimaginable anguish, with a whirlpool of human passions seething and roaring like a hell below; the heavens above darkened by the frown of an angry God. Oh! truly can He say, "All ye that pass by the way attend and see if there be sorrow like unto My sorrow."

Yes, my Brothers, sons of men, you have all your own griefs, your own trials, your own several afflictions. But be assured they are slight in comparison with Mine; My heart has absorbed your griefs and added them to its own. For this I came into this world, for this was a body fitted to Me that I might suffer the atonement due to each of you separately, and might bear in My own single frame, as the holocaust that must be consumed for the sins of all, the chastisement alloted to every living child of Adam. "Truly," cries out the prophet Isaias, "He has borne our infirmities and carried our sorrows—despised and the most abject of men—a man of sorrows and acquainted with infirmity. And we have thought Him a leper, and one struck by God and afflicted. But He was wounded for our iniquities, and bruised for our sins. The chastisement of our peace was upon Him and by His bruises we are healed. All we like sheep have gone astray, every one hath turned aside in his own path, and the Lord hath laid upon Him the iniquity of us all."

ON PALM SUNDAY.

AGAIN, beloved Brethren, the day has come round which ushers in the most solemn and eventful week in the history of the world. For the thoughtful Christian, we are on the eve of a period teeming with motives for adoring wonder, penitent grief, hope, love and confidence. Not without a sigh, indeed, can we approach the hour of the passion, when the envy and malice of men, long struggling for a rent, broke in tempests and whirlwinds of fury over the innocent Lamb of God, when He was torn with scourges, mocked, spit upon, and finally nailed to a tree, hand and foot, and left to bleed to death in naked immolation between earth and heaven.

But before we come to that last scene, our hearts are rejoiced to see the triumph of our dear Redeemer, even before the eyes of His enemies. He, whose voice smote to the ground the men that came to apprehend Him, and who, nevertheless, submitted to their violence, after asserting His power, was not to undergo the humiliations and horrors of death, until He had enjoyed the glory of a triumph; that so the world might see that He was in truth offered because He himself willed it. Often and often, when the people would have Him king, He had slipped from their hands. But now that the end was near, He wished, before leaving them, to receive their public homage, to have their public acknowledgment of His mission as the Messiah of God; so that He, over whose drooping head the ironical testimony should by and by be written "Jesus of Nazareth, King of the Jews," should first have a testimony of His kingship from the sincere of heart.

Arise then Jerusalem, and come forth to meet your king: for God says, by the prophet:—" Tell ye the daughter of Sion: Behold thy king cometh to thee, meek, and sitting upon an ass, and a colt, the foal of her that is used to the yoke" This, then, is the day chosen for His triumph. And what a triumph it is! How different from that which awaits Him eight days hence, when, the trial over and the work done, He shall rise up out of the jaws of the tomb, strong, glorious, and immortal, the light of earth and the lamp of Paradise. Nay, how different from the pomp and pageant with which earthly kings and conquerors celebrate their exploits! No gilded chariots, groaning with the spoils of war, adorn this procession; no long line of sculptured busts, borne by vassals of noble blood, exhibits the ancient ancestry of the Conqueror; no clanking of captive chains makes grim music in the ears of the people. No, "They brought Him the ass and the colt; and laid their garments upon them, and made Him sit thereon. And a very great multitude spread their garments in the way; and others cut boughs from the trees, and strewed them in the way; and the multitudes that went before and that followed, cried, saying: 'Hosanna to the Son of David. Blessed is He that cometh in the name of the Lord.'"

And so this strange procession passes along. From every quarter of the city crowds of people, attracted by the shouts of joy, pour into the street along which the poor King and His motley subjects are advancing. And as they come in by road or lane or alley, many of them hasten to join the throng before or after, swelling the chorus of blessings, and waving the branches which are being distributed among them. From housetops and windows faces peer in eager curiosity, mingled, according to the character of the persons, with gladness, admiration, love, contempt, or diabolical hatred. On the skirts of the advancing crowds here and there stands a scowling Pharisee, conspicuous by his band of inscribed piety upon his brow, and his broad fringe bearing embroidered texts of Scripture. Here and there a Scribe, or a group of Scribes, fix their malignant eyes upon the central figure. And as He smiles upon His apostles and disciples, or looks round graciously upon the multitude, or fondly observes the little children, whose innocent lips are shaping His praises and whose tender hands are struggling to raise the branches, to them cumbrous as banners; these Scribes and Pharisees remember, with a shudder and a pang of hate, how the tranquility of that divine face was once terribly broken, how those meek eyes flashed with a superhuman fire, and the voice, ringing like a trumpet of doom, poured out on their heads before all the people its torrent of woes: "Woe to you, Scribes and Pharisees, hypocrites!" With trembling hands they clutch their showy garments—the whited side of the sepulchre—mutter curses between their grinding teeth, and swear to have His heart's blood. Too soon, alas! will that dark vow have its fulfilment!

But turn from these frowning faces, stamped with an expression of hatred such as Cain's bore when he went forth with his confiding brother upon the fatal journey; turn to the more pleasing features of the procession. Trophies are not wanting, the living and breathing trophies of His saving power over body and soul. Here you may see those who had once been cripples skipping joyous as the roe, and sending up peals of blessings upon the hand that had effected their cure; those who had been blind beaming their gratitude upon the kindly face whose smile is to them a foretaste of heaven. Creatures once palsied, or scaled with leprosy, or tormented by evil spirits, press forward to hail their deliverer. And around them, wherever they go, a little knot of friends or acquaintances, well versed in the story of their miraculous recovery, throng and bustle, with renewed congratulations and redoubled joy. Nay, those who had passed the dark door of death and had been summoned back by the voice of Him who is Master of Death and Author of Life are there. And streaming eyes, too, may be seen, that tell of hearts which once had been hard as flint, but which the grace of that Saviour had turned to fountains of sorrow and of love. Many a Magdalen, whose story is unrecorded except in heaven, conveyed her profound and inexhaustable grief and thanksgiving through swimming eyes to that sweet King Who alone had power to snatch them as brands from the burning fire. Many a soul, weaned, by a word or look of Jesus, from a passion for the passing world, its riches, its honours, or its pleasures, again sent up to heaven a cry of gratitude, and blessed the God of all mercies, Who, having spoken by the prophets, had at length chosen to speak by the voice of His only Son. Others there are, too, faithful hearts, but timid as yet, like Nicodemus, whose love and admiration break forth, not in acclamations that startle the sense, but with the inward voice of praise and jubilee, not unheard amid the tumult by our Saviour's ear. At length all the city is poured along the line of the procession; strangers and denizens, witnesses of the extraordinary spectacle, or sharers in it: "And when He was come into Jerusalem the whole city was moved; saying, Who is this? And the people said; This is Jesus the prophet, from Nazareth of Galilee." And thus the journey's end is reached; the crowd disperse to their homes, bearing their branches with them as momentoes of the day; and as night falls the Saviour of the World nerves His strength for the coming trial; His enemies are devising plans for His ruin.

The Church, beloved Brethren, is not content that you should give a transient thought to the events of our Lord's life. She brings them vividly before the mind, in her various functions and services, joyous or sorrowful, and in a certain sense makes us participators in them. She is not like those so-called Christian communions that can be so dead and callous in their sympathies as to turn Good Friday into a day of feasting and revelry; and to allow their people to dance and sing and flock to picnics, when our Divine Redeemer is crying out in grief and loneliness: "O all ye that pass by the way, attend and see if there be any sorrow like to my sorrow." Every joy and sorrow of His awakens a kindred feeling in the breast of the Church. And so to-day she puts the new-budding twigs into your hands, as she did in the hands of your grandfathers and great-grandfathers, and bids you join in the triumph of your humble King, and unite your hosannas to those of the children of Sion throughout the world. Praise and bless Him from the bottom of your hearts. Recall the many kindnesses He has bestowed upon you since your birth, both those which you have received in common with your fellow-Christians and those which have been peculiar to yourselves. If you have already been reconciled to Him by a good Confession, rejoice His heart by renewing with fervour your good resolutions, and asking Him to bless them. And if you have not as yet complied with the precepts of the Church, be assured that you can give Him no greater consolation, no greater return for His bounty, than by fitting yourselves without delay through the life renewing sacraments to join with those whom He had raised at once from their varied diseases of body, and from the more fatal disease and death of sin, and with His faithful disciples and the guileless children in crying "Hosannah the Son of David! Blessed is He who cometh in the name of the Lord. Hosannah in the highest."

EASTER SUNDAY.

Regina Cœli, Laetare.

THERE are indeed, beloved Brethren, many motives for rejoicing to-day, when the new-risen sun spreads abroad from East to West the glad tidings that the King of Glory has arisen from the captivity of the grave, and broken the brazen fetters of death. Of those motives, I will select one for a brief meditation before we part.

Of all the hearts to whom the events of the first Easter Sunday brought joy and rapture, there was none so full, none so jubilant, as Our Lady's. To her, tradition says, He first appeared after His resurrection; and well may we believe it; or rather, it would be incongruous to suppose otherwise. No one had been so desolated, so harrowed, by His passion as she, the mother who had borne Him and fed Him from her own substance, brought Him up a sweet, tender, and obedient child; and even during his public life, when separation was unavoidable, had lived in His occasional smile, and followed Him with an imagination which was an instrument of joy and sorrow by turns, through all the chequered vicissitudes of His public career—His labours, His triumphs, and His dangers. Finally, no one had been admitted to such a share in the torments of His passion as she. God had so willed it, that the Man of Sorrows should involve in His painful expiation the gentle, mild, affectionate mother, whom He loved beyond all creatures, and to whom He owed his existence as man. Over the heads of both the thunder of God's justice roared, and His lightning flashed. And why should she be drawn into the awful circle of atonement? Beloved Brethren, it was, amongst other reasons, that our Lord might be able to show us that He had not spared Himself a single pain; that he had not even shrunk, for our sakes, from seeing His best-beloved, dearest mother, agonizing and breaking her heart. Thenceforth he could say without danger of contradiction that He had loved us to the end, to the extreme limit of love. If the Father had not spared Him, neither had He spared His own mother. And oh! beloved Brethren, it needed no special decree to rack that mother's heart at the sight of her Son's sufferings. She could not endure less than she did without loving Him less. You will never know how much she suffered, until you know how much she loved. You have often meditated, but never can fathom or conceive, what a deathlike agony seized her soul, when, on learning that at last the expected blow had been struck, and her love was in the midst of His raging enemies, as the lamb amid hungry wolves, she tottered forth with reeling head and burning brow, and met Him face to face at the turn of the road, along which He was staggering to death.

Oh! mothers, you alone can dimly picture her feelings. Her darling amid a circle of fiends, vying with each other in inflicting cuffs and blows and outrages, every one of which she feels more keenly than if it were inflicted upon her own pale cheek or delicate frame. He raises His drooped head; for His heart tells Him she is there—the mother He loves. Their eyes meet; and oh! the eclipse of that sun-like countenance. It is life in death. She would fain call the mountains to fall upon her; but she must bear up. She follows Him as He stumbles step by step, with frequent heavy falls, to the place that is called Calvary. And there—it is by a miracle that her heart does not burst asunder—she sees His garments torn from His back, His naked body, all one wound, flung upon the hard bed of the cross, the nails struck in with brutal eagerness through quivering flesh and sinew; and then, amid hoarse cries of sated vengeance, He is reared up into the air, and pants pitiously over her head. All the three hours she stands by Him, hearing His moans and sobs of pain; she cannot give Him relief; she cannot offer Him a drop of water to quench His fevered thirst; nay, she knows that, though her place is by the Cross, and under the shadows of Him she loves, her very presence adds bitterness to His cup. At last, amid the gathering darkness, and the first rumbling threats of earthquake, she sees Him move convulsively. "It is consummated," He cries; with one great sigh He yields His spirit, and His stark body hangs senseless from the tenacious nails. The earthquake comes; many leave the ground beating their breasts, and shaping their steps tremblingly towards the hushed and frowning city. But she abides there, heedless of all but that livid and crimsoned corpse. She is there, and cannot interfere, when the soldier strikes his lance into the side. Evening closes, and Joseph and Nicodemus come with spices and fine linen. Then softly, as one bereaved beyond hope, she assists in washing and embalming the poor ruin; raining her tears thick and fast into the trenched gashes and wounds, that score it all over. Too soon, the sad, but soothing task is done; and the shades of night give warning she must bid farewell to the treasure, around which her heart clings. They lay Him in the grave; and she composes the limbs in their obscure resting place, covering them fondly and lingering with the linen shroud; and kissing the clammy and discoloured lips, dull now and insensible as the sod she stands on. One last farewell; and she tears herself away; and like one in a trance she bears her bleeding heart home to her desolate dwelling.

All the Friday night, all the long, long Saturday, all the heavy night that followed, her soul was watching in His grave, nursing her sorrow in its congenial darkness. But as the first grey streaks of dawn began to wake on the horizon, ushering in the day of joy, a wondrous change came over her spirit. She heard the loud sound with which the stone was rolled away by the two angel watchers; and oh, glorious heaven! her Son, her beloved, her joy, her life. He comes forth mighty as a conqueror, bright beyond the brightness of earth, with the freshness and youth of eternal life upon His brow and in His limbs. A moment and she is locked in His embrace, as happy as she had been wretched; too happy to live were it not for the strength He gives her. He is risen indeed, to die now no more. His wounds, that had so defaced His beauty, did but add now to its splendour and glory. Here I must pause. Let the angels who witnessed that interview, if any were privileged so far, describe its rapture. Human tongue must falter here, human conception grows feeble.

Give her joy, then, beloved Brethren, along with holy Mother Church to-day, upon the event which has dried her eyes and turned her mourning into gladness. Rejoice with her to the utmost of your power, and thank God, who has blessed her sacrifice with so ample, so indescribable a reward. But if you would give her joy indeed, you must promise her to strive henceforth and live a life more worthy of the lavish and infinite aids to virtue bestowed upon you. In particular, promise her that you will not stain the season of her glad triumph by a relapse into your past evil habits, that you will not profane it by any excess of worldly feasting or merriment. Pray most earnestly that you, her guilty child, so often in the past giving grief to her heart, may bring her joy at length, in that you have risen to a life of grace and true repentance, and left the swathing bands of sin behind for ever in the tomb.

LOW SUNDAY.

Joy of a Cleansed Conscience.

NOW, beloved Brethren, that you have all, as I sincerely trust, cleansed your consciences from the stain of sin by a good confession, it behoves you to ponder well what a treasure you have acquired in recovering the grace and favour of God, and what precautions you must take to keep that treasure for the future safe from the attacks of the devil.

Consider, then, the wondrous condition to which you have attained if you have cast off the burthen of sin and taken upon you the light yoke of Christ—the yoke of obedience and self-constraint. You are no longer a captive of the devil, bound hand and foot with the chains of iniquity, awaiting only the signal of death to be hurled into the dungeon of eternal woe, where the worm dieth not, and the fire is not extinguished. Trusting in the mercies of the God Who for your sake spared not His only-begotten Son, you no longer fear to look death in the face, you no longer shudder in despair and blank dismay at the prospect of the judgment. Your enjoyments are no longer tinged with bitterness and troubled with alarms, like a man who should strive in vain to forget that he was tracked and followed by a phantom. For in truth death and its dark train are no longer spectres from which you avert your eyes; you can now say courageously, " Death, where is thy sting? Death, where is thy victory?" For the sting of death is sin. When night falls upon the earth you can commit yourselves, in trustfulness and hope, to the keeping of God, as a child finds its safest cradle and its sweetest sleep in its mother's lap. " He that dwelleth in the aid of the Most High shall abide under the protection of the God of Jacob. He shall say to the Lord: Thou art my protector and my refuge; my God, in Him will I trust. For He hath delivered me from the snare of the hunters, and from the sharp word. He will overshadow thee with His shoulders, and under His wings thou shalt trust. His truth shall compass thee with a shield; thou shalt not be afraid of the terror of the night, of the arrow that flieth in the day, of the business that walketh in the dark, of the invasion of the noonday devil." And when you rise in the morning your first feeling will not be that which springs from morose indifference, sullen recollection of your guilt, renewed hardness of heart, and reckless forecasting of the future; but rather a sense of joy and vigour, a healthy welcoming of the hours of labour, a grateful memory of God's kindness, and a new resolution to walk before God, and to work with Him. "I will always keep Thy law for ever and ever." And oh! the fortitude which a good conscience inspires in the hour of failure and adversity. To the wicked this world is all-in-all; their pleasure, such as it is, may gallop as the far as the churchyard gate; beyond the grave there is no hope for them. Is it any wonder, then, that they should be crushed to the earth beneath worldly disasters, knowing as they do that they have no friend in God, who alone can repair the evil and lighten the cross.

In such visitations, they may maintain an outward show of courage, nay, they may be supported to a certain degree by their strength of nerve, and their natural bravery, qualities inherent in their flesh and bone, thews and sinews; but there is beneath all an inward gnawing that passes beyond the body and eats at the very marrow of the soul, an aching sense of the hollowness of all things, a feeling that this pain may be only the foretaste of the eternal torments, which are the wages of a life of sin, the fruit of an habitual indifference to salvation. How often do they, under these trials, strive to buoy up their sinking courage with deep potations; killing their reason, to keep their fortitude alive; and drugging themselves with strong drink until they cannot look steadily at their misfortunes. Call this courage, call it manliness, if you like—but watch the poor wretch as he emerges, ghost-like, from his unnatural debauch; hang over him, as with trembling limbs, and head clouded and aching, he cons over anew in ghastly silence all the circumstances of his misery! It is a picture easier to conjure up, than to paint.

How, on the other hand, does the man whose conscience is clean, regard the woes and crosses of life? He needs no pot-valour. His hope, his trust is in God; the same God, whose voice stilled the raging storm, the Master of life, and all its ups and downs; the same who said, "Seek ye first the kingdom of God, and all other things shall be added unto you." The good man knows that God strikes only to heal; and that if He decrees earthly losses, it is only with a view to bestow infinite and eternal gain. Thus, whatever be the forfeit required of him, he cries out with holy Job: "The Lord hath given, the Lord hath taken away: Blessed be the name of the Lord for ever." However dense the darkness that envelops him, however grievous the troubles, however threatening the danger, his prayer is that of the Psalmist "The Lord is my light and my salvation, whom shall I fear? The Lord is the protector of my life: of whom shall I be afraid? . . . . It armies in camp should stand together against me, my heart shall not fear. If a battle should rise up against me, in this will I be confident." Knowing that soon this world, and its joys and sorrows, will fall from about him, and he will find himself in a strange land, where those who have suffered in patience shall be crowned with joy, and reap in exultation, he is anxious only to keep in the grace of God and to submit to His will: "One thing I have asked of the Lord, this will I seek after; that I may dwell in the house of the Lord all the days of my life. That I may see the delight of the Lord and visit His temple." The very Pagans recognised the sublime and unshaken fortitude derived from uprightness of life. "If a man be virtuous," says one of the poets, "and persevering in his resolves, the fiery passions of the mob will never shake his will; the frowns of tyranny will never move him from his rooted purpose; the stormy winds that rule the sea; the thunderbolts of heaven, will not terrify him. Nay, if the earth's huge frame should fall to pieces, and the universe crack asunder, all undismayed, he would see the hideous wreck, and meet his doom without a tremor."

As for prosperity, beloved Brethren, there can be no greater scourge to the wicked. The gifts and the goods, the honours and enjoyments, which ought to make them thankful to God, do but exalt their self conceit; do but raise them up to give them a heavier fall. Their good fortune, which to their fellows is an object of envy, is only a surer prelude to their final destruction. It is the opiate that drowses their souls and leaves them in a lethargy and a stupor, while death and the devil, stealing upon them, are drawing near without being perceived. Listen to the awful passage in Job and it will make you exclaim. "May the prosperity of the wicked never be mine": "Why do the wicked live, and are advanced and strengthened with riches? Their seed continueth before them, a multitude of kinsmen and of children's children in their sight. Their houses are secure and peaceable, and the rod of God is not upon them. Their cattle have conceived and failed not; their cow has calved and is not deprived of her fruit. Their little ones go out like a flock, and their children dance and play. They take the timbrel and the harp, and rejoice at the sound of the organ. They spend their days in wealth, and in a moment they go down to hell."—Chap. xxi.

Take then, beloved Brethren, every care of that treasure of a good conscience, which will lighten the weight of adversity, and make success powerless to harm you. Prize above all things the peace of a good conscience, that peace which the world cannot give, that peace which sin alone can take away. Let this be in your eyes the pearl of price. Often repeat the words of our Lord: "What doth it profit a man if he gain the whole world and suffer the loss of his soul." To make sure of a happy death give up every earthly toy and hobby, every entangling pleasure, every blinding interest, which has injured your past. Remember, it is better, as Thomas à Kempis says, to lead a good life than to be afraid of death. Let every obstacle to your salvation be unhesitatingly put aside; every tie which binds you down to sin ruthlessly cut. Though it wound you to the heart abjure for ever the company that stood between you and God and made your salvation more and more doubtful every day of your life. He that clings to the dangerous occasions of sin, he that loves the haunts and breathes the atmosphere of his former vices will soon lose his innocence, soon part with his peace "If thy right eye scandalize thee pluck it out and cast it from thee. For it is expedient for thee that one of thy members should perish rather than thy whole body be cast into hell. And if thy right hand scandalize thee cut it off and cast it from thee; for it is expedient for thee that one of thy members should perish, rather than that thy whole body go into hell." —*Matthew*, v. 29.

THE GOOD SHEPHERD.

SECOND SUNDAY AFTER EASTER.

IN to-day's Gospel, beloved Brethren, our blessed Lord presents himself to our minds in the character of the Good Shepherd who, when the ravening wolves assail His fold, instead of flying to secure His personal safety at the cost of the flock, like the hireling, cheerfully lays down His life to secure them from danger. To us of these cooler climes, that image brings little hint of the fond tenderness of which, to the Oriental mind, it was and still is the type. Among the people of the East, the shepherd was no rough keeper of the fold, who looked upon his fleecy charge as brutes worthy of his care only for the profit they were likely to afford. There, the shepherd loved his sheep, as a poor helpless thing, capable of affection for the hand that fed it, and liable, if his watchful eye were turned, and withdrawn awhile, to quit his safe guardianship, and foolishly wander away outside the enclosures that sheltered it, thus running the risk of being entangled among the brambles and briars and thick underwood of the forests, or to fall from fatal heights, to which its curiosity had attracted it, or to be torn to pieces by the wild beasts that prowled among the desert rocks for their prey. These accidents the shepherds of those times feared, not only because they deprived him of valuable property, but even more because he was knit with kindliest feelings to the poor foolish creatures, which had been born under his eye, and skipped in the joy of their first conscious life around his feet, and which had been led by him, not driven, from one green place of luscious pasture to another, until he knew them well, and all their peculiar ways, and, so to speak, their individual characters; and day by day became more studious of their comfort than of his own. Under this sweet figure then, our blessed Lord would fain have us to regard Him, while we look upon ourselves as bound to Him, and claiming His care and supervision, because, to use the words of the Psalmist, "we are the sheep of His pasture." And under this aspect the prophet Isaiah had long before described Him, in words that seem to palpitate with living emotion. "He shall feed His flock like a shepherd," said he, "and He shall gather them together with His arm, and shall take them to His bosom."

And in the Epistle of to-day, beloved Brethren, St. Peter follows out the same thought, still in the lines of the sublime prophet whom I have quoted. "We have all gone astray like sheep, and have wandered every one into his own path; but God hath laid upon Him the iniquities of us all." This thought the prince of the Apostles repeats almost in the same words; adding, however, an encouragement appropriate to this season of reconciliation: "But now you are reconciled to your Pastor and to the Bishop of your souls."

And often must we ponder, beloved Brethren, when we come forth from the tribunal of penance absolved from our sins, how wayward we have been, and how misguided in our wanderings. Often must we repeat, with deep feelings of regret for the trouble which we have entailed upon the loving and devoted Pastor of our souls, the beautiful words of the old Psalter of Jesus: "Jesus, Jesus, Jesus, have mercy on me, O God of compassion, and forgive the many and great offences which I have committed in Thy sight. Many have been the follies of my life and great are the miseries which I have deserved for my ingratitude. Hear me, O Lord, for I am weak; heal me, for I am unable to help myself." Yes; many have been the evil ways which, weary and footsore, perhaps tired even of life, but still obstinately flying from our Good Shepherd, we have already traversed, though our years be but few. Often has His tearful eye, that sought us in every devious path and secret gully, and upon every jutting and dangerous crag, caught sight of us, as torn and bleeding and breathless in a prison of thorny and tenacious boughs, we waited for death, scarce caring whether it brought us oblivion of pain, or a mere exchange of misery for misery. And O! how thrilling was His voice when Hè called to us, how heart-piercing, how full of new hope and joy, as if it opened fountains of refreshment in our arid souls! We felt His tender hands as they extricated us; they were bleeding from the rough and pointed thicket boughs, and we were red with the falling drops, as He lifted us upon His shoulder and laid our poor soiled faces to His; and bore us back joyfully, with many a cheering word and many a caress, to the fold where the ninety-nine that had never wandered awaited His coming.

But, beloved Brethren, it is not my object this morning to extract from the parable of the Good Shepherd motives for contrition, but rather to direct your attention to the consoling words of St. Peter: "But now you are reconciled to your Shepherd, and to the Bishop of your souls." If you have confessed your sins in sincerity and sorrow, and formed the determination to avoid them henceforth, as well as every occasion which might frustrate that determination, you are, beyond the shadow of a doubt, again the friends of Jesus Christ, the beloved sheep of His pasture. This is a happiness which, if rightly estimated, should make a heaven of this work-a-day earth. It is a privilege that crowns you with bliss even in this land of cares, this valley of tears. For has not the Psalmist said: "Blessed are they whose iniquities are remitted and whose sins are covered." Yes, the blessing of God descends upon you at your rising and your retiring to rest; it is spread over you in your sleep like sheltering wings; it follows you at your going out and your coming in; it is with you in your labour and in your relaxation. And this is true no matter how wild you may have been your wanderings in the past. All your follies, all your wickedness, are now forgotten, though your soul should have been seared and blackened with the fire of your iniquities. Though you were found in the wilderness, or on the precipice, or in the chasm, foul with mire, torn, blood-stained, faint and hopeless, far from your Good Shepherd's protecting hand, you have been now washed snow-white, your wounds and bruises have been healed, you have been admitted again into the company of the gentle and docile flock, and no hour passes but the Shepherd gives you some token of His loving care; at one time caressing you and fondling you, as the prophet says, in His bosom, at another carrying you on His shoulders to the nook where the herbage is rich and juicy, or setting you down by the clear fountain to slake your thirst in the mid-day heats. It is thus that He provides us with abundant grace for our consolation and refreshment when we commune with Him in our morning and evening prayer, when we turn our hearts to Him in loving ejaculations from hour to hour, when we hear Mass devoutly on week-day or Sunday, above all when we approach the Sacraments, which that Good Shepherd has provided for us at the cost of His precious blood.

But more than this. No matter how you may have wandered in the past, you may now become a Saint. Your past remissness, your indifference, nay your malice, in sinning, contain no necessary prediction of future falls. God calls each one of you to be a Saint, and gives you each sufficient grace to make you so. "This is the will of God, your santification." Our blessed Lord never could have said: "Be ye perfect as my heavenly Father is perfect," without furnishing us with ample means to do His bidding. You can be perfect. And how? Simply by using the agencies of sanctification, which He has provided, viz :—prayer, the frequentation of the Sacraments, and the avoidance of those things which have been to you an occasion of sin. Employ these means perseveringly, and you must be saints. Though you should have been monsters and prodigies of vice, satanic in your pride, effeminate in your vanity, a griping wretch in your covetousness and rapacity, like shameless dogs in your lust, like tigers in your anger and vindictiveness, like swine in your helpless and untamed gluttony, consumed with the canker of jealousy and envy, and sunk in the slough of spiritual sloth, it still remains true, that if you use the means of sanctification—if you pray earnestly, approach the Sacraments at proper intervals, and shun the traps into which you have fallen—you will one day sit in the kingdom of heaven, beside sinless Confessors and Virgins, pure as radiant lilies, and the white-robed army of Martyrs, the blessed friend and favourite of your Master. Take the means: leave the rest to God. You need not be pierced to your heart's core by the sweetness of our blessed Saviour's human look, the speaking compassion and tenderness of His divine eyes, like the poor Magdalen when, in an instant of time, she was transformed from a demon of licence into the broken-hearted penitent, whose after-life was one long wail of sorrow and of burning love. You will not need to be stunned by the thunders of a celestial voice, like Saul, and smitten to the ground, blind and writhing; that from the furnace of a three-days horror you may come forth refined as gold. If you take the means, and persevere in their use, the miracle of your transformation is secure. As sure as the arch of heaven bends above you, and the earth is beneath your feet, as surely as the Almighty lives, in whom you can do all things, your old sinful predilections, your evil habits, the strong overruling bias that seemed to carry you into vice as the torrent carries a twig, will cease to sway you; and you will find yourselves, sooner or later, like the patriarch, walking before God in blamelessness, and attaching day to day like pearls by one continuous thread of merit.

And if, beloved Brethren, you would see this lesson embodied in flesh and blood, you have only to read the life of the great St. Austin. Who that knew him in his youth could have predicted that he was to become one of the purest, holiest, humblest souls, that earth ever gave to heaven; and that the genius, which he had in many ways abused, should at last be dedicated on the slter of God, and should be the glory and pride of the Church in every succeeding age. He spent his early years, notwithstanding the admonitions and the example of his saintly mother, Monica, in all the fashionable vices. He was handsome, and vain of his personal attractions. He was proud of his intellectual superiority, which he exhibited to win applause when opportunity offered. He was careless of religion, and critical of its claims, and quick to dispute its tenets; until at last, in the blindness which intellectual pride engenders, he enrolled his name among the followers of an impious, falsely-subtle, debasing sect, called the Manichees, who believed that all material things are in their essence evil. As might have been foreseen by such a nature, he was delivered up to the corrupt desires of his own heart, and became a captive to impure love, the galling chains of which he wore for many a year. You see in him, therefore, to all appearance, a dashing young man of the world, such as you may meet any day flaunting himself in the public eye on the pavement or in the theatre, with a reputation for extraordinary parts, but known to be living an immoral life, and having no savour of religious principle, though he may in his eccentricity and his love of admiration link himself for a while to the kindred vagaries of an absurd creed. He is, in short, a brand for the burning, and the demons may well calculate upon sooner or later possessing him.

It is a long tale—the tale of his wanderings, in which, at every turn, we meet the mother's form still praying for him in sorrow, but in hope. At last, slowly, and with desperate effort, under the influence of grace, like a man wrestling for life, he casts off the oppressive burthen of his sins; and though he can scarcely realize how his heart, so long a slave to the desires of the flesh, is to be freed from its vicious propensities, he courageously adopts the means pointed out for his improvement. And God rewarded him for his manly and trustful self-immolation. He tells us that he knew now, as he never had known it before, that the saying of the pagan poet was true: "He who makes a beginning has half done the deed." "How sweet," says he in his confessions, "how sweet in a moment it became, to forego the pleasure of those toys that had so long beguiled my fancy! What I had been so fearful of losing, I now threw from me with joy: for Thou, O Lord, didst become my sovereign source of pleasure; the light of my soul, brighter than all other lights, and the highest dignity that could crown my ambition." Thus insensibly, and almost without pain, when once he put his hand manfully to the plough, he found the obstacles which he had feared insuperable, like a heavy soil, giving way before him; and became aware that it is the difficulties we conjure up in our imaginations, rather than those which exist, which scare us from a good life. By a necessary law, he did but adopt the means of sanctification, and his sanctification followed. He had but to put the seed in the ground, God gave the increase; and the holy Monica, who had been to him, as he says, a two-fold mother, having giving him birth in the spirit as well as in the flesh, breathed her last, with his hot tears falling upon her, and his broken accents of heartfelt prayer making music in her ears, as she sang her "nunc dimittis."

THE ASCENSION.

IN the Gospel of St. Luke we read that Jesus, forty days after His resurrection, led His diciples as far as "Bethania, and lifting up His hands He blessed them. And it came to pass whilst He blessed them He departed from them and was carried up to heaven. And they adoring, went back into Jerusalem with great joy,"

This, beloved Brethren, was the fitting termination of the Redeemer's earthly career. It was the triumphal crowning of His life foreseen by holy David, when in prophetic rapture he cried out, "God went up in jubilee and the Lord with the voice of the trumpet." The enthronization of the King of Kings in the palace of heaven at the right hand of the heavenly Father Whose will He had so heroically accomplished, had also been foreseen by the royal prophet: "The Lord said to my Lord, 'Sit Thou at my right hand, till I make Thy enemies the footstool of Thy feet'" This wondrous ascension had been foreshadowed, too, by the patriarch Enoch, "who," says the holy Scripture, "pleased God and was translated into Paradise." Still more nobly was it prefigured by the prophet Elias when he was swept up to heaven as on the wings of a whirlwind in a chariot of fire, yoked with fiery horses; and the words of his attached disciple Eliseus, addressed to him as he rose from the earth, might have been intended for the apostles of Jesus Christ when they bade their divine Master adieu—" My Father, my Father, chariot of Israel and its charioteer."

It was indeed a fitting sequel to the dark tragedy of the Crucifixion, with its hellish ferment below, dreadful as the frenzy of fiends; and above, its inky and troubled sky; and deep in the bowels of the earth the rumblings of earthquake and the movement of dead men in their graves, called up from their resting places to walk through the guilty city. The frowning rock of Calvary, the dreary hill of skulls, is now forgotten in the scene which greets the eyes of the Apostles upon the richly wooded acclivity of Olivet, that smiles over against it. Great was the contrast. *There* was consternation, panic, fear, and precipitate flight: *here* is joy and content blending indeed with the pensiveness and the yearning memories natural to such a parting. *There* was the grimness and the rigour of a painful expiation: *here* is glory, for here heaven and earth share in the joy, and echo each the other's acclamations —" Lift up the gates, O ye princes; and be ye lifted up, O eternal gates; and the King of Glory shall enter in. Who is this King of Glory? The Lord, who is strong and mighty; the Lord mighty in battle. Lift up your gates, O ye princes, and be ye lifted up, ye eternal gates, and the King of Glory shall enter in. Who is this King of Glory? The Lord of Hosts, He is this King of Glory." Instantly heaven's portals are opened wide; far beyond the dimly lighted stars, that burn wan and sickly, like lamps that burn in the dawn, the halls of light are seen widening, as the Incarnate God approaches to claim His undivided supremacy over the myriad spirits of the angel choirs. Above all the heavens, and all the orders, and hierarchies that fill them, He rises to the throne placed for Him at His Father's right hand. And then the venerable of days, the great Father, raises His voice to address Him, and heaven is hushed to hear. "With Thee am I the principle of Thy Sonship, the eternal giver of Thy eternal being; in the days of Thy strength, in the brightness of the saints; from the womb before the day-star I begot Thee. Behold Thy throne, O God, one with me in substance, behold Thy throne for ever and ever. A sceptre of justice is the sceptre of Thy kingdom. Let all the angels adore Him." And then, O spectacle of wonder, O sight to lift human nature in our eyes, and to make human flesh sacred to them that wear it, O sight full of consolation, and hope, and confidence, He, the Eternal Son of God, clad in our poor humanity, uniting in His own person the essence of the divinity with the very bone and tissue which had been tainted by Adam's sin, and which He shared with the basest sinner amongst us, takes His place upon the seat of empire, high over all created things; and the majestic spirits of God's court, fleshless and endowed with bodiless creations, gifts of nature beyond the reach of our thoughts, bow down in deepest and most reverent homage before this divine representative of our lowly race, whose flesh and blood, though our own, are adorable in the eyes of the very cherubim and seraphim!

But there are others who participate in these rejoicings, and themselves add to the magnificence, as well as the enthusiasm of the scene. It is the saintly souls:—patriarchs, prophets, nazarites, solitaries, kings, judges, warriors, matrons, maidens, who in all the ages past, since the first man's sin, had won their way, through broil and battle, through self-suppression and the conquest of their native concupiscence, to peace and contentment beyond the grave, though they were forced to await this hour for the realization of their hopes and the full satisfaction of their longings. Now at length the First-born of the dead, has opened the way to heaven for His languishing and long-expectant brothers. What transport is theirs, as they mingle with their fellow-vassals, the angelic hosts, and vie with them in the adoration of their King and swell the acclaim of congratulation that fills the vast presence-chamber with their heart-felt Hosannahs!

It is well for them that they are in the hands of the Almighty Father; else would the thread of life be snapped under this sudden and overwhelming weight of gladness and happiness, so far transcending all their anticipations. It is only St. John who can paint this spectacle of rapture, which we fruitlessly labour to conceive. "And I beheld, and I heard the voice of many angels round about the throne, and the living creatures and the ancients; and the number of them was thousands of thousands, saying with a loud voice: The Lamb that was slain, is worthy to receive power, and divinity, and wisdom, and strength, and honour, and glory, and benediction. And every creature, which is in heaven, and on the earth, and under the earth, and such as are in the sea and all that are in them: I heard all saying: To Him that sitteth on the throne, and to the Lamb, benediction, and honour, and glory, and power, for ever and ever."—*Apoc.* v. 11-13.

On Mount Olivet, meantime, the disciples of Jesus stood gazing upwards, "Then behold," the Acts tell us, "two men stood by them in white garments, who also said: 'Ye men of Galilee, why stand you looking up to heaven? This Jesus who is taken up from you into heaven shall so come as you have seen Him going into heaven.'" Yes! He has ascended in majesty, and in majesty He shall come again to judge mankind, and to give to every one according to the works done in the body, be they good or evil. Tarry not, then, the angel seems to say; break this trance of wistful contemplation; remember the call He has given you, correspond with the graces you have received; devote yourselves without delay heart and soul to the work He has marked out for you, that having shared His labours and drunk of His bitter chalice, you may, by the path of glory He has opened to you, follow Him to His kingdom at the appointed time, and sit with Him on the thrones which the Father has prepared for you. And so, full of wonder and thankfulness, they made their way back to Jerusalem, where they persevered with one mind in prayer, say the Acts, preparing themselves for the coming of the Paraclete, whom our blessed Lord had promised to send them, to illumine their intellects and to strengthen their hearts for the arduous duties of their sacred ministry. "You shall receive the power of the Holy Ghost coming upon you," were among the last words of Jesus, ere He left them on the brow of Olivet. "And you shall be witnesses unto Me in Jerusalem, and in all Judea, and in Samaria, and even to uttermost part of the earth." Nor did they receive that Spirit of God in vain. They had a twofold work bestowed upon them to perform, and they performed it faithfully and resolutely. They had first to preach Christ crucified, "unto the Jews indeed a stumbling block, to the Gentiles foolishness, but unto them that are called both Jews and Greeks, Christ the power of God and the wisdom of God"—the only means devised by the wisdom and power of God for the salvation of man, the only antidote of that poisonous corruption that fermented in his blood, and his only title to a joyous immortality. But this work could not be carried out successfully unless it went hand in hand with another, viz., the establishment and maintainance of God's kingdom in their own hearts, That was the first object of their efforts, for they knew that from this all the rest would follow. Their maxim, therefore, was laid down in those striking words: "I chastise my body and bring it into subjection, lest when I have preached to others I should myself become a castaway." Mortification of the bodily appetites, vigilance in controlling the movements of passion, absolute self-distrust, constant recourse to God in prayer—these were the vivifying principles, the daily spring of life that fed their apostolic spirit. Never forgetting that their Master was to come again so judge, to examine, to sentence, to punish, and to reward, they went forth to strange lands and alien peoples under the inspiration of God and in pursuance of their high vocation; burning with charity, consumed with zeal, grudging no labour, hesitating at no sacrifice, deterred by no danger; aiming with simple and undivided purpose, while breath was left in their bodies, to win to Jesus Christ the lost, deluded sons of Adam—their brothers, and to imprint upon their immortal souls the character and virtues of the Eldest Born, as their passport to future bliss. The world seemed scarcely wide enough for their hungry and all-devouring love.

Under the restless urging of this holy madness they crossed seas, they penetrated forests, they wandered over pathless wilds, they braved the torrent, the swollen river, the tempest, the icy fangs of northern winters, the haunts of wild beasts, the scorching heat of the tropics. They plunged into populous cities and shrank not from contact with the worldly and the cynical; they did not lose their self-possession in the presence of pretentious philosophies, nor quail before angry rulers, nor heed the clamours raised by self-interested votaries of false creeds. And why? Because they cultivated both the love and fear of God; therefore the fortitude of the spirit of God bore them up, and Jesus, the lover of mankind, the Saviour of the world was united to them, living in them, speaking and working by them, carrying out beneficent designs through them, and each of them was able to say what one of their number so well expressed: " Behold I live, now; not I, but Christ, liveth in me."

Wherever they roved, the admonition of the Angels, on Mount Olivet, followed and influenced them :—" This Jesus, who is taken up from you into heaven, shall so come as you have seen Him going into heaven."

No wonder, with the vision of that dread and august Judge perpetually before their eyes, they should have persevered in the faithful and difficult duties connected with their holy and most responsible vocation, and that, dying as they did, under various circumstances, and in lands widely sundered, they should, all alike, have welcomed death, the messenger of the Judge, with the exultant burst of feeling, for which St. Paul found words: "And the time of my dissolution is at hand. I have fought a good fight, I have finished my course, I have kept the faith. As to the rest, there is laid up for me a crown of justice which the Lord, the just Judge, will render to me in that day: and not only to me, but to them also that love His coming."

And we, beloved Brethren, how far do we bear in mind the judgment which awaits us, and in few, yes, in very few years, the Judge Who will sum up our lives for weal or for woe to all eternity? Does the recollection of the inevitable ordeal fill us with a fear of the all-holy God and a horror of sin, which alone can separate us from Him, and bring down upon us our terrific sentence of rejection: "Depart from me, you cursed!" Do we recognise that the fear of God is a distinct grace? "The fear of the Lord is holy," says the sacred Scripture, abiding for ever and ever." This fear is the basis of all solid goodness.

The fear of the Lord is the beginning of wisdom. It is enumerated by the prophet Isaias among the endowments characteristic of the Messiah, our Supreme Model: "He shall be filled with the Spirit of the fear of the Lord." Do we ever ask for this grace, as the royal Penitent did?:—"Penetrate my flesh, O Lord, with Thy fear, for I have trembled at Thy judgments." Does the account we shall soon have to give to our severe Judge, shape and mould our daily conduct. Does it make itself felt in our thoughts, and words, and actions? Or is it not rather swallowed up in the distractions of our environments, in the cares of business, in the headlong chase after pleasure, in the tyranny of habit, in the blinding whirl and dust of the world's chariot-wheels? Alas! it is even so! The one end for which they were born into the world, is forgotten by the mass of men; the thought of it is thrust aside impatiently as though it were some ill-timed interruption to the more serious purposes of their being. Naturally, therefore, the warning of our blessed Lord falls on deaf ears: "Watch ye and pray, that ye enter not into temptation." Watch! We must leave watching to the monk and the nun, and to the denizens of the cloister, whose avocations are no hindrance to such discipline. Pray! Where can we find time to pray (beyond hearing Mass on Sundays and Holidays) with the many things which claim our attention? Our worldly concerns absorb us; we must make a living; we must lay by money; we must educate and provide for a family; we must weary our brains over the interests of the business which depends upon us for success; we must suitably fill our positions in society, we must achieve those honours which our birth, our character, our abilities, our influence, our antecedents mark out for us; we must, in short, move amid the moving crowd, and so God is virtually bidden to stand aside. He is treated superciliously, as if He were an exacting and troublesome beggar at our gates, instead of the Giver of all that we have, and all that we are. His will, and the real work He has allotted to us, have no place in our crowded programme, are no element in our restless life. O vanity of vanities! Ah, beloved Brethren we may dupe ourselves with specious pleas; we may use what opiate we like to stupify our conscience; but God's day will come at last; and to those who have habitually and persistently turned aside from the thought of His coming it will indeed be a *dies iræ*: a day charged with wrath, and misery, and despair, and the tardy and fruitless recognition of the object of their life. Oh! beloved Brethren, if each of the dead were given a tongue to warn us, what a weird and tremendous chorus would rise and fill the universal air—from the tombs of buried nations, from mound and barrow, from urn and stony monument, from long-forgotten graveyards and charnel-houses, from the mould of ancient battle-fields and from the bed of the mighty ocean.

Ye sons of men, how long will ye be dull of heart? Why do you love vanity and seek after lying? One thing is necessary. Seek ye first the Kingdom of God and His justice, and all other things shall be added unto you. What doth it profit a man if he gain the whole world and suffer the loss of his own soul?

THE HOLY GHOST THE SPIRIT OF PEACE.

Whit Sunday.

TO-DAY, beloved Brethren, we unite with the faithful throughout the whole world in commemorating the descent of the Holy Ghost upon the Apostles, and the manifold and momentous consequences which flowed from that mysterious visitation. In compliance with the instructions of our blessed Lord, the Mother of Jesus and the disciples had been waiting in Jerusalem ever since the Ascension for the promise of the Father, "which you have heard," said He, "by My mouth. For John indeed baptised with water, but you shall be baptised with the Holy Ghost not many days hence."

Swiftly in fervent prayer and profound contemplation did the hours go by for that little community in their still retreat, until at last the time was ripe, and every heart was expanded to receive the outpouring of the Spirit of God. The days of Pentecost were accomplished, when "suddenly," says the inspired narrative, "there came a sound from heaven as of a mighty wind coming, and it filled the whole house where they were sitting. And there appeared to them parted tongues, as it were, of fire, and it sat upon every one of them; and they were filled with the Holy Ghost, and they began to speak with divers tongues, according as the Holy Ghost gave them to speak."

The mystic pageant, beloved Brethren, which accompanied the advent of God's Spirit, was worthy of the great event. That scene was one well calculated to inspire the soul, to kindle the imagination, and to quicken the intellect to a vivid sense of the great work which had been accomplished. First the stillness of brooding meditation, or the low murmur of prayer, with the distant hum of the great city perhaps just audible from without; then the sudden blast, as of a tempest sounding in the heavens, bursting into the chamber, filling every nook and cranny of the building; then, lit by invisible hand, the bi-forked flame quivering over the head of each of those chosen ones, and proclaiming that the substantial charity of the Father had taken up his abode in their bosoms. Yes! the Spirit had taken possession of His living temples for evermore. Consider the meaning of that ceremonial, which was not a thing of chance, but the result of deliberate design.

He came to them as wind, an unseen element, which, like thought itself, is a proverb of quickness. He came as the wind, which, in its gentler mood, fans the feverish brow of labour, and breathes health and freshness over the earth; but, when roused to exert its strength, tears up the giant of the forest by the roots, lashes the great ocean till it roars and foams, and scatters the wrecks of mighty armadas over its yeast of waters. Like the gentle breeze, He came to refresh the weary and to purify the air we breathe; like the hurricane-blast, He came to overthrow the towering, deep-rooted growth of paganism, which had so long overshadowed the earth. He had come, too, as fire, for His work was to resemble the work of fire. Like fire, he would penetrate to the very marrow of the soul, take possession of its every fibre, and inflame the coldest hearts with devotion's ardour. Like fire, He would consume sin, as so much straw and refuse, in every corner of man's being. Like fire, He would cleanse and purify until the precious metal was separated from all the dross of human infirmity and of human malice. Like the flame, He would light up the dark places of the understanding, and by His heavenly ray reveal, as no human wisdom could reveal it, the grandeur and glory of the Creator, and the feebleness, meanness, and dependence of the creature.

Such were to be the functions of the Holy Ghost, as typified in the rushing wind and the tongues of fire.

He came as the spirit of refreshment, comfort, and joy. He came as the spirit of compunction and salutary fear. He came as the spirit of sanctification and as the author of that twofold charity which looks at once to God and to man; a virtue without which all other virtues are as sounding brass and as a tinkling cymbal. He came as the spirit of light, of wisdom and understanding, of council and of knowledge.

And now consider the mystery of the Holy Ghost's coming

and the work He was commissioned to perform from another point of view.

In the first stage of creation, beloved Brethren, this beauteous earth still lay an undeveloped and shapeless mass of crude materials, which bore the same relation to the world we see, that the block of unhewn marble bears to the noble statue which some great sculptor's genius evokes from its shapeless mass. In that period of blank darkness and weltering chaos, the Spirit of God began His work. "In the beginning," says the book of Genesis, "God created the heavens and the earth. And the earth was void and empty, and darkness was upon the face of the deep. And the Spirit of God moved over the waters." That first work of His in the material world was a figure of the office which He was now to undertake in the spiritual kingdom and the spiritual man. His function it was, to bring to an end, by His silent and unseen operation, the strife of conflicting elements, to substitute the reign of order for confusion and perplexity; and thus to elaborate what is called "Cosmos," or harmonious world, every part of which, as it came forth fresh and glittering from the darkness, should win that praise which Almighty God, in the days of creation, bestowed upon each successive work of His hand "He saw," says the holy Scripture, "that it was good." Even so, on the day of Pentecost, did God's Holy Spirit create in the hearts of the Apostles, out of the imperfect materials which He found there, a kingdom in which justice and holiness held sway.

And in that realm of their souls, they felt already that peace which surpasses all understanding, and which springs from the purifying and the proper adjustment of all the soul's powers. Darkness and doubt; the stirring of many irregular passions, like the blind motion of chaos; ignorant prejudices, and falsehoods ingrained by education; worldly hopes and unspiritual yearnings; the foolish vision of an earthly kingdom in which they would be crowned with dignity, and vested with power; all these sources of unrest were banished from the kingdom which the Holy Ghost established within them, or were counteracted by the effects of His grace. In short, where there had only been the materials of virtue, crude and unreliable, where even the love they felt for their divine Master had been wavering and inconsistent, and unequal to the strain of temptation, no sooner had the Spirit of God moved over the mass, than every faculty, every view, every belief, sentiment, attraction and ambition, became refined and sublimated, and ranged in due subordination; so that divine peace could not but fill those hearts, which had before been haunted by wild dreams and earthly aspirations.

Even more important, beloved Brethren, than His function in bringing forth this lovely world out of its original ooze and darkness, was that divine and most miraculous operation which, as Spouse of our blessed Lady, He performed at the Incarnation, when He shaped in her spotless womb the frame of the Man-God, the Prince of Peace, whose expiation was destined to reconcile the human race to its offended Maker. In like manner did the Holy Ghost, at His descent, form in the souls of the Apostles the new and perfect man, Jesus Christ, having destroyed in them the old and corrupt Adam, in whose image and under whose ban they had come into existence. Thus, by the power of the Holy Ghost, each of the Apostles became as it were "alter Christus"—a second Christ—pleasing and perfect in the sight of the Father, and each of them could say what St. Paul said later: "I live, now not I, but Christ liveth in me."

Now, therefore, beloved Brethren, that the Promise of the Father had come down upon them, they knew what was meant by the baptism of the Spirit, for which our blessed Lord had bade them to prepare—a baptism so different from that of St. John, which was of a character symbolical and suggestive, but not sacramental or self-operating. For now their souls were immersed, bathed in a flood of supernatural light, which made things clear that before had been veiled in obscurity, and brought back, as our blessed Lord had promised, all the myriad teachings, which they had heard from His lips, and but dimly realized at the time He had uttered them — luminous now as the sun in heaven, and mutually harmonious as the stars in their courses. Again, as at the dawn of creation, the Word had said: "Let there be light; and there was light." Tranquillizing and joy-inspiring was that beam from heaven—a foretaste of that bright and all-satisfying Presence, which forms the happiness of the blessed; and well was the saying of the beloved Master fulfilled: —"Peace I leave you; My peace I give you."

But note, beloved Brethren, the significant addition. Our blessed Lord did not say merely: "Peace I leave you; My peace I give you"; but He added: "Not as the world gives, do I give unto you." No. The peace which Jesus Christ bestows through the Holy Spirit is not such as the world covets, or labours to acquire. The world says—Peace! Peace! and there is no peace. Its gratifications are superficial and evanescent. The draught of pleasure, which it offers to the lips of its votaries, is mixed with the bitterness of many cares, disappointments, and misgivings. It dares not look beyond the grave; its be-all and end-all of happiness is this small span of life, like an insignificant oasis, beyond which stretch the interminable tracts of an eternity which will bear for them no fruit nor flower of contentment. But the peace of the Spirit is the peace of a conscience that knows no truce with sin. It is the peace of a soul, whose warfare with self is unremitting. It is, therefore, a peace which implies perpetual contentment, because it looks not for repose in this life, but is willing to labour and toil now, that it may receive the wages of its industry and its patience in eternal bliss hereafter. Thus it fears not to bear the pricking and tearing of life's thorns; nor to peer into the noisomeness and corruption of the tomb, where earthly beauty and earthly grandeur are conquered by the trailing and slimy worm; nor to contemplate the rigours of the judgment that awaits us all, when every man shall receive according to his works done in the body, be they good or evil. Sin alone it fears; suffering, persecution, the hatred and contempt of the world, all these it accepts as its allotted portion in this vale of tears, and its recompense is the peace that the world cannot give nor take away; the peace that passeth all understanding. For earthly sufferings our blessed Lord himself had fully prepared them. "Behold, I send you," said He, "as sheep in the midst of wolves. (Be ye, therefore, wise as serpents and simple as doves) But beware of men. For they will deliver you up in Councils, and they will scourge you in their Synagogues.— The brother shall deliver up the brother to death, and the father the son; and the children shall rise up against their parents and shall put them to death. And you shall be hated by all men for My name's sake." Now, beloved Brethren, attend to the continuation of this prophecy, and ponder well the paradoxical words of our Prince of Peace :— "Do not think," says He, "that I came to send peace upon earth : I came not to send peace, but the sword. For I came to set a man at variance against his father, and the mother against her daughter, and the daughter-in-law against the mother-in-law. And a man's enemies shall be those of his own household." The instinctive malignity of the world against the work of the Holy Spirit will penetrate even to the hearts of those who are bound to the faithful by the nearest and dearest ties of kinship. The Church must therefore be prepared to sleep, like our blessed Lord, in the storm-tossed bark, while tempestuous winds whistle in the cordage, and angry waves drench her with their spray.

Since that day, beloved Brethren, when the Holy Ghost took up His abode in the bosom of the Church, how marked has been the contrast between the spiritual peace which she has enjoyed and the stormy vicissitudes of worldly fortune that have threatened to engulf her! For the first three hundred years there was the howling of one great hurricane, with occasional relaxations of fury, when the winds seemed to have exhausted themselves with their own violence. Persecution swiftly followed persecution, and rivers of Christian gore flowed in the public streets. Yet all the while, deep down in the bowels of the earth, beneath the trampling of Rome's pagan population, the august sacrifice was daily offered, the rites of Holy Church were administered, the great festivals were celebrated as jubilantly as in the vast cathedrals of mediæval times, and the far-reaching galleries that tunnelled the earth beneath the seven hills resounded to the heartfelt hymns of those servants of God, who knew not but that, ere another sun had set, they might be transported beyond the stars, chanting with the angelic choirs the praises of the holy, holy, holy! Lord God of Hosts. Persecution and torture and every form of outrage was the sum of their history as recorded in the chronicles of men; but in the eyes of God their story had been one of peace, contentment, joy, mutual love, burning zeal, tender devotion; in short, it was the story of the Holy Spirit's sweet and silent ministrations and the fostering of all virtues in the hearts of the faithful by a process as hidden and mysterious as the growth of fruitful seed in a favouring soil. In due season the Spirit of God waved, as it were, His banner in the sky; when the vision of the blazing cross promised victory to Constantine, and all the world was thunderstruck to see the dove of peace bearing back to the storm-battered ark the olive branch, to announce that the waters of the great deluge without had subsided. Then it was that the Cross became a symbol of honour; then it was that great basilicas, shining with costliest stones, and gold and silver, took the place of the dark catacombs; and kings and princes were proud to be numbered amongst the vassals of Jesus Christ. This sunburst of worldly prosperity, however, was destined to pass away, and to be succeeded by many a cloud and by many a sorrow. Even when, in the course of the 1,500 years which have elapsed since the days of Constantine, it pleased the Spirit of Peace to allow the Church a term of temporal triumph or tranquility, it almost always happened that in some clime, near or remote in its relation to the centre of unity, the fetters of the Christian confessor were clanking in some loathsome dungeon, and the blood of the Christian martyr was flowing beneath the persecutor's knife. And as the worldly prosperity of the Church has been qualified in its character, so has it been limited in its duration. The days of Leo X., unexampled as they were for splendour and power, were followed almost immediately by the days of Clement VII., when the eternal city was sacked and a horde of barbarous men, drunk with hatred of the Papacy and oblivious of all law, human and divine, plundered and desecrated the most ancient and venerated shrines, and almost under the eyes of the captive Pope perpetrated for more than half a year the most unheard-of crimes and abominable sacrileges. Nor has it been only from without that trials have come upon the Church. Her own children have often laboured to bring back the reign of chaos by challenging the truth of revelation, or by breaking away from the bonds of her discipline. Her garment has even been rent by a schism which long severed the eastern from the western section of Christendom, and saints have been found clinging to rival pontiffs. But, ever and always, the Holy Ghost has been moving over the waters, and when a certain number of suns had risen and set, it was found that strife was at an end, and that the Spirit of Peace had evolved order, harmony, and tranquility out of the entanglement and confusion of human passions and of human intrigues. Thus the Church, looking back upon her past history, may say, even in the midst of storms and misfortunes, what the Psalmist said, but with greater confidence than the Psalmist:—"In pace in idipsum dormiam et requiescam: quoniam tu, Domine, singulariter in spe constituisti me"—"In peace in the self-same will I sleep and take my rest: for Thou, O Lord, hast established me singularly in hope."

And now, beloved Brethren, let us not allow this hallowed season to pass without begging the Holy Ghost, the Spirit of Peace, to take up his abode in our hearts; and to kindle the fire of His love in every member of our household and family. And as we owe a special debt to our relations, so do we owe a special debt to the times in which we live. Let us therefore frequently ask Almighty God, in the words of the Church's petition : "Da pacem, Domine, in diebus nostris.—Grant us peace, O Lord, in our day." Let us pray that the Holy Spirit will multiply His gifts and fruits in the souls of all the faithful throughout the whole world. Let us pray that He will grant the Church that measure of worldly prosperity also, which He sees to be most conducive to her sanctification, and to His honour and glory. Let us pray that in those countries where the children of the Church have been seduced by infidel teachings, licentious literature, and the action of secret societies, they may return to their allegiance, and become the loyal aderents of the Church they have abandoned. Let us pray that earthly governments may be brought to understand that to remove all obstacles to the freedom of the Church is the best means of securing their own temporal interests; for the Church never yet taught anything but obedience to lawful authority. Let us pray, in fine, that the Holy Ghost may direct our Holy Father, and fill him with peace and consolation in the midst of all His troubles. Let us resolve to do what we can towards forwarding the wishes of our holy Pontiff, by reciting with the greatest fervour those prayers which he has ordered to be said after every Low Mass for the welfare of the Church. In fine, let us pray that God may prolong his term of life, till he sees his projects and desires crowned with success, and his efforts and anxieties bearing their long-expected fruit. May the Spirit of God, the Spirit of Peace, descend upon you all, and fill your souls with His manifold grace.

FEAST OF PENTECOST.

The Use of the Tongue.

THE tongue, beloved Brethren, was given us to honour and glorify God. It is set in the head, as a bell in a church belfry, to sound the praises of its Maker and to minister to His service. The office and function is a high and noble one; to give outward expression to our thoughts, emotions, and reasonings; to dart to heaven the fiery aspirations of the soul—its faith, its hope, its love, and its penetential sorrow; to communicate to our fellow creatures the glow of divine charity burning within us, and win them to goodness by the charm of righteous conversation, sound counsel, salutary warnings, unworldly comments on the daily occurrences of public and private life. Have you ever thought, beloved Brethren, how wondrous is that faculty of speech which has the tongue for its organ? Manifold are the phases of thought—more various than the changing clouds of heaven. Many are the feelings and emotions which accompany the march of our waking hours, seldom single and simple, for the most part complicated and interwoven like the many-coloured threads of some curious fabric. These thoughts and images, in all their combinations, though conceived in a spiritual substance, and as unmaterial as the soul they spring rom, actually find in the tongue an agent to convey them to others almost exactly as we feel them, so that they listening to the articulate sounds can enter into our thoughts and realize our feelings, and are conscious of a chord of sympathy which vibrates in unison with our inward emotions. Here, certainly, is one of the marvels of God's power. A number of different sounds, easily counted and classified, are enabled actually to bring home to me what is passing in the mysterious and unseen soul of my neighbour! A few modifications of the voice throw open a marvellous world—the world of another man's thoughts. If you have never thanked God for this wondrous faculty of speech, do so now on this feast of Pentecost; of Him Who is styled in the Church's hymn for to-day "Rite promissum Patris, sermone ditans guttura"—the truly promised one of the Father, enriching man's tongue with speech.

Now we are bound to use this gift of God for God's glory; first of all by employing it directly to celebrate His praise; and secondly in a negative way by abstaining from all profanation of so noble a member.

Let me then, this evening, say a brief word as to the positive duty of praising God with the tongue—I need not tell you, beloved Brethren, the tongue should praise God both when we rise in the morning, and when we compose ourselves to sleep at night. Both day and night are full of dangers; for the devil never sleeps; the evil fascinations of the world, and the uneasiness of the carnal appetites are not put off with the days clothes. Our waking, as a new birth, should be consecrated to God; and prayer, as a lesser baptism, should hallow each day, which is our life in miniature, and too often the evil image and counterpart of an evil life. The days are the links out of which our life's chain is wrought; no link should go unconsecrated.

Then the night, as is often remarked, is a striking type of death. How often does the sleeper startle us by his resemblance to a corpse—still, rigid, insensible, open-mouthed, sightless, sealed up as it were in the harmless extinction of a few hours. Rest should always remind us of our last repose, in which these bodies of ours shall lie, after the toils and troubles and noise of life, in some quiet cemetery, with less of vitality in our poor remains than there is in the slow-rising grass that pushes its way upwards out of our graves. Be not heedless of this gentle warning, which sleep addresses to you, as you feel your limbs growing numb and heavy under its gathering influence. But rather remembering the hour, which sooner or later shall come, when you will feel your soul parting out of your members one by one, from the feet upwards, and when not all the shocks of earthquake will arouse you, not all the applause and prizes of the world will win you back from that final lethargy, cross yourselves devoutly, and giving to your Maker the praise of heart and tongue alike, cry out:—

"From a sudden and unprovided death, Lord Jesus, deliver us."

And do not tell me that the heart is the temple of prayer, and that God wants no lip-service. It is true that He values not your prayer and praise, unless the heart give them substance, any more than the shop-keeper respects the Queen's head upon your coin, if he knows that, in spite of its gilding, it is made of base metal. But if God made the body as well as the soul, He has a right to the homage of the body. And surely if the heavens show forth the glory of the Lord, if holy David calls upon Sun, and Moon, and Stars to praise God by their varied light, surely, I say, this body of ours, with its unparalleled mechanism, witnessing to the infinite skill of the divine artificer, ought to render its periodic service of thanksgiving and praise to Him who made it, by the agency of the tongue, its natural and constituted spokesman. And if you would have Gospel warrant for this, has not our Lord Himself left us the holiest and most beautiful of all forms of prayer—not for silent use in the depths of the soul, but for constant vocal recitation. For, as His great Apostle tells us, "By the mouth is confession made unto salvation."

Have then your times for vocal prayer; and let your houses murmur and echo to the sound of the Rosary, the Psalter of Jesus, the Universal Prayer of St. Thomas, and those other traditional vocal exercises which, in earlier days, alas! found a more frequent echo in the houses of this country than now.

Again, beloved Brethren, the tongue is not only the main instrument of speech, but the main auxiliary in vocal music. The flood of sound poured out from the chest, and laden with the emotions of the heart, from which, as from a fountain, it seems to well, is trilled forth by the tongue in strange vibrations that touch the feelings of every listener. The very beast in the field, as you have sometimes, perhaps, seen, will pause in its browsing, and raise its wondering eyes, and follow the notes, spellbound, when its ears begin to tingle to some well-framed melody, rendered by the human voice. Here again is something to offer God. Consecrate your own taste for music to Him who gave it for your comfort, joy, and recreation. Accustom yourselves to sing, at least, when alone, some verses of the noblest of all sacred songs, these wonderful psalms and canticles, in which of old the leaders of the chosen people of God, the kings, and priests, and prophets were inspired to give utterance to faith and unshaken trust in

Him, to their love, their thankfulness for His boundless and unceasing mercies, their deep spirit of repentance for ingratitude and sin—songs in which the countless generations of His believing children have sounded forth His praises, round the bleeding sacrifices in His Temple, and before the Altar of His Church, in which the pure and august oblation of the New Law has been offered up in every age and clime, and will be offered till the world has run its course.

Or again, take up the strain of love of those sweet hymns which your large-hearted Mother, the Church, has composed for you, and which come to us as Apostles of soothing and consolation after going through life, and to the gate of death, with many a Christian before us. Fittingly on this great day when the Paraclete came down in the manifest form of tongues of fire, does the admonition of His Apostle re-echo in our ears, bidding us consecrate this gift of melody, as well as speech, to our all-bountiful Creator. "Wherefore He came not unwise, but understanding what is the will of God. Be ye filled with the Holy Spirit—speaking to yourselves in psalms, and hymns, and spiritual canticles, singing and making melody in your hearts to the Lord: giving thanks always, for all things in the name of our LORD JESUS CHRIST to God and the Father."—*Eph.* v. 17-20.

TRINITY SUNDAY.

THE whole world, beloved Brethren, material as well as spiritual, teems with mysteries; in other words, with facts which we know and acknowledge, but cannot comprehend or fully explain. The most obvious and familiar objects in which we are set, as in a framework, are all mysteries disguised, because there is none of them but carries the intellect to a point beyond which it cannot pass. The whole mass of the earth on which we live is indeed marked off into its constituent materials: its strata of various kinds of stone, its minerals, its living plants, its fields of dead and metamorphosed vegetable matter. But when you have given the various species the names that belong to them, there remains the question which cries halt to the master of physical science: What is it that forms the basis of all this accumulation? What is undermost? The chemist bids us follow him into his laboratory and decomposes these substances into molecules of various kinds, with their respective properties, powers, and affinities; but when he has done his work he finds mystery under all, for he is as ignorant as the babe of the real nature of his ultimate chemical elements. The metaphysician proposes to take up the work where his brother, the natural philosopher, stops; but when he opens the door which is to reveal to him the innermost mystery, lo! "darkness there and nothing more." From that recess, indeed, he and his tribe trumpet forth the discoveries they profess to have made, but when we listen to their words we find that each gives a different account from his neighbour, and so we are left as wise as before. If you wish to know what it is to be entangled inextricably in a thorny hedge of theories, opinions, wild assertions, and blank mutual contradiction, consult metaphysical treatises under the heads: being, essence, existence, substance, matter and form. The wisest of men find a mystery in the benches you are sitting on, the floor under your feet, the bricks of the wall, the slates on the roof and the strong niche of the belfry; for the final question proposed by every material thing for solution—What then am I?—places these sages of the world in a babel of controversy.

If the core of brute matter, beloved Brethren, be thus steeped in mystery, small wonder that we should be more deeply involved as we ascend the scale of being. I omit the thousands of riddles to be found in astronomy and other sciences, and deal with illustrations obvious to all. The cat at your hearth and the dog in the kennel are to be classed as mysteries. Who will explain to me the nature of their souls, the sphere of their thoughts, the extent of their intercommunication by speech or its substitutes, the scope of their intelligence, the limits of their instinct, and its relations to the human reason? There seems little to exclude the more cunning animals from the category of rational beings, except their non-advancement through ages, and the absence of that power of devising fresh combinations which reason implies. They do not break fresh ground; they go round and round in the same ring, and present the same study to-day which they presented centuries and centuries ago. There is not a move of Tobias' dog that is strange or unfamiliar to us. But when we reach man we are lost in an abyss of mysteries. Answer me, if you can, the countless knotty questions which are written in the substance of our bodily frame. Where is the power that has woven the elements of that body into chemical combinations not found in dead matter, and which maintains them through our years of life in the same proportion? Explain to me the endless activities that work beneath the quiet surface of the body, like a vast company of experts, carrying on the vital operations on which the life and health of the body depend, without cessation, without mutual embarrassment, jarring, or inconvenience; without any noise, or ado, or proclamation of their tireless industry? What power is it that separates and secretes from the many ingredients of the blood—first, those particles which are needed in one place for the structure of the bony skeleton, in another for the gristle or the cartileges of the joints, in another for the different bands that hold and brace the skeleton together —the tendons, the ligaments, the sinews and muscles, all delicately discriminated to serve their purposes? What power is it that draws from the blood the material which forms the elastic piping of the veins and arteries and capillaries, through which the current of life pulsates all over the body; or selects the precise mixture and composition that keeps up the supply of nerve filaments which spread themselves, more intricate than the finest network, inside and outside the system, and on which our sensations, or intelligence of the outer world, and our power of self-movement depend? What power eliminates from the one same stream of the blood the peculiar substance required for the maintenance of the great organs of the body—the brain, the lungs, the heart, the stomach, the liver—and the special fluids with which they require to be stored for the most diverse functions? What shall we think of the intelligence of that agent which snatches out of the ever-moving contents of the blood vessels the very measure of adipose tissue which is needed to cushion the organs specially subject to friction, like the rolling orbit of the eye and the unresting muscular machine of the heart? Who is there that duly recognises the world of mysteries in which and by which we live from day to day, or the large assortment of forces that are at work within us—all inexplicable—more busy, more responsible, more various in their functions, more microscopic in the nicety of their judgment, more accurate in their calculation, more quiet and undemonstrative, than the most skilful and able staff of officials ever known?

And if this body of ours is a home and nest of mysteries, what shall I say of the unseen spirit, without which it loses all these forces, and is drawn down by the blind and jealous earth into a companionship with the clod? Can you fathom your own souls? Shallow, you may be reckoned, but the poorest and most contracted soul is deeper than the deep sea! Can you explain that wondrous unseen life, the spring of your whole vitality, which is all in the whole body, and all in every part; and is so knit with the material frame, that each alike, whether matter or spirit, is included under the grand personal "Ego—I." Have you disentangled the complex web of your own passions and desires, and indefinable mental movements; have you bottomed the science of your intellectual faculties, your faculty of knowing, comparing, analyzing, reasoning, building up great edifices of reasoned conclusions, of calling up before your mind, through the imagination, things palpable and impalpable, things absent and past, things yet unborn in the future? Do you comprehend that crowning faculty of deliberate will, in which the soul sits God-like, above this crowded court of retainers ruling, all for good or ill? I say nothing of the profound problems suggested by your inherited likings and dislikings, passions and tastes, and proclivities, which seem to show you, in the light of a re-incarnation of some ancestor, near or remote, perhaps buried in the grave for centuries.

Such, beloved Brethren, in the meagrest outline, is this universe in which we find ourselves: a mass of conundrums, a sphinx's riddle, a museum of mysteries. Wherever we turn our minds we are met with an impassable barrier of darkness, beyond which nothing but airy conjecture is free to wander.

And oh! beloved Brethren, if this be man, and man's state, and man's surroundings, who shall be so silly and so blind as to expect that the great God, from Whose wisdom and power this complicated scheme has emanated, shall be easily understood, readable as a child's primer, exempt from all attributes of a nature which involve any difficulty to our understanding. Oh! foolish man! to turn away in contempt or dissatisfaction from the idea of a revealed Creator and Ruler of all—because, forsooth, His Being contains mysterious depths; when all nature, around and within him, from the furthest star to his own beating heart, tells him that mystery is the law, because his own intellect is limited; and none can penetrate to the kernel of created things but Him who created them. Solve the mysteries of your own finite being, nay, count up, merely number the insoluble questions which gape at you from the depths of your body and soul alike, and then object to the conception of a mysterious Godhead. He who made you, alone understands you. "He who fixed your heart, shall He not understand?" To Him there is no mystery in you: His hands moulded you: you are His work, open to His all-seeing eye; He penetrates to the innermost marrow of the nature He gave you. God is searcher of the reins and the heart! "Darkness shall not be dark to Thee," says holy David, "and night shall be light as the day: the darkness thereof and the light thereof are alike to Thee. For Thou hast possessed my reins; Thou hast protected me from my mother's womb. I will praise Thee, for Thou art wonderfully magnified: wonderful are Thy works, and my soul knoweth right well. My bone is not hidden from Thee, which Thou hast made in secret: and my substance in the lower parts of the earth. Thy eyes did see my imperfect being, and in Thy book all shall be written."—*Ps.* 138.

And He, the mighty Artificer, whose finger-marks are on thee, and who alone knows thee in all thy height, and depth, and breadth—both soul and body :— He alone, with much more reason, is able, in His consciousness, to traverse the abyss of His own perfections. "The things also that are of God, no man knoweth, but the Spirit of God."—I *Cor.* 2. 11.

If our conception of the Supreme Being contained no mystery, that would be the greatest mystery of all; nay, on the face of it, would be a condemnation of the idea as necessarily false. It would mean that our puny intellects have capacity enough to measure the measureless, and that an egg-shell can hold the tides of the world-wide ocean. I care not therefore what be the ability of a man in any department of study, I care not what is his reputation for learning among his fellows; if he cast God out of his system, or pretend that he is justified in rejecting his Creator, because the Divine Nature requires him to believe what he cannot fully explain. I hesitate not to call that man, what the Scripture calls him—a fool. " Dixit insipiens incorde suo, non est Deus: The fool hath said in his heart thereis no God."—*Ps.* 13.

Besides acknowledging the unity of God, beloved Brethren, Holy Church reminds us to-day that we must also acknowledge and adore three divine persons in that unity. The notion of one Supreme God is written on the face of creation; is attested in the unity and harmony of its design. It is rooted in the intellect, for there must be one Being from Whom all others proceed, else we have an indefinite series of creative beings going back and back for ever into an eternity in which they never began. If such a series be started, you will never reach a given point; the long succession will have beengoingon for ever, before reaching one; and therefore it will never reach one at all. This is not mystery, but a contradiction which the reason will not tolerate. One Being there must be, then, who came from no other; Who is the "ratio," the cause and explanation of His own existence; Whose nature has been moulded and circumscribed by no one; Who is, therefore, without limitation in His attributes—infinite, all-powerful. A mighty spirit is He; above matter, which is the creation of His hands, and having in His nature no admixture of matter to foreshadow change and dissolution. A mighty spirit indeed, pervading all the unimaginable spaces of the sun-strewn universe with His tranquil and unruffled Being, whose activity is as untiring as His repose is uninterrupted. Changeless in Himself, yet weaving a changeful web all round Him, in which, as in warp and woof, He has wrought the image of His own manifold grandeur. He, this glorious Being, is around us, more closely enwrapping us than the casing atmosphere; He is within us, more intimately associated with us than the air we breathe, more vital to us than our own hearts. In Him truly we live and move and have our being.

But more than this: In the bosom of this Godhead, one and indivisable, the new revelation of Jesus Christ has opened to us a wondrous Trinity of persons, perfectly distinct one from the other, each equally divine in essence and nature, each with its definite relation to the other, each with its appropriate functions and special operations. "The first Person, the Father, was made by none," says the creed which bears the name of St. Athanasius; "the Son is from the Father only, not made nor created, but begotten; the Holy Ghost is from the Father and the Son, not made, nor created, nor begotten, but proceeding. Therefore there is one Father, not three Fathers; there is one Son, not three Sons; there is one Holy Ghost, not three Holy Ghosts. And in this Trinity there is nothing first or last, nothing greater or less; but the whole three Persons are co-eternal and co-equal." The Father created the world; the Son took the flesh of Adam, its fallen lord, and redeemed it; the Holy Ghost brought order instead of chaotic turbulence and sanctified the race that was redeemed in the blood of the Divine Lamb. And profound as this mystery is, it does not cross reason, it only baffles it; it does not trample reason underfoot, it only soars above its ken; it does not forbid us to know the fact, it only defies us to fully comprehend or adequately explain it. For God is one and God is three, in two different senses: He is one in substance, He is three in personality. Willingly then, at the bidding of the oracle of Truth, the living organ by which the living God communicates with us, do we bow down in deepest adoration before this Godhead, Three in One, these poor, weak, narrow, circumscribed intelligences which He, the Giver of all good gifts, has assigned to us; willingly do we sink our pride, that pride which ruined us as a race, while we repeat with firmest faith and most fervent love, the rapturous words employed by Holy Church in to-day's office: Let us bless God the Father, God the Son, and God the Holy Ghost, let us praise and exalt Him for ever. "O, the depth of the riches, of the wisdom, and of the knowledge of God! How incomprehensible are His judgments and how unsearchable His ways. For who hath known the mind of the Lord, or who hath been His counsellor, or who hath first given to Him and recompense shall be made. For of Him, and by Him, and in Him, are all things: to Him be glory for ever. Amen. *Rom.* xi. 33-36.

CORPUS CHRISTI.

IT is now, beloved Brethren, about six centuries and a half since our blessed Lord made known to His Church the desire He felt that a special feast should be instituted to honour His sacred body in the Sacrament of His love. Already, from the earliest ages of the Christian era, the faithful had made that life-giving Body the object of their homage, veneration, praise, and thanksgiving, on the Thursday in Holy Week, or Maundy Thursday. For a portion of that day, to commemorate the fond legacy which He had bequeathed us in the Blessed Sacrament, as an everlasting reminder of His passion and death, the Church threw aside her trappings of woe, called up the whole pageantry of her ceremonial; ordered the bells to ring, and the organ to burst forth in jubilant strains, and carried our blessed Lord in joyful procession to the tabernacle prepared for Him, amids: the blaze of multiplied lights and the perfume of many-coloured flowers. But that ceremony was only as a gleam of sunshine amidst the overwhelming gloom of the week; and the Church seemed to mingle the music of the festival with half-suppressed sobs of grief, and to smile with the tears undried in her eyes. Centuries passed away before a celebration dedicated in honour of the Sacramental Body of the Divine Victim was removed from that context of sadness and mourning.

It was an era when men were attacking the doctrine of the Real Presence. This great truth had been denied explicitly, for the first time in the history of the Church, by Berengarius two centuries before. The heresiarch was condemned again and again; and after repeated recantations and repulses, by an extraordinary mercy of God, died contrite at last, and doing penance for his sins and the scandals he had caused, in 1088. But the seed of error had been scattered far and wide, and continued bearing bitter fruit.

To stimulate the faith and devotion of His people, at this critical time, our blessed Lord decreed at last that another festival, full of pomp and spiritual enthusiasm, should be held throughout the Christian world. The unfaithfulness of a few was to be counter-balanced by a vast and splendid demonstration, held in the very season of nature's luxuriance—the leafy June. The murmurs of disbelief were to be drowned in one cry of jubilee echoing all over the world, and proclaiming the grandeur of God's Being, as revealed in this masterpiece of His wisdom and goodness. As often happens, He chose a humble instrument to convey His will to the faithful. It was a young novice, of Liège, in Belgium, named Juliana, only sixteen years of age, but remarkable for her virtues. To this young girl our blessed Lord appeared; and, under His direction, she confided to her Superiors the message that He gave her. God's work is always sure, but often slow, as we make measurements of time; and especially in the introduction of new devotions, and the institution of new feasts. In the course of time, however, the work was accomplished. Urban IV., who had known Juliana before his elevation to the papacy, published a bull, in the year 1264, in which he ordered the feast to be kept throughout the Church on the Thursday following the first Sunday after Pentecost. This decree was confirmed by subsequent Pontiffs, who promoted the devotion by granting copious indulgences to those who joined in it; and the council of Trent commends the feast, and pronounces an anathema upon those who condemn it, or censure the procession with which it was, perhaps, from its first institution, associated. The office which is used on the festival day, is worthy of its high and noble purpose. It is from the pen of the Angelic Doctor St. Thomas; and in the whole range of her hymns, the Church has nothing more lofty, more triumphant, nor beating more fervently with the pulsations of a holy rapture than the procession canticle: "Lauda Sion Salvatorem": "Praise thy Saviour, O Sion."

The object of our devotion on this great festival, beloved Brethren, is the body, the flesh of Jesus Christ in the Sacrament of the Holy Eucharist. By means of this feast the Church reminds us of all that we owe to that most sacred and divine body, which came whole and entire from the virginal womb of Mary,

R

and yet was the body of God made man—the Word made flesh. We are reminded that this material flesh, which was torn for us in the scourging, punctured and lacerated by the crown of thorns, gored by the rough nails, and pierced through by the soldier's spear, was the cause and the agent of our redemption from the tyranny of sin and the endurance of eternal wrath. Of old, to prefigure its saving power, the brute victims had fallen under the knives of the priests, and their flesh been either consumed in the flames of the holocaust, or eaten by the priest and the offerer, as a banquet of peace, reconciliation, and gladness, prepared by the great Lord of heaven and earth for His children and subjects. Through those animal oblations, for the sake of this divine flesh, the offerer won the favour and countenance of God, made atonement for sins, voluntary and involuntary, performed the duty of worthily adoring God, as Creator and supreme Master of all, returned an acceptable thanksgiving for blessings received, and solicited the graces which his circumstances required, with every prospect of success. It was not the gashed throats nor blood-streaming carcases of ox, or calf, or sheep or lamb, kid, dove, or pigeon that earned such happy results and moved the heart of God. No. It was this most venerable flesh of the Lamb of Sacrifice, which was to be one day offered on the altar of the Cross. It was this flesh which He had brought under every species of pain that can torture the poor fabric of the human body and send madness through its nerves, that this anguish might secure us immunity from the vengeance we deserve. It was this thrice-blessed flesh which He had given freely to the executioner, and which He had "made a curse for us" on the cursed tree, that we might be rescued from the eternal malediction, that keeps lighted the undecaying fires of hell. This was the flesh that appealed to God in behalf of His sinful creatures through all the gory victims of the old dispensation. It was upon this flesh—the flesh of God the Son—that God the Father smiled when He accepted the offerings of His people, and answered with showering benedictions the ascending smoke of the sacrificial fires.

It was meet, beloved Brethren, that the divine flesh which was bruised and wounded for God's children in the old law and the new, should be exalted and honoured in proportion to the humiliation and outrage to which our blessed Lord submitted it in the excess of His passionate love. And hence the magnificence with which this festival of the Body of Christ is surrounded, the glittering processions in which It is borne in Catholic countries and more favoured spots; the triumphant hymns that soar to heaven; the candles and wreathed incense, and flowers outpoured upon the path, which are the features of this august solemnity. He hath emptied Himself, therefore shall He be exalted. The body that was trodden underfoot like a worm shall be raised aloft in the face of heaven as the flesh of God, whose rule is from sky to earth, and over all the depths beneath the earth; and, instead of the old cry—"If He is the Son of God, let Him come down from the Cross"—a loud, triumphant burst of faith and love rises from every land under the sun, and every lip repeats 'my Lord and my God.'

Again, beloved Brethren, the body of Christ commands our homage and admiration, not only because it has served the purpose of a perfect atonement for our sins, but also because it has been made the food and sustenance of our souls. Wonderful are the qualities of that Body. It possesses, in the first place, all the noble attributes of a body glorified. It is impassible; for no pain or ache can touch it; no sickness can undermine its vigour; excess of heat and cold cannot incommode it. It is no longer dull and opaque, as painted clay, but radiant, like the sun, and a centre of brightness. It knows no trammels of slow and constrained action, but flashes through space between the most distant points with the swiftness of thought; a quality which is technically known as agility. It has bidden adieu to material grossness, and puts on a subtlety, which carries it, as if it were pure spirit, through barriers impenetrable by the earthly frame. But these high attributes, though they belong in an eminent degree to the Sacred Body we adore to-day, will be shared by the blessed when matter and spirit shall be re-united in them after the general resurrection. One endowment belongs to the flesh of Jesus Christ, which no one can share with Him. That flesh has the property—a property altogether divine and unspeakable—of being the nourishment of our souls, of maintaining in them a spiritual life, of communicating to them powers and energies, of adorning them with loveliness and grace, which far transcends human nature, and stamps upon them the image of the loving God himself. These wonderful effects are produced directly by the flesh and blood of the Son of God—made man. It is His flesh which directly vivifies our souls, which is the "*panis vivus et vitalis*"—the living and life-giving sustenance. True it is that where His body is, there also is His soul, there is His Divinity. But it is not His soul, it is not His divinity, that directly supports the life of our spiritual nature: it is His adorable Body, it is His divine flesh. He is the source of our vitality as the children of God, and the pledge of a happy immortality. "Labour not," said our Blessed Lord, "for the meat that perisheth, but for that which endureth to life everlasting, which the Son of Man will give you. I am the living bread which came down from heaven, if any man eat of this bread he shall live for ever, and the bread that I will give is My flesh for the life of the world."

Is it not, then, beloved Brethen, in the highest degree fitting and reasonable, that we should give special honour, in a feast overflowing with joy and thankfulness, to that Body of Christ which shows the scars of sacrifice undergone for our salvation, and which ever abides in our tabernacle to serve as the food of our souls? What pomp and magnificence can we command to match with the titles to this enthusiastic love and loyalty, this delight and gratitude which are presented to our minds by this most adorable, most holy Body? How shall we worthily express to Jesus Christ the regrets that well up in our hearts, when we think of the coldness and indifference with which we have viewed that life-giving flesh, that was first our ransom, and then our food? Nay, with what deep veneration and spirit of devotedness, with what keen compunction and tearful acts of sorrow shall we make amends for the positive disgrace, perhaps the reckless outrages, of which we have been guilty in neglecting this sacred Body, or even receiving it in unworthy dispositions. Let us, beloved Brethren, resolve within this Octave to enkindle our faith in the divine mystery of the Altar, and to ponder seriously on the miracles of God's goodness which it contains; let us resolve that we shall not in future leave our souls to starve for want of a due participation in the banquet of this heavenly food, nor thwart its effects by a careless preparation or a listless, unloving attitude when we approach the Altar to renew the life of our souls by means of this flesh of the Son of Man. Let us resolve to do everything in our power to keep His tabernacle surrounded with flowers in their season, and to contribute when the chance offers, that there may be no lack of splendour in the services of the blessed Sacrament. If we saw through the veil which it is the will of God to draw over the mystery of the altar, we should not grudge to give our aid in beautifying the house of our God on earth, the sojourn of His sacred Body, the storehouse of this living and and life-giving bread which preserves the soul unto eternal happiness.

JESUS IN THE BLESSED SACRAMENT, OUR PHYSICIAN.

TO-NIGHT, beloved Brethren, I purpose devoting a short time to a few reflections, which we shall make together, on a subject connected with this noble festival—a festival which thrills the heart of Christendom to its minutest cord, and sends pealing allelulias to heaven from every point of the compass. The subject shall be "Jesus in the Blessed Sacrament, as the Great Physician or Healer." While we ponder on this theme, beloved Brethren, let us unite ourselves in a spirit of devotion and gratitude, to all the members of the mystical body throughout the world: and form the intention of adding our mite of thanksgiving and love to the boundless offerings which the Universal Church has laid to-day at the feet of our Blessed Lord in the Sacrament of the Altar.

After Adam's fall, beloved Brethren, there was great need of a Healer. The human body and the human soul alike felt the shock and ravage of that sad catastrophe. That frame which had once stood a masterpiece of soundest mechanism, a stranger to disease and ignorant of death, was now subject to a very different fate. As a penalty for man's rebellion it became a law that the race, as a race, should be afflicted with distempers and pains and divers forms of bodily distortion; and every generation was destined to know of agues and palsies, fevers and asthmas, gouts and leprosies, and many organic diseases, both named and nameless. Every generation was to be familiar with the moaning of the blind beggar by the wayside, with the beseeching accents of the halt and the crippled, and was to see written upon the forehead of the race, in these uncouth characters, the sentence of outlawry and condemnation. Some of these bodily ills were found to be, wholly or partially, under the dominion of healing herbs and distilled juices, prepared potions and extracts; and men arose who made themselves acquainted with the virtues of roots and leaves, minerals and springs. Thus the physician was destined to live in every age, and it was to be as true of him as of the ruler of the tribe: "the doctor is dead; long live the doctor." The skill of the physician was at best extremely circumscribed, for he could not make the lame walk nor the blind see; nor even within his province was he all-powerful, since disease was capricious, and at times baffled his efforts, and seemed to scorn his most recondite preparations. And at no time did his experiments upon liquids or solids enable him to arrest the progress of natural decay, which seized the bones and tissues, as autumn seizes the leaves on the trees, withering them ere they fall. Still less could the secrets of his science enable him to banish death from the threshold of the world, or to confer upon the children of Adam an earthly immortality. In spite of all physicians, the truth was every day exemplified afresh—"It is appointed for all men once to die."

But if man's body fared ill, beloved Brethren, his soul, the immortal half within him, fared even worse. All the beauty and the symmetry which belonged to the body of the unfallen man had been, in the early days in Paradise, but a poor setting for that sparkling and priceless jewel, the soul, on which God had stamped His own image with His own hand. It was the soul which, in its original splendour, before the fall, had entitled man to say, not in pride, but in gratitude: "Thou hast made me little less than the Angels: Thou hast crowned me with glory and honour." Amid a world of wonders, which elicited the praise of the divine Architect himself, "when He saw," as the Holy Scripture says, "that it was good," the soul was the best and brightest creation of all. There was an understanding, calm, clear, penetrating, and profound: darkened by no cloud of ignorance, and disturbed by no breath of passion. There were feelings manifold and airy, that waited, like winged attendants, dutifully obedient, upon reason; radiant joy, and vehement yet tempered love, calm hatred of wrong, and cheering hopes, that made all beautiful things more beautiful. Thus these passions came to reason's beck like tame birds to the hand of the fancier. And, as the complement and perfection of all these gifts, there was a will alert and facile in its obedience to the dictates of the judgment. So that the soul was a kingdom, where justice held rule, and where all the powers and faculties conspired to promote the glory of God.

But alas! after the fall, this wondrous kingdom became a prey to anarchy; this fair garden, in which, more than in the material Paradise, God loved to walk, became disordered, weedy, and desolate. The intellect became darkened, so that the vision of truth was obscured and perverted; and the dictates of conscience were like inscriptions on an old moss-grown monument, to be deciphered only with difficulty. Every generation brought in its stock of error, to swell the bulk, and add to the embarrassment of poor bewildered mortals. Philosophers increased men's perplexity by axioms and sayings, which were more frequently the offspring of passion, than the indications of a love of truth. At last, the highest things were confounded with the lowest, and the noblest ideas of man's mind were trailed in the mire. Divinity was found to reside in the works of man's genius, wrought of stone or wood, or precious metal: nay, in the bulbs that grew out of the earth, and the loathsome creatures that had their birth in the slime. Worse than that—a degradation, beyond which it was impossible to descend — man's vilest passions were set up, unveiled and shameless, upon the altar, as objects of supreme adoration. Cupidity was there, the mad ferocity of war, the brutal license of lust, all claiming the worship of man, and expanding their nostrils to the incense of sacrifice, and the steam of victims. And if such was the state of man's understanding—so basely fallen and hopelessly down-trodden—I need not say that his passions were rampant and flagitious. Those passions, I have said, were originally as tame birds that waited on reason; now they were as savage brutes, which reason dared not thwart, or balk of their meal of offal. And under such direction it is needless to say that the will did but pander to the worst of vices.

Such was the world when the Healer came, who was promised from the beginning. For thousands of years, through each century of wickedness, the guilty race seemed to bellow to the skies: "would that Thou wouldst rend the heavens and come down."

He came at last, a vision of gentleness and mercy, Whose hand had not only the healing quality of the physician, but the tender softness of a mother. And yet this vision of Him, Who was beautiful beyond the children of men, was not all a vision; for lo! the sovereign and heavenly Physician was become our own brother

—flesh of our flesh and bone of our bone. And having once come upon earth, having entered the reeking hospital of pestilence and misery, he wished never more to leave it, for "His delights were to be with the children of men." He was not content to say: "Come to Me all you that labour and are burthened, and I will refresh you," but He must add: "Behold I am with you all days, even to the consummation of the world." And hence He devised Himself a means of remaining amongst us, even after His visible presence had been withdrawn, by the institution of His wonderful Sacrament. Here He would abide, unseen save by the eyes of faith, under the meanest and most abject disguise; to the senses of men a little white wafer of bread, yet in very truth, under that veil, the self-same Physician and Healer who traversed Judea eighteen and a half centuries ago, healing the sick and raising the dead to life. His work is little altered now; though in some of its features it may be modified. In the days of His visible presence He wrought many miraculous cures. He made the lame to walk; He gave sight to the man born blind; He restored the widow's dead son to her desolate hearth. Such miraculous manifestations had their own transitory purpose. They were attestations of the divine sanction upon His teaching, and convincing and merciful arguments vouchsafed to an unbelieving generation. And this purpose was clearly pointed out by our Blessed Lord Himself. To the man who was brought to Him, sick of the palsy, He said: "Be of good heart, son, thy sins are forgiven thee." And behold, some of the scribes said within themselves: "He blasphemeth." And Jesus, seeing their thoughts, said: "Why do you think evil in your hearts? Whether is it easier for me to say, thy sins are forgiven thee, or to say, arise and walk? But that you may know that the Son of Man hath power on earth to forgive sins, then said He to the man sick of the palsy: Arise! take up thy bed, and go into thy house. And he arose and went into his house." It was to establish His mission, then, as the Saviour of Mankind and the Destroyer of sin, that He wrought these wondrous works; his power over bodily ailments was merely a testimony to His power over the maladies of the soul. Except these miraculous interpositions, His office as the Healer remains unchanged in the Sacrament of the Eucharist. Even yet, He has not withdrawn His promise that our faith shall move mountains; and that whatsoever we ask, nothing doubting, shall be granted to our prayers. But extraordinary or miraculous bodily cures, as they are no longer needed to establish His mission, can no longer be reasonably expected. Nevertheless, even the disorders that torture our frames and the frail organs of our body, do not escape His healing influence. For if He does not banish them He gives us great fortitude to bear them ; and keeps us constantly in mind that the inheritance of pain, if accepted with patience, will pave the way to eternal joy. The beatitude, with which He startled the ears of the Jews in the sermon on the mount, is still whispered from His tabernacle through the world, and amid the world's tumult penetrates to many a heavy-laden heart. "Blessed are they that mourn, for they shall be comforted." And as with bodily pains so with bodily defects : He bids us look forward to the time when the shame and trial they beget will be exchanged, in reward for our resignation, for a special dowry of perfections, in the land where there shall be no blemish or blight, and will be crowned with a reward which "eye hath not seen nor ear heard, and which it hath not entered into the heart of man to conceive."

But what shall we say of the power this hidden Physician wields over the spiritual diseases, the festering sores, that sin engenders? Ah, here indeed is his proper department. The earthly physician can apply his remedies according to his own favoured system, and follow up the disease in many cases with appropriate remedies, until it is expelled from the affected organ or the ailing member. But where is there a remedy in all the world that can touch the distempers of the spirit ? Where is the medicine that can cure the morbid swellings of pride, the consuming fever of covetousness, the delirium of lust, the fitful madness of anger, the unwholesome greed of gluttony, the pining of envy, the lethargy of sloth? These are beyond the reach of earthly treatment. These no finger can touch but the finger of our Healer, Jesus Christ, to whom all power is given in heaven and on earth. And no matter how deeply these seven diseases may have struck root in the soul, His hand is able to eradicate them. Let them have expanded and developed for years and years until there seems no hope of cutting them out, and, even so, it is not too late for this all-powerful Physician. He has but to speak and the vice is torn up by His word, as a tree by the force of a mighty storm, and cast forth root and branch. "Lord," said the Centurion, "I am not worthy that thou shouldst enter under my roof; say but the word and my servant shall be healed." And these words the Church has slightly altered so as to form a prayer for the cure of our spiritual ailments; so that every poor sinner, conscious of his slavery to one or other of these deadly diseases, can use no better prayer than this: "Say but the word, and my soul shall be healed." If then we feel within us the gnawings of these guilty passions, and the tyrannical grasp which long years of dominion have given them, what must we do? Must we cast out hope, and yield ourselves to despair? No. We must do as the Jews did in the desert, when the plague of deadly serpents was sent upon them. When the venom of the sting had entered their bodies and their veins began to burn with the poison, they were directed to turn their glazing and languid eyes towards the brazen serpent which was lifted up in the sight of all, and at once the effect of the virus they had received into their frames was cancelled, and the heart-weariness and pain and mortal debility left them. So we, as long as we can raise our eyes, our hearts, and our voices towards the occupant of this tabernacle, have no reason to despair. For on the face of the tabernacle the words seem written: "Is there no balsam in Gilaad, is there no physician?"

In conclusion, beloved Brethren, let me ask you to look into your own souls for the symptoms of any spiritual disorder that may lurk there. And if you recognize in yourselves the seeds of disease, be not slow in presenting yourselves to this Physician and Healer—Jesus, in the blessed Sacrament. Here pour forth your moans into His ear, and call upon Him, with the importunity of the blind man in the Gospel, poor Bartimeus, who, the more he was chid, cried out the more vehemently—"Jesus, have mercy on me." If you do so, He will give you grace to approach the Sacrament of Penance, and to cleanse yourselves of your sinful leprosy in the healing bath of His precious blood; He will give you Himself for your food in the Sacrament of Life, and bestow upon you a pledge of health and strength here, and immortal happiness hereafter. And no matter how you have weakened and defaced your soul with sin, if you persevere in frequenting the Sacraments, you will be strong enough to resist every evil impulse, and to overcome that perverse nature, which habit has created in you; so that you will realize the meaning of the Apostle's words: "I can do all things in Him that strengthens me." You will be re-constituted in the calmness and clearness of the Christian's intellect; your passions and feelings will bend to the yoke of reason; you will turn to follow the will of God, as faithfully as points the compass to the pole. Faith will shed its light on all things; and reveal the shams of life; hope will whisper comfort in your ear; charity will draw you in delicious bondage along the narrow way, which leads to eternal life.

THE SACRED HEART OF JESUS.

THE Church, beloved Brethren, has her emotional as well as intellectual side. In her intellect are most clearly mirrored all the unchanging truths of revelation; and these she formulates in her creeds and ever accumulating dogmatic pronouncements, according to the times and the varying needs of her children. On the other hand, the feelings and emotions which are awakened by the successive contemplation of the truths of which she is the guardian, find vent in her devotions: and that not by any agency of fluid chance, nor the promptings of caprice, but by the special providence of God, which sways the will of the faithful, even as the moon rules the tides. No epoch is exactly similar to any other; and, roughly speaking, these devotions are adapted to the characteristics of the epoch. But this property all devotions have in common: they all spring from dogmatic truth, and to dogmatic truth they owe their specific form, as the leaves and blossoms of a tree owe their existence, their luxuriance, and their special type of beauty, to the sap that circulates in the trunk and branches they adorn.

I have said, beloved Brethren, that the devotions of the Church are directed by the special providence of God, through the operating of His Holy Spirit, for the sanctification of the faithful. And this explains why it is that the Church is so cautious and deliberate in dealing with them Before she stamps them with the seal of her approval, she looks for some conclusive token of the divine authorization. This token is vouchsafed to her, either by a private revelation made by God to his eminent servants, or by the testimony of miracles, or by a general and spontaneous movement of the wills of the faithful, which can be explained only by the powerful influence of the Spirit of God.

Among the devotions practised at the present day there is none more conspicuous than that which has for its object the Sacred Heart of Jesus, It is a devotion which has been specially reserved by the fatherly thoughtfulness and solicitode of God for these days of languishing faith and earth-bounded hopes, and of half-extinguished love. "It is in the last era of the world," said St. John the St. John the Evangelist in a vision to St. Gertrude, "that God has decreed to make known the sweet mysteries of the Sacred Heart of Jesus, in order to re-kindle the fire of charity then decaying in the breasts of men."

Now this devotion comes to us, beloved Brethren, with every species of authorization. It was inaugurated by revelation; it was confirmed by miracles; it has successfully stood the test of the world's malignant opposition—an opposition that was organized with unexampled ingenuity, which varied its methods of attack with diabolical cunning, in support of which were employed the most brilliant and venomous satire—an opposition, again, which received additional momentum from the weight of theological lore, and which was sanctified in the eyes of the undiscriminating crowd by the external mortifications and austerities practised by many of its sworn partizans. In one word, the devotion has battled successfully through a hurricane, or rather through a series of hurricanes, which would have sunk for ever, fathoms deep, any undertaking not upheld by the hand of the Most High. And, lastly, its rapid, enthusiastic welcome, and thankful acceptance by the faithful, in all climes and countries, in spite of so many obstacles, triumphantly prove that it has its origin in the decree of God, and in the counsels of His Holy Spirit.

With good reason, therefore, does the Church stimulate us to the practice of devotion to the Sacred Heart of Jesus; with good reason does she set it, as a telling and impressive symbol, constantly before our gaze; with good reason has she established a solemnity in its honour, and consecrated to it the thoughts, the ponderings, and the pious ejaculations of one month out of the twelve. And she has urged her pastors in every part of the globe to direct the minds of their faithful flock to the Sacred Heart of Jesus as their model, their strength, their asylum, their comfort, and the foundation of their everlasting hopes.

The devotion to the Sacred Heart grows naturally out of the doctrine of the Incarnation of Jesus Christ; it is an inevitable corollary of the dogma. When God wrought that prodigy of wisdom and power which the divine Intellect alone could conceive and the divine Omnipotence accomplish ; when He united a human soul and a human body—the latter derived exclusively from the womb of the blessed Virgin Mary—to His own infinite and all-perfect Godhead, so as to form out of the two natures one individual or person ; every power and faculty, every member, organ, sense, and attribute belonging to the inferior nature thus admitted to a personal union with the Divine Essence, was entitled to exactly the same adoration as was due to the Godhead itself. Thus every power and affection of the soul of Jesus was adorable. And what is said of His soul applies equally to His body. Every organ of the Son of Man, as He loved to call himself, was also the organ of God. It was the eternal God that saw by the eyes, and heard by the ears, and felt by the hands of Jesus. It was the eternal God that hungered and thirsted, that ate and drank, that laboured, and preached, and prayed, that held mournful vigil beneath the starlight in the garden of Gethsemane, that sorrowed and wept, that bled and suffered, and died in the person of Mary's Son. And it was the eternal God whose mercy, and compassion, and love, palpitated and burned in the heart of Jesus.

When God decreed to become man, beloved Brethren, who, by the mere light of reason; could have anticipated the astonishing form in which He would come amongst us ! That mighty Being, who had whelmed the guilty world in the seething downpour of the deluge ; that mighty Being, who had rained down torrents of roaring sulphur upon the moral lepers of the plain ; who had hung up the foaming crests of the ever-swelling sea like a beetling mountain-range over the march of the Israelites, and had buried their ill-starred pursuers beneath the deadly mass of waters ; who had made His voice heard in the thunders of Sinai, and had scattered carnage and desolation from the Ark :—in what precise mould of our human nature will He present himself to us ? Surely He shall come as a vision of majesty and glory : surely He shall erect His throne above the thrones of the earth, as King of Kings, and Lord of Lords, and make all the rulers of the world His tributaries. His wisdom shall flash forth as the all illuminating sun, eclipsing the paltry lights and grimy lanterns of earthly philosophy. His authority, no less than His power, shall bend all to His behest. He shall establish peace and harmony among the chaos of unbrotherly races, and the clash of conflicting human interests; all men shall swear fealty to Him as the Emmanuel, the God come down from heaven to reign in our midst: "all flesh shall see His glory—the glory, as it were, of the only begotten of the Father, full of grace and truth."

Ah! beloved Brethren, how different is the guise the eternal Word chose for His manifestation in the flesh! Mysterious appointment of the infinite Wisdom and the infinite Love of God! "Who hath known the mind of the Lord, or who hath been His counsellor?" Behold, by the door of a humble cottage, in Nazareth, a young man, in his teens, dressed in a workman's garb. Beside Him, bending over a piece of wood-work which He is fashioning, is a grave, elderly man; and close by is a young woman of singularly sweet and modest face. Oh! take off your sandals, ye pilgrims of humanity in every age, as you approach that woman; for she is the very creation—joyous mother, yet spotless maid — whose union of virginity and motherhood was prefigured in the flame enveloped bush, that fire could not consume, and therefore, on her account alone, thrice holy is the ground you tread. And He—that slender youth, so gentle in His aspect, and so reverent to His mother and His guardian—He who re-produces her very features and reflects her air and bearing, her attitude and gestures—for He had no earthly father to modify the mother's stamp on countenance and form—He is the Son of the living God —God of God and Light of Light—co-eternal and co-equal with the Father—begotten before the day star—the omnipotent Word, that called forth from nothingness the solid earth beneath His feet and the boundless firmament that canopies it overhead. This quiet boy is the long looked-for Lion of Juda, whose voice was expected to awaken all the echoes of the earth; this unpretending youth is the mighty Son of David, of whom the royal Psalmist sung: "The Lord said to my Lord, sit Thou at my right hand until I make Thy enemies Thy footstool." This silent workman's helper, is the greater Solomon, of whom the world-renowned sage is but the shadowy presentment; this foster-child of a carpenter, so unnoticed and unknown, is the same of whom Isaias spoke, when he said—"For Sion's sake I will not hold my peace, and for the sake of Jerusalem, I will not rest till her just one come forth as a brightness, and her Saviour be lighted as a lamp."

Yes, be astonished, ye heavens, He, who deemed it no rapine that He should be equal to the Father, has indeed thus emptied himself, taking the form not merely of a man, but of a servant, the helper of a poor struggling carpenter. Long enough had men been familiar with the power and grandeur of the God of Hosts, and that paternal rigour which if relenting to forgive, was swift to chastise. Too long for the love of the eternal Son had been the slow-rolling ages, obscured by the smoke and stained with the blood of brute sacrifices, that had no value save what they borrowed from His pre-ordained expiation. At last they had passed away, those years of guilt and misery, and the eternal Word had whispered in the ear of the Father: "Burnt, and sin-offerings Thou didst not desire; then, said I, behold I come!" Yes! the long-expected era had arrived at last, when God would reveal, in all its unspeakable tenderness, the love which He had always felt for the children of men. He would incarnate that love for sinning and suffering humanity, which was, in very truth, one substantially with His divine essence. He would make the cry reverberate through the centuries—"God is Love." He would teach men what is meant by "the bowels of the mercy of our God," through which the Orient from on high hath visited us. He would be kinsman, brother, comrade, friend, to the meanest beggar, the most forlorn sufferer, the most abandonned sinner in this vale of tears. For He had said to Himself, "I will draw them with the cords of Adam, with the bonds of love."

And so a body was fitted for Him, and he became the owner of a heart, human as our own, yet divine and adorable. Like ours, it was the chief and central instrument of vitality, and its office was to propel through the veins and arteries the sacred stream of life. But its function did not end here. It was the bodily register of every emotional act of the soul. Every feeling, every break of passion, told upon it instantaneously, sometimes by relaxing its energy, sometimes by stimulating its pulsations and imparting to it unusual strength and excitement. Hopes and anticipations, joys and sorrows; fears, alarms, despondency, despair—all induce, in spite of our efforts, as we know, not only temporary tumults or derangement, but sometimes permanent injury in this most delicate of organs. So sensitive is it, indeed, that sudden shocks of powerful feeling have been known to shatter it altogether. It has been found ruptured in the breast by some terrible agitation to which it has been subjected.

It is this living heart of Jesus, then, beloved Brethren, the witness of His passionate love, the partner of His anguish, especially in his sufferings and death, that claims our adoration. We pretend to settle no philosophic question as to the seat of the feelings in the human frame. We do not stultify ourselves by approaching that heart as if it were a mere structure of flesh, abstracting, which can never be, from its union with the person of Jesus Christ, God and Man. We bow down all our senses and faculties before it, as the living and adorable heart of the living and adorable God. We select it as the organ which, in truth and reality, is most intimately associated with the emotions of its possessor and, in the common esteem and utterance of men, most vividly symbolic of his affections and dispositions. We offer it our homage in the breast of Jesus Christ, as at once a most fitting emblem of His divine compassion and love, and the living instrument which never failed to thrill to every yearning, every joy and sorrow that stirred His soul. So that the history of that heart reflects the history of His feelings.

It was, indeed, the most human of hearts, but God alone knows how so fragile an organ in the breast of Jesus could bear the conditions of its intimate association with the Eternal Deity. As easy would it seem to concentrate in a hollow stalk of grass, unconsumed in the process, the white heat of a thousand glowing furnaces, as to bring to bear on that frail human heart the inconceivable ardours of the divine nature. But to infinite love nothing is impossible, either to devise or to accomplish, and God the Son, in His eagerness to be one of us, made light of every difficulty, and came "skipping over the mountains, leaping over the hills."

Behold, then, beating under the coarse garment of the young carpenter of Nazareth, the noblest heart ever framed by the hand of God. There is the shrine of God's compassion for man : there is the true mercy seat. With what joy, with what happiness, does that heart throb as the hands of that divine workman ply the implements of His toil, for He is knit to our race by a new and everlasting bond ; He is now flesh of our flesh, bone of our bone ; He is now our brother, without any figure of speech, and His delight is to be with His brothers, the children of men. How deep must be His affection, how tender His pity for the sons of Adam, when He—the God, before whom the angels are not spotless—He, the Infinite purity, is able, I will not say to tolerate, but even to rejoice in their companionship. How great must be the interest of this heavenly physician in the plague-stricken dungeons of this vast lazar house of the world, when He has chosen to make His abode in them, undeterred by the foulness of our sores, undismayed by the sickening atmosphere that envelopes us, unappalled by every hideous sight and dismal sound, unchecked by the insensibility and ingratitude of those to whom He ministers so graciously. After growing to maturity, in mechanical labour, He will give three years of His life to preaching and teaching, and short though that term may be, it will suffice to stamp the image of His kind heart on the world's records indelibly; to win the affections, and soothe the sorrows, and mould the characters, of millions of His fellow-men in all generations to come, till time shall be no more. That noble, that generous, that self-oblivious heart, overflowing with the tenderest sentiments, to each single member of the human race, will indeed draw men in every age "by the cords of Adam—by the bonds of love."

Brief and incomplete are the fugitive notices of His public life, of His words and works compiled by the Evangelists; yet how wondrous is that heart of His they reveal; a light to all the ages; a study that can never be exhausted; an influence ever living and fresh. "Come to Me," is the cry of this most human of hearts. "Come to Me, all ye that labour and are heavily burthened, and I will refresh you." Far from avoiding the guilty, He avows that it is for their sake that He has come into the world. In how many pathetic forms does His heart reveal its sublime compassion! He is the Good Shepherd seeking the lost sheep; He is the ever-fond and forgiving Father of the prodigal, longing daily for his return from his weary pilgrimage of sin and hardship. He is the God that accepted the humble prayer of the repentant publican. His heart, bleeding with pity, devises a means of escape still for the woman taken in adultery; it prompts the tears which he outpoured by the grave of Lazarus, whom He called His friend; its love trembles in the accents with which He proclaims the acceptance of the poor Magdalen, and the undying fame of her conversion; its pulses throb with the anguish of a baffled love and a fruitless yearning as He washes the feet of Judas and receives his kiss of basest treachery. Out of that heart rises the lament with which He foretells the doom of the city He loved so fondly, and which so cruelly rejected Him. The all-forgiving impulse of that heart lends strength to His lips, now livid with the hues of approaching death, to promise from His cross to the penitant thief the certain joys of paradise. Truly "the bruised reed He shall not break, and the smoking flax He shall not extinguish." "Behold My servant, I will uphold him ; My elect : My soul delighteth in him."

ON THE HUMILITY OF THE SACRED HEART.

OF all the virtues that enrich the Sacred Heart of Jesus, beloved Brethren, there are two in particular that are most characteristic, which imply all the rest, and which our blessed Lord has proposed for our special imitation. "Learn of Me," He said, "because I am meek and humble of heart." These two are its master attributes. But the root of all its other virtues, furnishing nourishment even to meekness itself, is humility. If the heart of Jesus had not been humble, it could not have been meek. It is by pride that the flashing eye of anger is enkindled, the brow of defiance knit, the stinging insult darted, the sudden blow struck, and the longing for revenge sown and cherished in the mind. Let me speak then, first, on the humility of the Sacred Heart. It was humility that lent a uniform character to the whole career of the Son of God made man. He knew that, amongst angels and men, it was pride and the ambition begotten of pride that had been the first agents of disaster. He would, therefore, leave behind Him an ideal of humility that should live in the memories and haunt the imaginations of men—more persuasive than the exhortations of preachers or the treatises of the learned. Hence His providence shaped all the events of His life so as to earn for Him the contempt of the world. Who was His mother? A poor maid whose virtues were her dowry. His pedigree, indeed, included names that were famous and revered in Jewish story, but He came down from heaven only when all the splendour and prestige of His ancestry had vanished and faded away among the phantoms of the past. He was born not in a palace as would seem to become the babe of prophecy, upon Whose shoulders is empire; not even in a poor man's humble cottage or a beggar's hovel; but in a bleak stable, like a vagrant's child, His only cradle a rude pallet of straw spread in a manger, and gladly utilised for the emergency. He was not many days old when He would fain let His blood flow beneath the knife of circumcision, as though He were one of the brood of sinners out of whose nature the corruption of the fall required painful cutting. He fled into Egypt before the violence of Herod, as though He had no force to oppose to the relentless and inhuman tyrant; as though heaven's myriads of legions were not ready to sweep away His foes, if He but raised His infant hand. Out of a career of thirty-three years, for every day spent in works such as were calculated to make His name known and honoured, ten were spent in retirement. He was not only reputed the son of a carpenter, but Himself earned His bread as a common workman with the sweat of His brow. When at length He bade farewell to the beloved home of His retirement, in which He had spent so many years of His precious and saving life, He strangely contrived in His wisdom to blend publicity with seclusion, and fame with obloquy. He inaugurated His public life by mixing with the "brood of vipers" that gathered to the Jordan to be baptized by His Precursor, and was baptized even as one of them. And who were His favourite apostles? Were they distinguished in the schools? Were they men of refinement, or culture, or family? No; several of them were fishermen, who wrested a precarious livelihood out of the heaving waters of the inland sea, men of small account in the district to which they belonged. What would be thought nowadays of a sage whose favourite disciples and associates were a few labourers of the commonest stamp; who would propagate his doctrine among the wise and learned through unlettered rustics—at any rate, men with the least tincture of education? Would not the world gibe at such a fellowship?

It was thus that He bade pride stand abashed; that pride which turns away in fastidiousness and scorn from the poor and vulgar; which scarcely allows to the substratum of society the attributes of our common humanity; which hangs its whole happiness on the smile of the great, and seeks it in the company and conversation of the fashionables of this world. This is why He drew around Him rugged faces, bronzed from exposure and beaten by many a storm; this is why the hands He grasped were so many of them rough and horny; why the voices most familiar to His ear had some of the hoarseness of the roaring gale; why the very odour of their despised avocation, which clung to the garments of His earliest followers, would provoke the contempt and the scorn of the learned Scribe and the arrogant Pharisee, whom He yet offered to enlighten and teach. "For the foolish things of this world hath God chosen that He may confound the wise: and the weak things of the world hath God chosen that He may confound the strong. And the base things of the world, and the things that are contemptible hath God chosen; and things that are not, that He might bring to naught things that are. That no flesh should glory in His sight."—I *Cor.* i. 27. And then what gentleness and sweet tolerance did that heart exhibit, when the divine Wisdom took His seat in the grimy school-room of the world to play the part of humble Rabbi; the drudging pedagogue to the rude scholars whom He came to teach. How He stooped to bear with their coarse material characters, and unspiritual instincts, their slowness of faith and selfishness of aim, the coldness and harshness of their nature. And as Jesus turned not from the rude, neither did He avoid contact with the guilty. On the contrary, His heart went out to them even more than others. They were the special objects of His quest. "I come," He said, "not to call the just, but the sinner to repentance." So that His enemies, in their perversity, made it a reproach that He ate with publicans and sinners. Yes, they were His brothers, however defiled and degraded; and the more pitiful, the more loathsome, the more desperate their plight, the more did the Brother's heart feel and bleed for them.

How cheering, how encouraging, are the words in which He refers to them. They are sheep that have gone astray: He is the Good Shepherd that follows them, sorrowing, through brake and bramble. Their return makes heaven festive; "there is joy before the angels of God over one sinner doing penance, more than over ninety just that need not penance." Did the woman taken in adultery, and rescued by His device from the sentence of death which the hypocritical Pharisee, at least, invoked upon her, ever forget His gentle words: "Hath no man condemned thee? Neither will I condemn thee, go now and sin no more." They were so different from the rebuke she was prepared for. How many diffident sinners has He attracted to Him by the story of the contrite publican pouring out his sorrow humbly behind the pillar. How many eyes have wept during these eighteen hundred years and more over that pathetic picture presented by the poor Magdalen, when torn with self-reproach, shrinking from His sweet face as the shrine of purity, yet irresistibly drawn to it as the throne of compassion, she prostrated herself with streaming eyes and hair dishevelled, and felt a new life within her at those words of tenderness, which so strangely interrupted the indignant exclamations of the company: "Many sins are forgiven her because she hath loved much;" and again, "Amen I say to you, wheresoever this Gospel be preached in the whole world, that also which she hath done shall be told for a memorial of her."—*Mark* xiv. 9.

We cannot, beloved Brethren, look directly into that heart—we can only learn its sentiments and feelings from what our Lord said and did whilst He walked on earth; and His whole life in its every moment and act was an exhibition of humility. "I came not to do My own will," He declared, "but the will of Him that sent Me." He sought not His own glory, but the glory of His Father. When men were filled with wonder and awe at His stupendous miracles, He imposed silence on them. When they would have made Him king He disappeared from their midst. When the evil spirit cried out loudly and confessed Him the Son of God, Jesus rebuked him. When the woman, rapt with the power and unction of His preaching, cried out in ecstatic admiration that the mother who bore Him was surely blessed, He would turn her thoughts and the thoughts of the crowd from Himself as man, to that which should be the end of every human act, the glory of His Father. "Yea, rather blessed are they that hear God's word and keep it"—the essence and perfection of humility. Before He entered on the last and bitterest stage of His life, the hour of His passion, His final lesson to His disciples, still swayed by worldly emulation and jealousy, was a rebuke to their petty ambitions and love of precedence, but a rebuke conveyed with the most loving tenderness as He abased Himself before them as their very servant. He girt Himself with a towel and washed their feet—even the feet of the traitor, which (as the revelations of His servants tell us) He bedewed plentifully the while with tears of sad regret and disappointed love. But who, beloved Brethren, shall speak of the humiliations of His long agony, from the moment He received the treacherous kiss of His false friend and favoured disciple, till He buried His head and died in shame on the tree of infamy? He presents to us a picture of humility, the most complete that with our present powers of understanding we can take in. What can the most vivid imagination conceive that could be added to the ceaseless insult and ignominy of the last day and night of degradation in the house of Annas and Caiphas, in Herod's court, in Pilate's hall? All this we can in a certain measure realise, however faintly and inadequately. Even when we remember that this innocent sufferer, meekly silent amidst the taunts and scornful jeers of His enemies, is the eternal Son whose word called all creatures into existence, "through Whom God made the world;" that the countenance so bruised and defiled is the face on which the angels love to dwell; that the helpless victim, clothed in mockery with the ragged purple coat, and crowned with the cruel diadem of scorn, shown to the crowd in vain to move their pity, is the King of ages and immortal; that this Man of Sorrows, rejected as more criminal than a lawless homicide, and exalted to the highest place of infamy between the two malefactors crucified at His side, is, in His human nature, seated on His Father's right hand. All this was, if dimly, seen in the vision of the prophet. He foretold that the Redeemer, the Holy One, should be reputed with the wicked; that He should be a worm and no man; a leper and an outcast, and one struck by God and afflicted—yea, one accursed for our sake. This, I say, God in His infinite wisdom has allowed us to apprehend, and in some measure to understand.

But there was a humiliation deeper still which we shall never fathom, on earth or in heaven—which the highest Spirit of Knowledge, that sees furthest into the splendour of the divine purity, will never realize through all eternity. He, the God of Holiness, would have imputed to himself all the hateful iniquities of His creatures, from the first sin of Adam, to the last revolt of the perverse human will, till iniquity shall have filled its measure, and sin and the possibility of sin shall be swept away by the avenging flames, that will precede the awful judgment. Only the infinite knowledge of the Almighty can understand, as only His infinite purity could feel, the shame and humiliation of the last moments on the Cross, when the Eternal Father abandoned—turned, as in loathing, from the Son, in whom He was well pleased No word shall ever tell, no mind shall ever know, the uttermost anguish of shame and desolation which found vent in His piercing cry—"My God! My God! why hast thou forsaken Me?" And that sacred gentle heart was broken instantly beneath the crushing weight of gathered human crime, which pressed upon it with a mightier strength than that of pent-up waters.

Can we ever think enough then, beloved Brethren, of the humility of the Eternal Son, God made man, the fullest revelation we can receive, as it was the first effect, of the incomprehensible love that burnt in His sacred heart. Being God, "He emptied himself, and took the form of a servant—He humbled himself—becoming obedient unto death, even the death of the cross." And we are to learn of Him, and to imitate Him in this mysterious humility. The thought of it is not to be a barren recollection, or an empty wonder. It is a seed that must sink into, and take root, and flower, and fructify in our own hearts, as it has done so wonderfully in His great servants, in whom self-distrust and self-abasement was the most conspicuous virtue, the foundation of the saintly character in every one without exception. They were men who were not content with the sincerest conviction of their own weakness and unworthiness in the sight of God; they laboured strenuously to make the world conform its estimates to their own. They sought contempt and ill-treatment with an avidity which, to the ignorant, appears morbid and fanatical. They permitted no momentary elation, they checked the first pulsation of self-complacency, and referred all to God. Think of St. Philip Neri, who seemed perfect from the cradle, and when he was old had reached the highest degree of sanctity intelligible to the world, famed for his miracles, raised aloft in frequent ecstasy, with the love of God shining in his face and actually enlarging his breast beyond the wont of nature, to allow free play to the excessive beatings of his heart. Surely he was confirmed in grace; yet we know his self-distrust was such that, during the celebration of the divine Mysteries, he would grasp the chalice, and, as his hand shook and his voice faltered with emotion, would exclaim: "Have a care of poor Philip, O Lord, this day, or he will betray Thee." Like all his saintly compeers, in gazing into and in sounding the unfathomable abyss of the Sacred Heart, he had reached a depth which we shall never reach. But if we cannot hope to attain to the perfection of the saints, if we seem as far short of them as they knew themselves to be of their divine model and original, we can at least yearn and strive to think oftener, to reverence more deeply, to imitate more earnestly, to possess in fuller measure this first virtue of the divine Heart of Jesus. Feeble as we know ourselves to be, weakened and scarred, and disfigured by endless sins, yet inflated at every turn, swelling with the very things that should be our shame, and are sure signs of our deep corruption, even as the mouldering carcase is distended with the gasses that are engendered only in decay, we may well begin at last. Can we not check ourselves sometimes, as we fall into our customary self-complacency, dwelling with such pleasure on our endowments of body or mind, taking such sinful satisfaction in any good we have done or seem to possess—our past successes, our present position and influence, our empty day-dreams and vain anticipations for the future. Shrink we shall still, no doubt, unlike the saints, from contempt and ignominy. But surely even now we may cease seeking so ardently, surely we may be more resigned and cheerful if we fail to attract the notice, the esteem, the praise and acclamations of men. We can accept with gratitude, and consistently with the thorough performance of the duties of our calling, be content to remain, if so God wills it, in our obscure and lowly station in life. Above all we can soon form, by frequent acts, the habit of referring to God every atom of good and estimable we think we detect in our being. Thus we shall show a true love and reverence, and may trust we are sincere in our efforts to imitate the sacred heart of Jesus. Everything else is at best the expression of a mere sentiment, shallow, and passing, and fruitless—till we feel its mysterious humility, pondering, as we have tried to do to-day, on the profound meaning of those words of the Apostle; "He humbled himself, becoming obedient unto death—even the death of the Cross."

SACRED HEART OF JESUS.*

HARDLY have the hymns proper to the Octave of Corpus Christi ceased to echo in our ears, when the Church summons us to honour and glorify the Sacred Heart of Jesus, which is the divine source of that wondrous gift, as well as of all other spiritual blessings. This morning I will lay before you, beloved Brethren, a few considerations with a view to show how deserving is that heart of all the admiration, devotion, and fervent love we have it in our nature to bestow.

And first, beloved Brethren, we must remember that this heart of Jesus, though it is through the personal union truly divine, is no less the heart of the Son of Man, and as truly human. Within our own bosoms, therefore, where our own human hearts are beating, we have the key to the appreciation of all that is noble and excellent in that great heart which burns in the breast of our Elder Brother, the divine Son of Mary. We know that whatever exertions we make, whatever sacrifices we submit to for the sake of others, it is the heart within that prompts us to do and to suffer generously. And it is by those actions and sufferings that we are to estimate the quality of the heart which originates them. What then are we to say of the Sacred Heart of Jesus, in what fitting words are we to proclaim its goodness, which blossomed out into a thousand forms of benevolence and self-immolation? Test that heart by the events of this life. Conjecture its boundless generosity by all that it actuated Him to do and suffer

---

* This third Sermon on the Sacred Heart has been included as having a special personal interest. It was the last preached by Father Kelly. It so impressed a non-Catholic gentleman who heard it, that he sought an interview with the preacher, to make further enquiries as to the Church's teaching.

for our welfare, from His conception in the virginal womb of Mary to His passion and death upon the Cross. Years of humiliating bondage to the constraints of infancy and childhood; years of absolute obedience and submission to His creatures; years of labour and sweat, of hunger and thirst; the privation of a poor man's life; the endurance of contempt and insolence from those whom His providence had placed in a higher station: all these hard conditions of life He embraced of His own free choice, because His loving heart would have it so. And then when His time had come to preach the glad tidings to the world, His heart intervened again to shape His public career. That heart would mix bitterness with every sweet draught which His success commended to His lips. If His virtues elicited admiration from some, they extorted from others malignant and blasphemous abuse. If He healed the sick and raised the dead He was challenged to say by what power He worked the wonders, and His divine control over nature did but make His enemies swell with spite and envy. If He cast out devils, it was by Beelzebub, the prince of devils. If He won from the populace a spontaneous acknowledgment of His inborn Kingship, it was but to provoke from the priests and scribes and pharisees a howl of resentment and hatred, and an outcry against the spirit of sedition which they alleged must have ruled Him. If He received from the poor and simple a triumphant ovation, sitting upon an ass, with palm branches waving about Him, and palms bestrewing the path of the procession, nay, the very garments of His humble admirers, the scene had its contrast in the jangling objections raised to His doctrine by the learned and powerful of the land, ending in a sudden movement to stone Him as a blasphemer of God. If He received the homage and affection of the apostles and disciples, and valued their attachment and found consolation in their company, He allowed Himself to suffer from the abiding knowledge that one of them was a devil to whom He would owe His death. Thus His life was thorny at all times, and that by the imperious decree of His Sacred Heart, which would fain be a sharer in every form of trial and every sting of affliction, in every mortification, disappointment, and woe to which His beloved brethren were liable to be subjected to the end of time. Honour, then, and glory, praise and thanksgiving to the virtues of that great Heart of Jesus, which are indicated by the events of a life entirely absorbed in love of us, and dedicated to our welfare and happiness as its predominating object. All the treasures of effort and of suffering contained in His life testify to the nobility of that heart out of which they were, so to speak, unearthed to glitter before the eyes of His children. Truly "a good man" is He, and out of the good treasure of His heart bringeth forth that which is good.

Again, beloved Brethren, that heart deserves our deep reverence, and love, and thankfulness, because it has not only imprinted its character, so fond and self-forgetting, upon all the actions of His life, but even more because it had the chief place in working out our redemption. It was that heart which submitted the whole Being of Jesus to the merciful decree of the Heavenly Father for man's salvation at the cost of anguish untold, and a cruel and ignominious death, borne by the Lamb of God, who taketh away the sins of the world. "He became obedient unto death—even to the death of the Cross." What that heart suffered for us, in carrying out the behests of His heavenly Father, is witnessed by the sweat of blood in the garden, when He cried out, in the distress of His poor human nature: "Father, if it be possible, let this chalice pass away from Me: yet not My will, but Thine, be done." It is attested more clearly still in the last cry which was wrung from His dying lips, when all earth and heaven seemed in arms against Him, and the very face of His beloved Father was shrouded from His fading sight: "My God! My God! why hast Thou forsaken Me?" O, beloved Brethren, if we reverence the nails that fastened His hands to the Cross, the lance that pierced His sacred side, the Cross itself on which His agonized Body awaited death, how much greater shall be our veneration and our fond attachment for the human Heart of Jesus, which worked out our salvation at such a price? O, Heart of Jesus, we adore Thee, and we offer Thee our unworthy thanks; for were it not for Thy love, and Thy heroic exertions, Thy anguish and Thy out-poured blood, we should still be unredeemed, weighed down by the yoke of sin, thralls of the demons who hate in us the image of their Maker and ours, walking in dark ways, unregenerate, and dominated by the flood of transmitted custom, links in the long chain which forms the history of the lost generations.

And this work of Redemption, beloved Brethren, wrought through the loving impulses of the Heart of Jesus, reminds us that

that Heart is divine, and, like the essence of the Godhead, adorable. Therefore it is that the sacrifice it prompted availed to save us; for no power but that of the Divinity itself could offer worthy atonement for our sins. That Heart, united as it is in the personalty of the eternal Son of God, demands our adoration as surely as does the divine substance of the self-existing Deity. And every act of that Heart—every feeling and emotion, every throb of pain or pulsation of joy, every hope and disappointment that proceeds from it, or has proceeded since it was formed out of the pure blood of Mary—is as truly divine in its character, as precious and valuable in itself, and as capable of giving the life of grace to a lost world, as the wonder-working fiat of the Eternal Wisdom, which flooded the dark abysses with splendour by its omnipotent power. "Let there be light; and there was light." Before that Heart, then, let us bow; for though it is in form and tissue like our own, it is the Heart of the Son of God, and as adorable as Himself.

And deep is the veneration we owe to that Heart of Jesus, ardent the attachment it merits, as not only the author and prompter of our salvation, but the living symbol of the love which achieved that miracle of mercy. In this heart we see embodied that divine charity which yearned for man's welfare before the creation of the world. That heart is the organ by which the boundless goodness of God operated and found scope for its action. As we see with our eye, and hear with our ears, so we love with our hearts. It is in the heart that whole broods of loving and gentle thoughts nestle like doves. This Heart of Jesus, then, is the type of all His heroic devotion to the human race. It is with His bosom bared and that heart revealed within, wrapt in flames and crowned with the thorns of affliction which it most willingly bears, that our kind Redeemer speaks to us in enticing accents, saying: "Son, give me thy heart. It is thy love I seek; it is for thy love my heart craves. Thou shalt love the Lord with thy whole heart."

Oh, beloved Brethren, how old is the love of that heart for each one of us! What ages of tender thought and longing desire has that heart gone through for the meanest, the most despicable, the most uninteresting amongst us! Before the foundations of the world were laid, you and I were in the mind of God the Son, known through and through to the marrow, the familiars of His solitary meditations; more dearly cherished than ever babe was cherished by the most doting mother. Yes! God first loved us. He loved us before the sun or moon shone, before the history of our race began. And then, when sin was rampant and the world was living at war with Him who made it, His love would fain remodel our destinies and renew the face of the earth. "Burnt offering and sin-offering Thou didst not desire, then said I, Beloved I come." And that charity which constituted His being —for God is charity—that unimaginable fire of love which had burnt through eternity, was by a stupendous act of His omnipotence enclosed, shut up, compressed, into that human heart which Mary the Virgin gave Him of her substance; and there it glows, it blazes, it throbs, it fiercely consumes itself, without ever wasting away, through all the nineteen centuries which have passed since the gentle word of assent was heard all over heaven: "Behold the handmaid of the Lord. Be it done to me according to thy word!"

Yes! it is an old love, to which the amatory romances of human life can bring no parallel. It is to all other loves, in duration and intensity, as the vast all-reaching ocean is to the teardrop in the eye that scarce has weight to trickle. It was a love that broke forth in endless and restless manifestations. It made Jesus poor that we might be rich; it made Him mean and contemptible that we might shine glorious amongst the princes of His people; it made Him a man of sorrows that joy might be ours for evermore. It laid the Cross upon His shoulders, pressed the thorns upon His head, hammered the nails through hands and feet, it drove the lance that pierced His lifeless heart. For as He was offered up because He Himself wished it, so was the manner in which He offered Himself the choice of His insatiable love. He died for His friends, and greater friendship no man hath; it is friendship's seal and consummation. But more than that: He died for His enemies, love's deeper depth and undermost abyss of charity; that by His wounds they might be healed, and by His death they might have life everlasting.

"Charity," says the Apostle, "never faileth," and this Sacred Heart has proved the saying true. His visible career closed, His heart still found means to manifest its incomprehensible love throughout the recurring centuries. Yes, in the Sacrament of the Blessed Eucharist, in the silence and humility of the tabernacle, in the bread of angels dispensed to the faithful as their spiritual food, which makes them gods, and no longer men; in the throne of the monstrance, where He delights to sit in the midst of His poor brothers, listening to their prayers, their plaints, their longings, their pleadings, for their friends and foes; His heart is ever revealing itself from day to day in renewed manifestations of love; and the fire which burns within it is perpetually pulsating with the throes of its indomitable and inexpressible energy. With that heart to live is to burn. Like a raging and unquenchable fire, it has burned since its first throb of life, and must burn on throughout the ages of eternity. And the fuel that feeds it is the infinite love He bears to you and me.

FOURTH SUNDAY AFTER PENTECOST.

No Salvation outside the Church.

"GOING into one of the ships that was Simon's, He desired him to draw back a little from the land. And sitting, He taught the multitudes out of the ship."—*Luke* v. 3.

The multitude had gathered around the margin of the lake Genesareth, "to hear the Word of God," and our Blessed Lord, to gratify their desire, looked about for a boat from which He would be able to address them to advantage. There were two empty ships moored near the land; and of these our Blessed Lord chose the ship belonging, as it is stated, to Peter, to serve as His pulpit. In all likelihood, the ship belonged equally to Andrew, for the two brothers were partners; but it is called Peter's, though Andrew was the elder brother, because it was intended to typify that Church which was to the end of time to be indentified with the name of Peter. And this selection of Peter's boat was the more appropriate at this time, because the discourse of Jesus was to be followed by the miraculous draught of fishes, which was a figure of the souls that Peter's ministry was destined to save, and the call of the two brothers to be fishers of men and Apostles, and to leave their boat "and all things," to follow the Divine Master whom they had already acknowledged as the Messiah.

This incident, beloved Brethren, reminds us that Jesus Christ teaches the doctrine of eternal life out of one boat alone—and that the bark of Peter. It is to that bark that men must gather if they would hear the great Teacher, who has promised to be with His Church all days, and to speak by the voice of His Apostles and their successors: "He that heareth you, heareth Me." It is into that bark that men are to be drawn by the heavenly nets; it is in that bark alone that they can find salvation. This seems a hard saying, that outside the Church of Peter, the Catholic Church, salvation is not to be found. But it is only an imperfect comprehension of that doctrine which makes it appear difficult and illiberal. Ponder upon the question without prejudice or haste ; and the difficulty disappears, the harshness and inhumanity are softened down.

We certainly cannot be saved except through Jesus, the Mediator and the Redeemer. That every truly Christian sect will readily admit. "As there is but one God and Father of all men," says St. John, "so there is but one Saviour, who is the Way, the Truth, and the Life." He, and no other, must show us the way ; He, and no other, is qualified to teach us the truth without the danger of error ; He alone has the key to eternal life. "There is no other name under heaven given to men, whereby we must be saved."

It follows, therefore, that salvation can be attained only by those who believe in Him, and who obey His commandments. He is the way, and all other ways lead to perdition ; He is the truth, all theory and speculation that contradicts Him is falsehood ; He is the life, all other means of originating or maintaining a supernatural existence, or obtaining a supernatural happiness are futile and illusory. In Him only we live; apart from Him we die.

And He Who has the disposal of His gifts has promised the reward of eternal life only to those who accept Him as the unerring teacher of truth : "I am the light of the world," He said, "He that followeth Me walketh not in darkness, but shall have the light of life." But that supernatural life shall be withheld from those who disbelieve, distrust, or doubt Him : "He that believeth not shall be condemned," said our blessed Lord. And St. John tells us : "He that doth not believe is already judged, because he believeth not in the name of the only begotten Son of God." Here our blessed Lord, the kindest and most humane of beings, and St. John, the disciple of love, who had no drop of sourness, no fibre of harshness in his nature, register the distinct and rigid declaration that some shall be judged, that some shall be condemned ; in short, shall forfeit their salvation, viz., those who reject the teaching of that Master Who not only delivers truth, but is truth itself.

Now, where is that truth to be found ? Where is the Church that still teaches as the mouthpiece of Christ, without risk of misleading mankind ? Where is that Church with which Christ is pledged to be to the consummation of the world ; in which the words are fulfilled, he that heareth you heareth Me; and he that despiseth you despiseth Me? For it is certain that He founded only one Church; that He taught truths and not mere opinions; that, because they are truths, guaranteed by His teaching, He has no choice but to require from all the most undoubting acceptance of every tittle of doctrine. Where, I say, is that one Church? For, if we find it, our duty is plain. We must believe its doctrine as the doctrine of Christ; we must submit to its precepts as the precepts of Christ. And if we refuse to believe her, it is not we, but our blessed Lord Who has said "we shall be condemned;" it is not we, but St. John who has said we are "already judged.'

There is one Church which bears upon it the manifest and striking evidences of an origin derived from Jesus Christ. It is the old, old Church, carrying the memory back through all the ups and downs of history, the overthrow and re-construction of empires, the blending of races, the slow modelling of different forms of civilization, the decay and reflorescence of literatures and schools of thought, the endless metamorphosis of habits and customs. It is that old, old Church that lived in the catacombs; that confronted Frank and Hun and Goth; that preached to every race; that set the Cross up in every land; that roved the whole earth over, winning in one continent if she lost in another; that had her day even in Japan and China, where, till envy assailed her, she could boast of royal favour, and neophytes among the highest nobles. It is that old, old Church which can trace its finger upwards through the long centuries over the line of the pontiffs who successively took the place of Peter in Peter's bark. It is the old, old Church which has outlasted the age of persecution, and stands foremost now amongst Christian denominations, outnumbering them all. She alone claims to teach with unerring accuracy the very truths that her Founder taught. She alone has remained unaltered with the altering times. Her attitude to the world, the prerogatives she vindicated as her own, her action in the more explicit revelation of the truths entrusted to her charge according to the needs of the time, her action in the shaping of her discipline with maternal kindness to suit the varying characters of the age without sacrificing one jot of principle; her action in promulgating new devotions bearing the signs of divine approval, for God's honour and the salvation of souls, without deviating in the smallest degree from her received dogmas, or the fixed sentiments she has cherished from the beginning : all these characteristics mark her off from everybody that has adopted the name of Christian, and beyond them all she challenges, by her preternatural career, the attention of every thoughtful and candid enquirer.

This Church, then, beloved Brethren, proclaiming herself as she does to be the one Church which Christ founded, as the means of saving mankind, is bound at the same time to proclaim herself the only Church in which salvation is to be obtained. This claim she is not free to waive. If you suppose her to be, as she professes, the one Church by which Christ teaches, you cannot acquit those who reject her doctrines, or spurn her authority, of that disbelief and repudiation of the truth, which brings condemnation upon those who are guilty of it. If she is the one Church by which Christ teaches, then most certainly he that despiseth her, despises Him that sent her : and the doom is inevitable. He that believeth not shall be condemned.

The Church then cannot leave men free to reject her teaching : because what she teaches is not mere opinion, not mere speculative probabilities, not mere theological conjectures ; but the very truth, delivered to her by her divine founder. She can no more allow mankind to question or to doubt that truth, than our blessed Lord himself could. If His followers had disputed any doctrine He taught, would they still be disciples? No! He could have but one answer for every doubter and unbeliever : " He that is not with Me is against Me. I am the Way, the Truth, and the Life." Otherwise, He would have made truce, and effected a pleasant compromise with the Jews, who said, upon His promise that He would make His flesh their food—" How *can* this man give us His flesh to eat ?" But no. There is no alliance between light and darkness. They went their way, and He could not prevent them ; for what He said was true ; and He would not gloss it over, much less recall His words. His Church has to act as her divine Master acted ; and when she teaches what her children do not comprehend, and the worldly and unspiritual leave her, the faithful bow their heads, with St. Peter, and say : " If we forsake Thee to whom shall we go ? Thou hast the words of eternal life." These believe unto life everlasting ; those, because they believe not, are, as St. John says, already ' judged.'

We see then, beloved Brethren, that man is not privileged to disbelieve the doctrines proposed by the Church, any more than the doctrines proposed by our Lord ; and that salvation is promised only to the believers, while condemnation and judgment are the lot of those who believe not.

But, beloved Brethren, observe what I am going to say. The Church does not judge the individuals of any creed ; it is not for her to judge them ; but their maker, God. He alone sees into the conscience, and weighs the responsibility of His creatures He knows their lights and their opportunities upon which the Church presumes not to pronounce. The function of the Church is to declare by *what means* Almighty God has appointed that men should be saved ; she pretends not to lay her hand upon those who are predestined to life, and those who are doomed to eternal misery. She does, indeed, declare that all who *wilfully* and *deliberately*, that is with full knowledge and consent, reject her teachings, forfeit their salvation ; but she is not in a position to say that, because a person belongs to an heretical sect, he is knowingly and wilfully rejecting the truth of God. She does not presume the individual Methodist, or the Quaker, even the Jew, or the Mahomedan, to be necessarily sinning against the light. She leaves his case to the all-seeing God who searches the reins and the heart. She condemns the system under which they live ; she condemns the error, not those who err, perhaps without any consciousness of their pitiable condition. She hopes for them, she prays that God's mercy and goodness may gather them to His bosom, knowing that, as the apostle says, " He will have all men to be saved, and to come to a knowledge of the truth."

This, surely, beloved Brethren, is no savage doctrine. We hold that no one will be lost save by his own fault, whether within the visible fold or without. Of those who are outside the pale of the Church there are two widely-different classes. One class consists of such as are outside the pale of the Church through their own fault. For them the words of our blessed Lord leave no hope : " He that believeth not shall be condemned." Whatever be the motive of their disbelief, it matters not ; they cannot be saved except by making their submission through the Church to Him Who is the Way, the Truth, and the Life. It may be spiritual pride that actuates them, and the conceit of spiritual discernment ; it may be intellectual pride, which refuses to accept doctrines mysterious in themselves, or to all appearance contradicting the conclusions of science or the facts of history; it may be the pique of a resentful disposition, which finds fault with the words and acts of some minister of religion, and discards the Church because of the man; it may be disappointed ambition in those called to the pastoral offices; it may be the frivolous longing for notoriety—the bane of a superficial age; it may be allurements of the flesh, which run counter to the discipline or the principles of the Church of God. In some cases we cannot but fear that, in the present state of religion in this country, there are ministers of the Established Church who would join the Catholic Church this very day, were it not for the domestic ties which hold them back, and the fear of plunging wife and children into poverty and hardship. But the unbelief is grievous, no matter what its root, though the degree of its guilt may vary in the sight of God.

As to those who err without any fault of their's, God cannot condemn them, the Church does not censure them, if they sincerely desire to know the truth, and are willing to embrace it at all cost, when it reveals itself to their minds. Not only does the Church not censure them—she even numbers them amongst her children. They do not belong to the visible body of the Church, and would not swell the census of the Catholic population. Nevertheless, they belong (as theologians would say) to the soul of the Church, and are in the sight of God members of the fold, fish in the net of Peter. That soul of the Church comprises all, of whatever communion, who love and seek the truth, and who obey the dictates of their conscience, and so walk blameless before their Maker.

Beloved Brethren, let us follow the example of the Church, and refrain from judging anyone who differs from us in creed. Such persons may be dear to God, and moving by hidden ways, unsuspected by themselves, towards the bark of Peter. It is revolting to hear Christians, as we do sometimes, say of this or that public man: He has had the grace of conversion offered to him, and has rejected it; there is no hope for him. But while we foster a sentiment of genuine charity towards those who belong to a different denomination, let us not forget that it is the part of a true and lively faith to condemn every false sytem which contradicts or repudiates any of the teachings of the Church, to lament its existence, as to some extent an agency of evil, no matter how close may be its resemblance to the Church of Christ; to guard all those under our care from its influence, to banish from our household the books, the tracts, the leaflets which advocate its doctrines or principles; to prevent children and servants from keeping company with those who are likely to instill religious indifference into their minds; and last, not least, to be humbly cautious ourselves, lest in a country whose people and whose literature are non-Catohlic, if not anti-Catholic, we should abate anything of our intense attachment, our love, our loyalty to the old, old Church, and our heartfelt gratitude to Him for the gift of belonging to it.

EIGHTH SUNDAY AFTER PENTECOST.

IN to-day's Gospel, beloved Brethren, we have depicted in one of our blessed Lord's parables, an opulent and liberal master, who, having discharged his steward for his neglect of economy and his guilty wastefulness, is nevertheless struck with admiration upon finding how deftly and cunningly this unscrupulous servant provides for his future, by fraudulently diminishing the liabilities of the creditors, and thus winning their favourable and grateful recognition for his services, when he is thrown upon the world and forced to begin life again. Though his dishonesty is revealed more glaringly in this audacious stratagem, his readiness of resource, his promptitude and energy in retrieving his fortunes, even in the moment of calamity, is made a subject of commendation. "And the Lord commended the unjust steward," says the Gospel, "not, indeed, for his injustice, but for his worldly wisdom; forasmuch as he had done wisely, for the children of this world are wiser in their generation than the children of light": that is the professed worldlings, who seek their own selfish ends without scruple, employ more thought and ability, and display more vigour, and are more ungrudging of labour, in their own dark pursuits and the attainment of their guilty ambitions, than the adopted sons of God, the children of light, in their efforts to reach the goal of their desires—God's grace here and His eternal companionship in glory hereafter.

To the thoughtful mind, beloved Brethren, this fact becomes clearer and more surprising as the years go by; when we look into our own past experiences, and scan the daily lives of the Christians with whom we come in contact, and compare their lukewarmness in the spiritual life with the consuming and unresting energy which the votaries of this world bestow upon their cherished purposes. What a busy, fermenting, bustling hive it is, this world of the worldlings; how many elaborate schemes are turned over in the brains of men in the twenty-four hours; what feverish solicitude burns in their veins; what jealousy of emulation spurs them on, invading the very hours destined for repose, and possessing their heated fancies even when weariness closes their eyes in a troubled sleep; what fears and apprehensions start up before them, making them tremble lest any unforeseen stroke of ill luck should dash the full cup of success from their lips untasted; what keen study, what profound thought, what diligent canvassing of the methods by which others have succeeded, occupy their minds and absorb their attention, even when they seem in the full career of thoughtless pleasure. "I will be rich," says one man; and he leaves no stone unturned to add shilling to shilling and pound to pound. "I will not stop until I attain to such and such an honour or dignity," says another; and every engine is set to work to achieve this object; dinners are given, men of influence are flattered, popular manners are cultivated, public benefactions are trumpeted through the medium of the papers, the labour and harass of public appearances and platform harangues are submitted to with exemplary patience; life, in short, is squared entirely to the one end in view. "I will make a name as poet, or orator, or philosopher, or man of science," is the cry with others. And behold! the enthusiasm of their resolve is like an intoxication in their veins; they undergo fatigues that would break down a man who had only the sober forces of nature at his back. The midnight lamp, and the hush of the sleeping midnight, are congenial accompaniments to the straining and striving of their thoughts, and the nursing of their ardent and inextinguishable aspirations. They make light of austerities, which are mocked at in the lives of God's saints, as unnatural and inhuman. Leibnitz, the great thinker, with his wicker cage on his neck, so contrived that if he drops asleep amidst his studies, he will be caught abruptly, and awakened again with the sudden sharp pain of throttling; Kant, in his withered old age, protracting his studies till his nodding head, full of long-resisted sleep, drops his wig into the candle and sets it on fire; these are pictures of the fanatical power of such ambitions, to fight against the limitations which nature itself has imposed, and to triumph over every obstacle that thwarts the realization of their desires. Well does Milton describe "that last infirmity of noble minds, which makes them scorn delights, and live laborious days." What incredible hardships have the great military captains of the world endured, to leave great names on the page of history! Napoleon scaling the Alps, and spurning the colossal barriers of nature, to surprise his foe; or trusting himself to the horrors of a Russian winter, to experience the romance of dating his letters from the Kremlin: these are but typical pictures of the deeds of daring and the prodigies of patient endurance which a love of fame has prompted in every age. It is inconceivable even what pains, what efforts, what hours of hard work, what wrestling against disadvantages, what ingenuity and boldness in retrieving lost ground, and renewing the combat against adverse influences, are to be met with in the lives of the criminals whose names are recorded in the calendars of guilt in this country and elsewhere, in the pursuit of their nefarious enterprises of violence, cunning and blood.

But the children of this world are wiser in their generation than the children of light. Yes, alas! it is too true. Remissness and indifference seem the law instead of the exception, in the attitude of Christians towards the real aim of existence and the means by which it is to be attained. They call themselves Christians, that is, followers and imitators of Christ, yet it is to the world and not to Christ that they turn for their ideals, and it is from the books of this world's wisdom that they derive the maxims upon which, in practice, their lives are modelled. The Church is the kingdom of Christ, and Christians are professedly the subjects of this great kingdom, and the lieges of their great king. But that kingdom is, as our blessed Lord reminded us, not of this world. Yet, if we look at the lives and weigh the characters of multitudes who own subjection to that monarch, and are proud to be subjects of that kingdom, we find that their lives contradict their professions; that their kingdom is really of this world; that this world is practically the only authority to which they bow. They believe that God made them, and made them to save their souls, that this is the only end of their existence. They admit that if we die out of friendship with God, if we die with grievous sin unrepented upon our conscience, eternal separation from God, our Sovereign Good, will be the undoubted consequence, with all the dreadful facts implied in that separation. They are as sure of this as they are that they live and breathe. They are as sure of it as they are of anything, otherwise they are not Catholics at all. Yet look around you, and tell me could you gather from the conduct and the conversation of many, many Catholics that the awful nature of their future has any great influence upon their lives? Could you in many cases tell that they realise, that they even believe, in the stealthy approach, hour by hour, of that momemtous reckoning day when the great Lord of all shall say: " Give an account of thy stewardship, for now thou canst be steward no longer"? Is there anything in the character and the bearing and the tone of these people, Christians by name, which marks them as believers in a judgment when life is over, and a destiny shaped by their fidelity to God here which will last for all eternity, more than their fellows who proclaim their belief that death is extinction, and that judgment is a myth, and that the soul is, as Tyndall said, "a gross, pagan superstition." If they believed in the coming judgment which will sift their every word and deed, and set everything in its true light, and remove every illusion that veiled their actions from their own eyes, and silence every hollow excuse and attempt at self-justification ; would they live without a thought of God, from morning till night, for days together? Would they be so quick to find reasons for staying away from Mass on Sundays and holidays? Would they attend Mass by a sort of constraint, as if it were some work of superogatory labour imposed upon their patience ; some boring observance which the habits of society require, and which seem to their uninterested and weary spirits endless in its length, and tedious in its monotony? Would they, if they took any heed of the future which faith reveals to them, stay away from every Benediction and every service not of rigorous obligation ; and, not content with that negative disdain, positively ridicule as unmanly, as childish, as slavish, as silly, the persons who, acting on what they sincerely believe, do not think it beneath them to cultivate the friendship of their future Judge by giving Him a homage which He does not rigorously exact.

The people of whom I speak live in the midst of temptations ; they believe (or they are not Christians) that the frequenting of the Sacraments is their great safeguard against spiritual falls ; yet they are seldom seen to approach the Altar, to receive the Living Bread that giveth life ; and are apt rather to laugh forsooth at the humble devotees, as amusing specimens of weak-mindedness, who labour from week to week to make their calling and election sure. Yet God is to them truly like a man who has gone into a far country; and their souls are the very last objects of their thought or interest. They profess to believe that their bishops and priests, with the Pope at their head, are the successors of those whom our blessed Lord sent forth to teach the truths He had revealed, that they are the pastors, commissioned to feed the flock; that they are the infallible "magisterium," the mouthpiece of Him who said: "He that heareth you, heareth me, and he that despiseth you despiseth me." Yet in their cowardly human respect, which they call liberality and breadth of mind, they set themselves up to criticize the teaching and the discipline of that Church which is surely divine, or there is nothing divine on earth. They presume to regard her machinery as old-fashioned, her discipline as unsuited to the nineteenth century, her views as the unenlightened dicta of narrowly educated clerics, who have no knowledge outside their books. They quickly brush aside the law of fasting without seeking a dispensation; even laughing at the ordinance; and freely speaking of such mortifications as if they were a silly and obselete idea, which a sensible person is almost ashamed to avow as still surviving. They do not treat abstinence with much more consideration; especially if they find themselves in protestant company. They effect to smile superciliously at the ignorance of the Church in denouncing freemasonry, though the Church, whose eyes are all over the world, sees into the heart of that movement, as these wretched scientists and shallow critics can never do. Many other of the Church's ways, and practices, and judgments, these miserable half-Catholics, who have scarcely any one tie of feeling or spirit to attach them to the ark of salvation, will discuss, to the scandal and pity of their brethren, in a semi-contemptuous manner, swelling with the proud consciousness of their freedom from prejudice and bigotry.

It is difficult, indeed, to see why some of these people continue to call themselves Catholics at all. For many of them it is to be feared that the summing-up will be: "Amen, I know you not. He that will deny Me before men I will deny him before My Father in heaven." But other Catholics have some fear of the consequences of such an attitude towards the Church of Christ. Their offence is that, admitting their duty, and the momentous nature of it, they have no courage, no heart, to embrace it. They are like the old pagan who said: "I *know* what is right, but I *do* what is wrong." They know that their salvation depends on prayer; that if we would receive we must ask; if we would find we must seek; if we would have the door of a happy eternity opened to us we must knock. Yet they don't pray at all, or they pray very little, or they pray without earnestness. They know that, when their passions tempt them, they should call upon God for help, and withdraw themselves from the dangerous occasions of sin. In vain does their conscience dictate this course: their cry is not heard in heaven, their angel guardian sees them, with terror and sorrow, again and again in the company, or in the place where spiritual death awaits them. They are told by their directors that the Easter confession and communion alone do not suffice, in their peculiar circumstances, with their violent predisposition to sin, or with their long-formed evil habits, or with their surroundings of peril, to heal the spiritual diseases which they have contracted, and to enable them to walk blamelessly before God. They promise to act on the advice given to them, but after a few weeks of effort they fall away again, and remain bound hand and foot, willing captives, till Easter time returns; thus giving to God scarcely a tithe of the year, and bestowing the bulk of their lives upon Satan, their adversary. Can such persons pretend that they care for their salvation? Do they believe that as the tree leans so it shall fall? Do they think that our Lord meant what He said, when He warned us that death would come as a thief in the night? Do they think that their lives may claim, as a fitting consummation of all their indifference and disregard of divine help, that welcome with which our blessed Lord will receive His elect, when the grave closes over their earthly remains: "Come, ye blessed of My Father, receive ye the kingdom which was prepared for you from the foundation of the world. Well done, thou good and faithful servant, because thou hast been faithful over a few things. I will place thee over many, enter thou into the joy of thy Lord."

THE TENTH SUNDAY AFTER PENTECOST.

The Pharisee and the Publican.

TO-DAY'S gospel, beloved Brethren, contains a parable, or short story, full of instruction as to the attitude of humility which we must assume when addressing the great Lord of the World, if we would make our prayers acceptable in His sight. It was addressed by Jesus Christ to His disciples in the last year of His mission, when He was paying a farewell visit to His dearly loved Galilee, before going to Jerusalem to triumph, to suffer, and to die. He had observed, even amongst His followers, that restless spirit of rivalry and self-assertion, which marks the men of this world; they were apt, in spite of His precepts and example, to make a vain display of their virtues, to claim credit for their good works, to arrogate to themselves a superiority over their fellows, in fine, to look down upon them with a feeling akin to contempt. To correct this failing, our blessed Lord shows them their reflection in the conduct of the proud and self-sufficient pharisee, as in a mirror; and warns them of the futility of the prayers which are accompanied by such dispositions. The story which is framed for this purpose may have been drawn from the imagination, like others of our blessed Lord's parables; but there are some who think that the occurrence was not fiction, but fact; and that Jesus knew the circumstances which He relates by virtue of His divine and all-embracing knowledge.

"Two men," He says, "went up into the Temple to pray: the one was a Pharisee, the other a publican." Our Lord selects two extreme types from amongst the various classes into which Jewish society was divided. The Pharisee was a type of the puritanical devotee, scrupulously exact in carrying out every observance laid down by the law, and every ceremony imposed by tradition. He belonged to a sect of old-standing, originally aiming at a healthy precision in their religious practices, and calling themselves by a name which signifies "the *separated* section" to betoken their aspirations after a more than common purity of religious life. By degrees, their scrupulosity in the observance of the Mosaic law degenerated into a petty and puerile emphasizing of the minutest points of ritual, a tendency to set the letter of the law above its spirit, and an ostentatious regard for the traditional, as distinguished from the written, ordinances : those handed down by tradition being in the highest degree complicated, and embarrassing in daily life, and in some instances smacking of superstition. The greatest circumspection was necessary hour by hour to secure the pharisee from the taint of uncleanness; so multifarious were the ways of incurring it, according to their code, by eating or by touching objects which they reckoned unclean. The effect of the uncleanness, against which they thus guarded themselves, was to cut them off from every religious privilege, and to make their presence in the temple a defilement, till the rite of purification had been performed, which restored them to their lost status. Thus, if they ate any meat which had been killed by a heathen, it brought upon them the ban of uncleanness like that fixed by the Mosaic law, as the penalty for partaking of the carcase of an animal that had died of itself by disease. Endless were the cases, and most complicated in their distinctions, in which the mere touching of objects brought this legal uncleanness with it, and all its harassing consequences. You remember how shocked the pharisees were when our blessed Lord sat down to eat, without attending to their rule of washing first, as a preparation for it. And in rebuking them for their preference of empty ceremonial to solid virtue : " You pharisees," said He, " make clean the outside of the cup and the platter, but your inside is full of rapine and iniquity." And on another occasion He pointed out to them how some of their traditional usages were absolutely opposed to the law of nature itself. "Why do you transgress the commandment of God," He asks, "for your tradition ? For God said : Honour thy father and thy mother— . . . . but you say : whosoever shall say to father or mother : the gift whatsoever proceedeth from me shall profit thee ; and he shall not honour his father or his mother : and you have made void the commandment of God for your tradition."—*Matt.* xv. 3-6. Our Lord here alludes to the teaching in vogue among the pharisees, that a man need not give anything to the support of an indigent father or mother, provided he bestows his spare money upon the service of the altar: a doctrine which tended to enrich the pharisee at the expense of a poor starving parent. Thus their consciences were darkened by their pride and presumption; even to the extent of losing their discernment of the primary duties of nature.

The other type chosen by our blessed Lord in this instructive parable is the publican. The very name of publican came with hateful suggestions to Jewish ears. It meant a betrayer of his country and his race, an apostate, a tool in the hands of an alien power to oppress and beggar his own people. For the Jews were subject to all-devouring Rome, and were forced to contribute their share to the burdens of the empire, like the natives of other dependent provinces. Many of the Jews resented the payment of tribute as a violation of the inherent right of the chosen people to be exempt from such exactions. The central government farmed out the revenues of each province for a fixed sum, and left it to the individual or the company who paid for this right to make what profit they could in the process of collecting the dues, whether direct taxes, or customs. The tax-farmers generally lived in Rome, and had publicans or agents in the province, and these again their sub-agents, to meet the requirements of the business. Among these officials there was no limit to dishonesty and extortion. As the goods came into port or went out, they placed an arbitrary value upon them for assessment, and there was no gainsaying their decision. They stood by each other in every dispute; they had power enough to make interference a dangerous experiment; they procured the framing of savage laws in their own interests; they forced the execution of these laws with remorseless rigour; they brought false charges of smuggling to blackmail their victims; in fact, there was scarcely a form of dishonesty and oppression in which they did not freely indulge.

These, then, beloved Brethren, are the two classes represented by the men, who went up to the temple to pray, in our Lord's parable: to all appearance, the saint and the sinner. But God does not judge by appearance, He searches the reins and the heart; and the seeming saint was flawed and rotten, like the contents of a whited sepulchre, through corroding pride; the sinner, from self-hatred and sorrow for his sins, was on the way to justification. They were both drawn to the house of God, presumably to offer homage to its Master and to solicit his favour. But behold the contrast in the demeanour of the two men. The pharisee makes his way with great pomp and grandeur, conscious of the admiring notice of the worshippers present, to a conspicuous position; for one of the characteristics of the sect was to love the first places; such a position, say close by the altar of sacrifice in the temple court, as became a member of the body who shunned the vulgar and styled themselves the Separatists. It is open to him to kneel or stand while making his prayer; both postures are common enough amongst the Jews, but we may be sure that the pharisee will not make choice of the posture which betokens humiliation. And so, with head erect, he revolves these thoughts in his mind and calls them prayer. "O God," says he, "I give Thee thanks that I am not as the rest of men—extortioners, unjust, adulterers." There is no feeling of awe in the presence of the God who made him, the Infinite Majesty whose almighty power hovers over that temple, the God of hosts who had wrought so many wonders in defending His house, His city, and His people. All such associations are eclipsed in the mind of the pharisee by his own manifold perfections. He stands before the altar to praise, not God, but himself. He begins, indeed, with a formula of thanksgiving, but the formula is empty and vain, and merely throws the cloak of a religious phrase over his self-laudation. "I give Thee thanks," says he, "that I am not as the rest of men; I came to ask for nothing, for there is nothing I am conscious of as wanting to my perfection: I seek not forgiveness for sin, for I am no sinner; I ask not for an increase of virtue, for, looking into my life, I see nothing to improve; I do not crave Thy assistance in the time of temptation, for I am satisfied that my virtues make me proof against its onset; I do not petition for perseverance in Thy grace, because my past experience teaches me that I am secure against overthrow. I rest on my own merits; I am a contented man. And with good reason. The world is full of extortioners, men who have no regard for justice, men given up to their lusts; but I am not like the multitude." And here his eye is caught by the entrance of the poor miserable publican, who creeps into the court with diffident step and abashed demeanour, like one who intrudes upon forbidden ground, and stations himself near the doorway, his head bowed and his eyes fixed upon the pavement.

His air of dejection and shame stirs the pharisee to fresh exultation; "No; I am not as the rest of men—extortioners, unjust, adulterers, as also is this publican, who presumes to mingle with the saints in this place of prayer. I fast twice in the week." You remember that the pharisees were ambitious to achieve a reputation by this form of self-denial, and that they made known their mortification by sadness of visage, and disfigured their faces that they might appear to men to fast. "I give tithes of all that I possess." You know, beloved Brethren, that the Israelites were bound to give the tithes or tenth part of their herds and their harvest to the maintenance of the Levites, who served the altar and who were not allotted a portion of the land like the other tribes. "I have given to the sons of Levi all the tithes of Israel for a possession; for the ministry wherewith they serve me in the tabernacle of the covenant."—*Numbers* xviii. 21. But the pharisees, with their usual affectation of superior piety, were not content with the payment of tithes upon their cattle and the produce of their fields, but surrendered the tenth part of the most insignificant herbs which they cultivated for household purposes, such as mint and rue, which served as condiments and sometimes medicine. Upon this ostentatious generosity they plumed themselves more than upon works of sterling virtue. "Woe to you, Scribes and pharisees, hypocrites," said our blessed Lord, "because you tithe mint, and anise, and cummin, and have left the weightier things of the law—judgment, and mercy and faith."—*Matt.* xxiii. 23. This self-eulogy closes the so-called prayer of the pharisee. From first to last, his thoughts never glanced for a moment at his dependency upon God as the creature of His hand, at the gratitude which he owes to God for such gifts and endowments as he prides himself on possessing, at the necessity of God's grace and continual protection to save him from danger of soul and body, and to enable him to accomplish the destiny for which he was born. The proud man stands up unblushingly in the presence of his Maker, simply to proclaim his own all-sufficient virtue and strength.

Very different is the tone of mind with which the poor publican addresses himself to his Maker. The publican standing afar off would not so much as lift up his eyes towards heaven; but struck his breast, saying: "O God, be merciful to me a sinner." He feels his own nothingness in the sight of the Sovereign Lord of all; he feels his own sinfulness in the holy precincts of the temple chosen as a dwelling place by the all-holy God; his memory is filled with the visions of his past misdeeds, and his heart is crushed with sorrow and overwhelming regret at the spectacle of his baseness, recklessness, folly and ingratitude. Along with these feelings, too, there is a sense of God's infinite goodness and mercy, which wills not the death of the sinner, but rather that he should be converted and live. We are not therefore, surprised to hear the judgment pronounced by our blessed Lord: "I say to you, this man went down to his house justified rather than the other: because, every one that exalteth himself shall be humbled, and he that humbleth himself shall be exalted." Yes! I say it, who know God's dealings with man: that the prayer of the humble man brought him justification, that is, reconciled him to his offended Maker, re-instated him in the grace and the privileges of a good conscience; whilst the prayer of the proud and self-confident pharisee, far from benefitting his soul, does but deliver him more certainly to ultimate destruction.

Let us take to heart, beloved Brethren, the lesson contained in this parable. Humility is the very first requisite for effectual prayer. It is the necessary attitude of the supplicant. It is the recognition, underlying our petitions, that God is infinite, and we, mere worms, animated dust, of less account in the sum of things than a drop of water in the boundless sea. It is the recognition that we are beggars, absolutely dependent upon His bounty; that we have nothing, and shall have nothing but what we receive from Him; that we can do nothing save by the strength He metes out to us; "that we are not sufficient,' as St. Paul says, "even to think anything of ourselves as of ourselves, but our sufficiency is from God." To fit ourselves for prayer, that is, to be acceptable, three things are necessary; we must prepare ourselves, and not be as men tempting God, by casting off, as far as possible, every distraction and preoccupation that would have the effect of withdrawing our minds from God; secondly, we must abjure every thought of uncharitableness, every prompting of resentment or revenge, in accordance with our blessed Lord's instructions: "If thou offer thy gift at the altar, and there thou remember that thy brother hath anything against thee, leave there thy offering before the altar, and go first to be reconciled to thy brother, and, then coming, thou shalt offer thy gift." And lastly, we must pluck from our hearts every root of pride and self-confidence, every overweening estimate of our own importance, remembering this saying of Him, to whom we make our petition, "God resists the proud, and gives His grace to the humble."

TWENTIETH SUNDAY AFTER PENTECOST.

"Redeeming the time because the days are evil."—*Eph.* v 16.

THESE words, beloved Brethren, were addressed to the inhabitants of Ephesus, the capital of Asia Minor—a city which, in the days of St. Paul, had reached such a pitch of material prosperity, that a contemporary, Strabo, says of it:—"It was the greatest place of trade of all the cities of Asia, west of the Taurus." It was famous for the worship of the goddess Diana, whose temple, containing works from the chisel and the brush of the greatest masters of Greece, was renowned as one of the seven wonders of the world. St. Paul had preached to the Ephesians for three years, and received into the pale of the Church many Jews and Gentiles. But after his departure, teachers of false doctrine arose, who, favouring the myths of the Eastern races, sought to blend Christianity with Oriental superstition, denying the divinity of our Divine Founder, and trying to compound for this error by giving Him a pre-eminence among certain high and angelic natures—the creation of their own fancy.

With this heresy they combined many unsound theories of morality, and bid for popular support by allowing a larger scope and freedom to the vilest passions of our nature. But these were not the only ones occupied in oversowing cockle among the wheat.

The Jewish converts would fain ingraft rites and ceremonial observances of the Old Law upon the precepts of the Christian dispensation. They had a large following among those who, like themselves, had been reclaimed from the rejected house of Israel.

St. Paul accordingly wrote his Epistle to the Ephesians to commend the fidelity of those who had been steadfast to his teaching, to confirm them in the practice of Christian virtue, and to exhort them by the holiness of their lives to present a living contrast to the corrupt morals of the society surrounding them, and to brand the special vices of the time, by abstaining, not only from all indulgence in these vices, but even from the mention of them. From his bondage in Rome, therefore, thirsting for the martyr's crown, and despising more than ever the fleeting pageants, pleasures, and intrigues of earth, its ambitions and its love of pelf, he cries aloud in his own emphatic and fiery manner—"Redeem the time, the days are evil." Every moment of it is all-valuable and fraught with interests that stretch into eternity. Avail yourselves of it to discipline your souls in all virtues, that your lives may so shine in the midst of the prevailing darkness, as to make that darkness more hideous and gloomy still. The days are evil, and sin holds sway over the masses of men. All the more must you redeem the time that, though your tongues be silent, the routine of your daily lives may speak aloud in condemnation of the reigning wickedness.

And ever since the days of the great Apostle, his successors in the ministry, from pulpits and platforms, by word and by writing, have dinned the same lesson into the ears, have printed the same lesson upon the minds of the successive generations entrusted to their charge. "Redeem the time because the days are evil." Alas! there has been only too much justification in every age for that ill-omened repetition. The Psalmist seems perpetually, through garish day and secret night, through all the sinful pulsations of time, to murmur sadly over this busy God-forgetting world, "O ye sons of men, how long will ye be dull of heart? Why do you love vanity and seek after lying."—*Ps.* iv. 3. In every generation, while the Spirit that filleth the whole earth breaks into the hearts of men soft invitations to holiness, and salutary aspirations after things unseen and celestial, the still, small voice is drowned in the cries of the world; the good seed is choked by the thorns and the brambles, or rejected by the stony soil; and at the close of every volume of man's advancing history, the dread words, new written and more amply proved, are—"Many are called, but few are chosen." But in every age the chosen few have redeemed the time, and witnessed against the evil day.

The days were evil in those three hundred years of stormy persecutions, during which the infant Church was cradled in the womb of the earth. Ten times the storm rose into a hurricane, and the gutters ran with blood that fell like winter rain. And all the while Paganism, with its consecrated orgies, its deified vices, its mask turned heavenwards, and the eyes beneath gloating on earth and its pleasures, ruled over the whole world. Yet the chosen few redeemed the time, for they feared God rather than man; they stood steadfast in the ranks though death should decimate them; having no portion on the earth, they looked the more hopefully beyond the grave to the kingdom prepared for them; and they loved one another like brothers, who, praying to-day shoulder by shoulder, might to-morrow be called upon to march together to martyrdom.

The days were evil when, liberty proclaimed and the fetters struck off, many of the children of the Church abused their new-found freedom; contradicted her teaching, set up false prophets, went after the theories of men, and desecrated many a venerable see by the intrusion of heresiarchs—Arians, Donatists, Pelagians, Eutychians, Photinians: these are names symbolical of evil days that have passed away. But amid dissensions, and troubles, and manifold disorders, the chosen few redeemed the time; for the falling away of many made them the firmer and more loyal; they clung to the rock of Peter the more tenaciously, the more the winds and waves of false doctrine raged and roared, and for the loss of the souls that were torn from the centre of unity and the pillar of truth, they sought to compensate by wandering afar among strange tribes, savage and rude, winning them to the Lord, until the sheepfold, left half empty by the desertion of the lost ones, was filled again to overflowing; till once more the Church was the gladsome mother of a multitude of children.

They were evil days again, when under feudal lords the greater part of Christendom was cut up into a thousand petty clans at war with one another, and like adverse wild beasts preying upon one another's vitals; when might pretended to be right; when law was disregarded, and justice laid down her scales and sword; when cities were protected by strong walls, and deep moats, and massive gates, instead of the universal sense of right and humanity: and when the tocsin sounding to arms was an alarum familiar even to the youngest.

But amidst these evil days of darkness and violence, the time was redeemed by a spirit of simple faith which exhibited itself in many marvellous phenomena; in the five great military crusades which stirred Europe to its depths, and sent the cry of "Deus vult"—God wills it—over rock and valley, and across many a plain, eastward to the Holy Land; in the fair ideal of chivalry with its exalted standard of action, its honourable mission, its ennobling range of duties, and its high and generous impulses; in its many miraculously multiplied orders of religious, whose retired and mortified lives were a constant exhortation against worldly intrigue and lust of power, avarice, and thirst for sensuality.

But more evil days still were in store; when from those very monasteries came forth Satanic pride and brutish sensuality, and proclaimed a great rebellion against the representative of God; when, as Lucifer led the angels, a monk raised the ensign of mutiny against the Church; when stars fell from Heaven; when Christendom was rent in twain; when the watchword became private judgment; and when, as a natural consequence, hosts of usurping teachers arose, hating the Church, yet no less at feud with one another, until half Europe was like a tossing sea, on which men floated hither and thither, each knot holding to some few planks of the old doctrine, and risking their salvation on the crazy raft they themselves had joined together. But the time was grandly redeemed by that greatest of Councils—the Council of sound reformation, the Council of Trent; by the virtues and merits of many a saintly bishop; by the renewed zeal and sanctity of the clergy; and by the revival of discipline among the religious orders; so that the tumult of rebellion was only as the sound of rushing wind on the day of Pentecost, showing that the Paraclete was coming to renew the face of the earth.

And we, beloved Brethren, can say, at least with as much truth as the generations that have gone before us, that the days are evil, and to us, as to our predecessors in the faith, the Apostle calls from his tomb: "Redeem the time." It is our duty, as Christians, to examine the colour and texture of the society in which we move, and to learn what are the characteristic vices marking it off from other epochs. And this we may best do by a constant and diligent hearing of the Word of God, the one standard of truth and holiness; by giving heed to the warnings of the Church as to the special dangers that surround us. She is ever bidding us beware of the false optimism, the vaunting and self-glorification of the world at the wondrous miracles of science and invention; the increase of knowledge, the spread of education, of comfort and prosperity. The highest temporal gains and improvements, far exceeding, if we can conceive it, anything this age, so fruitful in amazing discoveries, has witnessed—even if they could secure peace and content for the toiling masses, which, in spite of the jubilant prophecies of enthusiasts, they have miserably failed to do—all would be a poor set-off for decay of faith in our Lord Jesus Christ as the eternal Son of God made man. Everywhere is Agnosticism; unbelief in all its shades and forms. More, perhaps, than at any other period of the world, must we be alert and keep our ears open, as she warns us against the poison in the air we breathe—more deadly as it is unsuspected; against the pitfalls—more fatal because they lie in our daily path, that seems so straight and safe. Hear her, as she cries out again in the words of the Apostle: "See therefore, Brethren, now you walk circumspectly—redeeming the time, for the days are evil."

TWENTY-FOURTH SUNDAY AFTER PENTECOST.

THE passage extracted from the Epistles of St. Paul to form the lesson of to-day's Mass, beloved Brethren, is well deserving of our serious consideration. It is taken from the letter which the great Apostle penned from his prison in Rome to the faithful of Colossæ, a town in the province of Phrygia, which is at present a portion of Turkey in Asia. It is, therefore, a letter which has always been held in special reverence, and read with special attention, since it breathes the spirit of a soldier of Jesus Christ, who felt that at any moment his life might pay the penalty of his attachment to the cause of his great Captain.

Blent with its noble and pathetic words, we seem to hear the clanking of the confessor's chains, the barring and unbarring of prison doors, and the rough voices of unsympathetic guards. Indeed, its style soars to the height of sublimity, in proportion to the depth of worldly hardship and contempt to which the Apostle was subjected for the love of his divine Master. The hero who has made his life a holocaust speaks unmistakeably in every line. In every line is revealed the depth of affection, and the tenderness of heart, which characterised St. Paul, "his daily instance, that solicitude for all the churches" which he couples, as the sources of his ceaseless trial, with "his labour and painfulness, his much watchings, his hunger and thirst, his fastings often, his cold and nakedness."—II. *Cor.* xi. 27.

He had never, in all probability, visited the people to whom he then wrote, but they had been the subject of his anxious thoughts and fond projects; and, though he had never seen their faces, yet he cherished them in his heart. He had sent them the holy priest Epaphras, whom he styles his own "most beloved fellow-servant," to take charge of them as bishop, and to be "for them," in the words of St. Paul himself, "a faithful minister of Christ." Nor did his affectionate interest in the people of Colossæ go unrequited. Through their bishop, they communicated to the saint the love with which they viewed him, and enkindled in his kind heart a more paternal affection still. "Epaphras," says he, "has manifested to us your love in the spirit. Therefore," he continues (here the day's Epistle begins), "we also, from the day that we heard it, cease not to pray for you, and to pray that you may be filled with the knowledge of His will, in all wisdom, and spiritual understanding, that you may walk worthy of God, in all things pleasing; being fruitful in every good work, and increasing in the knowledge of God; strengthened with all might according to the power of His glory, in all patience and long-suffering with joy. Giving thanks to God the Father, who hath made us worthy to be partakers of the lot of the saints in light. Who hath delivered us from the power of darkness and hath translated us into the kingdom of the Son of His love, in whom we have redemption through His blood, the remission of sins."

His thanksgiving, beloved Brethren, for the grace bestowed upon himself, in common with those whom he addressed, by the bountiful Giver of all good gifts, the Father of Lights, in admitting them from the outer darkness into the kingdom of light, was intensified, if not inspired, by the dangers which threatened the Colossians at the time when the Apostle wrote. Scarcely does the echo of our Lord's words appear to our imagination to have died away—"False prophets shall arise and false Christs"—when already the prediction was fulfilled. The town of Colossæ had even then become the school of false teachers, who sought to darken the faith of the new converts. At the prospect of such a peril all the solicitude of the Apostle is aroused. And thus it is that in the very front of his letter he reminds them of the precious boon of supernatural light, which baptism had conferred upon them, and which could never have reached them save through the incarnation and death of Jesus Christ. "Giving thanks to God the Father," said he, "who hath made us worthy to be partakers of the lot of the saints in light. Who hath delivered us from the power of darkness, who hath translated us into the kingdom of the Son of His love; in which we have redemption through His blood, the remission of sins." He hastens to combat the teachings of darkness, which threatened the extinction of that gift of burning faith.

For observe, beloved Brethren, St. Paul was not of the number of those, in our day so numerous and loud voiced, whose only tenet is that it matters not what we believe, provided only we lead good moral lives. He felt that the truths which our blessed Lord had revealed, were not to be mixed with the fables or fancies of men. He recognised that if our divine Master took so much pains to instruct His Apostles in the doctrines of revelation, it was that the Apostles might proclaim from the house tops what they had heard in the ear. He knew that the spirit of truth, whom that divine Master had sent down upon the Apostles, was sent not only to bring to their minds all things whatsoever he had taught them, but to preserve, in all their freshness and identity, those same doctrines, for the regeneration of the world. St. Paul could no more tolerate an attack upon the doctrines taught in the name of Christ, by His appointed ministers, than Christ Himself, the Way, the Truth, and the Life, could have tolerated the contradiction or doubt of his doctrines on the part of His Apostles.

And hence St. Paul, in this letter to the Colossians, performs the same function which we have seen the sovereign Pontiff performing in our day: he lays down, not the theories of the learned nor the speculations of the philosophers, nor the so-called dictates of common sense, which are oftentimes only the cunning maxims of an ant living in the circle of an ant-hill; but the very teaching of the Incarnate Word of God.

Against the Simonians, who were exerting themselves to divert the adoration of the faithful from our blessed Lord to the angels, he lays down in language, the most beautiful and forcible, the divine and eternal generation of Jesus, and the redemption we have won through his blood. He tears to pieces irresistibly, but without passion, the ridiculous doctrine that the angels had made this visible world, that they had rescued man from the death of the spirit, and that they were the appointed mediators to lead us to God. "He (Jesus Christ)," he exclaims, " is the image of the invisible God—in Him were all things created in heaven and on earth, visible and invisible." "Ay," he contiuues, "even the angelic hosts themselves, whether thrones, or dominations, or principalities, or powers, all things were created in Him and by Him." And as He is the Creator, at

whose word all things spring into being, so He is the Saviour, without whose mediation our being would have been a curse:—
"It hath well pleased the Father through Him . . . . . to reconcile all things unto Himself, making peace through the blood of His Cross, both as to the things on earth, and the things that are in heaven—blotting out the handwriting of the decree that was against us, which was contrary to us. And He has taken the same out of the way, fastening it to the Cross." And so also, the Apostle makes a determined stand against those Jewish converts, who would fain combine the Old Law and the New, to cling to the types and shadows when they had the reality. He spurns the burthens which they would impose upon the children of Jesus Christ, who had been transferred from the twilight of the old law, who worshipped in spirit and in truth, and who needed not a system of carnal observances and disabilities, to withhold them from the picturesque and licentious ritual of a Pagan worship. "Let no man judge you," says he, "in meat or drink, or in respect of a festival day, or of the new moon, or of the Sabbaths, which are a shadow of things to come, but the body is Christ's."

Against these two classes of teachers, no matter how plausible in speech and subtle in reasoning, against the philosophers who seek to seduce them from "Jesus Christ, in whom are hid all the treasures of wisdom and knowledge," and against the judaizing Christians, who superstitiously cry out: "Touch not, taste not, handle not," the Apostle sets his face, as firmly as ever did the Popes of Rome against the false teachers whom later ages, with their changeful circumstances, brought forth. In *his* treatment of heresy you have the prototype of theirs. Again and again, they have been obliged to warn the faithful, almost in St. Paul's words, against the popular and fashionable creeds which the powers of darkness have pressed from time to time into their service. "Beware, lest any man cheat you by philosophy and vain deceit; according to the tradition of men, according to the elements of the world, and not according to Christ." The princes and rulers of the Church have in all ages regarded as a motive for their most heartfelt thanksgiving, that steadfastness in the dogmas of the faith which made St. Paul proud of the Colossians, when he found them "grounded and settled, and immoveable from the hope of the gospel which you have heard, which is preached in all the creation that is under heaven, whereof I, Paul, am made a minister." "Though I be absent in body," they have seemed to say, in every crisis that threatened the faith of a nation or people, "yet in spirit I am with you; rejoicing and beholding your order and the steadfastness of your faith which is in Christ." "As therefore ye have received Jesus Christ, the Lord, walk ye in Him. Rooted and built up in Him, and confirmed in the faith."

To us, beloved Brethren, it is nothing new or strange to hear the voice of Christ's delegate dictating to us what we are bound to believe, and pointing out with authority what we are bound to renounce as the vagaries and falsehoods of the powers of darkness. He who said: "He that heareth you heareth Me, and he that despiseth you despiseth Me; and behold I am with you all days, even to the end of the world"—He, the Way, the Truth and the Life, has made His unerring voice heard through the teaching body, the living "magisterium" of the Church, whenever the people needed his direction, as surely as He did in the Apostolic age by the mouth of St. Paul and his fellow-preachers. And the admonition of St. Paul comes home to us at this remote age just as powerfully as it did to his people at Colossæ, that it behoves us to give "thanks to God the Father, who hath made us worthy to be partakers of the lot of the saints in light, having delivered us from the powers of darkness, and translated us into the kingdom of the Son of His love." We have precisely the same reason for thankfulness as the Colossians. Not only have we in common with our fellow men the light of reason to guide us, from the bounty of Him who enlightened every man that cometh into the world, but we have through the virtue of His precious blood, communicated in baptism, the supernatural light of faith, to direct our steps that "we may walk in all things pleasing, and fruitful in every good work." We are rescued, like the Colossians, from the powers of darkness; we are not left to wander, like travellers belated, through a country enveloped in gloom, and beset with pitfalls and precipices. We walk in the broad daylight of dogmatic truth; no doubts overcloud our way, no human theories, like will-o'-the-wisps, mislead our steps into bog or quagmire; the boasted march of science has nothing new to teach us about our salvation. We know all that the Apostles taught to their flocks; we need to know nothing more. For this light of faith, and for all the rays that dart from it, we ought never to cease thanking God. We should thank him for the light of instruction in our early years; for the early knowledge His providence gave us of His being, and His attributes; for all that we learnt of His angels and His saints; for the glimpses vouchsafed to us of His dealings with the world; for the winning examples of virtue which He set before us in our parents, our teachers, our pastors, and our friends, for the warnings and checks, and the chastisements by which he opened our eyes to dangers we were overlooking; for the profuse and prodigal generosity with which He enriched us from His holy temple, where He so often welcomed us from His tabernacle, so often offered Himself for us, a victim of propitiation in the Holy Sacrifice of the Mass; where He so often gave Himself to us as the all-satisfying manna of our souls, the living and life-giving bread that came down from heaven; our nourishment and our strength here, and the guarantee of immortal life hereafter. O! who shall reckon all that we have to be thankful for; gathered as we are into the halls of light, where we fear no snare for our feet, where we are safe from the wiles of Satan, "who transformeth himself into an angel of light" (II. *Cor.* xi. 14)—where all doubts cease and mistrust vanishes; while without, in the exterior gloom, the powers of darkness are weaving their clouds of delusion, and the Father of Lies, by the agency of self-sufficient men, is throwing his pall of error and deceit over the world.

ALL SAINTS.

TO-DAY, beloved Brethren, we are surrounded as it were by the glory, and bathed in the splendour of a great feast. Raised up from the turmoil and darkness of the earth awhile, we seem to breathe the fragrant airs of heaven, and through the half-opened portals of paradise to hear the heavenly Alleluias, that tell of everlasting joy and content. Like Peter, and James, and John, when they were favoured with the vision of our Lord's supernatural radiance on Mount Thabor, and when they beheld His face darting forth beams of light like the sun, and saw His vestments become dazzling white, like the driven snow, and were witnesses of the mysterious converse that passed between Him and the representatives of ancient law and ancient prophecy, Moses and Elias, we too are prompted to exclaim in the excess of our gladness "it is good for us to be here." Yes! too soon will the happy time pass away; with all its unearthly influences and half timid anticipations, its whispering of hope, its prognostics of future happiness, such as eye hath not seen, nor ear heard. Too soon will the spell be broken, which holds our spirits, as we think of the myriads who have been saved through the blood of the Lamb, and who are now reigning with God in heaven; some of them once as unlikely as the most unlikely amongst us to reach that desired goal; yet after sin and repentance added to that great multitude (seen by St. John), which no man could number, of all nations, and tribes, and peoples, and tongues, who stood before the throne, and in the sight of the Lamb, clothed with white robes and with palms in their hands; crying with a loud voice—Salvation to our God, who sitteth upon the throne, and to the Lamb. And all the angels stood round about the throne, and the ancients and the four living Creatures ; and they fell down before the throne on their faces and adored God: saying :—Amen, Benediction and glory, and wisdom, and thanksgiving, honour and power, and strength to our God for ever and ever, Amen.

If earthly courts, beloved Brethren, on occasion of high state pageant, are one scene of dazzling and splendour, what will the court of heaven be, when all the angels and saints, in all the splendour that comes to them by nature and by grace, assemble around the throne of their great Father to testify their gratitude for His innumerable bounties. High above all the fountain of life and beauty, on a throne of stately design, in all its joints and columns, and steps, compacted mosaic-like of winged spirits, is the Ancient of days, the eternal God, the Alpha and Omega, the Beginning and the End of all things. Think not that your imagination, though alive with noble and poetic beings, can conjure up the form or semblance of that incomprehensible Being, can even darkly reflect His grandeurs, or faintly picture His perfections. These faculties of ours must be enlarged, these senses etherealized, these hearts cleansed from every speck and stain, in short, the whole man, by God's omnipotent power, transformed, and, as it were, deified, before we can be admitted to that vision, or even realize its overwhelming effect. If we could imagine that Being, He would not be God. And the saints themselves, if they were not glorified, and raised above the feebleness of human nature, could not gaze upon that awful majesty without annihilation. "No man," says the Scriptures, "can see God and live." There He is, the eternal Sun of this great system of happiness, the origin of its light and heat, the source of the brightness that irradiates those boundless halls, and the light that illumines the myriads of clearest intellects that feast upon the contemplation of His attributes; the source, too, of that burning ardour of love which, even as the white heat holds under its sway the incandescent charcoal, kindles and flows in that multitudious array, and fuses them, as it were, into one great fiery heat. Ever revealing new qualities, which startle and delight, and forbid the shadow of monotony or weariness, He sits smiling upon His children, in the mysterious manifestations of His three-fold personality. For there is the eternal Father, pouring down fresh benedictions from His upraised hand ; there is the Son, His substantial wisdom ; there is the Holy Ghost, the spirit of unfathomed sanctity.

And high above the myriad courtiers that throng the palace of heaven, elevated at the right hand of His Father, is the sacred humanity of Jesus Christ, recognisable by the wounds that once disfigured, but now adorn Him, so glorious that the light of His countenance penetrates the remotest limit of that unimaginable circle, and adds brightness and beauty to every face. "The City," says St. John, "hath no need of the sun, nor the moon, to shine in it. For the glory of God hath enlightened it, and the Lamb is the lamp thereof." And beside the throne of the Redeemer, drawn mother-like near to her dear son, whom once in days gone by she nurtured at her virginal breast, is the Queen of Heaven, the Queen of angels and of all saints; eclipsing by the endowments of her nature, the nobility of her mein, the sweetness of her smile and the richness of her apparel, even the highest princess of God's kingdom. On her head is the diadem, which is the fitting ornament and reward of her transcendent humility, and round it attendant stars are ever turning, while beneath her feet the silvery moon is made her footstool. "And a great sign appeared in heaven," says St. John, "; a woman clothed with the sun, and the moon under her feet, and on her head a crown of twelve stars. And she brought forth a man child, who was to rule all nations with an iron rod; and her son was taken up to God and to His throne." Near her again, and completing that household which had its foretaste of heaven in the humble village of Nazareth, is her loving spouse St. Joseph, the patron of the universal Church.

Beneath this central group, battalions of angels stand in their nine orders, superb beings embodied and God-like, swifter than light in the play of their intelligence, prompt in their obedience to God's will as the clay is plastic to the hand of the modeller, reflecting the tranquility of the Godhead, yet terrible when roused to righteous indignation in the cause of God, more terrible than the blasting thunderbolts, or raging fire, or the convulsions of earthquakes. And there too, conspicuous in their companionship, are the twelve, whom our blessed Lord called to be His heralds to the world, when He walked the land of Palestine, in poverty and hardships, and who, discovering His divine nature through the garb of man's flesh, left all and followed Him. Upon their brows is set the mysterious seal of the priesthood, borne by the great high-priest himself, a badge which gives them a singular likeness to Him, while it distinguishes them from all their fellow courtiers, even the Cherubim and Seraphim, who yield ready precedence and offer their veneration to that august token of the Priesthood of Melchisedech. Numerous as the twinkling points of light upon a rippling sea beneath the blaze of the midsummer sun, is the far-reaching and countless multitudes that display that sacudotal badge; popes and patriarches, arch-bishops and bishops, priests and deacons in endless array.

Among them are men of apostolic gifts, whose names have, like those of the twelve, penetrated to the ends of the earth; men who won whole tribes and nations to God, and begot them, as one family of children, to the Church. There, easily distinguishable, is the great St. Augustine, who baptized the Saxon Ethelbert, and laid the foundation of Christianity in this Island. There, with his fervent and passionate nature speaking in his radiant countenance, is the patriarch of the Irish race, who stamped his own character upon the people he saved unto Christ, and whose prayer for their perseverance has kept them, through unparalleled persecutions, true to the faith he bequeathed to them. There are St. Willibrord and St. Boniface, sons of the Saxon race, who, urged by the promptings of their divine Master, devoted their lives to their kinsmen of Germany.

And wherever the eye turns over the ocean of faces, we see forests of waving palms, emblems of the martyr's death, and they who bear them are clothed in white garments. "I saw a great multitude," says the Evangelist, "which no man could number, of all nations, and tribes, and peoples, and tongues, standing before the throne, and in sight of the Lamb, clothed with white robes, and with palms in their hands, and cried with a loud voice, saying:—Salvation to our God, who sitteth upon the throne, and to the Lamb. And one of the ancients said to me: These that are clothed in white robes, who are they? Whence come they? And I said to him: my Lord thou knowest. And he said to me: These are they who come out of great tribulations, and have washed their robes, and have made them white in the blood of the Lamb. Therefore they are before the throne of God and they serve Him day and night in His temple; and He that sitteth on the throne shall dwell over them. They shall no more hunger nor thirst, neither shall the sun fall upon them, nor any heat. For the Lamb, which is in the midst of the throne shall rule them, and shall lead them to the fountains of the waters of life, and God shall wipe away all the tears from their eyes." Ah! how slight now seem all the torments that once made their human flesh to quiver and to creep; how unimportant and brief, passed like a momentary pang, yet winning them joy unlimited and endless.

And associated with the martyrs, are those who suffered with patience and meekness the manifold ills of life; and who witnessed to the divinity of their creed and the strength of grace, if not by shedding their blood, at least by bearing their trials and crosses in a spirit of gentle and uncomplaining fortitude. Cast your eyes over this great palace, with its swarming multitudes, and see how amply the promises of Christ are fulfilled—Blessed are the poor in spirit, for theirs is the kingdom of heaven. Behold St. Francis of Assisi, St. Thomas Aguinas, and thousands upon thousands besides, who stripped themselves here of all riches, and all things that could purchase honour, now vested with regal dignity, crowned and sceptred, like vassal kings in the train of the eternal King of Glory. "Blessed are they that mourn, for they shall be comforted. Blessed are they that suffer persecution for justice's sake, for theirs is the kingdom of heaven. Blessed are ye, when they shall revile you and persecute you, and speak all that is evil against you untruly for my sake. Be glad and rejoice, for your reward is very great in heaven."

Oh, see how it is all fulfilled now in this land of gladness! Yes, Lazarus had his day of sorrow, but it is long gone by. No more he sits, fainting and famished, at the rich man's gate, the dogs licking his sores. His supereminent reward above is proportioned to the sorrows which he bravely bore below for God's sake; and every tear which misfortune pressed from his eyes has its own special reward, because he, though his human nature shrunk from pain, repined not at the will of his Maker. No longer does the good St. Elizabeth wander homeless and despised, under the winter blast, vainly seeking the shelter of a friendly roof. For the relatives who sent her out she has found myriads of loving friends; and every desire of her heart is satisfied. And then the saints who, though they suffered little from without, became their own executioners, and followed the injunction of the Apostle by crucifying the flesh and all its concupiscences—how great is their delight and exultation now; for all the harass is over, the painful watchings and the stern se'f-discipline; the jealous custody of pleasure seeking senses; the spiky chain and the hair shirt, the thin raiment that betrayed the shivering body to the cold; the scanty crusts washed down with water—all these are grown into dim and shadowy memories, or motives for joyous reminiscences, like the hardships of a past campaign to a stout soldier, when the acclamations of his welcoming countrymen are deafening his ears.

And with what a glow of fond recollection will the hermit recall the long days and nights in which he mortified his body, and toiled upwards along the rugged path of virtue, with what rapture will he picture to his fancy the uncouth cavern that re-sounded to his prayers, the murmuring river from which he slaked his thirst, the tree that furnished him with food, the stone pillow that supported his heavy head, when the sleep of weariness fell upon him; how he will bless that *regime* which to the world seemed folly, but which has brought to him the peace of this eternal Sabbath. Those, too, who dedicated to their Maker the sweet blossom of their virginity, and guarded it from every evil influence, by the thorns of self-denial, how thankful they are for the grace which upheld them, and saved them from the tempest of the world. Numerous are they as the stars that stud the firmament; they are drawn as a girdle of light close to the throne of the Lamb. And their lips are privileged to sing a canticle which none but they can sing. "I heard a voice from heaven as the voice of many waters, and as the voice of great thunder, and the voice which I heard was as the voice of harpers harping on their harps. And they sang as it were a new canticle before the throne, and before the four living creatures and the ancients; and no man could sing the canticle but those hundred and forty-four thousand, who were purchased from the earth. These are they who were not defiled with woman; for they are virgins. These follow the Lamb whithersoever He goeth. These were purchased from among men, the first fruits to God and to the Lamb. And in their mouth was found no lie, for they are without spot before the throne of God."

But to us poor sinners, what sight can be so encouraging as that of the noted penitents, like Mary Magdalen and St. Mary of Egypt, whose grief, inspired by love and gratitude, was so intense as to unite them inseparably to the God they had offended; and to place them among the number of those to whom apply the words of our blessed Lord:—" Many sins are forgiven them, because they have loved much." Strange is the spectacle too, and as inspiring as it is strange, of those who stained their hands with bloodshed in the paroxysm of rage, or even in the deliberate cunning of vindictiveness; men who were tracked by the law like mad dogs, and were cut off from life by the steel or the rope, as unworthy to breathe the same air as their fellow-men : malefactors, whose brutal lives inspired horror, and whose death was incapable of moving pity—Yet, because they did not reject the grace of the all-merciful God, which visited them as it visited the thief on the Cross at the last gasp, are numbered for evermore with the blessed

But look around once more, beloved Brethren, are there none in this vast concourse for the sight of whose faces your sad soul thirsts? Yes! There is many an old friend, many an old playmate and companion, whose pale corpse you kissed years ago for the last time ; ere it mingled its dust with the clay of the graveyard. There is father or mother, brother or sister, wife or husband—all think of you—all praying for you—even as I speak. Oh! beloved Brethren, they are not lost to us those dear, dear friends, but gone upon a pleasant voyage, where we shall soon join them ; and when grief shall be no more. " Blessed are the dead who die in the Lord : from henceforth now," saith the spirit, " they may rest from their labours, for their works follow them."

ALL SOULS

THE songs of triumph, beloved Brethren, which hailed the great feast of God's servants in glory, have died away upon the ear, and a solemn hush has settled over the Christian world, in the midst of which we seem to hear, faint, distant and vague, wails of suppressed woe, and moanings and sobbings of patient pain. It is the eve of that day which our fond mother, the Church, has set apart to commemorate, and to aid those of her children whose race on earth is run, but whose souls are still in darkness, awaiting the dawn of the eternal day. She is not like earthly parents, whose tears are soon dried, and whose wounds, inflicted by the sad human law of death and bereavement, soon find a healing balm to close their red lips, and to allay the throbbing of pain which the poor victims of sorrow feared would be eternal. Parted by the hand of death from the spiritual battle which rages above ground, severed from the throng of Christian warriors in whose company they laboured, fought, and suffered—vanished though they be from the eye of flesh, they are ever present to her memory, ever dear to her heart. With her there is no forgetting : immortal in her vigour and vitality, she is immortal in her love. Death may snatch her poor child away and give his body to the worms, but cannot tear him from her communion, nor call him to a region where her influence may not reach him. Her arms stretch beyond the grave, and gather to her bosom the living and the dead. Her tears and supplications, as they avail in this world to cleanse the soul and to multiply grace, so in that dolorous region of trial and pining expectation, through God's mercy and loving kindness, they assuage the misery of the captive and shorten the term of his constraint and bondage. Let us to-night hearken to her summons, and withdraw our minds for a brief space from the distractions and cares of life, that we may ponder on the condition of the poor sufferers who have fought the good fight, but are still too stained by the dust and grime of battle to receive the wedding garment, and to be admitted into the light of splendour and joy of the great banquet hall. Let us conjure up the forms and faces of those whose lives were woven into our own in some past phase of our little story, but whose chapter was brought too soon, alas! to an end; and the memory of whose friendship, once so cherished, perhaps is growing unfamiliar in the swift-passing years, and apt to startle us in the solitary hours, as by the sudden rising of a phantom.

This doctrine of Purgatory, beloved Brethren, rests upon one of the mysteries of God. You know that God is one with his attributes, unlike man. A man may be truthful; but his truth is not so essential to him that he cannot be imagined without it—nay, that he cannot part with it in reality. There was only one man that could ever say: "I am the Truth," and He was God as well as man. And as God is truth itself, so God is mercy and justice essentially. He is All-just, and yet He is All-merciful. How to reconcile these two attributes, so that I shall understand in what manner the claims of the one do not interfere with the claims of the other, is a problem beyond the reach of man's intellect. God alone, operating freely and without effort, can solve that problem in act, by displaying His mercy and His justice in due proportions, according to His own high and inscrutable standard. Suffice it to us to know that He could not be unjust nor unmerciful without ceasing to be God.

Another mysterious attribute of the divine nature, upon which the doctrine of Purgatory is based, is the sanctity of God. God is not holy as men are: He is the law, the fountain, and the measure of holiness. He is holy by doing his own will; we are holy in proportion as we conform our will to His. "There is none," says the Book of Samuel (i. 22), "holy as the Lord. The angels themselves in His sight are not pure," and this attribute of holiness prompts that perpetual hymn of praise, which, shading their faces with their wings, and bowing down in awful reverence, they sing in ceaseless concert: Holy! holy! holy! And it is this sublime and incomprehensible holiness of God which imparts to sin its guilt and its hideousness. Sin is as infinite as God, and as unfathomable.

To understand sin, we must comprehend God; and that, no created intelligence can do. No one but God can know the divine nature, and its infinite attributes. And hence it was said of the Holy Ghost by St. Paul: "The spirit searcheth all things, yea, the deep things of God. For what man knoweth the things of man, but the spirit of the man that is in him? So the things also that are of God no man knoweth, but the Spirit of God."— 1 *Cor.* ii. 10. And as God alone comprehends His own holiness, so God alone can sound the depths of the malice and turpitude of sin. Indeed, if it can be truly said that "no man can see God and live," it may be said with equal truth that "no man could see the vileness and degradation, and deformity of sin," without dying of fright and horror, unless God exerted a special power to secure the bonds which unite soul and body in the unity, which we call life. The revelations made to the saints on this subject show that even to the purblind vision of mortals, there is no apparition so scaring and appalling as that of a soul in the death and corruption of sin.

Now, beloved Brethren, God has given us His own perfect will as our law, and has given us the power to follow that will or not, as we choose. In this ordinance His mercy is conspicuous; for the gift is most gratuitous; and though the abuse of that gift will bring ruin upon our heads, yet the divine Giver has furnished us with ample aids to prevent such a catastrophe, and has encouraged us during our short-lived trial by the prospect of a reward "such as eye hath not seen, nor ear heard"; no other, in a word, than that which forms His own supernal bliss; the vision and enjoyment of His perfections.

But if we reject His mercy, and transgress His law, we call into play that awful attribute of justice, which is as much one with Himself as His mercy. God, the tender, the gentle, the compassionate, the sweet, whose hands are opened to fill every living thing with benediction—He, the generous and bountiful Giver of all good gifts, becomes the God of wrath, the God of battles and of hosts: the God, mighty and strong, visiting the sins of the father upon the children unto the third and fourth generation, the Almighty and the Omniscient, against whose rage no being can stand up, from whose eye no covert or gloom can curtain the guilty. "Whither shall I go from Thy spirit?; or whither shall I flee from Thy face? If I ascend into heaven Thou art there, if

I descend into hell Thou art present. If I take my wings early in the morning and dwell in the uttermost parts of the sea; even there also shalt Thy hand lead me, and Thy right hand shall hold me. And I said, perhaps, darkness shall cover me, and night shall be my light in my pleasures. But darkness shall not be dark to Thee, and night shall be light as the day; the darkness of night and the light of day are alike to Thee."—*Ps.* cxxxviii. 10.

Oh, the awful mystery of sin's defilement and heinousness, which clouds the face of the God of beauty and love, and draws forth from the mercy-seat stupendous thunders, that make the powers of heaven quake, and resistless bolts of destruction for the eternal ruin of the sinner.

Mysterious then although it be, beloved Brethren, we must bow down our poor, scared, and troubled intellect before the truth of God. Turn to the Sacred Scriptures, and what will you find there—certain, and clear, and indubitable? You will find that Almighty God inflicted the most terrific punishment for even venial sins; in other words, those offences which do not sever the soul from Him completely, and which, therefore, may be termed minor offences; what the world calls peccadilloes. These sins, however light and trivial they appear, are, when viewed in themselves, and in the dazzling splendour of God's sanctity, heinous and hideous. They are slights and insults offered by man to the Being of beings, who has designed to make man His friend, nay, His adopted son. They are as running sores and noisome cancers, which disfigure the soul's loveliness, and which interfere with the fond caresses of our heavenly Father. His disgust of these blemishes is stamped in unmistakeable characters upon holy writ. I will omit the many other examples by which I might illustrate this truth from the old Testament, and confine myself to one—old and familiar though it be. You know that King David was tempted by a motive of vanity to number his people. "Go," said he to Joab, the general of his army, "through all the tribes of Israel, from Dan to Bersabee, and number me my people, that I may know the number of them." Joab expostulated; but in vain. Nine months and twenty days he went through the land on this foolish errand. On his return, David recognized the unworthiness of his motive, and turning to God, said: "I have sinned very much in what I have done." And the word of the Lord came to Gad, the Prophet, and the seer to David, saying:

Go and say to David: thus saith the Lord: "I give thee thy choice of three things—either seven years of famine shall come to thee in thy land, or thou shalt flee three months before thy adversaries and they shall pursue thee, or for three days there shall be a pestilence in thy land." And David said to Gad, "I am in great strait, but is it not better that I should fall into the hands of the Lord, for His mercies are many, than into the hands of men."—II. *Kings*. xxiv. 10-15. And the Lord sent pestilence upon Israel from the morning unto the time appointed, and there died of the pestilence, from Dan to Bersabee, 70,000 men.

Behold, beloved Brethren, the merciful God with the scourge in His hand! How heavily He smites, when His anger is aroused! What a sum of suffering is comprised in the words, "there died of the people from Dan to Bersabee 70,000 men." How many heart-strings are torn by a single death! What tears are shed over one rigid corpse—the pride, ornament, and support of a household! But here are hecatombs, armies of pest-stricken victims, breathing out their agonized spirits in the midst of the families who had woven their affections around them, and learnt to feel that life would not be tolerable with their loss! How many fathers and mothers were wringing their hands and pouring their scalding tears upon the remains of the sons, who had been the prop and consolation of their old age; how many children were gazing in sad wonder at the motionless, speechless forms of the sires, who, a while ago, were full of life, and geniality, and affection; how many young wives tore their hair, and wailed over their premature widowhood; how many friends were left to mourn the loss of the comrades they had loved! Ah! where was there ever a lachrymatory large enough to hold such a rain of tears? And the whole of that vast flood of grief had its spring and origin in one little sin of vanity! O God of justice and of mercy! how deep is the mystery of sin!

And if God's justice exacts such severe retribution for these offences, which, in spite of all their inherent heinousness, do not dissolve the bonds of friendship between Him and His creatures, He is no less severe in the penalties which He inflicts upon those who have been guilty of grievous or deadly sin, even after He has blotted out the guilt of their transgressions. I am not preaching a controversial sermon, so that I will simply remind you of what you know already, viz.: how King David, after being assured by the prophet Nathan that the guilt of his murder and adultery was remitted, was nevertheless condemned to suffer most bitter loss in the death of his child, and that seven days and nights of fasting, and tears, and prayers, and penitent prostration in sackcloth and ashes, did not avail to ward off that blow.

You know too, beloved Brethren, that if we leave this world before we have satisfied the justice of God, both for the venial sins we have committed, and for the grievous sins forgiven but not expiated in their consequences, we are not received into the joy of the Lord, but consigned to a lot of temporary suffering, from which there will not be release by God's mercy until His justice has cried "Enough." What the exact nature of that atonement is we do not know for certain, because the Church has never defined it. But that it comprises sorrow, uneasiness and unhappiness, is beyond all doubt. Else, why the dark and mournful weeds which the Church assumes at this season, the melancholy plaints that break forth in Her liturgy for the dead, and the funeral chan's and dolorous strains of music in which she seeks to relieve the burthen of her feelings? Yes, Purgatory is a place of harass and tribulation; and hence she sighs: "Eternal rest give to them, O Lord. My soul is troubled exceedingly, but do Thou, O Lord, succour it." It is a prison of gloom, rayless and cheerless; and hence her prayer: "Let perpetual light shine upon them" It is a place where ingratitude and malice will weigh heavily upon the memory, and torture the soul with regrets; and hence the Church in her office calls out in the name of her poor stricken child: "I am horrified at my misdeeds, and am covered with shame in Thy sight. Remember not, O Lord, the offences of my youth and my ignorances. Woe is me, O Lord, for I have sinned exceedingly in my life." It is a place where the abuse and waste of grace will be brought home with horrible force to the undistracted mind, and hence she says: "I have done nothing worthy in Thy sight, therefore I deprecate Thy majesty."

But as the great pain of hell is the sense of the loss of God, beyond all the tortures of that prison house of atonement, beloved Brethren, is the enforced separation of the soul, even for a time, from the God of all beauty. The soul has now parted with every earthly thirst, and the scales have fallen from its eyes; its views and feelings are no longer coloured and clouded by the bodily senses, its thoughts are no longer entangled by earthly distractions and cares. It once loved creatures inordinately; it once set too much store by some particular satisfaction, was too much enslaved by some particular fault, was too much at the beck of the concupiscence of the flesh, the concupiscence of the eyes, or the pride of life. But now all is changed. As the river turns to the sea, and sweeps onwards day and night with strong and restless current, till it is absorbed into the great centre, so every force and faculty of the soul sets towards God, and struggles to reach Him. Oh! how beautiful, how glorious, how desirable, how necessary, how indispensable to the poor soul's happiness, will He then appear—the sumnum bonum—the essence of all loveliness, and amiability, and joy! As the wild forest-bird, whose delight is in the sunshine and fragrant air of heaven, and whose song is a homage to the fair free world, when it is caught in the toils of the fowler and pent up in the small circumference of the cage, beats its palpitating breast against the bars of its little dungeon, in the vain hope of reaching again the home of light and liberty which it has lost; so will the poor soul long and pant for the face of God, and pine away with the sickness of deferred hope. Yea: "as the hart panteth after the fountains of water, so my soul panteth after thee, O God. My soul hath thirsted after the strong living God, when shall I come and appear before the face of God." Oh for the opening of the gate of glory! Oh for the ending of this tormenting solitude, where no word of comfort is softly instilled into our ears, no tender hand of friendship smooths our sick pillow, no alteration of day and night brings a sense of relief.

Do not relax your efforts then in behalf of the holy souls. By labouring for their relief, you soften your hearts, and open them to every tender sympathy. Freely have your received, freely give. Remember that you really assist them by your prayers; especially those indulgenced for this end by the Church; you assist them by your charities and alms to the poor and destitute; you assist them by your Confessions, by your Communions, by hearing Mass devoutly, and by procuring that the holy Sacrifice should be offered for their deliverance. On selfish grounds alone, you ought to busy yourselves in this pious and sacred industry. For the day will doubtless come when you, yourself, will clamour for relief; and if, in your day, you have forgotten the dead, even so in turn shall you be forgotten. The God of justice decrees this retribution. Wise are they who devote all the merit of their works to the object of releasing those poor suffering souls, so dear to God, by hastening their passage to bliss; for in their own turn they may with perfect confidence resign themselves to the mercy and goodness of God. There is no truth more certain than this:—" Blessed are the merciful for they shall find mercy."

ST. JOSEPH, PATRON OF THE UNIVERSAL CHURCH.

TO-DAY, beloved Brethren, our holy mother, the Church calls upon us to celebrate the feast, to ponder upon the virtues, and to glorify the name of St. Joseph, the illustrious foster-father of the Word made flesh. It is not merely in consequence of the spotless life and the high supernatural character of the saint that this festival day challenges our interest, and appeals to our feelings. Besides the claim which St. Joseph has upon us, in common with the other saints of God's house—the elder brothers of our race, and the heroic captains of our army—he commands our special reverence, admiration and love, as the patron of the universal Church, and therefore the guide, guardian and protector of every child of the Faith. For this title, conferred upon him by the late Pontiff of happy and sainted memory, is more than a token of the high regard in which St. Joseph is held by Christendom, or a mere agency for enhancing his accidental glory, and crowning him with fresh laurels in his celestial home. By virtue of the word of Christ's vicar, which penetrates heaven as it searches to the ends of the earth, that title assigns to St. Joseph a new sphere of duties, linked with a weightier influence in behalf of his votaries, and a larger power in the spiritual world. In the old Roman times, the Patron and his client were united by the closest bonds and the most sacred ties, which it was impiety to violate. The clients formed a retinue of honour for the Patron; in the early morning they thronged his hall to pay their respects and tender their dutiful homage; they were proud to accompany him in his progresses and walks through the city; they gloried in his power, and felt themselves sharers in the honours that fell to his lot; and they strained every nerve to promote his purposes and advance his prestige.

And, on the other hand, the Patron showed to the humblest of his clients a fraternal affability and kindliness, which the stranger could not claim. He interested himself in their prosperity; he watched over their safety and shielded them from their foes; he helped them with material succours in seasons of distress; he made them partakers in the joy of every welcome incident and fortunate event of his life by banquets and personal gifts; in short, he was willing that the happiness and wellbeing of his clients should be taken as the criterion and the measure of his own opulence and power.

In like manner is St. Joseph, the Patron of the universal Church, bound to each one of us by the most sacred of ties. While we are, as clients, obliged in duty to honour him by our frequent salutations, steadfast loyalty and undeviating devotion, by wearing as it were his livery and imitating his character, and striving to make ourselves worthy of his patronage, he, on his side, is equally obliged to exert his power in our behalf, to shield us from perils both visible and invisible, to stand between us and the archenemy that thirsts for more than our blood, and to mould and fashion us by his constant intercession and his silent influence into that form and figure of sanctity which our Creator has designed us to attain, and which will fit us for our place in God's kingdom hereafter. With good reason, then, do we hail the return of this glad anniversary, in which all the children of the Church throng, in their millions, into the palace halls of their great Patron, the second and the greater Joseph, the Prince of God's household, and the dispenser of His treasures, to raise their loud cry of praise and joy, of gratitude and thanksgiving, to Him who has raised up St. Joseph to be the embodiment of the divine bounty, and minister of His unlimited munificence.

Although St. Joseph's position in heaven is so high to-day, yet when we look, beloved Brethren, into his life, we cannot but be struck by the scanty materials for biography which it presents, and by the homely, unimposing virtues of which it furnishes record. If you except his surpassing dignity as husband of Mary and foster-father of Jesus Christ, and the two or three touching incidents which that office brought in its train, his days passed like those of the millions upon millions of poor toiling artisans, whose brief epitaph might be comprised in the words: "They were born to labour and to die." Among those of his own contemporaries who knew him, he was but an insignificant unit in the sum of human existence. He had no mission to dazzle the world by the display of supernatural pre-eminence nor by the exercise of miraculous power. He did not, like Elias, call down the devouring fire from heaven to consume the enemies of God, nor, like Eliseus, summon springs of water from the bosom of the arid earth to re-invigorate a perishing army. He did not make the desert his home, and by his alienation from human society, fix the attention and compell the wonder of men, like St. John the Baptist. He did not persecute his flesh with fierce and phenomenal austerities, like St. John of the Cross or St. Peter of Alcantara. He did not make himself famous by winning a nation or a race to God, like St. Patrick or St. Francis Xavier. He did not, like St. Benedict, raise up a family of religions, to whom he bequeathed the distinctive features of his sanctity, and in whose lives he lived again. Though a cheerful son of toil, and a willing victim of poverty, he did not exhibit his spirit of detachment in a form of heroism which could rivet the minds of men, like St. Francis of Assisi. In one word, his virtues bloomed for God alone; his life was a plain and unadorned casket, that told no tale without of the riches it enclosed, but which was filled to bursting with the most inestimable gems, with the rarest pearls, and diamonds of the purest water.

Already he had passed the meridian of human life, beloved Brethren, when impelled by the stimulus of God's Holy Spirit, he unconsciously contributed to the realization of that merciful scheme which rescued man from eternal misery, by becoming a suitor for the hand of a beautiful and gentle maiden, like himself a descendant of the royal race of David, and like himself poor; yet marked out for a destiny which would fill with wonder and awe the sublimest of heaven's hierarchies, and make a new heaven and a new earth to all eternity. Those nuptials, which knit his virgin soul to hers, were of small moment in the eyes of the world, although they changed its destinies. Two simple, foolish mortals, enacting once again the old, old drama which had been so often rehearsed before in the theatre of the world—that stale drama, whose climax was love and whose closing scene was death—such would be the comment of the passing moralist, who saw the carpenter clasp in his labour-hardened palm the maiden hand which God's Incarnate Son would kiss with filial love. Even that unspoken vow, so well understood between them, which consecrated the home of marriage as another shrine of virginity, and made their union worthy of two unbodied spirits above, even that escaped the eyes of casual witnesses, who, perchance, beheld them plight their troth to each other. A most common ceremony then it seemed to common eyes. Yet, it is not more true that the genius of Cyrus changed the face of nations; it is not more true that the trampling of Alexander's hosts shook down empires and thrones, than that the simple marriage between a nameless workman and a poor dowerless girl affected the destinies of every child of Adam's sinful seed from the first to the last man. If no trumpet of jubilee thrilled the air, when the murmured promise of life-long fidelity made those two saints one, we may be sure there was no lack of triumph and gladness before the angels of God, and no lack of terror among the wandering spirits of darkness who plot man's ruin. For already they must have dimly discerned, if they were not allowed as yet fully to realize, that in the modest and shrinking maiden, whom that elderly workman took to wife that day, they beheld the dreaded woman of prophecy, whose foot would crush the serpent's head, and to whom the wondrous description of sacred writ would be applied till time itself should perish:—"Who is she that cometh forth from the desert, fair as the moon, bright as the sun, terrible as an army in battle-array?"

The dignity, beloved Brethren, to which St. Joseph was thus raised, pre-eminent as it was, and stupendous, was the crowning of a life, which, however ordinary in the esteem of men, must have been one long course of heroic virtue. The trials of the soul, though unseen, may be far more searching, and more fruitful of merit, than the external ordeals and achievements which address themselves to the senses. Though we know not one single passage or phrase of St. Joseph's earlier life, we know that he must have been placed by God's Providence in such circumstances, as fully tried and matured his virtue, and made him worthy to be the reputed father of the world's Redeemer, the husband of God's virgin mother, the daily and hourly companion and guardian of their lives, till death summoned him to his rest. He must, I say, have been placed in circumstances that enabled him to prove himself the possessor of a faith more unquestioning than Abraham's, of a hope in God and a trustfulness in God's goodness, exceeding that of the heroic Judith, of a meekness and forbearance greater than those of the paragon Moses, of a chastity and prudence transcending those of his prototype Joseph, and of a seraphic charity, to which David, in his most rapturous moods, could never soar.

You know, beloved Brethren, and I need not dwell upon it, how soon that disciplined virtue, acquired through inward trials and triumphs, was put to the test. With that timidity and reserve, so natural to her spotless maidenhood and her matchless humility, Mary had not divulged even to her beloved spouse the Archangel's visit, and the miraculous maternity, of which it was the harbinger. Doubt and trouble seized on the soul of Joseph. He saw, and knew not what to believe. Behold, how he acts towards her in his bewilderment, showing the depths of his charity, and the resources of his prudence. "Being a just man," says St. Matthew, "and not willing, publicly, to expose her, he was minded to put her away privately." What anguish of thought do these words betray! What agonizing fears and misgivings, when the laws of nature seemed to belie the justice of his esteem and affection. But the dark cloud soon passed, and the peace of his soul, and his admiration and love for his peerless spouse shone forth again, brighter and more cheering than the noon-day beam. "While he thought on these things," continues the Evangelist, "Behold the angel of the Lord appeared to him in his sleep, saying: Joseph son of David, fear not to take unto thee Mary thy wife, for that which is conceived in her is of the Holy Ghost."

I need not say, beloved Brethren, for you have often meditated on the theme yourselves, with what consolations this sorrow of St. Joseph was recompensed: when in the months that preceeded the nativity he adored the unborn Saviour in the tabernacle of Mary's womb; when he first saw the sweet face of his foster-child smiling upon him, and felt the first caress of those waxen fingers; when he nursed Him in his lap, and fondled Him in his arms, hung over Him in His balmy sleep, murmured soft prayers in His ears, and soothed Him in the trials of infancy with hymns that told of Israel's tribulations, and the mercy and compassion of Israel's God. What joy was blent with his sorrow, even when the angel's voice bade him carry his frail charge into the land of the heathen, the typical land of Jewish humiliation and bondage! In the remote region of his exile, he found a home that was dear to him, as long as he looked on the face of Jesus and Mary. In the seat and centre of a degrading idolatry, he scarcely sighed for the sacred city or its temple ; for behold the Lord God, to whom the great round arch of heaven is but a temple-dome, was enshrined in His humble cot. Whatever hardships he endured, he thanked God so long as his arm was strong enough to earn for his beloved companions, his growing child and his adored wife, the means of clothing and sustaining them.

Even his long and painful return to far Galilee, through dreary and perilous deserts, though it brought its tears and hours of deadly weariness, was soon forgotten in his hidden home at Nazareth. One terrible tempest indeed he was forced to breast ; and this was all the more unnerving and prostrating in its horror, because it consisted in the withdrawal from his little bark of the very anchor of his life, and the obliteration from the heavens of the guiding-star he steered by. Who can tell how sorely his courage was tried, how freely his tears flowed, notwithstanding all his efforts to control himself, how his very heart bled within him, to see the anguish of his poor wife, the robbed and desolate mother, when for three days he sought his foster-child through the sacred city, where the exigencies of His Father's business had concealed Him ? But again his sorrow was recompensed with joy, and in his little cottage at Nazareth, he found a heaven, which he would not have changed for the Paradise of the angels.

By the side of His grey-haired guardian, Jesus eventually tired His young sinews in the labour of an artizan. They wrought together on the same piece of work, and rejoiced to be able to give their joint earnings to the sweet lady, who, without commanding, ruled the humble household. If they were hungry ever, and work did not come in, they bore it in penitential patience, offering themselves as willing holocausts to expiate the sin, which brought poverty into the world. Thus no sentence was perhaps ever penned, which enclosed such mysteries of love, consolation, and pure earthly happiness, as are implied in the words of the Evangelist :—" And Jesus went down with them, and came to Nazareth, and was subject to them—And Jesus advanced in wisdom, and age, and grace with God and man."

But enviable, beloved Brethren, as St. Joseph was in his life, he was still more to be envied in ,his death. His death was the natural sequel to such a life. It was like a mellow sunset in the autumn, when the golden grain lies cut in the fields, and ready to be stored up in the granary. Death came not to him, as it comes to many, in the shape of a grisly and ill-boding phantom, that decrees heart-rending separations, stirs up bitter and hopeless remorse for past misdeeds, transforms indifference into despair, announces imminent and merciless judgment, and predicts in the world to come eternal trouble and unrest, and in this world the darkness and corruption of an unhallowed grave. Suffice it to say that the last impressions, which his failing senses brought him of this fleeting existence, were the farewell kisses imprinted on his furrowed brow and cold lips by his beloved wife Mary, and by his darling foster-child Jesus; that God-man, to whom all power is given in heaven and on earth; that Lamb, who is the lamp, the glory, the illumination, and the happiness of heaven; that Conqueror who, by accepting death in its bitterest form, has enabled us to challenge the grim tyrant of the human race, and to say:—"Death, Jesus has been thy death—Death, where is thy sting? Death, where is thy victory?"

Let us then, beloved Brethren, on this festival-day, mingle with the multitudes of votaries who, in every quarter of the globe, are pressing forward to congratulate holy St. Joseph on the return of this great anniversary. Let us, as his clients, recount to our powerful and affectionate Patron, our difficulties, our trials, our temptations; our fears for past sin, our resolutions of future amendment. Let us not be apprehensive of tiring Him by our supplications and entreaties. And above all, let us ask Him by His own most happy and holy departure from this world, to save us from that worst of blights and curses—a sudden and an unprovided death.

ST. JOHN OF THE CROSS.

WHEN I last addressed you, beloved Brethren, I spoke of the sign of the Cross as a Sacramental, and exhorted you to cherish and love the sacred symbol of salvation, and to imprint upon your hearts the lessons it conveys. Since then we have been called upon by our holy mother, the Church, to celebrate the feast of St. John of the Cross, whose whole life was distinguished by the spirit that flows from the contemplation and imitation of our crucified Master. And it has suggested itself to me, as a suitable subject for this evening's discourse, to sketch, as briefly as may be, the career of this saint as the model of mortification, charity, patience, and forgiveness—in fine, all the virtues of which the Cross is emblematic.

St. John was born in Old Castile in the year fifteen hundred and forty-one, about the middle of that stormy century, in which the greater part of Europe was convulsed and desolated by the Reformation. His devotion to the Mother of God actuated him to join the Carmelite Friars when he was twenty-one years of age ; and though his humility aimed at nothing higher than the grade of lay brother, he was forced by obedience to receive the sacred order of priesthood in his twenty-fifth year. During the period of his childhood, his youth, and his noviciate, his love for the Cross was already conspicuous. In his tender years, his patience and charity induced his superiors to employ him in waiting on the sick in the hospital wards, and ministering comfort and relief to our Blessed Lord in the persons of his suffering members. From his childhood he seemed beckoned forward by his divine Master along the most thorny paths of self-denial. It was as if he, beyond his fellows, had received the command : " Take up your Cross, and follow me." While a novice, he practised the most rigorous mortifications; his cell was the darkest hole he could find in the dormitory; his bed was a sort of coffin of planks; his fasts were constant and excessive; his hair-shirt, woven with his own hand, drew blood at every movement. It was his rule to deny his senses everything which did not seem to promote the honour and glory of his Maker. By these austerities, and still more by the spirit of prayer and contemplation which accompanied them, and of which they were but the outward tokens, he grew every day more fully into the likeness of him who, for the love of man, had put off all the glory and forsaken for a time the splendour and bliss of his heavenly existence; who had, in a word, emptied himself, and lived a life of pain and privation among men, that he might encourage them to die to themselves, as the only way of living to him, and being united to him in a joyful immortality.

Shortly after his ordination, the Spirit of God led the great St. Theresa to employ his services in the foundation of a house of reformed Carmelites, who were to receive the name of the "Barefooted Carmelites." The institute was blessed with rapid success; and its members so faithfully imitated the self-denial and the austenties of St. John, that St Theresa deemed it necessary to mitigate the rigours of their life. In his new position of responsibility, St. John kept his eyes ever fixed upon his crucified Lord, was never tired meditating upon the virtues, which His passion revealed, and grew more and more anxious to share in the pains, trials, and ignominies, mixed in the chalice of bitterness which our blessed Lord had drunk to the dregs. He was not long before his desire was gratified. First of all, that sensible devotion, which had made prayer sweeter than honey to his lips, and overflowed his heart with satisfaction and delight, was withdrawn from him by his divine Master; and every exercise of piety cost him an effort, as walking is painful to a man suffering from a sprain. But this was not all. He began to be devoured by scruples and fears, until his accustomed acts of devotion became formidable and repulsive; and at every step he trembled lest he should plunge into mortal sin. Heaven seemed to darken above him; hell seemed to open its devouring jaws beneath his feet. And to add to these trials, men were stirred up by the devil to calumniate him at the very time when heavenly succour appeared lost, and he seemed abandoned to his own feebleness and helplessness. These crosses were, however, but the first of a series, and were succeeded by light and joy, which broke over his troubled soul at first in uncertain gleams, like the hazy dawn of morning, and then in an overwhelming sunburst of consolation and spiritual delights. From this first phrase of predestined trial, his spirit came forth purified, having left all self-will and self-seeking behind, and thirsting only for the fulfilment of the petition "Thy will be done." But the storm was renewed with tenfold violence, when be had been refreshed by this brief period of comfort ; and a darkness more awful and depressing than death brooded over his being. Again the Master, who rules the winds and waves of the moral as well as the physical world, spoke the word, and a calm succeeded. Then it was that his poor wounded spirit was bathed in an ocean of happiness, and repaid by the unspeakable caresses of his divine Spouse for all the trouble and anguish of the past. From the second phrase of his trial he came forth with strong spiritual penetration, keenly alive in particular to the advantages of suffering, and more than ever longing to drink the cup of his Saviour's passion. The brawling of the storm was succeeded by a halcyon calm ; the ill-defined horrors of his period of dereliction and darkness were replaced by a sense of warmth and light, and an indomitable fortitude in the performance of the divine will. From that time to the time of his death, by the action of a sort of law, he never received any great favour from Almighty God, which he had not first paid for, as it were, by some great cross or trial.

To us, beloved Brethren, whom God has called to walk by no extraordinary paths to our heavenly destination, it may be difficult to realize these mystic afflictions, and periods of spiritual desolation and darkness. But there is no doubt that such trials as these are far more grievous and painful to the servants of God than mere external crosses. The very climax of desolation has come, when the disciple of Christ, wrapt in a cloud that hides from him the smile of his beloved, cries out, like his Master in the supreme stage of His anguish : " My God ! my God! why hast Thou forsaken me ?" A real saint recks little of the sleet and hail of outward troubles, so long as he feels the hand of his Father amid the storm, or discerns His benign face through the darkness.

And if it seem strange that God should bear so heavliy upon His servants, let us remember the object He had in view, viz : to detach them from the world, to steel their spirit against its insidious pleasures, and to turn their thoughts without reserve to Himself, as the only true and lasting spring of satisfaction and content. "And I will bring," says the prophet, "the third part"—in other words, the chosen majority—"through the fire, and will refine them as silver is refined: and I will try them as gold is tried. They shall call on my name, and I will hear them. I will say: Thou art my people; and they shall say: The Lord is my God."—*Zacharias* xiii. 8. And St. Peter has the same thought when he says that joy will be the reward of our present crosses, "if now you must be for a little time made sorrowful in divers temptations, that the trial of your faith (much more precious than gold which is tried by the fire) may be found unto praise, and glory, and honour, at the appearing of Jesus Christ."—I. *Peter* i. 6. In truth, the creature suffering at the hands of his Creator, is like the little child that must be washed by its nurse, in spite of its tears and appeals for mercy, if it would be kept sound and strong, and free from many forms of sickness.

With all these afflictions of the soul, which we can only imperfectly estimate, St. John was called upon to imitate his divine Master by suffering many worldly adversities, such as are more readily understood and appreciated. One of the duties, to which St. Theresa appointed him, was the office of director to the nuns of the house of Avila, where she had made her first profession. This community had always set its face against the reforms of St. Theresa, and in particular resisted any attempts to curtail the frequent visits of their secular acquaintance. In forcing the needful reformation of the Sisterhood, St. John incurred the resentment of the old Carmelite friars, who denounced him, in open chapter, as a renegade, although what he had done had been undertaken with the sanction of the General of the Order and the Bishop of the Diocese. These conservative friars, carried away by passion, sent a troop of soldiers to arrest the Saint, had his door burst open, and himself torn away to prison, where he lay for nine months, almost without light, and with scarce nourishment sufficient to keep body and soul together. Thus he tasted the anguish of that fiery trial of our Lord, when He was cast off, arrested, imprisoned, and tortured at the instance of His own misguided kith and kin. By the interest of St. Theresa, he was not only liberated from his dungeon, but raised up again to some of the most important positions in the Order. But his

was destined to be a chequered career, like that of our blessed
Lord, whom the people at one time sought to make their king,
and at another would fain have stoned. In one of the chapters
of the Order, his freedom in opposing certain projects of his
brethren, which he believed would be prejudicial to religion,
drew down upon him such a storm of odium, that by the intrigues
of some of the more powerful among his brethren, he was
deprived of every office. Two of the fathers of the Order, whom
he had forbidden to preach, when he was Provincial of Andalusia,
because in their ambition for applause they had neglected other
duties, now took advantage of his prostrate condition, and went
about everywhere publishing slanders against him, and scraping
together any scraps of imformation they could obtain to blacken
his name. Their efforts brought upon him the contempt and
aversion of many; and even those who had reverenced him
before, amazed and bewildered, turned from him with a painful
feeling that they must have been mistaken. His best friends
dared scarcely be known as such, and were forced to burn his
letters, lest they should be involved in his disgrace. All this the
saint bore without one word of complaint, only offering himself
to suffer, in imitation of Him, who had stood before His
persecutors as the lamb before the shearers.

But the end of his trials was fast approaching. In his forty-
ninth year, he was seized with an illness that grew upon him,
until it could no longer be concealed. His Provincial, seeing
that the convent, from which he had retired during his disgrace,
was in every way ill-suited for a sick man, gave him his choice
of two places of sojourn during his illness. In the choice which
he made, the saint gave signal proof of his love of humiliation
and his spirit of mortification ; for instead of choosing the more
convenient and comfortable house, the prior of which was his
own devoted friend, he preferred a poorer house, which was
governed by one of his bitterest opponents, a man who had done
his utmost to injure him. For three months he lay in most
acute pain, all his legs inflamed, and covered with sores and
ulcers, which were aggravated by the repeated application of the
surgeon's lance. The prior was not moved by the spectacle of
his poor brother's agony. He allotted him a miserable cell,
withdrew the infirmarian who showed him kindness, and allowed
him only the coarsest fare. To complete his misery, another
cloud of spiritual dryness came over him ; and he lay on his bed

of agony to all appearance abandoned by God and man. But in the depth of his utmost affliction, his weak hands clung to the image of his crucified Lord; that was his solace in woe, his hope in despondency, the source of his fortitude, the inspiration of his patience, the living principle of his charity. The only token of the intense pains, which he suffered in body and in soul, was the tighter grasp of his clenched hand upon the crucifix, and the more fervent pressure of it to his breast. Once more before he died, the veil was lifted, and sunshine flooded his soul. It was the breaking of the eternal day. In deepest contrition, he repeated the psalm, "Have mercy on me, O God"; and then with raptures of love he heard portions of the Book of Canticles. At last, the thanksgiving of a life-time broke from his lips in the cry, "Glory be to God!" and pressing the crucifix to his breast, as if he would fain force it into his heart, he gave his soul the word to go forth: saying with his dying Saviour—"Into Thy hands, O Lord, I commend my spirit."

May the Cross of Christ, which St. John loved so well, be your safeguard and sanctification here, and hereafter your salvation and your recompense for evermore.

ST. MARGARET OF SCOTLAND.

THE year 1070 witnessed an event which was fraught to Scotland with most important consequences. Malcolm Canmore, or Malcolm of the large head, whose father, Duncan, had fallen a victim to the ambition of the notorious Macbeth, and who had wandered a fugitive for seventeen years, had at last been restored to the throne, by the aid of good King Edward the Confessor. Nine years later, the Conqueror seized upon the English throne; and Edgar Atheling, grandson of Edmund Ironside, who was half-brother to St. Edward the Confessor, felt that his kinship to the Saxon kings, and his superior title to the crown, exposed both his liberty and his life to danger, while he remained in the dominions of so unscrupulous a despot as William. Accordingly he found means to embark with his family and all his treasures, unknown to his watchful foe, intending to return to the continent, but the weather was unpropitious, as Providence would have it, and the exiles found themselves, when the sky cleared, not far from the coast of Scotland. There they were received with the most genial and lavish hospitality by King Malcolm; who remembered his own long years of destitution, isolation, and dependence, as a wanderer in a foreign land. Before long, Margaret, the youthful sister of the Atheling, so won the affections of Malcolm, that he laid at her feet his crown, his fortunes, and his heart; and she agreed to be a sharer of his royal throne.

And so the marriage was celebrated, with pomp and rejoicing almost unknown before in Scotland; for Malcolm had learned at the Saxon Court how such an occasion might be most fittingly adorned with all that could delight the senses. The old palace of Dumferline, long the abode of the Scottish monarchs, situated in the midst of most picturesque scenery, echoed for days to the tumult of the festival, and the first nobles of the land rejoiced to do justice to the royal cheer.

But the centre of all eyes, was the young bride, Margaret, now twenty-four years old, whose surpassing loveliness was to be equalled only by her modesty and goodness, She had received an education, first at the court of Hungary, and then at the court of her uncle, St. Edward, which developed, in the highest degree, her great native talents; and now, mistress of all the accomplishments of her time, she was calculated not so much to occupy, as to reflect lustre upon a throne. Her sprightliness and wit were subordinated to a rare soundness of judgment; and her whole character was penetrated with a spirit of Christian charity, which knew how to turn every endowment to the honour and glory of God, and the good of her neighbour. No wonder indeed that she should have attained such perfection, while still so young; for her mother, Agatha, sister to the queen of Hungary, was herself a model of every virtue.

The omens of that wedding-festival, beloved Brethren, were not belied by the sequel—Margaret became not merely the queen, but the mother and the pattern of her people, the powerful foe of irreligion and disorder, the promoter of social refinement, the judicious patroness of all the arts of peace, the salutary friend and handmaid of pure ecclesiastical discipline : in one word, she became, in spite of her Saxon tongue, the pride and the darling of that rough but warm-hearted people ; who handed down her name and the memory of her works as a rich heirloom and a palladium of safety to their remotest descendants.

It would take a series of discourses to unfold her many exquisite virtues. We must content ourselves with culling a few specimens, like sweet flowers from a luxuriant garden.

And first : she was the best of wives. She regarded her various gifts as primarily a means of enhancing the peace and happiness of her husband's life ; and of winning him to God, through his human affection for her. Malcolm was perfectly unlettered ; and though free from glaring passions, was, as might be expected from his roving life in early manhood, somewhat uncouth and rude, and prone to outbursts of anger and resentment. But Margaret, by the great respect with which she treated him, as well as by her instant readiness to gratify his whims, and the caressing sweetness of her ways, all directed to his improvement, won him to her more and more, with ever fresh surrender of his simple heart; until he became himself by dint of his admiration for this matchless woman, and his half-unconscious imitation of her, not merely a good and pious man, but a saint, whose name is found in the category of God's great servants. Wondrous power of gentleness and virtue combined to mould the most intractable and unpromising of characters! Malcolm did not know how sufficiently to honour his beloved Margaret. He gave into her hands, without reserve, ths management of the palace household; left her the disposal of his revenues, which she showered upon the poor and the ailing; entered upon no state affairs of any moment without consulting her as an oracle of God; and he joined, so far as his duties permitted, in the exercises of piety, with which her life seemed filled, although the daily list of her good works would appear to leave little room for prayer or meditation. How beautiful is the picture presented by Malcolm, who, though unable to read himself, had Margaret's books of devotion bound for her in the most gorgeous ornamental bindings which the art of that day could produce; and who loved to signify his desire to unite with her in the employment of those aids to piety by imprinting fond kisses again and again upon the volumes she loved.

And as Margaret was an ideal wife, so was she a truly Christian mother. Five sons and two daughters were the issue of her marriage; and to the training of these children, in succession, she devoted herself with a loving diligence and solicitude, which only a good christian mother can feel. From their tenderest infancy she taught them to love God, and to hate sin, as the most awful of earthly evils. She prayed with them from the time when they could lisp the holy name; and insensibly her little ones caught her manner of deep reverence and attention and fervour in the time of prayer. She would not permit them to indulge in the softness and luxury too often encouraged in the scions of royalty; she knew that to pamper their bodies with delicacies was to foster the craving of the senses, and to open the door to early temptation; perhaps to warp their whole lives; in short, to play the part of an enemy, instead of a mother. She found for them the ablest and the most virtuous instructors, whose example was as valuable as their teachings. She most jealously guarded them against the corrupting influence exercised by vicious and unprincipled companions. When they grew up, she took them as partners in her deeds of charity; in her alms-giving, her attendance on the sick, her innumerable offices of benevolence. And bountifully did God, the giver of all good gifts, bless the efforts of this noble mother! Her children were all good; and centres of good, from which radiated all the brightness and sweetness of the Christian virtues. Three of them, Edgar, Alexander, and David, wore, in succession, the crown of Scotland; and left an unsullied name in its often-tarnished annals. The half-century, and upwards of that, during which they reigned formed an epoch of light; when the kings were models for their people; and ruled them with justice and with judgment; and when every year that passed furnished fresh reasons for coupling with benedictions the name of that mother, who had moulded them for the high and arduous position of responsibility to which it pleased God to call them. The name of David, indeed, is found in the old Scottish calendars amongst the saints. Remoter still, we come across a grandson, Malcolm IV. (called the maiden), whose supernatural purity and gentleness reflected the virtues of the saintly Margaret:—Maud, again, the daughter of Margaret, who married Henry I. of England, so faithfully reproduced the supernatural life of her mother, that her name also was inscribed in the calendar of the saints.

To her subjects, Margaret was more like a mother than a queen; and like a mother was she beloved by high and low, but especially the poor. Their souls and bodies, their spiritual and temporal welfare, were both alike objects of her tender solicitude. She fostered science, as I have said, and promoted the cultivation of those arts and industries which, while they advance the material well-being of a people, wean their minds from the perpetual turmoil of armed enterprise, and attach them to the pursuits of peace. But even more earnestly did she provide for their instruction in the truths of religion, of which great masses of them were densely ignorant. She sent zealous preachers everywhere to teach them, and to stimulate them to a faithful observance of the laws of the Church —which had been scandalously neglected. Gradually she had the consolation to see the people reclaimed from their ungodliness, and the burning abuses, which had sprung up like weeds, disappear from the face of the land. The money-lender sought a more congenial sphere for his operations; dealers in superstitious practices began to fear the light; the heinous guilt of trading in sacred things was brought home to the public conscience; marriages were no longer contracted in defiance of divine and ecclesiastical law. The clergy, too, felt the effects of her salutary influence. And wherever it was necessary, she caused her husband to enforce, by strict enactments, a due observance of those regulations which were called for by the condition of the country.

But above all the poor were the beloved objects of her care. Wherever her sweet face appeared, they waited upon her in crowds, urging their petitions, and calling down God's blessing upon her. Nay, more; they invaded the palace itself, claiming a sort of right to expose their wants to her sympathetic and kindly eyes. She never tired of them, notwithstanding their rags, their filth, their vulgar importunity, their frequent lack of gratitude. Many a time she emptied her own purse, and trenched upon her husband's stores, nay, emptied his private coffers; to relieve the army of mendicants that beseiged her: a liberty which he was only too happy to see her exercise. Her daily preparation for her meals was to wait on nine little orphans and twenty-four adults, while they ate their fill: after which, she was ready to sit down to her own meal, which was so spare and scant, that it barely kept body and soul together. No one could count the number of the wretched and footsore whose feet she washed, and to whom she administered refreshment, with her own royal hands. No one could describe the tenderness and humility with which she attended upon the sick in the hospitals, where no ministration was too lowly or menial for her charity. And all these works of mercy were sanctified by a spirit of prayer which penetrated her every action, and made every breath she drew an offering to God. For hours she would remain before the blessed Sacrament, entranced and still, as if her soul were already mingled with the blessed.

Before her death, it pleased Almighty God to visit her with a most painful illness, which she bore with a sublime serenity and resignation to the divine will; and which she turned to account as an incentive to compunction for the sins of her life. But even this sickness, which seemed like a protracted death, was not the worst she had to suffer. She was stricken to the heart, through her affection, as the fondest and faithfullest of wives and mothers. Contrary to her advice for once, Malcolm set out to recapture the town of Alnwick, which Rufus, the English king, had surprised and taken. The expedition was fated to disaster. Both Malcolm, and after him his son Edward, were slain in the seige: the Scots were fain to fall back from the town; and her son Edgar, who bore the sad tidings, found his widowed mother fast approaching her end. She had just overtaxed her strength in dragging herself to her oratory to receive the holy viaticum; and, lying exhausted, with the Cross in her hands, which she kissed repeatedly, and which was a most treasured relic in Scotland in after days, she joined her Confessor and other clergy in saying the psalm of the penitent : " Miserere." She seemed to divine the misfortune which had befallen her when Edgar entered the apartment. With uplifted hands she thanked God for sending her so heavy an affliction in the last hour of her life to purify her from the guilt of her sins; and soon after, feeling the cold hand of death upon her, she mustered strength to utter that prayer of the Church :—" O Lord Jesus Christ, who hast, by Thy death, given life to the world, deliver me from all evil." With this beautiful prayer, she breathed her pure soul into the hands of God, at the age of forty-seven, seven years before the eleventh century close; leaving behind her a name which is an honour to womanhood, a watchword of faithfulness and love to every wife and mother, a reminder of the duty of constant prayer, an encouragement to self-denial, and a stimulus to every work of mercy, spiritual and corporal.

www.ingramcontent.com/pod-product-compliance
Lightning Source LLC
Chambersburg PA
CBHW030408230426
43664CB00007BB/798